THE WILL TO IMPROVE

THE WILL TO IMPROVE

Governmentality, Development,

and the Practice of Politics

TANIA MURRAY LI

Duke University Press • Durham & London 2007

ADB	Asian Development Bank
APP	Asia Pulp and Paper
CCA	Community Conservation Agreement
HRW	Human Rights Watch
KDP	Kecamatan (subdistrict) Development Project
KPA	Konsorsium Pembaruan Agraria (Consortium for Agrarian Reform)
NEI	Netherlands East Indies
NGO	Non-governmental organization
PRA	Participatory Rural Appraisal
SPADA	Support for Poor and Disadvantaged Areas Project
STORMA	Stability of Rainforest Margins
TNC	The Nature Conservancy
UNDP	United Nations Development Program
USAID	United States Agency for International Development
VOC	Vereenigde Oost-Indische Compagnie (Netherlands East Indies Company)
WALHI	Wahana Lingkunan Hidup Indonesia (Friends of the Earth Indonesia)
YTM	Yayasan Tanah Merdeka (Free Land Foundation)

Adat	Custom
Akte Jual-Beli	Record of sale and purchase
Damar	Resin used in the production of varnish
Masyarakat adat	Customary community, translation of indigenous people
Masyarakat terasing	Isolated and estranged community
Petrus	Contraction of *penembakan misterius*, mysterious shooting
Provokasi	Provocation
Reformasi	Reform period following the resignation of Suharto in 1998
Sawah	Irrigated wet rice field

ACKNOWLEDGMENTS

In our busy, overstretched lives, the gift of sustained time and attention is precious. Thus I am very grateful to the generous colleagues who read a long and unwieldy draft of this book and gave me many, many pages of detailed, tough, critical comments that provoked me into clarifying, rethinking, and revising it. They are Arun Agrawal, Tim Babcock, John Clarke, Jim Ferguson, David Henley, Kregg Hetherington, Angela Keller-Herzog, Donald Moore, Jonathan Padwe, Nancy Peluso, Renee Sylvain, and Michael Watts. Parts of the draft were read by Scott Guggenheim, John McCarthy, David Mosse, and Albert Schrauwers. Peter Vandergeest and Shubhra Gururani at York University read a draft with their students and offered thoughtful feedback, as did students in my governmentality seminar at the University of Toronto. Participants in the seminars of Benedict Kingsbury and Philip Alston at New York University and Agrarian Studies at Yale commented on versions of chapter 7.

In Sulawesi Arianto Sangaji worked with me on fieldwork and analysis. Staff of YTM in Palu provided logistical support. Staff of TNC, WALHI, and other NGOs shared material and ideas. Many Sulawesi highlanders were generous with their time, insight, and hospitality. In Jakarta my brother Julian Murray and his wife Anne Banwell provided a warm welcome and spent many hours discussing with me the possibilities and constraints of their work inside the development apparatus. Scott Guggenheim sent me material and encouraged me to think that our dialogue was worthwhile. In Toronto, Kirsten Brown and Konar Arifin provided research assistance. Ken Wissoker at Duke University Press believed in the project and gave me sound advice. Colleagues at

Dalhousie University, University of Toronto, and several campuses south of the border—especially Gavin Smith, Pauline Gardiner Barber, Jim Stolzman, Michael Dove, Anna Tsing, Gillian Hart, Robert Hefner, Jim Scott, and Donna Young—offered support and encouragement.

Funding to support the research and writing was supplied by the Canadian Social Science and Humanities Research Council through a standard research grant and through the Canada Research Chairs program, and by the John D. and Catherine T. MacArthur Foundation program on Global Security and Sustainability. There was a hidden gift of time there, too, from unknown colleagues who read proposals and wrote references.

In Halifax, my friend Jana Wieder walked and talked with me through the rough and the smooth. From a distance, Donald Moore was there on the phone to inspire and guide me with his incomparable wisdom. As I labored at my computer screen, my siblings Julian, Rupert, and Lisa and my mother Anita popped up periodically on MSN to remind me that I am part of a far-flung but very close family. At home, Nicholas, Simon, and Allanah, nurtured me with their loyalty, and the warmth of our dinnertime conversations. Victor tolerated my absences and gave generously of his amazing intellect and loving care. These are the enabling conditions under which I wrote this book. Its burdens were shared. Its limitations are all my own.

MAP I   Indonesia

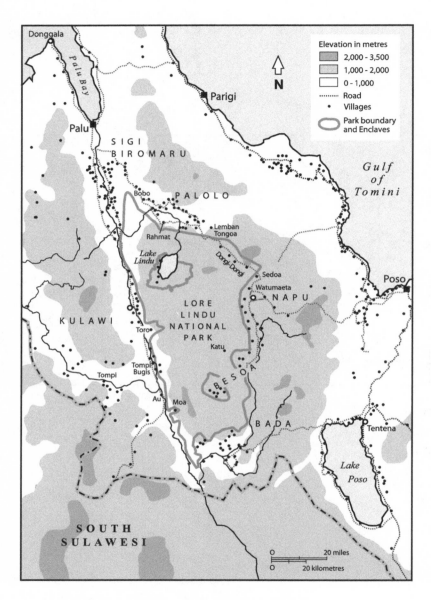

MAP 2   Central Sulawesi Highlands and Lore Lindu National Park

Introduction

THE WILL TO IMPROVE

Indonesia, a nation beset with poverty and violence, may seem a strange choice for an investigation of the will to improve. Yet talk of improvement is everywhere, in offices and villages across the archipelago. It is not just talk. Programs that set out to improve the condition of the population in a deliberate manner have shaped Indonesian landscapes, livelihoods, and identities for almost two centuries. Ironically, these programs, intertwined with other processes and relations, set the conditions for some of the problems that exist today. Programs to move populations from one place to another, better to provide for their needs; programs to rationalize the use of land, dividing farm from forest; programs to educate and modernize—all of these are implicated in contemporary sites of struggle.

The outcomes of improvement schemes are not always bad. Programs of improvement often bring changes that people want—more roads and bridges, fewer floods and diseases, less corruption and waste. My purpose in this book is not to condemn. Rather, I seek to understand the rationale of improvement schemes—what they seek to change, and the calculations they apply. I also seek to understand their effects, as they intersect with other processes shaping particular conjunctures. My title *The Will to Improve* draws attention to the inevitable gap between what is attempted and what is accomplished. It also highlights the persistence of this will—its parasitic relationship to its own shortcomings and failures. The will is stubborn, but it is no mystical *geist* or teleology. Indeed, I have often been struck by the rather mundane way it is expressed. After listening patiently to my account of the troubled history of improvement schemes in the highlands of Sulawesi, one expert summed up his position thus: "You may be right, but we still have to do something, we can't just give up."

There is no sign that schemes for improvement are about to be abandoned. There are always experts ready to propose a better plan. I do not dismiss their efforts. Nor, however, do I offer a recipe for how improvement can be improved. I take a critical stance, one that seeks to prize open expert knowledge and expose its limits. In so doing, I hope to expand the possibilities for thinking critically about what is and what might be. I argue that the positions of critic and programmer are properly distinct. A central feature of programming is the requirement to frame problems in terms amenable to technical solutions. Programmers must screen out refractory processes to circumscribe an arena of intervention in which calculations can be applied. They address some problems, and necessarily not others. Under pressure to program better, they are not in a position to make programming itself an object of analysis. A critic can take a broader view. I believe such a view has value, although its importance should not be exaggerated. As I will show, some of the more incisive critiques of improvement are generated by people who directly experience the effects of programs launched in the name of their well-being.

In the contemporary era, challenges to improvement programs are often framed in the language of unkept promises, or in the related language of rights, increasingly codified in national and transnational laws. Yet concepts of right are also embedded in commonsense notions that have, in Kirstie McClure's words, "more to do with felt sensation, with embodied perceptions of injury or abuse." The "subject of rights," McClure observes, is "a prickly creature, wary and willful, . . . a subject suspicious of those who claim to speak in its name."[1] I will describe prickly subjects of this kind in Sulawesi, subjects who clearly understand the relationship between their current insecurities and the defects of the improving programs carried out in their name, but who have been driven to act, individually and collectively, by injuries experienced as visceral, personal attacks on their ability to sustain their own lives. When processes of class formation, the damaging effects of improvement programs, and the failure of experts to deliver on their promises coincide—as they often do, for reasons I will explain—mobilization is apt to follow. Political economy and contestation thus stand alongside the will to improve as pillars of my analysis.

In the classic tradition of anthropology, my approach in this book is to make improvement strange, the better to explore its peculiarities and its effects. The discussions of improvement taking place in village meeting halls, in debates among activists, and in the offices of donors and officials might seem so banal to me after more than a decade of research in Indonesia that they would escape attention. Yet every time I meet someone with a plan to realign landscapes and livelihoods, or improve the capacities of villagers by supplying a technology or institution they are presumed to lack, I am amazed by it. I was especially struck by the concentration of expert attention focused on one of my research sites in the highlands of Central Sulawesi, an area that has received wave after wave of intervention over a period of a century. This site is striking partly because it is so different from my other highland field site, a few hundred kilometers away, where improvement schemes have been scarce and highland farmers make their own way as best they can. It is the busy site that forms my subject matter in several chapters of this book. The wealth of documentation about improvement programs, combined with a rich set of ethnographic and historical accounts and my own fieldwork, provides a unique opportunity to examine what each program sought to change and how.[2] Just as important, this material enables me to track the effects of planned interventions as they have layered up one upon the next and intersected with other processes to shape the landscapes, livelihoods, and identities of the highland population.

There is a second aspect to my experience of the strangeness of improvement. I find an ethnographic appreciation of the complexities of rural relations to be antithetical to the position of expert. This might seem counterintuitive. Surely a person like me, after more than a decade of research, has ideas about how to translate that knowledge into effective programs to help people? Indeed, I am sometimes asked by anthropologically trained development administrators in Indonesia to provide suggestions about what they should do. More specifically, they ask me to provide them with a bridge between my research describing the dynamics of rural life, which some of them have read, and the world of projects, which they inhabit. Such a bridge eludes me. Why is it, I ask myself, that so many experts can examine Indonesia and devise programs to improve it, whereas I cannot? This is not a matter of coyness or modesty on my part. Still less am I indifferent to the problems of poverty, disease, and ecological disaster that experts seek to resolve. I believe my predicament is diagnostic. It enables practice of excluding or, as Ferguson put it, "reposing political questions" in technical terms is itself an intervention with far-reaching effects. As I will show throughout this book, this exclusion both limits and shapes what improvement becomes.

A third dimension to improvement might also be labeled antipolitics: the design of programs as a deliberate measure to contain a challenge to the status quo. In Britain in 1847, for example, an observer argued for special programs for paupers because they were "the class of men injured by society who consequently rebel against it."[17] Another argued, "Assisting the poor is a means of government, a potent way of containing the most difficult section of the population and improving all the other sections."[18] In the Netherlands, it was a subsistence crisis in 1816–17 combined with the French Revolution—a ready reminder of the dangers posed by poverty and despair—that prompted the scholar-administrator Van den Bosch to devise programs to teach rural paupers how to work. These were programs he later adapted and transposed to the Netherlands East Indies, as I explain in chapter 1.[19] Social welfare programs in the global North arose from the convergence of expert concerns about the condition of the population, and the challenge of organized labor.

The transnational practice of development as it emerged in the 1950s responded to the threat posed by popular mobilization in the global South, witness the subtitle to Walter Rostow's book *The Stages of Growth: A Non-Communist Manifesto*.[20] It was intimately linked to counterinsurgency and the cold war, a battle for hearts and minds waged through promises to solve the problem of hungry bellies. In Southeast Asia in the 1960s, the U.S. concern with falling dominoes prompted support for repressive regimes prepared to squash a communist threat. In Indonesia, Suharto's role in engineering the massacre of up to half a million alleged communists in 1965 was rewarded by lavish support from international aid donors that helped sustain the New Order regime for more than three decades (1965–98). The New Order concept of development was an explicit attempt to contain the challenge presented by a mobilized peasantry demanding land reform and turn them into a "floating mass" that would vote as instructed, and concentrate on improved farming and other technical matters.[21]

Notwithstanding instances in which improvement is deployed to contain a political challenge, I do not argue that improvement is merely a tactic to

In the classic tradition of anthropology, my approach in this book is to make improvement strange, the better to explore its peculiarities and its effects. The discussions of improvement taking place in village meeting halls, in debates among activists, and in the offices of donors and officials might seem so banal to me after more than a decade of research in Indonesia that they would escape attention. Yet every time I meet someone with a plan to realign landscapes and livelihoods, or improve the capacities of villagers by supplying a technology or institution they are presumed to lack, I am amazed by it. I was especially struck by the concentration of expert attention focused on one of my research sites in the highlands of Central Sulawesi, an area that has received wave after wave of intervention over a period of a century. This site is striking partly because it is so different from my other highland field site, a few hundred kilometers away, where improvement schemes have been scarce and highland farmers make their own way as best they can. It is the busy site that forms my subject matter in several chapters of this book. The wealth of documentation about improvement programs, combined with a rich set of ethnographic and historical accounts and my own fieldwork, provides a unique opportunity to examine what each program sought to change and how.[2] Just as important, this material enables me to track the effects of planned interventions as they have layered up one upon the next and intersected with other processes to shape the landscapes, livelihoods, and identities of the highland population.

There is a second aspect to my experience of the strangeness of improvement. I find an ethnographic appreciation of the complexities of rural relations to be antithetical to the position of expert. This might seem counterintuitive. Surely a person like me, after more than a decade of research, has ideas about how to translate that knowledge into effective programs to help people? Indeed, I am sometimes asked by anthropologically trained development administrators in Indonesia to provide suggestions about what they should do. More specifically, they ask me to provide them with a bridge between my research describing the dynamics of rural life, which some of them have read, and the world of projects, which they inhabit. Such a bridge eludes me. Why is it, I ask myself, that so many experts can examine Indonesia and devise programs to improve it, whereas I cannot? This is not a matter of coyness or modesty on my part. Still less am I indifferent to the problems of poverty, disease, and ecological disaster that experts seek to resolve. I believe my predicament is diagnostic. It enables me to ask what ways of thinking, what practices and assumptions are required to translate messy conjunctures, with all the processes that run through them, into linear narratives of problems, interventions, and beneficial results.[3]

My reflections on improvement are conditioned, further, by my occasional work as a development consultant. I have observed the limited tolerance of elites for interventions that might actually restructure relations in favor of the poor. One example from the early 1990s will illustrate. Invited by a development agency to prepare a report on land tenure issues in a highland area, I found that a program to encourage hillside farmers to plant a new crop, cacao, was having some unintended effects. Most significantly, it was providing an opportunity for elites living on the coast to grab hillside land on the grounds that they could make efficient use of it, while the backward hill folk could not. When I exposed this problem, the project directors took it seriously. They initiated a program to help the hill farmers document their legal rights to the hillside land so it could not be stolen from them. This was a novel initiative at the time, some years before Indonesia's indigenous rights movement made talk of indigenous land rights familiar. The Indonesian legal consultant hired by the project began the uphill task of trying to persuade officials in the provincial capital that the hill farmers do indeed have legal rights to their customary land, and the Basic Agrarian Law (passed in 1960 under the populist president Sukarno) has provisions for recognizing those rights. The outcome of her efforts was a backlash. The implication of recognizing customary rights was recognized by the Governor as a threat to the status quo, and he issued a formal edict stating that there is no customary land at all in the province of Central Sulawesi. The edict is still being used to justify dispossession. Customary rights activists in the provincial capital, Palu, are still trying to get it rescinded. This incident is also diagnostic. It leads me to ask how programs of improvement are shaped by political-economic relations they cannot change; how they are constituted, that is, by what they exclude.

THE WILL TO IMPROVE

Many parties share in the will to improve. They occupy the position of trustees, a position defined by the claim to know how others should live, to know what is best for them, to know what they need. Trusteeship is defined as "the intent which is expressed, by one source of agency, to develop the capacities of another."[4] The objective of trusteeship is not to dominate others—it is to enhance their capacity for action, and to direct it. In Indonesia, since the nineteenth century, the list of trustees includes colonial officials and missionaries, politicians and bureaucrats, international aid donors, specialists in agriculture, hygiene, credit and conservation, and so-called nongovernmental organizations (NGOS) of various kinds. Their intentions are benevolent, even utopian. They desire to make the world better than it is. Their methods are subtle. If they resort to violence, it is in the name of a higher good—the population at large, the survival of species, the stimulation of growth. Often, their schemes operate at a distance. They structure a field of possible actions. They modify processes. They entice and induce. They make certain courses of action easier or more difficult. Many schemes appear not as an external imposition, but as the natural expression of the everyday interactions of individuals and groups. They blend seamlessly into common sense.[5] Sometimes they stimulate a more or less radical critique. Whatever the response, the claim to expertise in optimizing the lives of others is a claim to power, one that merits careful scrutiny.

The will to improve is situated in the field of power Michel Foucault termed "government."[6] Defined succinctly as the "conduct of conduct," government is the attempt to shape human conduct by calculated means. Distinct from discipline, which seeks to reform designated groups through detailed supervision in confined quarters (prisons, asylums, schools), the concern of government is the well-being of populations at large. Its purpose is to secure the "welfare of the population, the improvement of its condition, the increase of its wealth, longevity, health, etc."[7] To achieve this purpose requires distinctive means. At the level of population, it is not possible to coerce every individual and regulate their actions in minute detail. Rather, government operates by educating desires and configuring habits, aspirations and beliefs. It sets conditions, "artificially so arranging things so that people, following only their own self-interest, *will do as they ought*."[8] Persuasion might be applied, as authorities attempt to gain consent. But this is not the only course. When power operates at a distance, people are not necessarily aware of how their conduct is being conducted or why, so the question of consent does not arise.

The will to govern, and more specifically, the will to improve the condition of the population, is expansive. In Foucault's definition, it is concerned with "men in their relations, their links, their imbrication with . . . wealth, resources, means of subsistence, the territory with all its specific qualities, climate, irrigation, fertility, etc.; men in their relation to . . . customs, habits, ways of acting and thinking, etc.; and lastly, men in their relation to . . . accidents and misfortunes such as famine, epidemics, death, etc."[9] Trustees intervene in these relations in order to adjust them. They aim to foster beneficial processes and mitigate destructive ones. They may operate on population in the aggregate, or on subgroups divided by gender, location, age, income, or race, each with characteristic deficiencies that serve as points of entry for corrective interventions.

To improve populations requires the exercise of what Foucault identified as a distinct, governmental rationality—a way of thinking about government as the "right manner of disposing things" in pursuit not of one dogmatic goal but a "whole series of specific finalities" to be achieved through "multiform tactics."[10] Calculation is central, because government requires that the "right manner" be defined, distinct "finalities" prioritized, and tactics finely tuned to achieve optimal results.[11] Calculation requires, in turn, that the processes to be governed be characterized in technical terms. Only then can specific interventions be devised.

An explicit, calculated program of intervention is not invented ab initio. It is traversed by the will to improve, but it is not the product of a singular intention or will. It draws upon and is situated within a heterogeneous assemblage or *dispositif* that combines "forms of practical knowledge, with modes of perception, practices of calculation, vocabularies, types of authority, forms of judgement, architectural forms, human capacities, non-human objects and devices, inscriptions techniques and so forth."[12] Although there are occasions when a revolutionary movement or visionary announces a grand plan for the total transformation of society—the kind of plan James Scott describes as "high modern," more often programs of intervention are pulled together from an existing repertoire, a matter of habit, accretion, and bricolage.[13] There are of course individuals involved in devising particular interventions and programs of improvement. The position of programmers is structured by the enterprise of which they form a part. It is routinized in the practices in which they engage. What, then, are these practices?

Two key practices are required to translate the will to improve into explicit programs. One is problematization, that is, identifying deficiencies that need to be rectified. The second is the practice I call "rendering technical," a shorthand for what is actually a whole set of practices concerned with representing "the domain to be governed as an intelligible field with specifiable limits and particular characteristics . . . defining boundaries, rendering that within them visible, assembling information about that which is included and devising techniques to mobilize the forces and entities thus revealed."[14]

The practices of problematization and rendering technical are not separate. As James Ferguson explained in his landmark study of development in Lesotho, the bounding and characterization of an "intelligible field" appropriate for intervention anticipates the kinds of intervention that experts have to offer.[15] The identification of a problem is intimately linked to the availability of a solution. They coemerge within a governmental assemblage in which certain sorts of diagnoses, prescriptions, and techniques are available to the expert who is properly trained. Conversely, the practice of "rendering technical" confirms expertise and constitutes the boundary between those who are positioned as trustees, with the capacity to diagnose deficiencies in others, and those who are subject to expert direction. It is a boundary that has to be maintained and that can be challenged.

There is a second dimension to rendering technical, equally central to my analysis. Questions that are rendered technical are simultaneously rendered nonpolitical. For the most part, experts tasked with improvement exclude the structure of political-economic relations from their diagnoses and prescriptions. They focus more on the capacities of the poor than on the practices through which one social group impoverishes another. This feature led James Ferguson to describe the apparatus of planned development as an "antipolitics machine" that "insistently repos[es] political questions of land, resources, jobs, or wages as technical 'problems' responsive to the technical 'development' intervention."[16] Antipolitics of this kind is subliminal and routine. Experts are trained to frame problems in technical terms. This is their job. Their claim to expertise depends on their capacity to diagnose problems in ways that match the kinds of solution that fall within their repertoire. Yet the practice of excluding or, as Ferguson put it, "reposing political questions" in technical terms is itself an intervention with far-reaching effects. As I will show throughout this book, this exclusion both limits and shapes what improvement becomes.

A third dimension to improvement might also be labeled antipolitics: the design of programs as a deliberate measure to contain a challenge to the status quo. In Britain in 1847, for example, an observer argued for special programs for paupers because they were "the class of men injured by society who consequently rebel against it."[17] Another argued, "Assisting the poor is a means of government, a potent way of containing the most difficult section of the population and improving all the other sections."[18] In the Netherlands, it was a subsistence crisis in 1816–17 combined with the French Revolution—a ready reminder of the dangers posed by poverty and despair—that prompted the scholar-administrator Van den Bosch to devise programs to teach rural paupers how to work. These were programs he later adapted and transposed to the Netherlands East Indies, as I explain in chapter 1.[19] Social welfare programs in the global North arose from the convergence of expert concerns about the condition of the population, and the challenge of organized labor.

The transnational practice of development as it emerged in the 1950s responded to the threat posed by popular mobilization in the global South, witness the subtitle to Walter Rostow's book *The Stages of Growth: A Non-Communist Manifesto*.[20] It was intimately linked to counterinsurgency and the cold war, a battle for hearts and minds waged through promises to solve the problem of hungry bellies. In Southeast Asia in the 1960s, the U.S. concern with falling dominoes prompted support for repressive regimes prepared to squash a communist threat. In Indonesia, Suharto's role in engineering the massacre of up to half a million alleged communists in 1965 was rewarded by lavish support from international aid donors that helped sustain the New Order regime for more than three decades (1965–98). The New Order concept of development was an explicit attempt to contain the challenge presented by a mobilized peasantry demanding land reform and turn them into a "floating mass" that would vote as instructed, and concentrate on improved farming and other technical matters.[21]

Notwithstanding instances in which improvement is deployed to contain a political challenge, I do not argue that improvement is merely a tactic to maintain the dominance of particular classes, or to assert control by the global North over the South—an interpretation common to dependency theory and its variants.[22] Rather than assume a hidden agenda, I take seriously the proposition that the will to improve can be taken at its word. This is another important lesson learned from Ferguson's *Anti-politics Machine*. Interests are part of the machine, but they are not its master term. There are indeed hybrids, in which improvement schemes serve to enrich a ruling group or secure their control over people and territory. There are instances of bad faith. There are sound reasons to be skeptical of some of the claims made in the name of improvement. But for several centuries trustees have endeavored to secure the welfare of populations and carried out programs that cannot be explained except in these terms.

In my view, the rush to identify hidden motives of profit or domination narrows analysis unnecessarily, making much of what happens in the name of improvement obscure.[23] Trustees charged with the welfare of populations cannot support only the interests of a select group. They must attempt to balance all sorts of relations between "men and things." To govern, as Foucault made clear, is to seek not one dogmatic goal, but "a whole series of specific finalities." Diverse "finalities" may be incompatible, yielding interventions that are in tension with one another, or downright contradictory. As I will explain in chapter 1, concerns to secure orderly rule, entrepreneurial profit, revenues to support the state apparatus, and native improvement jostled awkwardly for more than a century in the Netherlands East Indies. In this colony as in others, they were the subject of continuous debate among colonial officials, missionaries, politicians, commercial lobbies, and critics of various persuasions. There was no unitary purpose to colonial rule.

In the Sulawesi highlands, my focus in chapters 2 to 6, some trustees have promoted capitalism in the earnest belief that "efficient" markets bring prosperity to the poor. Others have promoted subsistence, community self-help, and cooperation. Several schemes have focused on public health, education, and forest conservation. The profits to be gleaned from such schemes, if any, are modest and indirect. Indeed, many improvement schemes have no foreseeable prospect of yielding profits for anyone. If profit were the issue, no international donor or agriculture department would have invested in the rugged hills of Central Sulawesi. From the optic of profits, the transnational endeavor to conserve tropical rainforests is quite mysterious. One can make a link with bio-prospecting and pharmaceutical corporations, but it is tenuous. In the highlands of Sulawesi, conservationists attempting to protect the Lore Lindu National Park recognize that bio-prospectors have not materialized, and indeed, they may not come. They defend the park because, in their view, a park has a place in the proper management of relations between "men and things" and benefits the population at large. Similarly, the World Bank's billion-dollar scheme to make village planning more participatory and transparent, my focus in chapter 7, might help prepare villagers for the expansion of global capital, but the link, if any, is indirect.

POLITICS AS PROVOCATION

Although rendering contentious issues technical is a routine practice for experts, I insist that this operation should be seen as a project, not a secure accomplishment. Questions that experts exclude, misrecognize, or attempt to contain do not go away. On this point I diverge from scholars who emphasize the capacity of expert schemes to absorb critique, their effective *achievement* of depoliticization. Hubert Dreyfus and Paul Rabinow, among others, argue that expert knowledge takes "what is essentially a political problem, removing it from the realm of political discourse, and recasting it in the neutral language of science." They find expertise closed, self-referencing and secure once a "technical matrix" has been established. Resistance, or failure to achieve a program's stated aims, comes to be "construed as further proof of the need to reinforce and extend the power of the experts." Thus "what we get is not a true conflict of interpretations about the ultimate worth or meaning of efficiency, productivity, or normalization, but rather what might be called a conflict of implementations."[24] Similarly, Timothy Mitchell describes discursive practices that translate issues of poverty, landlessness, and hunger into problems of public health to be solved by technical interventions in social relations and hygiene. In his account, experts rule: much of the time, they succeed in disguising their failures and continue to devise new programs with their authority unchallenged.[25] Ferguson offers the qualified observation that development "may also very effectively squash political challenges to the system" by its insistent reposing of political questions in technical term.[26] Nikolas Rose stresses the "switch points" where critical scrutiny of governmental programs is absorbed back into the realm of expertise, and "an opening turns into a closure."[27]

Closure, as these scholars have shown, is indeed a feature of expert discourses. Such discourses are devoid of reference to questions they cannot address, or that might cast doubt upon the completeness of their diagnoses or the feasibility of their solutions. In particular, as Ferguson and Mitchell stress, they exclude what I call political-economic questions—questions about control over the means of production, and the structures of law and force that support systemic inequalities. I am fascinated by the question of how these questions are screened out in the constitution of improvement as a technical domain, and I examine this operation in detail in several chapters of this book. Yet I am equally interested in the "switch" in the opposite direction: in the conditions under which expert discourse is punctured by a challenge it cannot contain; moments when the targets of expert schemes reveal, in word or deed, their own critical analysis of the problems that confront them. I make a conjuncture of this kind the focus of my analysis in chapters 4 and 5.

From the perspective proposed by Foucault, openings and closures are intimately linked. He describes the interface between the will to govern and what he calls a strategy of struggle as one of "permanent provocation."[28] He writes:

> For a relationship of confrontation, from the moment it is not a struggle to the death, the fixing of a power relationship becomes a target—at one time its fulfillment and its suspension. And in return the strategy of struggle also constitutes a frontier for the relationship of power, the line at which, instead of manipulating and inducing actions in a calculated manner, one must be content with reacting to them after the event. . . . In effect, between a relationship of power and a strategy of struggle there is a reciprocal appeal, a perpetual linking and a perpetual reversal.[29]

As I see it, the unsettled meaning of the terms *politics* and *the political* hinge on this element of linking and reversal.[30] Is politics the name for a relation of power, or a practice of contestation? At what point does one slide into the other?

In order to pin down the relation of "perpetual reversal" that Foucault describes in rather abstract terms and to make it the subject of empirical investigation, I have settled on a terminology that distinguishes between what I call the practice of government, in which a concept of improvement becomes technical as it is attached to calculated programs for its realization,[31] and what I call the practice of politics—the expression, in word or deed, of a critical challenge. Challenge often starts out as refusal of the way things are. It opens up a front of struggle. This front may or may not be closed as newly identified problems are rendered technical and calculations applied. Government, from this perspective, is a response to the practice of politics that shapes, challenges, and provokes it. The practice of politics stands at the limit of the calculated attempt to direct conduct. It is not the only limit, however. In the next section, I examine the limit presented by force.

GOVERNMENTALITY, SOVEREIGNTY, AND DISCIPLINE

Foucault's essay "Governmentality" makes a useful distinction between the purpose of government—the well-being of populations—and the purpose of sovereignty. Sovereignty, he argues, is circular: its purpose is the confirmation and extension of the might of the sovereign, demonstrated in the size of the realm, the number of subjects, and the riches accumulated.[32] A sovereign's authority to issue commands, punish enemies, deduct taxes, and bestow gifts is absolute. A sovereign can choose who will live or die and wreak havoc with impunity. To govern, in contrast, is "to be condemned to seek an authority for one's authority."[33] When violence is used, it must be justified by a notion of improvement. Its purpose cannot be mere plunder or domination.

Although Foucault's essay on governmentality suggests a teleological unfolding toward government as a superior form of rule originating and taken to its highest form in Europe—an ethnocentric replay of modernization theory—the essay offers a second, more interesting possibility: that the analytic of governmentality be used to examine how practices of rule articulate elements of government, sovereignty, and discipline. At some historical conjunctures a sovereign's might is best confirmed—and secured—by ensuring the well-being of the population and augmenting its prosperity. Although the right of a sovereign may be absolute, sovereigns have often been judged good or bad according to their capacity to secure the welfare of their people. In India in the eighteenth century, for example, indigenous rulers kept sophisticated accounts and engaged in programs to increase the wealth of their realms. Their goal was not appropriation alone. "Popular prosperity," writes David Ludden, "was measurable and seen as the responsibility of rulers . . . who could be judged accordingly."[34]

In colonial contexts, as Achille Mbembe eloquently reminds us, rule was based on conquest. There was no liberal regime of rights to balance the sovereign's absolute authority to command and deduct. For Mbembe, "arbitrariness and intrinsic unconditionality" were the "distinctive feature of colonial sovereignty."[35] Yet violence was not the whole story. Merchant-colonial regimes were attracted by the prospect of hit-and-run profits, but in the long term, these could not be sustained. As Richard Grove explains, the greedy extractivism of the British and Dutch East India Companies caused ecological destruction and the dislocation of populations. The resulting droughts, famines, and rebellions threatened both profit and rule. Doctors and scientists on the staff of these companies were among the first to think systematically about the relations between "men and things" as an arena of intervention, and mobilized to persuade their employers to do likewise.[36] In the colonies as in the metropoles, when the complexity of the processes sustaining the population came into view, a governmental rationality concerned with balancing various ends had to follow.[37] So too did the concern to govern with economy— economy of funds, economy of force, and the minimum necessary intervention to achieve a given set of finalities.

As late colonial regimes came to include, among their objectives, providing native populations with the benefits of improvement and orderly rule, new calculations were required. Although David Scott identifies in Sri Lanka a clean break between mercantile colonialism in which the aim was to secure "extractive-effects on colonial bodies" and the late-colonial concern to achieve "governing-effects on colonial conduct,"[38] in many colonial contexts old and new objectives were combined in awkward amalgams, and means were also hybrid. Lord Lugard's "Dual Mandate" for nineteenth-century British rule in Africa was a case in point.[39] When scientific knowledge was hitched to imperial designs, experts argued that more efficient production "would necessarily confer the greatest good on the greatest number."[40] Yet the authority of experts, as Richard Drayton points out, did not stand alone. It was backed by the coercive might of the sovereign as "mobilizer of collective efforts, force and legitimacy."[41]

Discipline, similarly, was not displaced by government but reserved for subgroups of colonial and metropolitan populations deemed to merit or require detailed supervision. "Despotism," the political philosopher and employee of the British East India Company J. S. Mill famously declared, "is a legitimate mode of government in dealing with barbarians, provided the end be their improvement."[42] Similar arguments were made in the colonial metropoles to justify disciplinary regimes for defective populations—children, paupers, "lower orders," racialized others, women, prisoners, and people suffering from particular illnesses. They were excluded from the exercise of rights granted to other citizens on the grounds that they were incapable—or not yet capable—of exercising the attendant responsibilities. For some of these groups, experts justified subjection to intrusive discipline as a means to prepare them to take their place in the general population. They would graduate. For others, tutelage was permanent.[43] If one were to conduct a head count, Barry Hindess suggests, the "liberal government of unfreedom" was far more common, even in the metropoles, than the ideology of liberalism suggests.[44]

In the colonies, there was intense debate about which subgroups were more or less improvable, or whether racial others would ever become mature enough to be governed in a liberal manner. The consequences of these debates were profound, as were the contradictions. Although native difference and deficiency supplied an important rationale for colonial intervention, as Gerald Sider observes, beginning with Columbus, colonial powers were caught between "the impossibility and the necessity of creating the other as the other— the different, the alien—and incorporating the other within a single social and cultural system of domination."[45] If the colonized were utterly different from their colonial masters, the promise to bring improvement was an empty one. Discipline could not be improving, it was merely extractive. Alternatively, if colonizers and colonized were essentially the same, successful trusteeship would eliminate the distinction that justified colonial rule. Either way, the will to improve was in tension with the right to rule.[46] Colonial sovereignty and government were, in this sense, incompatible.

Colonial regimes addressed the contradiction between difference and improvement in various ways, all of them unsatisfactory. One, explored by Gary Wilder, was the "structure of permanent deferral," as native society was both "rationalized and racialized," its subjects "destined to become rights-bearing individuals, but always too immature to exercise those rights."[47] Natives were consigned, as Dipesh Chakrabarty puts it, to a "waiting room."[48] A second tactic was division: natives were sorted into categories that were more or less improvable, elites generally falling into the first category, layering a class logic upon a racial one.[49] But improved subjects, educated natives, made colonial authorities and settlers very nervous. They threatened the basis of the colonial right to rule. "Not quite/ not white," they were inappropriate, the object of a profound ambivalence that translated into the elaborate schemes for boundary maintenance explored by Ann Stoler.[50] The fate of people deemed to be unimprovable was serious indeed: in white settler colonies, groups defined as "hopeless cases" were exterminated, or left to die out by attrition, their "manifest destiny" according to theories of natural selection.[51] A third tactic was to argue that improvement for natives did not mean becoming like their colonial masters, it meant being true to their own indigenous traditions. It was the task of trustees to improve native life ways by restoring them to their authentic state.[52] Intervention was needed to teach (or oblige) natives to be truly themselves. All three tactics were deployed in the Netherlands East Indies, as I will later explain, with the third—the perfection of authentic otherness—especially well developed.

The structure of "permanent deferral" continues to pervade contemporary development agendas. Planned development is premised upon the improvability of the "target group" but also posits a boundary that clearly separates those who need to be developed from those who will do the developing. Deficient subjects can be identified and improved only from the outside; as Stacy Pigg observes, to know one, one cannot be one.[53] In many postcolonies, racial difference transmuted rather easily into divides constructed around locality, class, and status, in which city-based trustees distinguished by their education and technical know-how joined with the transnational development apparatus to expound on how deficient, tradition-bound villagers should live.

Late colonial and postcolonial states share in the "institutionalized configuration of power" defined by David Ludden as a "development regime": (1) ruling powers that claim progress as a goal, (2) a "people" whose conditions must be improved, (3) an ideology of science that proffers principles and techniques to effect and measure progress, and (4) self-declared, enlightened leaders who would use state power for development and compete for power with claims of their ability to effect progress.[54] Like their colonial predecessors, contemporary national development regimes sometimes resort to violence to achieve their objectives, but regular use of violence indicates weakness. It suggests that "the people" do not want the improvements on offer, finding them inefficient, damaging, or simply irrelevant. Although rejection is often attributed to the people's failure to understand what is good for them, some level of popular acquiescence is necessary for a development regime to retain a credible claim to be advancing popular well-being. For the transnational development apparatus (donors, development banks, consultants, and nongovernmental agencies), acquiescence is crucial. Lacking access to the means of violence, they can operate only by educating the desires and reforming the practices of their target population. For example, in the neoliberal development program promoted by the World Bank, which I describe in chapter 7, experts seek to render their target group entrepreneurial, participatory, responsible, and corruption-averse. These characteristics cannot be imposed—they can only be promoted by setting conditions to encourage people to behave as they ought.

All the elements of Foucault's triad continue to be in play in the global North and South alike. Minimally, control over territory, the classic concern of sovereignty, is a prerequisite for government. So too with law: law as a tactic to govern conduct is effective only because it is backed by the threat of punishment. If it was not so, few of us would pay our taxes. Arguably, despotism appropriately describes the punitive approach of welfare (now workfare) regimes in the global North that coerce people into improved behavior by threatening to withdraw their means of survival. Although they are supported by expert rationales, from the perspective of the victims these regimes differ little from the despotism of sovereigns who can take away life and liberty upon a whim. In Indonesia, as in the sub-Saharan postcolonies described by Mbembe, and the oil state of Nigeria described by Michael Watts, individuals, corporations, and other groupings operating with or without official sanction seize land, plunder resources, and imperil lives with impunity.[55] They are in league with the army and police, and with thugs and militias. Yet explanations of this state of affairs in terms of the failure to progress along a linear trajectory toward modern forms of rule overlook an important fact: the corporations protected by private militias include transnational enterprises listed on public stock-markets, valued at millions of dollars. Like the sovereigns of old, though differently dressed, contemporary transnational corporations, supported by self-described liberal regimes, take what they want because they can. They select victims at their convenience and write the rules to legitimate their actions. Thus the deductive powers associated with sovereignty are not subsumed within government; they coexist in awkward articulations, presenting contradictions I explore in several of the chapters to follow.

GOVERNMENTALITY'S LIMITS

To govern means to act on the actions of subjects who retain the capacity to act otherwise.[56] When violence is used, even when the rationale is improvement, the absolute authority of a sovereign to mete out punishment is brought into play. Violence stands at the limit where government and sovereignty articulate. I have already described another limit on government—the limit posed by politics, the ever-present possibility that a governmental intervention will be challenged by critics rejecting its diagnoses and prescriptions. Here I want to describe two further limits to government.

One is the limit posed by the target of government: population. Men in their relations, their links, their imbrication are not easy to manage. Men in their relations with wealth, resources, means of subsistence, recognized by Marx and others as the fulcrum of class-based injustice and political mobilization, must somehow become the target of technologies to secure optimal arrangements—a point to which I return below. Climate, epidemics, "territory with all its specific qualities"—these are not passive objects. They are, as Bruno Latour reminds us, actants, dynamic forces that constantly surprise those who would harness and control them.[57] Men in "their customs, habits, ways of acting and thinking" are no less refractory. The relations and processes with which government is concerned present intrinsic limits to the capacity of experts to improve things. There is inevitably an excess. There are processes and relations that cannot be reconfigured according to plan.

The second is the limit presented by the available forms of knowledge and technique. Foucault observed that governmentality's principal form of knowledge is political economy, by which he meant the liberal art of governing the polity in an economical manner—intervening in the delicate balance of social and economic processes no more, and no less, than is required to optimize them. The political economy of Adam Smith focused on the invisible hand of the market, understood as the hugely complex and largely self-regulating way in which economic processes coordinate the infinite range of individual wills. Just as experts should tread lightly in attempting to regulate the sphere that came to be known as "the economy," the art of government directed toward the population must recognize the delicate balance of its vital processes.[58] Programs of improvement must respect "the integrity and autonomous dynamics of the social body."[59] The social sciences emerged together with this new concept of population and its correlate, society. Their task was to devise a theoretical knowledge of the processes immanent in populations, a knowledge from which calculated interventions might follow.[60]

From the perspective of liberals such as Adam Smith, a claim of omniscience or the attempt to regulate society in totalizing fashion was counterproductive. Graham Burchell points out that the problem of excessive regulation was already evident in the eighteenth century, when critics did not fault rulers for their despotism: "You must not do this, you do not have the right." Rather, critics faulted rulers for their claims to omniscience and totalizing direction: "You must not do this because you do not and cannot know what you are doing."[61] As James Scott observes, the claim to totalizing knowledge combined with despotism is especially noxious. He exposes both the futility and the violence of detailed schemes of social engineering in which experts attempt to obliterate existing relations to build upon a clean slate.[62]

Rather than exercise total control, the objective of government is to sustain and optimize the processes upon which life depends. But beneficial outcomes cannot be guaranteed. Being "irreducibly utopian," governmental interventions can never achieve all they seek.[63] An important reason promised improvements are not delivered is that the diagnosis is incomplete. As I argued earlier, it cannot be complete if key political-economic processes are excluded from the bounded, knowable, technical domain. Further, governmental interventions routinely produce effects that are contradictory, even perverse. Indeed, the messiness of the world, its intractability to government, is caused, in part at least, by the overlapping of various governmental programs in historical sequence or, concurrently, one program at cross-purposes with another. Failures invite new interventions to correct newly identified—or newly created—deficiencies. The limits of each governmental intervention shape its successor. New thinking about how to govern arises not only from inspired ideas, but from the pragmatic observation of how things work out in practice.

The limits of government outlined here point to the limits of governmentality as an analytic—a way of understanding how power works, and what it does. To complement the insights of Foucault, I turn to Marx for a more robust way of theorizing the processes that animate the relations between "men and things." To attend to the ways people become mobilized to contest the truths in the name of which they are governed, and to change the conditions under which they live, I turn to Antonio Gramsci. My purpose in making these moves is not to construct a supertheory, an improbably seamless amalgam. Rather, I tolerate the untidiness and tension introduced by different theoretical traditions because of the distinct questions they pose, and the tools they offer to guide my analysis.

CAPITALISM AND ITS CONTRADICTIONS

In medieval England, the verb *to improve* meant to turn agricultural land to a profit, an operation often associated with enclosing "waste" or common land.[64] Enclosure is simultaneously an act of dispossession. It is central to the process Marx called primitive accumulation. Backed by a legal regime supporting the concept of private property, enclosure turns land into an asset that can be monopolized by an individual farmer, or a corporation. Possession of private property enables rural producers to become entrepreneurs who not only meet market demands, but accumulate land and capital. People who do not succeed in privatizing land, because they are slow to start, or unable to hold onto what they have in the face of violent exclusion or competition, are deprived of access to the means of production. They are obliged to become wage laborers, exploited by those whose command over capital enables them to pay workers less than the full value of their labor.

The transformational sequence appropriation-displacement-exploitation-accumulation, the core process explored by Marx in *Capital*, is operative in agrarian settings in many parts of the global South. In the highlands of Central Sulawesi that I will describe, farmers hold a concept of improvement very similar to that of medieval England: they recognize an investment of labor that increases the productivity of land as a form of enclosure that creates private rights. There too, some farmers have been more successful at accumulating land and capital than others. Yet the scale and rapidity of the appropriation-displacement sequence exposed by Marx has increased greatly in recent years. Tens of thousands of people who retained direct access to land a decade ago now find themselves landless. To understand why this is happening, I need the analytical tools Marx supplied. I also need to understand how the conditions for this transformation were set. This means examining the ways in which government and capitalism intersect. There are four elements to this intersection.

First and most obviously, capitalist relations serve double duty as a vehicle of extraction and a vehicle for imparting the habits of diligence, responsibility and the careful weighing of costs and benefits that characterize, in liberal thinking, the ideal, autonomous subject of rights.[65] It is, in part, recognition of the "improving" effects of capitalist discipline upon sections of the population deemed to lack these habits that prevents experts from proposing the restructuring of relations of production as a solution to poverty. Competition, the experts argue, spurs efficiency.

Second, as Marx recognized, capitalism is not an autonomous system. Primitive accumulation is a violent process. The laws that support private property, enforce exclusion, and produce "free" labor are violence by other means. In metropoles and colonies alike, the profits that accrue to capital have been subsidized by investments in infrastructure supplied by ruling regimes from the public purse. It takes intervention to keep capitalist economies growing. Experts justify intervention as a measure to optimize the general good. Even though they do not stand to profit directly from capitalist enterprise, they promote growth because they are convinced it is beneficial to the population at large. Yet interventions that set the conditions for growth simultaneously set the conditions for some sections of the population to be dispossessed. Winners and losers do not emerge naturally through the magic of the market, they are selected.[66]

Third, optimizing requires that experts pay attention to the displacement and impoverishment that are co-produced with growth. This is not an afterthought. Intervention is a condition of growth in the capitalist mode. The deliberate creation of markets for land and labor provokes what Polanyi called a "countermovement"—a demand for intervention grounded in the recognition that "leaving the fate of soil and people to the market would be tantamount to annihilating them." Demands for social protection have a broad constituency as variously situated groups concur on the need to alleviate misery and mitigate disruption and disarray.[67] Managing the fallout from capitalism's advance is one of the tasks assigned to trustees. Trusteeship does not translate into any permanent solution to problems of disorder and decay— indeed, as Michael Cowen and Robert Shenton stress, it cannot, since there cannot be security for everyone caught in capitalism's wake.[68] Trustees promising improvement must distance themselves from complicity in chaos and destruction. Their interventions are "always the cure, never the cause."[69] Trustees cannot address—indeed, may not acknowledge—the contradictory forces with which they are engaged. Thus attempts to render "men in their relations to . . . wealth, resources, means of subsistence" technical and governable are chronically incomplete. Capitalism and improvement are locked in an awkward embrace.

Fourth, trustees use a particular population's failure to improve (to turn nature's bounty to a profit), or to conserve (to protect nature for the common good) as rationales for their dispossession, and as the justification to assign resources to people who will make better use of them.[70] In the colonial period dispossession was backed by what Richard Drayton calls the myth of the profligate native: "Whoever was on the spot was wasting its resources, and . . . might legitimately be expelled, or submitted to European tutelage."[71] This myth is alive and well in national bureaucracies and transnational agencies promoting agricultural development and conservation. It continues to be used to justify dispossession, as I will show.

The intersection of capitalist processes and programs of improvement is a striking feature of the transformations currently occurring in the Sulawesi hills I describe in the middle of the book. Officials have assigned land used by highlanders since time immemorial to corporations promising to boost production, and to conservation agencies enclosing nature to save it from farmers' abuse. Displacement is also occurring as an unintended effect of programs designed to promote the welfare of highlanders, notably by resettling them out of the hills into valleys, better to provide them with roads and services. The land base for valley settlement, however, is insufficient. Unable to survive in the valleys and excluded from the forest, highlanders have become landless, and they have mobilized to reclaim their due. To explain how this mobilization came about I need to draw upon another set of concepts gleaned from the tradition of Antonio Gramsci.

CRITICAL POSITIONS

Critique, writes Nikolas Rose, has the potential to "reshape and expand the terms of political debate, enabling different questions to be asked, enlarging spaces of legitimate contestation, modifying the relations of the different participants to the truths in the name of which they govern or are governed."[72] The critic I picture, from Rose's account, is the academic whose primary medium for learning about and changing the world is text. In contrast, the critic conjured by Gramsci is an activist, interested both in studying and in helping to produce conjunctures at which social groups come to see themselves as collectivities, develop critical insight, and mobilize to confront their adversaries. There are also the "prickly subjects" I mentioned earlier—the targets of improvement schemes, who occupy an important place in my account.

A follower of Marx, Gramsci considered the fundamental groups driving social transformation to be classes differentiated by their access to the means of production. Yet he understood that the actual social groups engaged in situated struggles are far more diverse, reflections of their fragmentary experiences, attachments, and embedded cultural ideas. Thus for him, the question of how a collective, critical practice emerges could not be answered with reference to abstract concepts such as capital and labor. It had to be addressed concretely, taking into account the multiple positions that people occupy, and the diverse powers they encounter.[73] Building on Gramsci's work, Stuart Hall proposes an understanding of identity as the product of articulation. Rather than view identity as the fixed ground from which insights and actions follow, he argues that new interests, new positionings of self and others, and new meanings emerge contingently in the course of struggle. Thus a Gramscian approach yields an understanding of the practice of politics and the critical insights on which it depends as specific, situated, and embodied. An example may help to illustrate the kind of analysis this approach enables.

In 2001, Freddy, a young man from Lake Lindu in Central Sulawesi, recounted to me how he had "learned to practice politics" (*belajar berpolitik*). What this meant, for him, was learning to figure out for himself what was wrong and right in the world, and how to carry that assessment forward to bring about change. His epiphany occurred a few years earlier, when an NGO based in the provincial capital Palu began helping the people of his village organize to contest the construction of a hydroelectric dam that would flood their land and forcibly evict them. Home from Java, where he had worked and studied for some years, he was sent by the village Headman to observe the activities of this NGO, and report back on what kinds of trouble they were fomenting. So he started to attend their meetings, listening from the back, and came to the gradual realization that much of what they said about the importance of livelihoods, conservation, and the legitimacy of customary land rights made perfect sense. In contrast, the more he listened to officials promoting the dam as a step toward "development" in the province as well as a better future for the villagers, the less credible he found them.

The campaign against the dam occurred under the New Order regime, when individuals who had critical insights shared them frequently in the form of cynical jokes and asides but did not articulate them in public forums or engage in collective action. NGOs such as the ones assisting Freddy's village were threatened by the authorities and accused of being communist. But seeing the dedication of the NGO's young staff, and absorbing some of their intellectual energy, he became convinced that learning to practice politics was a positive step. He described his feeling as one of awakening from a long and lazy sleep. He began to look with new eyes at the people around him in his village and in the state apparatus who were too afraid to engage in political debate. When I met him in 2001, after the fall of Suharto, he felt the possibilities for practicing politics had opened up, but people were slow to grasp them. They had to unlearn habits of quiescence cultivated through three decades of New Order doublethink and doubletalk and start to think of politics positively, as an entitlement.

Throughout the struggle for independence and especially in the period 1945 to 1965, until the army-led coup that ushered in the massacre of half a million people labeled communists, many Indonesians had been active in conducting politics and vigorous in debating the shape of the nation. There were mass mobilizations of workers, peasants, women, youth, regional, and religious communities, all engaged in struggles over the distribution of resources and the recognition of differences (cultural, historical, regional, religious) that supplied points of distinction and alliance. But Sukarno, the first president, retreated into the paternalism of "Guided Democracy," paving the way for his successor, Suharto, to declare politics an unhelpful distraction to the work of development. *Politics* became a dirty word. The goal of Suharto's regime was to secure a stable state of nonpolitics in which nothing "untoward" or "excessive" would happen—the condition of eerie stillness memorably described in John Pemberton's ethnography about Java.[74]

In the hostile conditions of the New Order, reclaiming politics and giving it a positive inflection was no mean feat. To understand how it was achieved by a young man in a highland village in Sulawesi, we must examine both the process through which his political positioning emerged and the particular shape it took. Together with his covillagers, Freddy came to see himself as a member of an indigenous group defending its territory against the state—an identity he did not carry with him when he left the village to pursue his studies years before. That identity emerged when a set of ideas to which he was exposed by the NGOs supporting his village helped him to make sense of his situation, locate allies and opponents, and organize.[75] Identities, as Stuart Hall argues, "are subject to the continuous 'play' of history, culture and power." They are "unstable points of identification or suture . . . Not an essence but a *positioning*."[76]

In this book, I explore the positionings that enable people to practice a critical politics. I also explore positionings formed through the will to improve: the position of trustee, and the position of deficient subject whose conduct is to be conducted. Gramsci did not examine the position of trustee, which stands in an awkward relation to that of the "organic intellectual" whose job is to help subalterns to understand their oppression and mobilize to challenge it. Yet the work of the intellectual and the trustee are not entirely distinct. As I will show, Indonesian activists engaged in a critical politics find numerous deficiencies in the population they aim to support. Their support becomes technical, a matter of instructing people in the proper practice of politics. They too are programmers. They share in the will to improve, and more specifically, the will to empower. Their vision of improvement involves people actively claiming the rights and taking on the duties of democratic citizenship.[77]

The value of a Gramscian approach, for my purposes, is the focus on how and why particular, situated subjects mobilize to contest their oppression. This was not a question elaborated by Foucault. Conversely, Foucault has the edge on explicit theorization of how power shapes the conditions in which lives are lived. Although Gramscians turn to the concept of hegemony for this purpose, Gramsci's formulations were notoriously enigmatic and fragmented. In her critical review of the use of Gramsci by anthropologists, Kate Crehan argues that the term *hegemony* for Gramsci "simply names the problem—that of how the power relations underpinning various forms of inequality are produced and reproduced."[78] He used it not to describe a fixed condition, but rather as a way of talking about "how power is lived in particular times and places," always, he thought, an amalgam of coercion and consent.[79]

Foucault shared the concern to examine how power is lived but approached it differently. Gramsci understood consent to be linked to consciousness. Foucault understood subjects to be formed by practices of which they might be unaware, and to which their consent is neither given nor withheld. Further, Foucault highlighted the ways in which power enables as much as it constrains or coerces. It works through practices that are, for the most part, mundane and routine. Thus the binary that is compatible with a Gramscian analytic—people either consent to the exercise of power or they resist it—was not useful to Foucault.[80] I do not find it necessary to choose between Gramsci and Foucault on this point. Some practices render power visible; they trigger conscious reactions adequately described in terms such as resistance, accommodation, or consent. Other modes of power are more diffuse, as are peoples' responses to them. John Allen put this point eloquently when he observed that power "often makes its presence felt through a variety of modes playing across one another. The erosion of choice, the closure of possibilities, the manipulation of outcomes, the threat of force, the assent of authority or the inviting gestures of a seductive presence, and the combinations thereof."[81]

Powers that are multiple cannot be totalizing and seamless. For me this is a crucial observation. The multiplicity of power, the many ways that practices position people, the various modes "playing across one another" produce gaps and contradictions. Subjects formed in these matrices—subjects like Freddy—encounter inconsistencies that provide grist for critical insights. Further, powers once experienced as diffuse, or indeed not experienced as powers at all, can become the subject of a critical consciousness. Indeed, exposing how power works, unsettling truths so that they could be scrutinized and contested was as central to the political agenda of Foucault as it was for Gramsci.[82] Foucault did not elaborate on how such insights might become collective, although the connection is easily made. To the extent that practices of government form groups rather than isolated individuals, critical insight is potentially shared. One of the inadvertent effects of programs of improvement—the dam at Lake Lindu, for example—is to produce social groups capable of identifying common interests and mobilizing to change their situation.[83] Such collectivities have their own internal class, ethnic, and gender fractures. Their encounter with attempts to improve them forms the basis of their political ideas and actions. Scholars working in a Foucauldian mode have often observed the "strategic reversibility" of power relations, as diagnoses of deficiencies imposed from above become "repossessed" as demands from below, backed by a sense of entitlement.[84] Bringing insights from Foucault and Gramsci together enables me to extend this observation, and to put the point more starkly: improvement programs may inadvertently stimulate a political challenge. The way they do this, moreover, is situated and contingent. Floods and diseases, topography, the variable fertility of the soil, prices on world markets, the location of a road—any of these may stimulate critical analysis by puncturing expert schemes and exposing their flaws.

Studies that draw their inspiration from Foucault tend to be anemic on the practice of politics.[85] In Rose's *Powers of Freedom*, for example, discussion of politics is confined to the conclusion, "Beyond Government." There Rose argues that "analysis of the forms of contestation might help us understand the ways in which something new is created, a difference is introduced into history in the form of a politics." This is not, he says, to "seek to identify particular agents of a radical politics—be they classes, races, or genders—or to distinguish once and for all the forces of reaction from those of progression in terms of fixed identities. Rather, one would examine the ways in which creativity arises out of the situation of human beings engaged in particular relations of force and meaning, and what is made out of the possibilities of that location."[86] I find this a very clear statement of a critical research agenda worthy of attention, but it is not one that Rose himself pursues. The reasons for this are both theoretical and methodological.

I have been arguing that the practice of politics is best examined through a Gramscian approach alert to the constellations of power in particular times and places, and the overdetermined, messy situations in which creativity arises. This is a research strategy fully compatible with the analytic of governmentality, as I will show. However, it is strategy Rose rejects, as he wants to separate studies of governmentality from what he calls sociologies of rule—studies of the ways in which rule is actually accomplished, in all their complexity.[87] To study government, he says, is not to start from "the apparently obvious historical or sociological questions: what happened and why. It is to start by asking what authorities of various sorts wanted to happen, in relation to problems defined how, in pursuit of what objectives, through what strategies and techniques."[88] On similar grounds, Foucault argued that to study the genealogy of an institutional complex such as incarceration is quite distinct from ethnographic study of the "witches' brew" of practices that actually transpire inside prisons.[89]

I agree that study of the rationale of governmental schemes and the study of social history are distinct kinds of inquiry, and they require distinct sets of tools. My point is that we should not privilege one over the other. Further, I argue that bringing them into dialogue offers insights into how programs of government are constituted and contested. Rather than conduct two separate analyses, I make the intersection of governmental programs with the world they would transform my principal subject in this book. To explain how I propose to examine that intersection, I turn now to a discussion of method.

TOWARD AN ETHNOGRAPHIC METHOD

My research strategy brings together the two kinds of study Rose would keep apart: analysis of governmental interventions (their genealogy, their diagnoses and prescriptions, their constitutive exclusions) and analysis of what happens when those interventions become entangled with the processes they would regulate and improve. This strategy takes me beyond the plan, the map, and the administrative apparatus, into conjunctures where attempts to achieve the "right disposition of things" encounter—and produce—a witches' brew of processes, practices, and struggles that exceed their scope.

To examine the "beyond" of programming does not mean replacing a false object of study (the program) with a true one (the world). Foucault readily admitted that nothing happens as laid down in programmers' schemes. Yet he insisted that they are not simply utopias "in the heads of a few projectors." They are not "abortive schemas for the creation of a reality. They are fragments of reality." They "induce a whole series of effects in the real." They "crystallize into institutions, they inform individual behavior, they act as grids for the perception and evaluation of things."[90] I take up this insight to argue that programs, and the messy consequences of programs, are equally real, and both merit attention.[91]

To examine the effects of programs at particular conjunctures does not mean attempting to grasp all things at once. An ethnographic study is always selective. Nor does it mean treating places as isolates, complete unto themselves. Quite the opposite, since, as Doreen Massey explains, "What gives a place its specificity is not some long internalized history but the fact that it is constructed out of a particular constellation of relations, articulated together at a particular locus."[92] Thus I explore how governmental interventions configure ways of thinking and acting not by operating alone, but by working as part of a constellation. I attend to particular histories, landscapes, memories, and embedded cultural ideas, better to grasp how power is lived, produced, and contested.

My writing strategy tacks back and forth between examination of the emergence of a new target of governmental intervention and exploration of the effects of that intervention as it intersects with other forces and vectors on historically configured terrain. I conduct detailed readings of program documents and set them in the context of their constitutive exclusions. I use ethnographic and historical sources to expose the refractory processes screened out as programmers construct an arena amenable to management and calculation. I examine the fractures in that technical domain, uneasy collaborations between trustees and their target groups, and the compromised position of experts who promise improvements they cannot deliver. I attend to formal practices of planning, and to the "subterranean practices" through which programs are adjusted to respond to contingencies and reversals.[93] These practices include, among others, looking away when rules are broken, failing to gather or to use information that undermines the linear narrative of the plan, and constructing data to demonstrate unerring "success."[94] I explore the challenges presented by people at the receiving end of all this attention, as they weigh the costs and benefits of improvement schemes in relation to situated struggles over land, livelihood, and claims to place. I do not position them as heroes contesting power from the outside but show, rather, how their struggles have been formed within its matrices. I examine the ways political challenges are closed down by new programs of government, sometimes to be opened again in the moments of reversal intrinsic to power as a relation of "permanent provocation."

I begin in chapter 1 with an overview of how contradictions intrinsic to the will to improve played out in Indonesia over a period of two centuries, as one governmental assemblage yielded to the next. In chapter 2, I examine the first round of improvement schemes that were implemented in the highlands of Central Sulawesi, teasing out what it was that trustees sought to change, the techniques they devised, and the outcomes that emerged. In chapter 3, I focus on the processes of capital and identity formation that were stimulated by these projects, or intersected with them to produce the conditions in which violent conflict would erupt. In chapter 4, I examine a second set of improvement schemes that attempted to achieve "integrated conservation and development" in the sixty or more villages surrounding the Lore Lindu National Park. In chapter 5, I focus on political challenge, tracking how and why a group of farmers mobilized to contest the authority of the many trustees who had devised projects to help them and took action to bring about improvement on their own terms. In chapter 6, I examine a further intervention provoked by the challenge to the park: an attempt to use an elaborate system of managed consultation to persuade park border villagers to "buy in" to conservation. In chapter 7, I zoom out from Sulawesi to interrogate a billion-dollar, nationwide project of the World Bank intended to foster practices of transparency and accountability in the provision of rural infrastructure, and the use of mediation to manage the conflicts that emerge, according to World Bank social experts, as an inevitable byproduct of economic advance.

Focus and selection are necessary in order to make an argument, but I have endeavored not to reduce complexity or force everything neatly into a fixed framework. Rather, I see the specifics of my various study sites, their untidiness, as a provocation that enables me to put pressure on the conceptual repertoire I have adopted and confront theory with the world it would explain. Careful study of specific conjunctures—the kind of work conducted by anthropologists and social historians, among others—opens a space for theoretical work of a kind that is rather different from that of scholars engaged in the immanent critique of theoretical texts, or the production of general models. My hope is that readers interested primarily in governmentality will learn something by examining practices of government through the lens of an anthropologist committed to what Sherry Ortner calls an "ethnographic stance." This approach produces understanding "through richness, texture, and detail, rather than parsimony, refinement, and (in the sense used by mathematicians) elegance."[95] Conversely, I hope that readers interested primarily in Indonesia will find that thinking about the will to improve offers a new perspective on familiar terrain: so much of Indonesia's history has been shaped by this will, more or less directly. Finally, I hope that readers involved in enterprises such as rural development and environmental management find, in my account, grist for their own critical thinking about programs of improvement, their prospects, and their limits.

CONTRADICTORY POSITIONS

This chapter explores two of the contradictions I outlined in the introduction, contradictions deeply embedded in the will to improve. The first is the contradiction between the promotion of capitalist processes and concern to improve the condition of the dispossessed. I examine how this contradiction played out through a series of governmental assemblages, each with its characteristic diagnoses and prescriptions, its preferred way of balancing profits, native welfare, and other "specific finalities." The second is the way that programs of improvement designed to reduce the distance between trustees and deficient subjects actually reinscribe the boundary that positions them on opposite sides of an unbridgeable divide. This boundary is the contradictory foundation that makes colonial and contemporary improvement programs thinkable, anxious and doggedly persistent. Yet it is not self-evident. It is produced through situated practices that can be critically explored.

My examination in this chapter takes the form of a history of government, teasing out the problems that various authorities sought to address, the techniques they deployed, their contradictions, and their effects. It is an overview, covering in schematic form a period of two centuries (1800–2000), with particular emphasis on the island of Java, the focus of colonial attention before the Netherlands East Indies Empire was "rounded out" in the period 1900–1910. Subsequent chapters, focused on the highlands of Sulawesi, examine governmental programs of the colonial and contemporary periods at much closer range.

Although I have arranged the parts of the chapter in chronological order, this is not a narrative of governmentality rising. It is not the case that late colonial rule overcame the racism and despotism of earlier regimes, nor did independence bring all citizens into the nation on an equal basis. The governmental assemblage that took shape on Java early in the nineteenth century was far more optimistic about the capacity of Indonesians to develop their own capacities through a "normal" process of self-improvement than the assemblage that emerged under Suharto in the New Order, in which the boundary separating trustees from those they would know and improve was sharp indeed. Arguments about the racial superiority of Europeans, relatively inchoate for more than two centuries while the Netherlands East Indies Company (Vereenigde Oost-Indische Compagnie, or voc) competed with other parties for a share and eventual monopoly of trade in the archipelago, became much more pronounced after 1800 when the Dutch crown assumed sovereignty. They were entrenched in separate legal systems and reached their peak under the ethical policy (1905–30), precisely the moment when the white man's burden of improving Native lives was most clearly enunciated.[1] As I will show, this was also the period when the "otherness" of the Natives, their ineffable difference, was conceptually elaborated, empirically investigated, and made the basis for policies aimed to restore "tradition" and harmonious, Asiatic village life.

THE RIGHT TO RULE

As far as possible, the voc ruled indirectly. It reinforced the powers of local rulers so that they could extract more profits for themselves, and for the company, by intensifying existing systems of appanages, tax farms, forced labor, usury, and trading monopolies. In Java, it used Chinese as agents in its collection system.[2] Its objectives were not governmental—it did not intervene in native lives in order to improve them or make them more secure.[3] It reserved discipline for the population of the territory it ruled directly—a minute proportion of the territory that later became the Netherlands East Indies. Even then, it asserted detailed control only when this was necessary to maximize profits.[4] The predominance of the voc's extractive orientation is evident from its accounts. It paid stockholders an average of 18 percent per year for two hundred years (1602–1800), a return so high the company was eventually bankrupt.[5]

The bankruptcy of the voc obliged the Dutch crown to assume direct responsibility for the Indies in 1800. Thereafter, Dutch authorities became more deeply involved in the lives of subject populations in some parts of the archipelago—namely Java, parts of Sumatra, and the northern tip of Sulawesi. Over much of the rest of the archipelago, Dutch rule remained nominal, taking the form of treaties and contracts with local rulers to protect Dutch commercial interests. Only in 1900–1910 did the Dutch establish territorial control over the entire archipelago by the extension of existing contracts in some areas, and direct military action in others.

The reasons for the territorial extension and intensification of Dutch rule around 1900 are the subject of debate. Although some historians have argued that the Dutch were obliged to consolidate their hold over territory to ward off competing colonial powers, others argue that the spheres of influence of Britain, France and the United States were stable by 1900, and Dutch interests were sufficiently protected by the British as *arbiter mundi*.[6] The argument that commercial motives prompted intensification is persuasive for some parts of the archipelago but not others.[7] Many expansionary ventures "made little sense in terms of economic profitability" and some were "financially disastrous."[8] Costs could easily outrun returns. State-owned mines and plantations plus port duties added important sources of revenue, but European corporations paid little tax.[9] Military ventures could be ruinously expensive, the prolonged Aceh War (1873–1903) a case in point.[10]

Decisions about territorial expansion, argues Benedict Anderson, "were made in Batavia rather than The Hague, and for local *raison d'etat*."[11] What were these reasons? By the end of the nineteenth century, Robert Elson observes, the "right to rule was no longer a function of divine anointing, or possession of the palace or regalia, but rather of secular efficiency, formalized order, and getting things done."[12] Local rulers had always been awkward partners for the Dutch, routinely despised, critiqued, and sometimes unseated for their despotic ways and personal failings. What changed around 1900 was not the conduct of local rulers, but the practices and assumptions of the Dutch. As Dutch emphasis on regulation, enumeration, and bureaucratic compliance increased, so did the range of fronts upon which local rulers were found deficient. Concerns for the well-being of the colonized population, popular fare in the Netherlands, and "bureaucratic concerns about Dutch prestige and law and order" were conjoined in critique of the misdeeds and defiance of local rulers.[13] Colonial archives reveal "the fear of diminishing the prestige of the colonial government, and need to maintain vigorous Dutch authority."[14] Maintaining that prestige and authority came to require a set of practices different from those that had previously prevailed.

Security, improvement, and systematic administration were key, by the late nineteenth century, to how the legitimacy of government and the right to rule were defined.[15] Officials justified military action against the population in these terms. Violence was the prerequisite to welfare.[16] Sovereignty over territory and a concern with the condition of the population emerged together in the colonial situation, and remained entwined there as the focus shifted to the question of how to achieve not one dogmatic goal but a "plurality of specific aims," a "whole series of specific finalities," the problematic of governmentality exposed by Foucault.[17]

GOVERNING WITH ECONOMY

In the areas where secure control over territory was achieved early in the nineteenth century, the question of how to govern, and to what ends, soon followed. The approach of Sir Stamford Raffles, appointed to rule Java during a brief interregnum when control of the colony passed to the British (1812–16), was informed by liberal ideas about individual rights and freedoms, the self-regulating character of markets, and the capacity of the native population to bring about its own improvement once the necessary conditions had been set. Raffles's associate William Colebrooke wrote that the people of Java

> possess in aggregate as large a share of natural intelligence and acuteness, of patriotism and enthusiasm, as will be found among the lower orders of any country; & it goes for to confirm the universal doctrine that Mankind in the same circumstances is always the same. . . . Java might in 30 years or less be elevated into a respectable & eminent free state . . . [if Java was established] under the protection of England 'till by introduction of Arts and Education the people might be fitted to govern themselves.[18]

In addition to freeing the peasantry from what he saw as excessive control and exploitation by Native elites, Raffles sought to improve the peasants' capacity to consume the products of British industry, routinize administration, and stabilize revenue. He thought these diverse ends could be achieved through a single strategy: creating the conditions for free trade and free agrarian production. Farmers would prosper simply by following their natural interest. The state would obtain its revenue directly from independent cultivators and ensure it was collected systematically according to law, thus eliminating extortion by local elites. All these changes could be achieved, moreover, merely by adjusting the social forces that were already present.[19] A study of land tenure commissioned by Raffles found, conveniently enough, that all the land on Java was previously the property of the indigenous rulers, from whom it had passed into the hands of the successor sovereign power, namely the British crown. Thus the crown, as landlord, could derive its revenue as rent. Rent would not be alien to Java's peasants, already familiar with concepts of individual land tenure. The intermediaries known as *bekel*, currently operating as agents of a personalized and hierarchical appanage system, could serve as village Headmen, tasked with collecting rents and taxes on behalf of the landlord state.

Although Raffles presented his policies as the mere confirmation and systematization of existing tradition, they proved difficult to implement with the very limited administrative apparatus at Raffles's disposal. In the areas where his reforms were implemented, they did not produce the expected results because they "assumed a social structure that did not in fact exist."[20] Peasants were indeed tied into personalized extractive systems that did not disappear. Yet Raffles was not simply guilty of bad research. As with other programmers, his knowledge was shaped by the interventions he envisaged, and by the need to represent the domain to be governed as "an intelligible field with specifiable limits and particular characteristics."[21] The model was India, where the British sovereign claimed the position of superlandlord, and administration was conducted through village Headmen. Thus the historian Furnivall found it "difficult . . . to resist the suggestion that in the material collected for this enquiry Raffles found what he wanted, and expected." Other critics, Furnivall observes, put the point more strongly, arguing that "Raffles discovered in Java the economic system which the British had invented for Bengal."[22]

Rectifying the confusion, protest, and impoverishment created by Raffles's new system of land rents was one of the tasks facing the Dutch when the colony was returned to their control.[23] Johannes van den Bosch, assigned to the Indies in the role of Governor General in 1830, found Java's peasants in rebellion, and the colonial state weak. The Netherlands' economy was stagnant, and the costs of running the Indies empire exceeded revenues. Unlike Britain, the Netherlands had no industrial manufactures to export and was interested in the Indies principally as a locus for production from which revenues could be obtained. Van den Bosch's task was to make the Indies both profitable and secure.[24] To this end, he instituted the *Cultuurstelsel* (Culture System or Cultivation System) in Java and in Minahasa (the northern tip of Sulawesi), intervening to organize production as well as monopolize trade in key products: sugar in the lowlands and coffee in the hills. Working through "traditional" authorities and village units reconfigured for the purpose, the Culture System conscripted land and labor from around 70 percent of Java's households, supplying a third of the Netherlands' state revenue by the 1850s.[25] In Minahasa, colonial authorities laid out new villages and roads and subjected the population to an "unprecedented level of colonial surveillance and control."[26]

Successful as it was for the Netherlands in economic terms, critics at the time and subsequently have regarded the Culture System as a throwback to the coercive tactics of the VOC, a system out of step with the rising tide of liberal thinking emphasizing market principles.[27] Based on a careful study of Van den Bosch's economic ideas, however, Albert Schrauwers argues that Van den Bosch shared many of Raffles's liberal premises.[28] He too sought to govern through existing social forces, merely adjusting them to produce the desired results. His diagnosis, however, was different. He did not share Raffles's faith that market forces, set free, would be sufficient to reform Native conduct. He recognized that capitalism was contradictory. His analysis of rural poverty in the Netherlands led him to identify a problem—lack of a habit of industriousness—that could not be addressed through market forces alone. Rural paupers lacked industry, he argued, because any surplus they produced was quickly extracted from them by the owners of capital. Wage workers, similarly, were disciplined not by morality but by their lack of access to the means of production. They were wage slaves, not free men and women contracting to sell their labor as a matter of choice. From his analysis, a course of action followed. Rather than seek to displace capitalism, which he regarded as legitimate, or to eliminate poverty, which he regarded as an inevitable feature of a class society, he sought to use disciplinary means to create habits of industriousness, substituting for the incentives the "self-regulating" market failed to supply. His goal was to make the poor more productive, and less threatening to the state.

For the Netherlands, Van den Bosch devised a system of agricultural colonies, the first of which opened in 1818. These were parapenal institutions tasked with instilling discipline in the criminalized poor. Inmates were sorted into categories and permitted progressively more freedoms as their behavior conformed. Eventually, they were expected to graduate to become independent farmers. In Java, Van den Bosch understood the task of government in similar terms: how to discipline underproductive farmers to produce marketable surpluses, which would not only provide for their own limited needs, but also support the edifice of the state and capitalist profit. Since the system of detailed supervision in parapenal colonies he devised for the Netherlands could not be extended to the Indies population at large, discipline must be supplied by other means. Farmers should be obliged to pay rent for the use of land Raffles had conveniently declared the property of the sovereign authority, then British, now Dutch. Rent would take the form of agricultural commodities produced under a regulated system. Payment would be the collective responsibility of village communities, enforced through the "traditional" authority of Native elites. This authority would be strengthened by new administrative techniques, including the demarcation of village boundaries and the registration of populations to prevent flight. Thus emerged the blend of collective and hierarchical features that later came to be regarded as "traditional" village Java.[29]

It is ironic, as Schrauwers points out, that (invented) traditional authority and village-based communalism became the prerequisite for the coerced production of market crops, while tradition was also named the major obstacle that the Dutch civilizational mission had to overcome. Significantly, the traditionalism of Java's Natives was taken to indicate that they could *not* be expected to graduate into independent commodity producers, nor would the market become truly "free" as Raffles had anticipated. For Van den Bosch, their tradition-bound character rendered the Javanese permanent minors who would require the ongoing tutelage of a disciplinary state.[30] His strategy was premised on, as it produced, an indelible boundary permanently separating trustees from their wards.[31] Under such a system it made no sense to treat Natives as subjects of right, with means of recourse against the arbitrariness of the "traditional" authorities or the Dutch.[32] The system required, as Daniel Lev points out, an "unmistakable demarcation between the exploiters and exploitees."[33] This point was sharply expressed by J. C. Baud, Governor of the Indies in the period following Van den Bosch: "Language, color, religion, morals, origin, historical memories, everything is different between the Dutch and the Javanese. We are the rulers, they are the ruled."[34]

Despite the expressed intention to govern the Indies population through "their own" traditions, the changes introduced by the Culture System were far reaching. Some of these changes were intended, but many were not. The Culture System as it emerged in practice was not the product of Van den Bosch's ideas alone. It was situated within an assemblage of governmental objectives and techniques of diverse provenance. It intersected with economic processes already in play. In George Kahin's assessment, it deepened the structures of inequality set in place by the extractive practices of the VOC. These included an increased authoritarianism legitimated by tradition; a weakening of the economic and political bargaining position of the peasantry in relation to the nobility; a more communalistic (though not egalitarian) organization of village economic life as the extreme tax burden was portioned out; a dulling of the spirit of individual enterprise; a reduction of direct contact between peasants and the markets for their products; and the virtual elimination of merchant classes.[35] The material outcome was prosperity for some people, in some areas, reflected in increased purchase of salt, European cloth, more consumption of rice and meat, and a busier commercial life.[36] For others, Kahin records conditions of superexploitation in which the forced use of land and labor was far more than the stipulated limits, and famines resulted, especially in the period 1843–48. In one district of Java, the population fell from 336,000 to 120,000, in another from 89,000 to 9,000.[37] Further, the structural problem of tying the economy to production of primary commodities such as sugar and coffee destined for volatile world markets became all too evident with each downturn in international trade.[38]

MARKET FREEDOMS?

Under a barrage of criticism, variously citing the need to promote Native welfare and the benefits of market freedoms, the Culture System for sugar was phased out by 1870, although forced cultivation of coffee continued in some areas until 1918.[39] From 1870 to the end of the century, the colonial regime entered the so-called liberal period in which the principles of laissez-faire capitalism were widely enunciated. In practice, as in all liberal systems, the regime intervened repeatedly to set the conditions under which a nominally "free" market would operate, and favored groups would prosper.[40]

Land tenure was an important terrain upon which colonial officials debated alternate models of improvement for the Native population. Officials of a liberal persuasion favored transforming customary Native tenure into a system of private rights to facilitate the sale and lease of land for commercial purposes. They argued that Natives would benefit from participating in markets for land and labor. To progress, they must be set free to find their own destiny. Others in what was called the conservative camp argued that protection of Native welfare required retention of the old policies preventing the alienation of Native land to foreigners. The Agrarian Law passed in 1870 was a compromise that recognized some Native rights but declared the state to be the owner of forests and any other "wasteland" not under permanent cultivation.[41] In an interpretation of the law regarded by the conservatives as a travesty, officials ruled that the category wasteland included managed forests and the fallow land Native farmers used for rotational or swidden cultivation.[42] The effect was to remove extensive areas of land from Native control and make it available for long-term lease to large-scale commercial ventures, notably agricultural plantations in Java and Sumatra. No definitive maps were produced, however, showing where village territories ended and the state-claimed wasteland began. Over the next century, village territories were marked by default. They became defined as the areas not included in plantations, or left over after the demarcation of what Nancy Peluso and Peter Vandergeest call the political forest—the state-claimed forest estate. But these state territorializations were contested, and they remained a front of struggle throughout the archipelago.[43]

Administrators and scientists of the liberal period used Native profligacy as justification to assert state control over forests. An ordinance of 1874 prohibited swidden cultivation and required villagers to obtain official permission before clearing forest to extend village agriculture. Java's lucrative teak forests came under increasingly efficient "scientific" management.[44] Forest officials had villages moved to create continuous forest tracts.[45] The obvious tension between state responsibility to conserve forests and the interest of entrepreneurs in expanding plantation agriculture produced a synergy on another front. Natives excluded from the forests that were central to their livelihoods became available as labor for European enterprise. The Agrarian Law was unevenly applied. In some areas, notably the fringes of Java's teak forests, villagers who were classified as poachers and thieves could be arrested and evicted. Even if they escaped this fate, their "illegal" situation made them vulnerable. Thus they could be co-opted to work as forest labor on the most minimal terms and subjected to multiple supplementary forms of extraction and harassment.[46] In Sumatra, peasants were able to rearrange their productive activities on the margins of the colonial plantation economy, and reject wage labor.[47] To fill the labor gap in Sumatra's mines and plantations, indentured workers, mainly Javanese, were imported on a large scale under very severe contracts, bound by debts that were manipulated through routinized gambling, and subject to minute supervision and fierce physical discipline. Far from promoting "free" wage labor, the self-professed liberal regime underwrote profits by setting conditions for servitude at least as severe as those of precolonial slavery and the Culture System, and often worse.[48]

Colonial rule in the liberal period was not devoid of concerns for Native welfare, but the theory that capitalist growth would translate into Native well-being was, of course, incomplete. In addition to supplying administration, entrepreneurs expected the regime to supply the infrastructure for mining, forestry, plantations, and other industries. They wanted the state to set conditions so that commerce would thrive, but the rewards were reaped as entrepreneurial profit, leaving state coffers bare. Thus there were never sufficient funds for programs such as Native education. Nor did peasants and workers thrive in the boom times and support economic growth through consumption. They were exploited and taxed to the hilt, indeed more severely, according to later welfare surveys, than they had been under the Culture System, whose authoritarian abuses liberal rule was supposed to correct.[49] The contradiction was plain to see. The promotion of free markets and the unbridled search for commercial profits, wrote Furnivall, "released forces, moral and material, creating a new colonial world, which teemed with problems that on Liberal principles were insoluble."[50] As profits dwindled and liberal doctrines promoting market freedoms lost their allure, the voice of critics highlighting the poverty and insecurity of the Native population came to the fore, producing a policy shift in a direction the Dutch labeled "ethical."

ETHICAL RULE

A sense of official responsibility for the welfare of citizens was present in the Indies throughout the nineteenth century, as a permanent counterpoint to promarket principles and revenue demands. It was present in Raffles's concern to eliminate despotism on Java and in Van den Bosch's Culture System. It was present in a famous critique of the abuses of the Culture System penned by a Dutchman in 1860 writing under the name Multatuli. It was present during the liberal period, as officials of the conservative or "old-school" persuasion endeavored to protect Native land rights and livelihoods from rapacious entrepreneurs and tax collectors. In the Indies as in other colonies, the contradictions of capitalism and the dual mandate of profit and improvement continually reemerged and were debated, both on ethical grounds and on the practical grounds of how security for the regime and for the population could best be assured.

In the last decades of the nineteenth century, a public sense of guilt about the conditions of Natives in the Indies, and a duty to bring about their improvement—so long as the cost was low—became widely accepted in the Netherlands. The need for a change in direction was confirmed by the effects of the 1870s economic boom and subsequent bust, the evident vulnerability of Natives to hyperexploitation under state-supported capitalism, the skewing of laws to favor entrepreneurs, high taxes, and the greedy extractivism that had taken money from Java to support development in the Netherlands while providing nothing for the Natives in return. Pressures internal to the Netherlands included the rise of confessional parties stressing religious duty, and the rise of secular socialism in the Netherlands and elsewhere. Notably, it was the conservative Protestant Anti-Revolutionary Party that gathered these threads together in the platform of the ethical policy (1905–30). Its founder, Abraham Kuyper, formulated principles of trusteeship and moral responsibility in his party's colonial program (1879), and his pupil Idenburg carried the agenda forward as Minister for Colonies from 1909 to 1916.[51] Market-oriented liberals supported the ethical policy as it was intended not to substitute for capitalist enterprise, merely to complement it.[52]

Although it was presented as new, the goal of the ethical policy to "educate India in moral principles, to govern it for its best advantage,"[53] would have been quite recognizable to Raffles and Van den Bosch. What changed was the form of knowledge and technique. In the century before the ethical policy, the official instructions of the Residents (the senior Dutch officials in each district), reflected a diffuse paternalism concerned with protecting Natives from a multitude of threats, while stopping short of recognizing the complicity of colonialism itself in creating or exacerbating the problems that benevolent rule had to correct. The Regulation of 1854, for example, declared that the purpose of the colonial government was to "protect the Indonesians against tyranny and corruption by the indigenous nobility, to forestall internecine dynastic wars, to teach and educate the 'Natives' to overcome primitivism and poverty."[54] Residents were instructed to work through the appointed or recognized Native heads but take precautions against the abuse of Native authority. They were to supervise and relieve the burden of compulsory labor, regularizing the practice while decrying its "excesses."[55] They should attend to the planting of food crops, a task Natives were inclined to neglect in favor of new, more lucrative, market-oriented options. They should encourage the foundation of schools for Natives, but not finance Native education. They should encourage their staff to study Native languages and conduct scientific inquiries. They should scrutinize agreements between Native cultivators and European planters, to ensure the Natives were not pushed too far. They should maintain a register of properly qualified priests, so Natives would not be misled by charlatans. They should discourage begging. They should make provisions for care of the elderly, a responsibility Natives previously undertook of their own accord, but in the context of new temptations might easily neglect. Finally, and quite ironically in view of the long list of matters to which the Residents should attend, they should prevent encroachments on village "autonomy."[56]

Improvement of village life on Java in the ethical period took on a far more focused and technical character. It became the subject of increasingly specialized expertise. The bureaucracy increased vastly in size and scope, as experts in health, education, agriculture, and village development intervened in every aspect of daily life.[57] The express goal of the Village Regulation, passed in

1906, was to make villages into cost-effective instruments of welfare. It also sought to protect the village from what the authorities saw as excessive—and novel—individualism.[58] In a language strikingly resonant with the World Bank's neoliberal development programs I will discuss in chapter 7, the regulation proposed that experts should train villagers so that they could reinvigorate their natural autonomy and take on responsibility for their own improvement. For this they needed to learn new practices such as record keeping, accounting, banking, the conservation of village lands and customs, and democratic governance through elected village representatives. Not only did experts define the forms that culturally appropriate improvement should take, they recommended the use of "gentle pressure" to make recalcitrant and oddly ungrateful villagers understand what was good for them. Legitimate pressure included the use of coercion to extract the labor and resources that villagers—in their own interest—were obliged to supply for schools and other facilities.[59]

Dutch critics of the time argued that the autonomy promised by the Village Regulation was a myth, and the regulation merely an instrument for bureaucrats to get their way. Some argued that intervention in the details of village life was well motivated but suffocating of initiative and patronizing in the extreme.[60] Other critics noted that too much enforced welfare was prejudicial to Dutch rule, because it created friction in the relations between rural people and the colonial regime, a regime now present in everyday affairs rather than remaining distant as the benevolent protector against (Native) oppression—the role of the Resident in earlier times. The Saminist protest movement in Java embodied these concerns. The Saminists demanded "to be left free to lead their own lives unmolested by government interference." They refused to pay taxes or undertake corvee labor, and they attempted to avoid contact with officials and the "host of new and enforced duties designed to 'benefit' them."[61] They were particularly enraged by their exclusion from the forests, which they claimed as communal property, open to all.[62] Like the protest movement in Sulawesi that I will examine in chapter 5, the Saminists were a new community assembled around their rejection of attempts to dispossess them, to tax them, and to direct their conduct in the name of their welfare.

Ethical programs were expensive and increased the tax burden on the people who ultimately had to pay for them. Taxes collected in the Indies increased from 57.3 million guilders in 1900 to 361 million in 1928.[63] A survey of the Native populations of Java and Madura in 1920–21 concluded that the population was "taxed to the furthest limits of its ability." The official responsible for the survey reacted "with a shudder" to plans to increase taxes further. Still, the next seven years saw sharp increases in taxes.[64] Improvement was not a free gift. Fifty percent of state revenues were spent on the bureaucracy itself, including an increasing number of Dutchmen and, by 1928, a quarter of a million Native officials.[65] Money was also spent on roads and other infrastructure designed to facilitate control, administrative efficiency, and commercial profits.[66] Furnivall concluded that "despite all that had been attempted for the well-being of the people they were rather worse off in 1930 than in 1913."[67]

Ethical programs attending to Native welfare included no provisions to counter the growing inequalities within the Native population—inequalities in which Dutch policies were implicated. On Java, village Headmen whose position had been strengthened by their official role as tax collectors started to treat village land as their personal property, leasing it, selling it, or dividing it among their kin and supporters. As a result, in 1929 up to 25 percent of rice land in Java was under lease for sugar, and by 1932 83 percent of Java's rice land was privately owned.[68] Rural class formation in Java was further provoked by the closing of the land frontiers associated with the demarcation of forests. Flight became more difficult. The outcome of all these changes was to subject villagers to the twin hazards of more pervasive state control and reduced bargaining power in relation to local elites.[69]

DEFINING DIFFERENCE

Under the voc, unconcerned with the detailed discipline or improvement of populations, the legal apparatus defining distinctions between employees of the voc and the local population was light. All Christians and city-dwellers were subject to Dutch civil law, and villagers were left to follow customary practices.[70] Under the Dutch crown after 1800, Native became a legal category, alongside the categories European and Foreign Oriental, the latter mostly people of Chinese descent. Initially, Natives could choose to submit to justice under Dutch law, but this situation changed in subsequent decades as racial classification became "the cornerstone of the colonial administration . . .

deeply embedded in legislation, judicial practice and executive policy," a system Fasseur compares to South Africa's (much later) apartheid.[71] A statute of 1824 declared that all Natives including the residents of Java's major towns were subject to the Native justice system and hence to "customary" law.[72] This ruling racialized the axis of difference. From then on, Natives were Native regardless of where or how they lived. Among the economic objectives of this statute was the exclusion of Natives from independent engagement in commerce. It paved the way for the Culture System that relied upon "traditional" authorities to secure discipline and maximize extraction. The political stakes were equally clear. If Dutch law was extended to Natives, officials feared they would gain "so many rights, independence and control" that they might begin to question the premise of Dutch rule.[73]

Legal separation was supported by officials bearing Enlightenment ideas with a humanist orientation, who argued that Natives should be subject to "their own" judiciary and laws, assumed to provide them with culturally intelligible, appropriate, and speedy justice.[74] The administrative system was also separate: there were two bureaucracies, one staffed only by Europeans, the other staffed largely by Natives except at senior levels, the two linked in "an intimate hierarchy."[75] Yet the two groups separated by law, administration, and racial ideology were not so distinct in the flesh. As Ann Stoler's work has shown, the racial boundary had to be produced and maintained through a set of administrative prescriptions.[76]

The VOC had restricted the immigration of European women, recruited only bachelors, and promoted cohabitation with Native concubines as the most practical and cost-effective domestic arrangement for its employees. This policy was maintained by the Indies government throughout the nineteenth century. Concubinage was a confirmation of racial hierarchy: access to Native women was the white master's entitlement. It also compromised that hierarchy. By 1900, of the 91,000 people legally defined as European, three-quarters were of mixed-blood, blurring the racial divide.[77] So long as Dutch superiority was unchallenged, Stoler argues, mixed bloods posed a lesser threat to the axis of racial rule than the emergence of a class of "poor whites," average European salaries being insufficient to maintain white families in appropriate style. The authorities became more preoccupied with the whiteness of the white population from the 1920s on, as Native nationalist and labor movements gathered strength. Official policy shifted. New conditions were set to encourage Dutch officials to marry white women and cultivate a domestic sphere cordoned off from the mental and physical pollution of Native society. Living spaces were to be separate, although segregation was punctured by practices such as domestic service that brought Europeans and Natives into close proximity. In the late colonial period, Stoler observes, prescriptions concerning a "valuable life" for Europeans in the colony became more detailed, and they were specified in medical and psychiatric terms: "Eugenic statements pronounced what kind of people should represent Dutch . . . rule, how they should bring up their children and with whom they should socialize."[78] Whites who could not meet the standards of "superior health, wealth and intelligence" that became distilled as a "white man's norm" were sent home or hidden from public view.[79]

In the same period as the distinction of the white population was being conceptually elaborated and enhanced, the nativeness of Natives emerged as a parallel field of study and creative (re)construction. In Java, the essence of nativeness was associated with "the Javanese Village." In the rest of the archipelago, difference was associated with Native custom or *adat*. Experts argued that Native difference was innate, yet intervention was needed to restore Natives to their authentic state.

Since intervention in Javanese rural economic relations, authority structures, and spatial arrangements had been continuous since the arrival of Raffles, the late colonial project to restore Java's villages turned the wheel full circle. As Jan Breman puts the matter, "Village rehabilitation pointed the way back, not to tradition, but to the illusion of one, which was first evoked in the course of the 19th century in order to be modeled into reality."[80] Yet village reconstruction in the ethical period was not the first attempt to improve Javanese villagers by making them true to themselves. Dutch officials in the 1890s, convinced that Natives were naturally communitarian, had ordered the construction of communal rice barns. They envisaged this as a modest innovation fully in keeping with Javanese culture. The village would become "a cooperative society which manages its own finances and assists its members with loans, at first in *padi*, later perhaps also in cash."[81] It turned out, however, that villagers were individualistic and distrustful, lacking in the natural solidarity colonial officials had assumed.[82] They accused the committees charged with managing the barns of corruption. There followed a rapid slide from the attempt to govern through existing social forces to the assertion of a paternalistic control, a slide Furnivall neatly summarized as "let me help you . . . let me show you how to do it, *let me do it for you.*"[83] The communal rice barns and village banks that officials had imagined as autonomous expressions of Native culture would instead need to be managed and supervised by bureaucrats. As I will demonstrate, the World Bank's contemporary interventions into village life repeat this slide, setting out to build on the "social capital" already present in villages, but effectively replacing it with new practices experts have devised.

For the late colonial scholar and official J. H. Boeke, the essential difference of the Native population was confirmed by what he saw as their inability to change.[84] Their failure to develop under the market regime of the liberal period was proof, for Boeke, that the Natives of the Indies were not *homo oeconomicus*. They did not respond to economic stimuli in the same way as other peoples. The Indies comprised, he argued, a "dual economy" made up of two separate spheres, each driven by its own internal logic, interacting only slightly. Essential difference was confirmed by the failure of the ethical policy to bring about lasting change. As soon as the "gentle coercion" of the colonial power was removed, the Natives reverted to their old ways. If they were given credit, they quickly fell back into debt.[85] No exercise of authority, he believed, could bring about "a socially educative effect"; it would only rob the people of their sense of responsibility and initiative.[86] Thus colonial policy should abandon the attempt to change Native ways, and focus rather on restoring the harmonious village life of "an intrinsically Eastern community," an idea he adopted from Ghandi.[87] The objective of village reconstruction, in his view, should be to "convince the peasant that he should be satisfied with spiritual values which will enable him to feel contented with his present meager existence."[88] He thought the project of restoring Native life to its "natural" communal state would require specialized expertise. Campaign strategies must be drafted, and plans prepared. Native mentalities must be transformed while giving the Natives to believe that the necessary changes stemmed from their own desires.[89]

Dutch critics of the 1920s and 1930s challenged Boeke's model of difference on the grounds that *homo oeconomicus* exists nowhere in pure form. All economic activity is socially mediated, and European villagers were not so very different from Asian ones. The dual-economy model was too abstract and static, and it was not based on studies of actual economies, Eastern or Western, in all their flux and diversity. Moreover, the exploitative conditions of the Indies constrained Native economic development.[90] For these critics, Boeke's distinction between different forms of economy was nothing more than an attempt to rationalize the differential treatment of economic actors on a racialized basis: witness the protection of the interests of European rubber planters during the depression at the expense of Native smallholders.[91] One senior official argued that apparent stasis did not show that the Natives were unimprovable, only that the responsibilities of trusteeship had not yet been discharged: "To attain genuine progress the authorities must meet the precondition that the individual's capacities are developed by self-activity, but, assuming the validity of that precondition, it needs to be realized that the day it is met will at the same time mark the culmination of the work of colonial policy. What has been postulated as a *conditio sine qua non* is not the starting point, but the final and perfect proof that the administering nation has fulfilled its calling."[92]

CUSTOMARY OTHERS

Outside Java, the principal way of constructing racialized difference in the ethical period was in terms of the diversity of Native customary law or *adat*, a concept elaborated by Leiden professor Cornelis Van Vollenhoven.[93] *Adat* scholarship was guided by a nostalgic and humanist desire for the other to remain other, despite the disruptions of colonial rule. Peter Burns has traced Van Vollenhoven's orientalist ideas to the influence of Germanic concepts of an indigenous essence or *volksgeist*, mediated through the French writer Ernest Renan.[94] Leiden scholars, Burns argues, understood *adat* as a total worldview, completely alien to the European mind. They viewed *adat* communities as organic wholes in which relationships between people, nature, and the spirit world were governed by principles of balance and harmony. The role of customary law, as they understood it, was to restore this balance whenever it was upset.[95]

Like "the communal village" of Van den Bosch, "the Javanese Village" of Boeke, or Raffles's Java, populated by individualist, landholding peasants, Leiden's *adat* world was a myth. It was a myth, argues Burns, not because it lacked any empirical base, but because it became axiomatic: a conceptual framework so powerful that it subsumed contradictory evidence. *Adat* law scholars interpreted deviations in ways that brought them into line with their ur-*adat* framework or, more commonly, dismissed them as symptoms of the breakdown or pollution of a pristine *adat* that they were convinced once existed, even if it had never actually been observed.[96] Van Vollenhoven himself visited Indonesia only twice, in 1907 and 1932, both times briefly. He devised the essentialized framework of ur-*adat* and its variations by sifting through the materials collected by his students and associates, without encountering the messiness of Native life directly.[97] Leiden scholarship made a virtue of abstraction, arguing that only trained foreign experts could "discover" *adat* because Native informants were merely practitioners, incapable of synthesis.[98]

Leiden scholars shared the "old school" perspective that Natives needed protection from the destruction caused by the combined onslaught of colonial administration and capitalist encroachment. They needed to be protected from unscrupulous outsiders, and also from themselves, by being prevented from selling or mortgaging their land. Van Vollenhoven did not challenge the legitimacy of capitalism or colonial rule. Indeed he sought to secure them, by forestalling the upheaval that was sure to result from continued contempt for Native rights.[99] On the persistence of Native difference, his position was equivocal. On the one hand, he argued that collective customary land tenures would gradually be phased out by the Natives themselves, as their conditions changed and individualized tenure became more common. On the other hand, he did not see the protection of Native tenures as contradictory to capitalist development. If *adat* communities were consulted, treated with respect, and given the token payment for the transfer of rights known as *recognitie*, he believed they would comply with Europeans' requirements for concession land.[100] If not, they should be expropriated by due legal process, since "respect for the rights of the people at the expense of development and prosperity of the NEI would wreak greatest vengeance on the people themselves."[101] He valued *adat* ways as wholesome and worthy alternatives to European practice but recognized the need to rearrange them should expert investigation identify deficiencies, for "none of us regards *adat* law as a sacred cow."[102]

The model of difference elaborated in Leiden accommodated colonial authority, capitalist interests, and the premises of racial rule.[103] Nevertheless, it raised a political question so serious it was regarded in Van Vollenhoven's time as practically taboo. If *adat* worlds were indeed self-contained and they included a sovereign right over customary territories, what was the basis of the Dutch right to rule?[104] This question, writes Burns, threatened to "expose the contradictions at the heart of colonialism."[105] It potentially unraveled the sequence in which Raffles claimed to have assumed the sovereign right of eminent domain from the precolonial rulers, a right subsequently assumed by the Dutch, and later by the postcolonial state. It suggested that the precolonial rulers did not have sovereignty over territory. They had subjects, but no domain.[106] Customary communities exercised territorial control in their own localities by regulating matters such as access to farmland and forest products. The continued existence of autonomous, sovereign, *adat* communities in the late colonial period put the state claim of eminent domain into question. Since the 1990s, challenge to the state claim has formed a core platform of Indonesia's indigenous rights movement.

Leiden arguments were picked up by Dutch officials, entrepreneurs, and others pursuing divergent agendas. Some elements of organized capital supported the program of maintaining an unchanging *adat* world, worried as they were about the rise of nationalism, and unwilling to spend on Native education. For others, the legal protection of *adat* land rights in the 1870 Agrarian Law—however truncated in practice—still constrained the expansion of plantations and other capitalist ventures.[107] Many liberals continued to favor a unified legal regime, arguing that Natives would benefit from being drawn into competition with other groups under common rules, and commercial transactions would be more efficient.[108] Ironically, as Daniel Lev points out, the "real reformers" who would have radically changed the apartheid legal and administrative system were less sympathetic to the Native cause than Van Vollenhoven, who "out of genuine respect for Indonesian cultures . . . nevertheless helped to imprison them in a cage of elegant policy that rendered them even more vulnerable to outside manipulation."[109]

On a pragmatic level, Dutch administrators found *adat* a useful template through which to manage the new territories outside Java they acquired after 1900. They appointed "traditional" authorities to rule indirectly and created traditional offices where they were lacking.[110] They set about reviving *adat* law where it had lapsed, and they established formal *adat* courts with jurisdiction over civil matters. Decisions of these courts were monitored and reviewed by Dutch officials, and judges themselves were sometimes Dutch. The strategy of governing through what were understood to be customary communities was intended to create an appearance of unchanging tradition. The Dutch did not figure in closed *adat* worlds. They were present only on the outside, as experts concerned with the authenticity of custom and its restoration.[111] This is an approach reiterated in contemporary development interventions, as I will later show.

CONTINUITIES AND REALIGNMENTS

Independence displaced race as the axis of difference separating rulers from ruled, but elements of colonial apartheid were retained. The two separate bureaucracies of the colonial era merged into a new structure dominated by the stream the Dutch had designed to rule over the Native masses, its "patrimonial, discretionary, and authoritarian" character intact, its personnel and its political and ideological styles "shaped almost entirely by the colonial regime."[112] These characteristics lead Daniel Lev to conclude that "the independent state was not merely similar to the colonial state. It was the same state."[113] European racial domination mutated as Indonesia's educated, moneyed, and aristocratic elites replaced the Dutch.

Colonial assumptions were embedded in the 1945 Constitution of the Republic of Indonesia. Although it solemnly declared the equality of all citizens before the law[114] and made *adat* the basis of that law, the dual legal system was effectively retained. The *adat* of the constitution was *adat* in the abstract, *adat* as the embodiment of the zeitgeist, repository of the authentic Indonesian spirit, not the functioning customary practices of rural communities.[115] The elite lived in urban centers, in the legal world of civil, commercial, and criminal codes devised by and for the Dutch. *Adat* as customary practice, or, in areas of heavy Dutch influence, *adat* as a formal system of *adat* law, became the de facto basis for resolving local disputes among "lower class, mainly rural Indonesians." *Adat* also marked their status "more as objects of administration than as citizens."[116] Officials invoked *adat* to demand or enforce obedience, and to call upon villagers to engage in unpaid labor on village infrastructure framed as "self-help."[117] In the New Order, land and forest laws made reference to customary rights, but in practice overrode them with the claim of eminent domain established by Raffles.[118]

It was the Leiden-trained scholar Raden Supomo, principal author of the 1945 constitution, who inserted the organicist discourse of Dutch and German romanticism.[119] The constitution envisaged the state "as a family, organically united in love, and governed by a father-head who best understands the needs of its members." From this family model flowed "harmony and consensus rather than open debate and majority decision, unitarism rather than federal or contractual relations, the primacy of group needs over individual needs, representation through 'functional groups' rather than competitive parties, and rejection of the standard elements of liberal constitutionalism such as separation of powers and individual rights."[120] Although Benedict Anderson traced links between this conceptualization of power and a Javanese aristocratic worldview in which "leadership flowed naturally from wisdom and spiritual strength, and conflicts were overcome by cooperation and by recognition of wise leadership rather than by class struggle or majority vote," Europe's legacy of paternalistic orientalism was also apparent.[121]

The pronouncements of the constitution notwithstanding, consensus was scarce following independence, as were politicians and administrators capable of providing for the needs of the national "family." Japanese occupation, the collapse of the export economy, hyperinflation, and popular rebellion against the bureaucratic stratum regarded as corrupt and quisling led to a situation where, upon Japanese surrender, the state apparatus "almost disappeared in the face of popular insurgence."[122] The inherited bureaucracy was a "weak machine." Its Native officials had an uneasy relation to the nationalists they had opposed. There was no nationwide political party (no equivalent to the Indian Congress Party), nor was there an integrated army to fill the gap.[123] A range of ideological, ethnic, religious, and regional movements flourished across the archipelago.[124] By the 1950s, the state apparatus had stabilized and swelled, and leaders from many of the mobilized groups were recruited into the bureaucracy.[125]

The bureaucracy in the postwar period had limited capacity to devise and implement improvement programs. It served mainly as a backdrop to the charismatic persona of President Sukarno.[126] Under Sukarno's watch, the most ambitious program to restructure relations between "men and things" was probably the Basic Agrarian Law of 1960, which had provisions to recognize customary land rights, redistribute former plantations leased to Europeans, and distribute private land held by individuals in excess. Key implementing regulations were never passed, however, and the bureaucracy was incapable of carrying through with the reform agenda. The outcome was to raise expectations, fears, and tensions, without procedural means of redress.

Sukarno attempted to hold a fractious nation together by synthesizing divergent streams of thought into overarching ideologies and endowing them with his personal authority: NASAKOM (nationalism, religion, communism) was one such amalgam. He was in a constant tussle with the military, alternately relying upon them to suppress threats of succession and attempting to curb their powers. After a period of martial law, he permitted mass mobilizations by the three major political parties: Islamic, Communist, and Nationalist. He pursued an anti-imperialist foreign policy aimed at economic autarchy, but rampant inflation caused the state apparatus once again to collapse, with the exception of the army, which was able to sustain itself through its control over material assets.[127] Economic crisis increased the pressure on the Communist Party to deliver relief to the poor. It responded with a program known as *aksi sepihak*—unilateral mass actions to occupy land and force the implementation of the land reform provisions of the Basic Agrarian Law. This movement was resisted by aristocrats, army officers, and members of the bureaucracy who had invested in land.[128] It was also resisted by many ordinary villagers afraid of losing the little they had. The three main parties mobilized their mass organizations, pitting groups of villagers, or sometimes entire villages, against others. Old and new social tensions, party affiliations, and the direct intervention of the army supported by the U.S. government culminated in the massacres of 1965, in which at least half a million people were murdered. Most of the victims were alleged members of the Communist Party and affiliated unions, although these were legal organizations; a disproportionate number were of Chinese descent.[129] So began Suharto's New Order, its legitimacy staked on the destruction of the Communist Party and "a mountain of skeletons."[130]

The massacres of 1965 marked a significant rupture in the social body, dividing it in new ways. In Benedict Anderson's assessment, they ruptured the "imagined community" of the nation that took shape during the independence struggle and was nurtured by Sukarno and other leaders in the period

1945–65. Violence itself was not new—colonial authorities used violence to conquer territory, and they implemented extractive schemes that resulted in famines in which tens of thousands died. The shift, Anderson argues, was in the way the boundary was drawn. In 1965, death was caused by one group of Indonesians who turned upon another group, treating them neither as brothers nor as improvable wards but as "animals or devils," appropriate subjects for sadistic torture and murder.[131] The result, he concludes, was a rupture in the population at large, which was rendered more or less complicit in the massacres and the silence that still surrounds them. There was also a rupture in the culture of the Indonesian army, which went on to attack Indonesian citizens with impunity: in the invasion and occupation of East Timor, which resulted in the death of one-third of the population (200,000) between 1977 and 1980, and in Aceh and West Papua, in which at least 10,000 have died.[132] The notion of nationalism as a horizontal comradeship gave way to a hierarchy in which components of the population were deemed dispensable— in Anderson's words, mere " 'objects,' 'possessions,' 'servants,' and 'obstacles' for the Ogre."[133] The Ogre—Anderson's name for the greedy cabal of Suharto and cronies—was intent on controlling resources and extracting profits. Their methods were brutal. In addition to deploying the military and police against the population, they made use of militias, vigilantes, and gangsters to advance the interests of political parties, private and parastatal corporations, and officials appropriating land for "development" schemes.[134] It was little consolation if appropriation was backed by law, since the dispossessory legal regime Indonesia inherited from the colonial period enabled powerful parties to appropriate resources more or less at will.[135]

VIOLENCE AS TECHNIQUE

In addition to greed, there is a further dimension to violence that is worth pondering: the point at which, in Foucault's words, "massacres become vital"—necessary to secure the welfare of the population at large.[136] The Dutch justified violent conquest in the period 1900–1910 as a prerequisite to welfare. In the New Order, officials justified attacks on fellow Indonesians in terms of national security: the need to defend the nation from godless communism, or from regional separatism, or from the phenomenon of "criminality," conjured up by officials and the media as a diffuse and pervasive threat to the social order.[137] In the 1980s, the military murdered 7,000 alleged criminals on Java, dumping their corpses on the street before morning. Although labeled "mysterious killings" (*penembakan misterius*, shortened to *petrus*), there was no mystery about who was pulling the trigger. Amirmachmud, head of Indonesia's parliament, defended the killings with a cost-benefit equation: "If there are killings, that is the result of the presence of crime. . . . To secure the welfare of more than 146 million Indonesian inhabitants, it is preferable to sacrifice X hundreds of criminals." He went on to equate criminals to the Communist Party, confirming their status as absolute enemies who had to be eliminated to ensure security for the population—criminals, communists, and other designated enemies excepted.[138]

Fast-forward twenty years, to the post-Suharto period known as *reformasi*. In 2002, I attended a lunch-hour seminar on the topic of illegal logging at a U.S. Agency for International Development (USAID) office in Jakarta, together with the mainly Indonesian staff of donor agencies, consultants, and others concerned with the fate of Indonesia's forests. The guest speaker for the day was Suripto, former Secretary General of the Forest Department. He was talking about the need for execution. A metaphor, I thought. Or perhaps he meant execution of a law or policy. Clarification in the question period confirmed his literal meaning. The ten or so bosses of the main illegal logging syndicates, sometimes known as mafia, should be executed. He drew his index finger across his throat. He reeled off their names or nicknames, communicating their Chinese origins.

How should the executions be carried out, someone asked, in view of the deep complicity of officials—including the army and police—in illegal logging and its protection? Their complicity made it difficult to use the technique of the *petrus* campaign, another added. Who would *petrus* the kingpins of illegal logging? Suripto had an idea. He thought it might be possible to invoke Islam, or more specifically, the mass Islamic organizations. It would suffice for Gus Dur, the leader of the mass organization Nahdlatul Ulama (NU), to remind his followers that spoiling the environment is sinful (*haram*).[139] The next day, the illegal loggers would be dead. Alternatively, he said, one could call on students, who are passionate about justice and the environment. They would recognize that illegal logging jeopardizes the livelihoods of the poor. A numerical calculus was introduced into the discussion. Ten lives versus the tens of thousands affected by floods, drought, and other negative effects of illegal logging. No one mentioned the problem that the head "mafia" are elusive and well protected, while the frontline "illegal loggers" are ordinary villagers, including members of NU. I was too dumbstruck by the proceedings to make the point. So the discussion continued, as the forces and vectors for solving the problem of illegal logging were described and assessed.

Suripto proposed to exercise the sovereign's right to kill in order to protect life. A film I had seen about the Nazi Conference at Wansee came to my mind: a group of men sitting round a table, discussing how to solve the "problem" of a (racialized) threat to the population. The severity of the threat and the need to take drastic action appeared to be commonly understood. What was remarkable in the film was the cool calculation, the emphasis on system, planning, and method—as if what was at stake was the efficiency of the railway system, not the lives of the people who would ride those railways to their death. I imagined such meetings prior to the 1965 massacres, in which the army undertook a deliberate campaign to persuade Muslims that the "communists" were devils, people so utterly different that they must be violently excised from the nation.[140] Environment, terrorism—these are the new emergencies. Their solution requires expertise and calculated measures such as those being calmly discussed. Nazi techniques were different: solving a "problem" by using legal-bureaucratic means to create what Giorgio Agamben calls a "state of exception" is different from setting people up to attack "enemies" in person.[141] Yet to instigate a massacre within the population also requires calculation. The population, its social processes, its hierarchies and antagonisms, its fears and predilections, must be carefully assessed.[142] Only then can conditions be set so that people will do what they ought. This is not the converse of governmentality but its expression in a peculiarly intimate and malevolent form. That the participants in the seminar did not take Suripto's proposal very seriously and nothing actually happened to the illegal loggers is notable, but small comfort.[143]

THE NEW ORDER DEVELOPMENT REGIME

The political mobilization of the Sukarno period, and the violent ruptures that brought that period to a close, did not remain raw. They were reconfigured in the governmental assemblage of the New Order development regime. I have already mentioned the virulent antipolitics of this assemblage and its relation-ship to U.S. counterinsurgency in South East Asia. Taking the lead in na-tionalizing and legitimating the assemblage were Indonesian economists trained in the United States, sometimes referred to as the "Berkeley mafia," who helped to convince the military leadership that planned development was an efficient means to achieve multiple goals. Development of the form they envisaged would reduce the authority of old-style politicians and officials who mobilized people through emotional appeals; eliminate irrational and tradi-tional attitudes; reduce the poverty that fed communist support; and provide a framework through which the regime could communicate with the people and obtain their consent. A researcher who interviewed New Order technocrats in 1969–70 found that they supported the program to decimate or tame political parties, unions, and the press, replacing them with a national party loyal to the regime and dedicated to development. They thought democracy disruptive and unnecessary. They expected that the masses, once they properly understood the regime's benevolent purpose and the benefits of development, would acquiesce.[144]

Communication was a core feature of the New Order development regime. The people must be made to understand. Suharto, the self-styled "Father of Development," made speeches replete with phrases that assimilated develop-ment to stability, orderliness, and strength. He blended populist rhetoric—declaring development to be from the people (rakyat), by the people, and for the people, with statements about the need to instill the correct, prodevelop-ment mentality. The regime, for its part, needed no correction: its goals were set by principles, frameworks, plans, and stages, its achievements measured by lists of statistics. By declaring its legitimacy to be based on the number of bridges built, the tons of fertilizer delivered, and statistical measures of prog-ress that were always positive if not yet *optimal*—now an Indonesian word—the regime attempted to limit debate about the purpose of development and its distributive effects.[145] To ensure these messages were clearly relayed, a uni-form, hierarchical administrative structure was imposed across the archi-pelago. It comprised provinces, districts, subdistricts, and villages, the latter modeled on the *desa* of Java—an administrative unit that was, as I have noted, created by the Dutch in the context of the Culture System.[146] Village heads were responsible for delivering development, order, and votes for the ruling party, Golkar. "Mental guidance" (*pembinaan mental*) was a keyword in all official programs, reinforcing the boundary between trustees and their wards.

New Order proclamations about development were prone to emptiness. They were so repetitive and formulaic they had little relationship to peoples' lives and struggles, a feature critics such as Goenawan Mohamed had already noted in the 1960s.[147] Moreover, many Indonesians received no material benefits from development, and some suffered serious losses when officials backed by the military appropriated their land and forest resources and assigned them to others who could make more "efficient" use of them. To maintain order under these conditions, the regime made calculated use of punishments and rewards. People who resisted dams, toll roads, golf courses, plantations, transmigration schemes, mines, factories, timber concessions, and forest boundaries were labeled communist or traitors to the nation and subject to brutal treatment. Conversely, supporters of the regime were rewarded with jobs, contracts, licenses, subsidies, roads, schools, and other manifestations of state largesse. Beneficiaries ranged from Suharto cronies, who monopolized major components of the economy under contract, to village Headmen and groups of "advanced" farmers who were rewarded with subsidized farm inputs and other handouts in return for ensuring order in rural areas.[148] Many relatively poor people also benefited from public infrastructure such as schools and roads, which were channeled to villages compliant with the political requirements of development: not asking questions or demanding rights, but showing gratitude and patience while waiting for state largesse to come their way.[149]

International donors contributed to the New Order development regime. The United States, determined "to create loyal, capitalistically prosperous, authoritarian, and anticommunist regimes—typically . . . military-dominated," led a coalition of donors to support the New Order with funds.[150] The format of foreign aid was especially beneficial to the regime, because it was delivered directly to the central institutions of the state apparatus, whence it could be funneled out to cultivate loyal clients. Licensing fees from transnational corporations and oil revenues, especially important in the "oil decade," 1973–83, were also controlled from the center. These external sources of funding enabled the regime to reestablish and vastly increase the bureaucratic apparatus and spread state largesse without placing a tax burden on the populace, and with minimal domestic accountability.[151]

As I will show, New Order development-in-practice required compromises that muddied the sharp line dividing all-knowing officials from ignorant subjects.[152] As Michael Dove and Daniel Kammen observe, it was routine practice in the New Order to pay lower-level officials and village leaders to facilitate the flow of development handouts to relatively poor and remote communities to ensure that some resources actually reached their "target group." Villagers and officials shared a vernacular model of how development resources tended to flow, and the kinds of incentives needed to direct them.[153] The more ambitious the planned intervention into village life, the more officials required the cooperation of village elites "to perform well, or at least appear to perform well when higher officials came to observe."[154] In the New Order period, so long as officials were not too greedy, critics of project design and implementation were not too meticulous, and the regime delivered more to its various clients than it collected from them, the acquiescence of rural elites was assured.[155] The balance between these vectors could quickly unravel, however, as it did in the 1990s preceding Suharto's fall.

The emphasis of the neoliberal development assemblage that took shape in Indonesia post-Suharto was "good governance." It envisaged corruption and lack of accountability in the state apparatus as key problems to be rectified. The practices of both officials and villagers—notably the routine compromises that kept "development" funds moving under the New Order—became a new arena for expert scrutiny and correction. As I will show in chapter 7, the trustees' work is still not done.

CONCLUSION

This chapter explored programs of improvement in their colonial and national iterations, teasing out their contradictions. From Raffles onward, rule was understood to require attention not to one dogmatic goal but to a "plurality of specific aims," using multiform tactics—the problematic of governmentality described by Foucault. Over a period of two centuries, there was a series of distinct governmental assemblages, each with its characteristic way of balancing welfare, profit, revenue, and other objectives. Trustees set conditions for some to prosper, stimulating protest among the dispossessed. They prided themselves on bringing order, overlooking their own role in creating chaos.

They sought to improve deficient populations while maintaining a boundary separating rulers from ruled, and experts from the targets of correction. A recurrent theme was the attempt to preserve, reconstruct and perfect indigenous villages and customary ways. This theme reemerged a century later in the neoliberal development program to govern through community led by the World Bank, which I examine in chapter 7.

Tracking governmental programs across a huge expanse of time and space—two centuries, an entire archipelago—my analysis in this chapter has been necessarily synoptic. It is especially brief on the New Order period, and it says little about the governmental assemblages that took shape outside Java, on the "outer islands" of the archipelago. These gaps will be filled in the following chapters, as I narrow my spatial focus to the highlands of Central Sulawesi. These highlands have been prime sites for improvement programs, characterized as they are by multiple deficiencies: the persistence of shifting cultivation and "illegal" squatting on state-claimed forest land; the presence of people who are not just culturally distinct from the trustees who would govern and correct them—they are beyond the pale; and the limited reach of roads, schools, health clinics, and administrative supervision. A focus on one area will enable me to trace more precisely the ways in which particular improvement programs were devised, and how they intersected with the world they would transform. It will also enable me to examine the positions from which rural people have observed, critically and sometimes with appreciation, all that has been done, or omitted, in the name of their well-being. Chapter 2 initiates the five-chapter sequence in which I examine wave upon wave of interventions in this particular place.

PROJECTS, PRACTICES, AND EFFECTS

The highlands of Central Sulawesi were subject to violent conquest during the "ethical" period, when the Netherlands rounded out its empire. Officials and missionaries together initiated the first of several sets of intervention into the landscapes, livelihoods, and identities of the highland population. Their projects, and those of the New Order that were closely modeled on them, are the subject of this chapter. I explore the rationale of their interventions—what it was they sought to change, to what ends, and through what means—questions central to a study of governmentality. I also address the questions of a social historian and ethnographer, seeking to expose how these projects were implemented, the compromises that emerged, and the effects they had on their target populations. The projects described in this chapter had three main objectives: to improve the population, by reconstituting them as orderly villagers; to improve the landscape by protecting forests from use and abuse; and to improve the productivity of the land as a source of revenue and prosperity. The principal techniques were forced resettlement from scattered hillside hamlets into concentrated villages located in the valleys; the demarcation of the state-claimed "political forest" in which customary land uses were severely circumscribed; and the intensification of agricultural production. That authorities should be concerned with the details of how and where people live now seems obvious, and similar programs were pursued in other colonial situations. The need for such interventions was far from obvious, however, during the four centuries the Dutch had been present in and around Sulawesi before conquest, a period I review very briefly.

From the sixteenth to the nineteenth century, the voc extracted its profits from a distance. It placed itself at the apex of the existing system of tributes, fines, and the exchange of forest products for luxury goods through which coastal realms exploited the interior.[1] Company officials were not involved in the details of highland lives. They did, however, have a role in arbitrating disputes between warring factions. According to historian David Henley, this was a role they were invited to assume. Rejecting the idea of colonial power as a unilateral imposition, he argues that the near-Hobbesian state of "warre" in the Sulawesi highlands fostered a positive preference for entering into relations with other ethnic groups, coastal rulers, and "stranger-kings," including the voc, who would keep their social distance while acting as mediators.[2] voc officials were not expected to understand the details of how local groups were organized, their histories, customs, or claims. Indeed, it was the ignorance and indifference of voc officials that enabled them to treat contending groups with equal arbitrariness, breaking cycles of treachery and revenge. The armed force housed in the scattered garrisons the voc began building in the seventeenth century was minuscule, insufficient to make the company despotic, should it so desire. Thus the indigenous groups that invited the company's attention retained autonomy in their everyday affairs while making use of company services. Despotism was indeed not tolerated. When the company attempted to create a stable hierarchy by placing one group in a position of authority over others, jealousies were intense, and the outcomes disastrous.[3]

Beginning in the seventeenth century, in the northern tip of Sulawesi that became Minahasa, the form of colonial rule changed as the voc acquired a new target: access to rice produced in the highlands to feed its garrisons. For this purpose, the voc found the mediation of coastal rulers inefficient, and so began to intervene directly in the interior to establish territorial sovereignty, to prevent hill farmers from flight to areas outside voc control, and to buy rice directly from the highlanders.[4] The target shifted again with the introduction of coffee to the highlands as a compulsory crop in 1822. In Minahasa as in Java, compulsory cultivation under the Culture System required the detailed reordering of relations between territory and population. Colonial authorities laid out new villages and roads and began to worry about welfare.[5] By the end of the nineteenth century, David Henley explains, Minahasans had been "integrated into the international money economy, and subjected to the most intensive colonial administration anywhere in the Dutch Indies."[6] Almost all had been Christianized, and many were educated through the efforts of missionaries working alongside the administration.

In stark contrast with Minahasa, the highlands of Central Sulawesi had no direct Dutch presence until the end of the nineteenth century. There was no compelling target that required intervention. For this reason, archives on the history of the region in prior centuries are thinner than for some other parts of the archipelago. Nevertheless, Henley was able to construct an impressively detailed account of landscape, demography, and economic relations in north and central Sulawesi, including the area that forms my focus here (see map 2). Several anthropologists have also examined colonial and missionary archives and gathered oral histories from different parts of the highlands—Albert Schrauwers for the area around Lake Poso, Lorraine Aragon for the hills west of the Kulawi Valley, Greg Acciaioli for the area around Lake Lindu, and Johanis Haba for the hills east and west of the Palu Valley. These are the accounts from which I draw.

Before the nineteenth century, much of the population of Central Sulawesi was concentrated in the hills and valleys of the highland interior. The exception was the low-lying Palu Valley, already deforested, farmed, and settled in the seventeenth century. Southeast of Palu the population was concentrated in the highland valleys of Palolo, Napu, Bada, and Besoa, and there was a concentration around Lake Poso.[7] The broad Napu Valley is situated above 1,000 meters elevation. The Kulawi Valley, southwest of Palu, is narrow and offers little scope for settlement. All the valleys are surrounded by steep and rugged hills, rising above 2,000 meters at their peaks. Circa 1900, these hills were home to a significant population of swidden farmers living in fortified hilltop hamlets, or scattered in the forests. The Dutch attempted to resettle the hillside population into the valleys, but figure 1 indicates the limited effectiveness of their efforts. A decade into Dutch rule, there were still population concentrations in the hills east and west of Palu and west of Kulawi. These populations remain in place today, despite repeated attempts to resettle them.[8]

Before the colonial period, highland groups were mobile and porous. Each of the major valleys was associated with a distinct ethnolinguistic group,

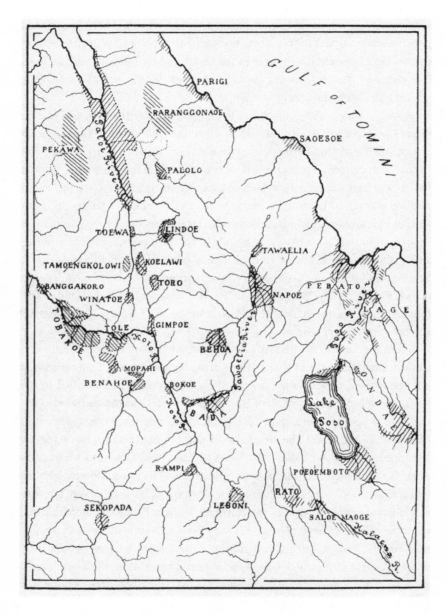

FIGURE I   Central Sulawesi population distribution circa 1920. Reproduced in David Henley, *Fertility, Food and Fever* (2005).

but mobility made many highlanders multilingual.[9] Clusters of households moved short or long distances for reasons of war, drought, epidemics, the search for good farmland and hunting grounds, and as slaves captured in war.[10] Social relations in the valleys were strongly hierarchical. Each village had its own elders, warriors, and ritual specialists, and one or more big men or nobles, as well as commoners and slaves. Hierarchy was marked by ownership of buffalos, used for marriage payments and fines, and for trampling the fields where wet rice (*sawah*) was grown. Commoners and slaves were responsible for tending the livestock and working the *sawah* of the nobles. The large herds owned by the elite were difficult to control and often ruined the *sawah*. When commoners were in a position to assert some autonomy, they preferred to make swidden farms in the hills where they could live and work undisturbed. Commoners collected rattan and *damar* (a resin) in the forests, as did slaves. Trade in these products furnished the wealth of nobles both in the highlands and on the coast.[11] Hierarchy among the hillside swiddeners was less marked than it was in the valleys. There were charismatic leaders who gathered small groups of kin to pioneer new forest land, took responsibility for harmony with the spirit world by conducting the necessary rituals, managed relations with other groups, and mobilized people for attack or defense.[12]

Since land was abundant, labor was the principal limit on production. Yet the spatial isolation of the highlands from coastal markets meant that farmers working *sawah* or swidden had little incentive to produce a surplus—a condition that older farmers in Napu and Besoa still recalled when I asked them about this in 2001. They described walking for many days to reach the coast, carrying a back-load of rice, and returning with some packs of salt, a piece of cloth, or a knife blade. They slept overnight in the trailside huts built for the purpose and cooked the food they carried with them in cooking pots stored there for common use. They did not dare to walk at night, for fear of attack by buffalos that had run wild. These trips were an adventure, but in the farmers' estimation, the time and energy expended were not matched by the economic return.[13]

When new commercial opportunities opened up on the coast toward the end of the nineteenth century, highlanders were quick to respond. Thousands of men left their homes, permanently or for years on end, to collect *damar* in the coastal forest. The result was a decline in subsistence production in the highlands and in some areas a net decline in the highland population. This was not the first population decline. In Napu there are remnants of the raised bunds surrounding wet rice fields that were abandoned long ago—evidence that the area once sustained a significantly larger population.[14] The pattern of out-migration from hills to coasts in the late nineteenth century was similar to that occurring elsewhere in the archipelago in the same period as an intensified Dutch presence ranged against "pirates" made the coastal belt safer, and new economic opportunities rendered it attractive.[15] On the downside, between 1884 and 1912 increased contact with the coast yielded serious epidemics of smallpox, cholera, and influenza among nonimmune highland populations.[16]

In the highlands before Dutch conquest, relations beyond the hamlet were based on intermarriage, myths of shared origin, trade, and occasional cooperation against common enemies. Political centers were weak. Even the so-called kingdoms of the Palu Valley were little more than clusters of villages recognizing one of their nobles as a *primus inter pares*.[17] With the exception of the kingdom of Sigi at the head of the Palu Valley, the more significant kingdoms of the region were located on the coast.[18] The Palu Valley became an Islamic enclave by 1790. Traders converted other coastal realms to Islam in the nineteenth century. The Netherlands East Indies authorities signed treaties with the coastal kingdoms (Palu, Donggala, Tawaeli) in 1854 but did not sign a treaty with inland Sigi until 1892. Administrative incorporation of the lowlands followed, and by 1905 Dutch officials were placed in Donggala, Palu, and Poso.[19]

The highlands were not so easily incorporated. They had to be conquered by force. The triggers for conquest were local and specific. In the Kulawi Valley, the trigger was the arrival in 1902 of two Swiss naturalists who had conducted explorations in the Poso hinterland in 1893–96, and wanted to extend them. Science and rumored gold drew them to Kulawi. They found their way to the Kulawi Valley blocked by the king of Sigi. The Indies government, "with the eyes of the world scientific community" upon it, was afraid "to give the impression that it exercised only nominal control in the hinterlands of its possessions." It authorized the landing of a company of infantry to pressure the Kulawi king to let the expedition proceed.[20] Occupation of the interior followed in 1904, beginning with the capture and exile of the recalcitrant Sigi king. His followers retreated to the hills to launch guerrilla attacks. The hinterland groups of Kulawi united to erect a fortress at the entrance to the highlands, but the Dutch army, consisting mainly of soldiers from Minahasa, used an alternate route, captured another key leader, and the resistance collapsed.[21] For ease of administration, the Dutch authorities unified the independent village clusters under a single, Dutch-appointed Raja, and installed him in the Kulawi Valley.

In the hinterland of Poso, the trigger for conquest was rather different. There, the missionary ethnographer Albert Kruyt and missionary linguist Nicolaus Adriani prepared the practical and moral terrain for military invasion. They lived and traveled in Central Sulawesi for a decade before Dutch control was established, conducting detailed research as a precursor to Christian conversion.[22] Making very slow progress among the scattered and independent highlanders, they became convinced that military conquest was necessary. They recommended this course to the Indies authorities. Thirteen ships bearing 3,000 men landed on the coast in 1905, subjugating the king of Luwu, who claimed suzerainty over the Poso interior. Although the Dutch did not expect armed resistance from the highlanders, it took many months to conquer the interior, and several hundred highlanders were killed in the process. Conquest in 1905 was followed by the forced resettlement of the population from isolated hilltop hamlets and swiddens into amalgamated villages, and the imposition of a Raja based in Poso Town.[23]

CONSTITUTING CHRISTIAN SUBJECTS

The project of the missionaries Adriani and Kruyt was to bring Christian salvation to the animist highlanders. As Schrauwers explains, the missionaries did not believe conversion could be accomplished by force. Central to their Protestant Reformist faith was personal piety, understood as an emotional link between the believer and God. They were convinced this link could emerge only from within a person's own language and culture.[24] Thus they faced a dilemma: how to loosen the hold of those beliefs and practices that blocked the progress of the new religion while retaining an authentic cultural core. Their strategy was governmental. They would change the conditions under which the highlanders lived in order to stimulate new practices and desires.

At the center of Kruyt and Adriani's "sociological" mission method was the careful study of language, practice and belief, and the selection of what was to be eliminated, changed, or retained. They thought this kind of study incumbent upon anyone assuming the role of trustee. As Adriani wrote:

> To mix in the affairs of a people a fixed program is required wherein the one thing is allowed, the other not, which is primarily a political matter and thus not something offered with free choice. Only knowledge of a people, and love for a people give insight in that which we may interfere in. . . . We cannot know beforehand what a people really needs, but we can discover it. This applies to both civil servants as well as missionaries, and the best service they can offer each other is to stand by each other in the search for that which they still need to become good leaders of the people who are entrusted to their care.[25]

Once trustees had decided on the appropriate "fixed program," the targets of that program would not be offered a "free choice." For Adriani and Kruyt, a decade of study had produced mounds of ethnographic data but limited results in terms of conversion, until they invoked the assistance of the Indies authorities to conquer the highlands and force the highlanders down from the hillslopes into the valleys. Resettlement, in the missionaries' calculus, would act on the actions of the highlanders in quite specific ways: (1) the spiritual understandings connected to the swidden cultivation cycle would lose their meaning when people were forced to work *sawah*; (2) intervillage feuds would be dampened by enforced proximity with former rivals in amalgamated villages under watchful missionary eyes; (3) supervision would eliminate headhunting and render its associated ritual complex defunct; (4) old curing practices requiring the intervention of spiritual forces would seem less efficacious in new surroundings, and new diseases would receive biomedical remedies; (5) ancestral lands, graves, spirits, and burial practices would be left behind in the abandoned hilltop hamlets, their relevance reduced. As people were obliged to grapple with their drastically altered conditions, and as they engaged in the new practices their survival now required, the significance of Christian teachings would be indigenized and localized. Conversion would thus emerge "freely" from the people's own (altered) beliefs and aspirations.[26]

For the missionaries Kruyt and Adriani, the use of the sovereign's right to kill and command was necessary to set the conditions for improvement. For colonial authorities operating at a panarchipelagic scale, the order was reversed: reformation of the highlanders was a tool to secure sovereignty. Fearing the rise of politicized Islam, they calculated that the Dutch position would be strengthened if there were compliant, Christian communities in the hinterland regions. Thus they encouraged missionary activity and were willing to supply the requisite force.[27] For Assistant Resident W. G. Englenberg, appointed as the senior official in Central Sulawesi in 1906, conquest had yet another rationale. He was of the view that the principal purpose of colonial rule was to enhance Native capacities. His goal was to teach the Natives not just how to live a better life, but how to govern: "I foresee our task as that of educators," he wrote. "I seek to bring here the power for self-determination. . . . What is self-government? Does it not imply the competence to foresee the needs of the people? This self-government must learn to understand what a territory, a people need to develop, to extend their own power, to exploit their own capital. It must learn to find the means to develop. Income must be found and the regulation of their finances must be set up such that a broad economic development therefore results." His plan was to gather the local rulers, the future "self-governors" of the region, into a federation that would have a "single common exchequer" and legal authority.[28] As it transpired, the highlanders did not have local rulers of an appropriate and educable kind. Colonial rule became a matter of paternalism, bureaucracy, and force.

IMPROVING PRODUCTION

For the missionaries in the Poso highlands, the elimination of swidden cultivation was an essential component of the integrated package of transformation they devised. With breathtaking guile, given his complicity in the military conquest that installed Dutch rule and coerced resettlement, the missionary Adriani wrote of the need to impose irrigated rice farming:

> In the old days, people only lived permanently in the village if their farmland happened to be very nearby. For most of the year they lived in their houses on the swiddens, visiting the village only for festivities and meetings, or when there were rumours of war. Now, however, this freedom was gone, since in the new villages everybody was under regular supervision. If the old type of agricul-

ture had been continued, the now much larger villages would obviously have required a very great area of farmland around them. Naturally, there could be no more question of moving constantly to and fro; the houses were now more solidly built, the plots of land around them well planted, most villages had a school and a teacher's residence, and it was desirable to concentrate the farmland in the immediate vicinity. It is, therefore, very fortunate that the Government has forced the Toraja to lay out irrigated rice fields.[29]

Force created arrangements that were "fortunate" or convenient from the missionary perspective, but less so for the targets of this program. The swiddeners in the Poso highlands were fully familiar with *sawah* cultivation, having long observed the farming practices of their neighbors in other highland valleys. Their reluctance to develop *sawah* stemmed from their assessment that their terrain was unsuited for it, or, put differently, that the labor investment was unwarranted for the limited returns it would produce. To oblige them to create *sawah* under unfavorable conditions required coercion.[30] Adriani did not address the question of whether or not *sawah* was actually more productive, whether it could sustain life, or the human costs of its imposition. He simply stated that swidden was ruled out by the spatial logic of the new concentrated valley settlements.

There was a second concern driving improvements to production. The missions and the entire edifice of colonial administration depended upon the capacity of the Natives to pay taxes, school tuition, and church dues. To increase production in the valleys, Dutch officials pressed for the adoption of the plough and extended irrigation in a few areas. They proffered instruction to farmers who, they presumed, lacked the relevant motivation or expertise to improve production for themselves. In the Palu Valley, for example, officials saw fit to require every household to plant fifty coconut trees, and an extra ten per additional family member.[31] Yet farmers in the Palu Valley had been planting coconuts since the seventeenth century and relied upon the copra and oil as a source of income and a means to pay tribute. From the 1880s onward they added millions more trees in response to good prices. Enthusiasm for the crop continued after conquest. Colonial officials must have observed this enthusiasm, since they issued further instructions that food production should not be neglected.[32]

In the highlands the authorities initially encouraged people to intensify

their collection of rattan and *damar* in order to pay taxes, or to migrate season-
ally for agricultural labor. They later discouraged these practices, favoring
instead a model that combined food and cash crop production on a stable
family farm.[33] They promoted coffee as the ideal cash crop for the highlands.
I mentioned earlier that the Dutch had introduced coffee as a compulsory
crop in Minahasa in 1822. In south Sulawesi, smallholders in the highlands
adopted the crop in the nineteenth century, and coastal and highland elites
vied for control over the coffee trade.[34] Coffee is mentioned as an export from
the Central Sulawesi port of Donggala in 1856, although there are no details
on the quantity or where it was produced.[35] In the highlands south of Palu,
farmers did not grow coffee for sale until after colonial intervention, and in the
more remote Kulawi hills the crop was reportedly unknown until Dutch
traders promoted it in the 1940s.[36] Coffee was well suited to the rugged terrain.
Farmers could plant it on the swidden fields after the harvest, or in small forest
clearings after a few large trees had been removed. Kulawi villagers nicknamed
the Dutch official who punished them if they refused to plant the crop "Mr.
Bitter Coffee." They became more interested in the crop when the price increased after World War II.[37] To bring down the coffee, footpaths were improved, some of which became bridle paths and eventually roads. Villagers did
this work as forced labor when they could not pay their taxes.[38]

Like the missionaries, Engelenberg envisaged the transformation of the
Natives in terms of a sequence. For him, conquest would beget peace, and
peace would enable indigenous economic development, a process that would
follow naturally so long as the Natives were granted sufficient autonomy to
manage their own affairs. His model for how *not* to proceed was Java, in which
excessive intervention by colonial authorities had caused famine and impoverishment. He thought economic autonomy would enable Natives to prosper through their natural inclination to engage in trade.[39] Recalcitrant Natives
who failed to progress should be disciplined by other means. Thus when the
authorities planned a road into the steep hills surrounding Palu to encourage
lowlanders to move up to grow coffee and legumes, some officials were aware
that the hillside swidden farmers would be marginalized by the influx of
lowlanders seeking land. They argued, however, that the have-nothing highlanders would benefit by having the opportunity to work on road construction
close to their homes as a means of paying their long-overdue taxes.[40]

Dutch officials and missionaries concurred that swidden systems caused soil erosion, land degradation, and the waste of valuable forest resources. This was (and still is) a common prejudice among officials and scientists alike.[41] It was perhaps exaggerated, in this case, by the relatively intense swidden system typical of Sulawesi, which involves a one- to three-year production cycle of rice, maize, and root crops, followed by a three-to-eight-year fallow. The short fallow produces a dense, bushy cover that is easy to cut and burn but sufficient to shade out grasses and provide a fertile ash. Henley found evidence of this system in colonial records from northern Sulawesi in the 1820s. It diverges from the model assumed to be "traditional" in Southeast Asia, in which forest is restored during fallow periods of fifteen to thirty years. Failure to understand the Sulawesi short fallow system led some colonial and later observers to argue that forest "destruction" was the recent and catastrophic result of population pressure and reduced fallows. In Minahasa, colonial officials reluctantly came to acknowledge that the Sulawesi swidden farming system was in fact sustainable. Yet this observation was not sufficient to change the colonial prejudice.[42]

Drawing from his observations in the Poso area, the missionary Kruyt concluded that forest loss was a crisis. In 1912, he wrote that the highlands would be denuded of trees in twenty-five years if deforestation continued at the same rate. But the landscape he imagined to be rapidly deteriorating already existed in 1895, when the Swiss naturalists reported agrarian land use with scrub-fallows, grassland, and cultivated fields all along the trail from the coast to the Poso Lake. The agrarian landscape of the hinterland existed even in 1865. Further, the human modification in the Poso area that so alarmed Kruyt was not unplanned. Highland elites systematically converted former swiddens into pasture for their livestock.[43] In much of the highlands, according to Henley, the deforested enclaves of 1990 still coincided with the cultivated basins an observer of the 1920s reported to have "long ago yielded to the chopping knife."[44]

The barren, treeless hills surrounding the Palu Valley and the spectacular Palu Bay were a focus of concern for Dutch officials. This landscape could be viewed and reported from very different perspectives. Not surprisingly, officials of the ethical period with a mandate to intervene highlighted the damage caused by profligate natives and the need for correction. Earlier observers were more inclined to recognize what the natives themselves had created on this terrain. In 1724, a Dutch writer recounted:

> The land around Palu, all the way to the mountains, is a beautiful land in much the same way as is Holland, as it is flat and has a black, clayey soil; it is surrounded by relatively high mountains and planted with thousands of coconut trees. This gives a gloriously beautiful view upon the fields, pleasant enough by themselves, which are full of all sorts of livestock: fatting cows, buffaloes, horses, sheep, goats and all sorts of wild animals. Above all they yield a great abundance of paddy and rice, as the paddy fields are usually worked by these buffaloes. It is a blessed land; but in the manner of life an accursed Sodom.[45]

This description, which was derived from an earlier account supplied by a VOC soldier sent to reconnoiter a land route across the peninsula in 1681, omits to mention what an even earlier VOC source (1669) confirms: that the steep hillslopes surrounding the Palu Bay were *already* treeless, bare, and grassy, "like a series of dunes."[46] In the twentieth century, Henley explains, the dry climate (among the driest in Indonesia), the cactus growing on abandoned *sawah*, and the presence of eroded sediments from the streams flowing down from the hills convinced Dutch officials that "the Palu valley was in the grip of a man-made ecological crisis." From the 1920s onward, proponents of what Henley calls this "apocalyptic view" have drawn support from the same, partial description.[47] They have also drawn on the mid-eighteenth-century scientific wisdom fundamental to the governmental assemblage of "green imperialism" described by Richard Grove: the proposition that deforestation is linked to dessication and climate change and can be remedied by forest conservation.[48] In relation to Palu, the forest official J. B. H. Bruinier declared in 1923: "I think there is indeed nowhere else in the archipelago where deforestation has had such a fatal influence as in this land, which could otherwise have been a little Egypt, lavishly watered by rivers flowing from wooded mountainsides."[49] The geologist E. C. Abendanon supplied a more measured assessment. His report of 1915–18 noted that subsidence of the Palu Valley floor led to accelerated erosion on the surrounding mountains, creating unstable, landslide-prone slopes, and heavy loads of eroded material around the edges of the valley and in parts of the valley itself. "The result is that extensive complexes of bountiful *sawah* alternate with dark coconut plantations, swamp forests, and areas of dry, barren terrain."[50] Abendanon attributed the abandonment of *sawah* in the Palu Valley not to problems of sedimentation or climate change, but to political conflicts and insecurity—the same conditions that had caused *sawah* to be abandoned in the hinterland valleys, especially Napu, where environmental factors had never been mentioned as a cause.[51] The rainfall measured in Palu between 1909 and 1941 showed no downward trend but this, again, did not alter the prejudice.[52]

Bruinier was determined to reforest the slopes around Palu, a project he began in 1923 with some success, based on the simple but severe technique of demarcating forest boundaries and excluding people.[53] A dissident official argued that this policy neglected the needs of the hillside farmers, but he was ignored and his report was censored.[54] As it turned out, it was not swidden farming but burning the grassland for livestock that had been the main factor preventing forest generation, and the livestock owners were the Palu elite.[55] But the swidden farmers from the hills were forced off the slopes they were presumed to have spoiled, and moved down to the Palu Valley, with sometimes devastating results.

CONSEQUENCES

Colonial-era resettlement from the hillslopes and hilltop hamlets into concentrated valley settlements with permanent *sawah* was imposed most drastically and forcibly in the Poso highlands, the focus of Kruyt and Adriani's attentions. Indies officials, backed with arms, moved distinct and sometimes hostile groups into amalgamated villages some distance from their ancestral terrains.[56] The effect was serious jeopardy to the lives and livelihoods of the highland population.

Managing "men in their relation to . . . accidents and misfortunes such as famine, epidemics, death"[57] was one of the objectives of colonial resettlement. Officials and missionaries argued that orderly, hygienic villages were the answer to the dirt, crowding, and limited access to water that characterized the defensive hilltop settlements.[58] Nature, however, failed to comply. Large numbers of hill people forcibly moved down into the valleys promptly fell ill and died. Adriani and Kruyt attributed the deaths to a "spiritual depression" that rendered the population "susceptible to disease."[59] A more likely explanation, Henley argues, is that the settlers succumbed to the different forms of malaria present in the valley environments.[60] A hygiene expert who visited Central Sulawesi in 1924 noted that one resettlement village had been relocated three times due to malarial mortality. Crowding was also a problem: families that had lived scattered in their farm huts for most of the year were more exposed to diseases such as cholera and tuberculosis in the concentrated settlements. Smallpox vaccination and free quinine later relieved the situation, but "even the muted missionary sources," writes Henley, "concede that for a period after 1905 there was an absolute population decline."[61]

Managing the highlanders' relations to "the territory with all its specific qualities, climate, irrigation, fertility" proved equally problematic. Official resettlement sites were selected for ease of administrative access, and on the assumption that any piece of land could be made productive with sufficient investment of labor and technology, especially irrigation. This was a mistaken assumption, especially in the Palu Valley where land quality was highly uneven as a result of the geological features. Already in 1898, most of the Palu Valley was a dense patchwork of farmland, pasture, and settlements. Since local farmers were adept at selecting fertile sites for *sawah* or short-fallow swidden, such sites were heavily farmed and settled long before Dutch intervention.[62] If land in the valley was unused, there was usually a good reason to avoid it. Hundreds of people from hills west of Palu died after they were forcibly relocated to the valley floor in the years 1912–15, as "a local famine was followed by a dysentery epidemic."[63]

"Men in their relations to . . . customs, habits, ways of acting and thinking" were also changed by colonial interventions, but not entirely as planned. Some groups retreated deep into inaccessible hillside forests in the attempt to evade Dutch authority. Their numbers were also much reduced, as a result of the hardships their refusal imposed.[64] Most of the groups that complied with resettlement efforts did not stay long. When colonial resettlement schemes proved untenable for reasons of health and subsistence, officials had little choice but to let the hill farmers return to the hills.[65] Ethical rule was difficult to reconcile with high mortality, although not, it seems, impossible. One Dutch official, convinced deforestation was the greater tragedy, applied a numerical calculus to the population under his care, arriving at policy through a cost-benefit equation. In a report of 1935, he wrote "I have given these people all freedom that I could let them, but the needs of the 10 times larger population of the plain go beyond those of some inhabitants of the mountain."[66] Yet despite repeated attempts to corrale the population from the hills around Palu, by 1936 most of them were back in the hills and only one resettlement site, Bobo, remained inhabited. The hillslopes, meanwhile, had been marked with forest boundaries that restricted swidden to limited areas, increasing human hardship and reducing the productivity of overused plots.[67] Even the success with resettlement at Bobo did not last. The resettled hill farmers fled back to the hills during the Japanese occupation, and their land, coconut trees, and livestock were taken over by the original inhabitants of the valley, who had never relinquished their claims to the sites on which the resettlers were placed.[68]

The failure of resettlement compromised the Dutch. It exposed their claim to have the technical knowledge and capacity to secure the welfare of the population under their care. It exposed their incapacity to enforce their own rules. The people living in the hills around Palu continued to practice shifting cultivation, forest boundaries notwithstanding, because they lacked a viable alternative. Some hillside groups were moved, or moved themselves, many times because, despite the promises, the reality was that resettlement jeopardized their health, their livelihood, and sometimes their lives. Yet colonial officials consistently blamed the targets of failed resettlement schemes for their lack of skills, gratitude, and willingness to adapt. With more intensive guidance, officials argued, the hillside farmers could still be improved, an interpretation that facilitated repeated resettlement attempts.

In the rugged Kulawi hills officials were less drastic in imposing resettlement, perhaps because the narrow valley had so little potential for *sawah*, combined with a forester's professional assessment that the ratio of people to forests was "balanced."[69] Officials obliged Kulawi hillside swiddeners to build a house at a central village site but permitted them to live in their field huts during the annual swidden cycle. They ordered some to move their settlements down from the hills to the vicinity of the nearest major village or footpath. Even then, the maximum village size was only twenty extended households.[70]

Experiences recounted to me in 2001 by Papa Eli, an old man living at the head of the Kulawi Valley, give an indication of what it meant to be at the receiving end of colonial-era improvement schemes that were, from his perspective, not undesirable, but impossible to realize. As we sat on the floor of his small wooden house one afternoon, he told a tale of a century of dispossession. "They got the body," he told me, "we just got the ear." Yet the others of Papa Eli's story, those who got the body, the wealth and power, were not the Dutch. They were Muslim Bugis who migrated into the Kulawi Valley from their homelands to the south, now the province of South Sulawesi.[71] In Papa Eli's tale colonial plans, compromises and unplanned processes intersected in complex ways.

His people originated in Tompi, a hamlet high in the Kulawi hills about twenty kilometers west of the Kulawi Valley. Sometime in the 1920s, the Dutch forced them to move down to the valley alongside the bridle path and the river. Many Tompi people evaded this command and remained in their original hillside hamlet, but his family and others complied. They formed a new hamlet in the valley they called Tompi, after the original, and duly laid out *sawah* as instructed. But their labor, in Papa Eli's words, "only fattened up the buffalo of the Kulawi Raja," whose huge herds trampled their fields. "We reported the problem to the Raja, but he was angry with us and asked why our fences weren't strong," the old man recalled. So the Tompi people continued the old practice of swidden cultivation on the slopes. They stayed close to the valley, but out of reach of buffalo hooves. They sold rice and later coffee to Bugis traders who plied the bridle path peddling salt and clothing.

In 1947, a Bugis man arrived in the valley. He lived in the abandoned rice warehouse that the Japanese had ordered the highlanders to build. After a while, he asked the Kulawi Raja for land and was directed to Tompi. "The Bugis knew how to ask for land from the Raja, bowing down to him, bringing him coffee and cakes; they asked to borrow land, but in the end it became concrete, complete with official papers . . . We didn't sell our land to the Bugis—they took it with permission of the Raja." More Bugis people came to Tompi. These Muslims succeeded in developing *sawah* on the valley land due to help provided, inadvertently, by rebel Christian soldiers who killed (and consumed) hundreds of buffalo on their way through the valley in 1952.

By 1959, the Tompi people were feeling thoroughly marginalized by the Bugis, who by then controlled the valley floor and the village administration. They decided to retreat from the valley slopes to found a new settlement, Tompi Bangka, fourteen kilometers back into the hills. They were joined by some relatives still at the original hillside hamlet. At Tompi Bangka, they developed *sawah*, planted coffee, and built their own school. Then in 1973 a severe flood swept everything away. The authorities resettled them back down in the valley about twenty kilometers up the road from their former valley site, which by then had been officially renamed Tompi Bugis. No Tompi people lived in Tompi Bugis in 2001. The name offended Papa Eli: "It should be Bugis Tompi, because they are Bugis who live in Tompi, Tompi is not a Bugis place— we are the ones who founded Tompi."

Papa Eli and other Tompi people may have to make do with the ear. There was no sign, in 2001, that they were planning to mobilize to reclaim territory from the Bugis who were ensconced on the valley floor. What exactly would they claim? True, they inhabited the Kulawi hills long before the Bugis moved into the valley. But the specific place in the valley where they settled and tried to develop *sawah*—the place they lost to the Bugis—was not a place in which their ancestors had lived and labored since time immemorial. It was land they were moved to by the Dutch. The Dutch-backed Raja then assigned the same land to others. He criticized them for failing to develop productive *sawah* in the valley, a failure that legitimized his decision to offer the land to the Bugis, whose farming efforts were more successful.

In Papa Eli's tale, improvement programs intertwined awkwardly with the powers of a sovereign to favor and punish, and with the peoples' own initiative. The Dutch used force to conquer the highlands, to impose resettlement, and to support the Raja they appointed. The Raja let his buffalos ruin peoples' fields with impunity and allocated land to favored clients. Yet despite the powers arrayed against them—powers of command, of nature, and the prowess of the Bugis who knew how to get what they wanted, the Tompi people did not reject the model of improvement the Dutch proposed. When they withdrew into the hills, they did not go far. Rather, they tried to secure the conditions for their own advance—land close to amenities such as roads, schools, and markets, in which they too could prosper. They wanted the body, not just the ear. Another actant, a flood, interfered with their plans.

In Central Sulawesi during the Japanese occupation, livelihoods were disrupted, some settlements were moved, and people were forced to labor in cotton fields and mines.[72] As elsewhere in Indonesia, the period between the Japanese occupation (1942) and the New Order (1965) was marked by the collapse of state capacity to implement improvement projects and an increase in popular mobilization. Two armed rebellions made Sulawesi especially unstable through the 1950s, one linked to the Darul Islam movement seeking an Islamic state in the archipelago, the other, known as Permesta, led by Christians of Minahasa seeking an independent Sulawesi. These rebellions provoked a stream of Christian refugees into the highlands from South Sulawesi, and—as we learn from Papa Eli's tale—there were also some Muslims who sought sanctuary in relatively remote locales. Highlanders periodically fled or went into hiding in the effort to avoid cooptation or punishment by rebel groups or the national army.[73]

In the New Order period (1965–98), attempts to reorder highland landscapes and livelihoods recommenced. To a remarkable extent, New Order programs replicated the techniques of their colonial precursors: resettlement, forest enclosure, and the intensification of agriculture. Here I discuss two New Order resettlement schemes that had a marked impact on the Sulawesi highlands: the scheme that continued the attempt to move hillside swiddeners down into valleys, and the transmigration scheme that brought in settlers from Java and Bali.

The New Order label for deficient hill farmers, *masyarakat terasing*, meant "isolated" or "estranged people." To replace the racial divide of the colonial period, the label posited an extreme social and cultural boundary separating the hill farmers from "ordinary average Indonesians."[74] The persistent presence of estranged people, officials argued, would "lessen the success[ful] image of national development."[75] Thus estranged people joined the list of other deficient subjects under the paternalistic care of the Department of Social Affairs (Depsos)—a list that included prostitutes, orphans, and the disabled. The task of Depsos was to normalize these people or, in Indonesian terms, to "socialize" them *(memasyarakatkan)*, the same term used for the rehabilitation of prisoners.[76] Significantly, graduates of the Depsos civilizing program were expected to become "ordinary villagers," rather like the Dutch paupers who were taught labor discipline in the parapenal colonies of Van den Bosch in the 1820s. They would no longer be distinct, but neither would they become the equals of the officials charged with their transformation—officials whose status was defined by the specialized knowledge and expertise required to bring this especially backward population up to standard.

To eradicate difference, Depsos first had to emphasize it. Depsos distinguished its target group from "ordinary villagers" along two dimensions. One was spatial. Depsos documents defined estranged people as those who lived in mountainous areas, in remote hinterlands, in coastal swamplands, or on the sea. The second dimension was their way of life. They were described as nomadic or living in scattered or impermanent settlements; they used limited and/or environmentally destructive production techniques, such as shifting cultivation; they had inadequate housing, nutrition, clothing and hygiene; they were culturally backward, closed, undynamic and irrational; they were animist; they were isolated from interaction with other people and from markets; they lacked knowledge of national affairs, the national ideology, and the concepts and obligations of citizenship; and they were without access to standard village services.[77]

At the core of the Depsos civilizing program was resettlement, an intervention that was calculated, like Kruyt and Adriani's program, to have specific, improving effects. Resettlement would physically remove the target group from their isolation and enable Depsos to furnish the conditions necessary for "normal" village lives: a small wooden housing unit per family on a half-hectare house lot; two hectares of farm land; basic food supply for one year; tools, household utensils, seeds, fertilizer, and clothing; a social activities building; settlement roads and bridges; a clean water system; religious buildings (church or mosque); a communal radio and television powered by a solar energy system; and a demonstration farm plot. The target group would be guided and supervised by resident field staff, religious personnel, and other officials. The purpose of this supervision was to impart new habits and routines, a detailed discipline of daily life. Settlers who failed to obey the rules could be punished by withdrawal of the food ration, the house, the land, or other goods. On the basis of this set of inputs, a modernity package for primitives, they were expected to move from isolation and backwardness to the status of "ordinary villagers," enmeshed in the regular system of village administration and national development within a period of five years.

Unlike the sociological mission method of Kruyt and Adriani, the Depsos program was not designed to work through the cultural orientations already present in the "estranged" population. Its purpose was to replace defective ways of thinking and acting with standardized, modern forms. The national ideology of "unity in diversity" notwithstanding, it was deficiency, not cultural difference, that Depsos took to be the defining feature of its target group. When domestic and foreign scholars criticized Depsos for seeking to homogenize villagers and eradicate legitimate cultural diversity, Depsos responded that primitives needed to be civilized, and only romantics failed to appreciate that fact.[78] In the 1990s, Depsos did begin to contract universities to conduct ethnographic research on the target populations, but the program did not change. Depsos had no use for information that might confuse the idea that primitives exist and need to be civilized. The researchers, alert to the premises of the program and desiring future contracts, seldom if ever concluded that the target group was already normal and needed no intervention.[79] More fundamentally, the idea that a program could instigate drastic changes in the conditions of peoples' lives while also retaining their cultural authenticity was as contradictory for Depsos as it had been for Adriani and Kruyt. As I will show in later sections, new conditions introduced by Depsos produced new practices and identities that often deviated from the program goals but were certainly different from what was there before.

Compared with the Depsos program, the interisland resettlement program known as transmigration took a milder view of difference and was less invested in discipline as a means to bring about transformation. This program moved people from Java and Bali, deemed to be overpopulated and scarce in resources, to areas such as Central Sulawesi, deemed underpopulated and rich in resources. In addition to supplying the transmigrants with land, houses, and support to start their lives in a new place, the program was also intended to benefit populations in the receiving areas. The new infrastructure associated with transmigration would stimulate regional development and attract spontaneous migrants and investors; and the local population would learn from the transmigrants' superior diligence and more advanced farming techniques.[80] The program assumed, in effect, that the local population, although deficient in modern farming skills and work habits, was sufficiently "normal" in its desires to learn from the transmigrants by emulation. They did not need to be disciplined, coerced, or moved about. Transmigrants were placed in areas thought to have agricultural potential. In my study area they were placed in the upland valleys of Napu and Palolo alongside "ordinary villagers" and hillside farmers resettled by Depsos.

COMPROMISING PRACTICES

Like their colonial predecessors, New Order officials made compromises that enabled them to continue to devise and implement resettlement programs, but these compromises exposed the fragility of their authority on many levels. The Achilles' heel of New Order resettlement schemes was the disputed status of state land. The land assigned to resettled populations was supposed to be free of competing claims. However, officials responsible for translating planning maps into on-the-ground reality were usually aware that the claim to grant the resettlers a new start in a "new" place was hollow: the place was never new. The state-claimed land designated for resettlement schemes bore physical signs and embedded memories of the labor invested by villagers previously resident in the valleys who held customary rights. Resettlers allocated this land were routinely harassed and intimidated by prior claimants. If they stayed at a resettlement site, it was because they lacked ready options, were numerous enough to keep counterclaimants at bay, or made payments to the customary owners for the land "given" to them by the state.[81]

Two practices reveal the tentativeness of the New Order land allocations. First, resettlement projects required the agreement of the customary landowners. Officials often obtained this permission coercively or fraudulently, by techniques such as appending the attendance list from a meeting as confirmation of consent. But the requirement to seek permission attested to some degree of recognition that villagers did indeed have legitimate, customary claims to the land and could be expected to protest if it was appropriated. Second, there was the practice of withholding land titles from resettled populations for a period in case there were successful counterclaims, and the settlers had to be moved to another location. The "estranged" populations resettled by Depsos were not promised formal title, but transmigrants were supposed to be

supplied with titles as a standard part of the program. Yet transmigration officials feared that titles would limit their room for maneuver. Settlers with title
would no longer be recipients of state gifts, they would be holders of rights.
The laws concerning private property in land would have to be applied.[82]

New Order officials knew that a state claim, however boldly stated, would
not necessarily prevail. The response was to compromise. As far as possible,
officials placed resettlement schemes on land that was currently unused. This
measure mitigated land conflicts and demands for compensation when customary landholders saw their productive gardens, the results of their labor and
sweat, being bulldozed by construction crews. The practice of appropriating
unused land enabled resettlement to proceed with minimal opposition. But
unused land, as I noted earlier, is unused for a reason: often it is unusable,
infertile, prone to flood, or otherwise problematic. Selecting this land compromised the program goal of intensified production and livelihood improvements for the settlers. It also exposed technical agencies to the accusation of
incompetence or bad faith—talking about improvement without the means to
deliver. It invited a series of further criticisms to the effect that officials wanted
resettlement projects only so that they could profit by appropriating land,
colluding with contractors, cultivating clients, and so on. Cultivating clients
was indeed part of the compromise that enabled resettlement to proceed:
benefits were channeled to local elites to minimize their resistance and garner
their support. This practice only deepened the cynicism of the villagers disadvantaged by the program.

The compromises surrounding resettlement are well illustrated by the fate
of a transmigration scheme of the mid-1990s that brought hundreds of families from Java into the highland valley of Napu.[83] Planners who observed
Napu's unusually large expanse of flat grassland, much of it uncultivated,
concluded that it would be suitable for intensive agriculture. They were wrong.
Although there are fertile pockets, land quality in Napu is diverse. Much of it
had been used for grazing until the elite's buffalo herds (and significant numbers of people) succumbed to the debilitating illness schistosomiasis in the
1950s. The land allocated to the transmigrants was infertile, prone to flood,
and at least one site was infested with the snails that spread the dread disease.[84]

Local observers were not surprised that the scheme ran into problems: it was
obvious to them that if the land was usable, someone would already be using it.

Instead of mastering floods and diseases by technical means, the transmigration scheme placed people in their path. There was another reversal: instead of educating the locals on improved agricultural techniques, transmigrants arriving in Napu learned from the locals how to survive there. Dissatisfied with the low productivity of their assigned farm plots and the failure of the Department of Transmigration to provide irrigation as promised, the transmigrants abandoned their land, sold up to others, resorted to wage labor, and began to collect rattan and clear more fertile land inside the state-claimed forest. They burned down an unstaffed health center in protest. There was conflict between transmigrants and Napu natives, and among Napu people who benefited unevenly from the scheme. Although plans were made to "prevent jealousy" by including some Napu households, supposedly those who lacked sufficient land, the spots were given to well-connected members of the Napu elite. They continued to reside in their original villages, treating the transmigration program as a mechanism to increase their landholdings.[85]

FOREST LINES

The process of forest demarcation began by the Dutch recommenced in the 1970s, after the passing of the Forest Law of 1967. Like resettlement, this intervention was characterized by compromise. Boundaries that looked solid on maps were breached in many ways. Forest officials could not effectively exclude highlanders from using the state-claimed forest to meet their livelihood needs, since they lacked the resources to maintain surveillance over large areas and the population lacked economically viable alternatives.

Compromise over forest boundaries can be illustrated by the process of designing the Lore Lindu National Park. The park occupies a significant portion of the Central Sulawesi highlands. The Minister of Forests declared the plan to designate the area a park at the World Parks Congress hosted by Indonesia in Bali in 1982, a moment when the New Order regime was concerned to demonstrate its modern, environmental conscience. The Ministry confirmed its official park status in 1993, and border demarcation began in earnest thereafter. The park combined three previously protected forest and wildlife areas dating from the 1970s, extending their spatial scope and intensifying restrictions on human access and use.

The conservation law that regulates national parks states that there shall be no agriculture within them. Parks are supposed to be natural, pristine, and biodiverse.[86] But a problem emerged during the design of Lore Lindu Park. The proposed boundaries enclosed swidden fields, fallows, and former settlement sites to which villagers claimed customary rights. These rights were quickly dismissed by the Forest Department, but it proved more difficult to ignore the hundreds of hectares of coffee planted by villagers beginning in the colonial period and continuing until the 1990s, when cacao became the preferred crop. As I noted in the introduction, colonial concepts of improvement were in step with an indigenous idea, common in the archipelago, that the investment of labor to make land more productive creates private rights. Colonial forest law had acknowledged perennials as "improvements" that merited compensation should land be appropriated for public use. The New Order forest law of 1967 contained clauses of a similar kind, although these were seldom operationalized.[87] This stance infuriated Sulawesi highlanders whose coffee was inside the park. Not only was their coffee decades old, they had planted it on Dutch command, in order to pay their taxes. Faced with opposition, the park planners had to devise a compromise.

The planners decided that a spatial compromise—drawing the park boundary to exclude the coffee—was unfeasible because there were small, scattered coffee groves deep inside the Park. Attempting to skirt around them would require "unrealistic and unjustifiable deviations of the boundary." Instead, they proposed a compromise that acknowledged that labor invested in coffee had created rights but sought to eliminate those rights over time. The planners argued that the coffee inside the park was already wild or "semi-wild." The compromise was that individuals would be permitted to register the coffee they claimed, stating the number of trees. They must sign an agreement which confirmed that they could continue to harvest from their registered trees, but they could not maintain the coffee groves, replace dead trees, or add to their holdings.[88] By implication, any coffee that was not fully wild would eventually become so. Preventing labor investment would extinguish the basis of the villagers' rights. Villagers could make no claim to wild coffee that had seeded itself or been spread in the droppings of birds. According to a team studying the park in the 1990s, the "coffee regulation" was "generally accepted by the affected households at the time, who recognized that their unregistered and semi-wild trees gave them a weak case for formal compensation from the Ministry of Forestry."[89] Acceptance of the 1982 compromise, if it ever existed, later evaporated. In 2003, farmers who spoke to me on this subject were adamant: coffee is the product of human labor investment. They planted it around the borders of their swidden fields with a purpose: to signal their private rights to the land.[90] They pointed out that their coffee grew in straight lines and could not possibly have been spread by birds.

INTO THE WITCHES' BREW

Following the colonial lead, the 1970s Depsos resettlement program for "estranged people" continued to focus on the people living and farming in the rugged hills east and west of Palu. Depsos moved about six hundred families from these hills to resettlement sites in the Palolo Valley at the edge of the forested hills that became the park.[91] By defining the hillside farmers as alien and primitive, Depsos licensed itself to coerce them. Its program was backed by the police and army. As one resettlement official put it: "These *to lare* do not understand the meaning and purpose of the national development plans. . . . The best way to bring them down is to force them with power. Now we can see the fruits of the program, where the resettlers gradually gain a better life."[92] The term *to lare* is a derogatory local usage that means hillbilly, although official Depsos documents used the term as if it named an ethnic group.[93] Yet the hill farmers were not the radically different, primitive others envisaged by the Depsos program. Their lives were configured, rather, by marginality— much like the Meratus people of Kalimantan evocatively described by Anna Tsing, who were also described as hillbillies by lowlanders who thought themselves superior.[94] The hill farmers from around Palu had long been familiar with money, markets, and clothing; since the 1920s they had been familiar with officialdom, and most were Christian as a result of the Salvation Army mission. Decades later, however, they continued to be marked by a low status both historically in relation to lowland elites, whose prestige was tied to *sawah* and buffalo, and on contemporary scales of education and access to material goods. Despite linguistic affinities—the hill farmers from around Palu speak Da'a, a variant of the Kaili language common to the Palu and Palolo Valleys— valley villagers treat them with derision. Long after they were resettled by

Depsos in Palolo, former hill farmers reported to me that they were still taunted by Palolo villagers native to the valley, harassed over their state-allocated land, and told to "go home."[95]

The experience of one Depsos resettlement site, Rahmat, captures many components of the witches' brew that emerged from resettlement plans and forest boundary lines. Rahmat was designed for 250 households, the first of which arrived in 1975. The contractor built the small wooden houses but left the designated farmland under forest. Gradually the settlers cleared land and devised basic drainage and irrigation systems, but there were frequent floods, some catastrophic, and much of the soil was acidic peat. According to settlers' accounts, those who were fresh from the hills experienced the same health problems as their ancestors who had been forced down to the valleys in the colonial period: scores of people became ill with malaria, and many died. The malaria problem was most acute in the early days, before the settlers cleared the forest and began to drain the peaty soil. A large number of the hill farmers fled back to the hills within months of their arrival. Resettlement officials reassigned their houses to people from the Palu and Palolo Valleys, arguing that if the feckless hill farmers did not want the gifts the program had supplied, these gifts should not be wasted.[96] Each ethnolinguistic group that eventually settled in Rahmat occupied a cluster of adjacent houses, built a separate church or mosque, and maintained a separate social circle.[97]

Many hill farmers resettled in Rahmat and other Depsos sites in Palolo subsequently claimed that they did not receive the standard two hectares of land they were promised. They explained to me that the boundaries of the land intended for them were never clear. Resettlement officials told them that they had to learn to use the initial half-hectare allotment "correctly" before more land would be allocated to them. When they demanded the additional land, there was none to be had. The officials responsible for the site meted out punishments and appropriated the settlers' land and labor. For some officials, improving deficient hill folk was merely a cover for theft. One settler told me that an official appropriated the land he had cleared and brought into production and sold it to a third party. When he challenged the official, the response he received was "you are still subject to guidance" (*masih dalam binaan*), "you have no rights." "Ordinary villagers" not designated "estranged" were also robbed of their land in the New Order period, so his experience was not unique. Nevertheless, he felt his standing as an immature ward of a social welfare department increased the jeopardy.

Not all settlers were equally intimidated. Nor were all of them coerced. There were compromises in recruitment, as I noted earlier—officials allowed in settlers who were already living in the valleys who wanted to benefit from the "free" land and houses. Pak Ato, a former Headman originally from the hills but resident in the Palu Valley for several decades, brought his covillagers into Rahmat in order to obtain better land. He confessed to me that he invented a fictitious tribal name for his group. When he and his people arrived at Rahmat the officials and other settlers recognized them and knew that they were not hill farmers. Still, the resettlement official let them pass "because he didn't want only hill people," who he thought were backward and difficult to control. Pak Ato helped the project staff by keeping order and organizing work parties, but he also used his charisma and skills as a leader to challenge the officials. On one occasion, he led a mass protest and threatened a walkout if a long-promised bridge was not built. In recounting his experiences, Pak Ato described the sense of social justice he and others of his generation formed during the independence struggle, strengthened during the Sukarno years, and maintained despite New Order oppression. "I didn't stop," he said. "I am a person with fire in my heart. I asked the official, 'is this the nation of beating people up, or the nation of *panca sila*?' I had read the book *Di Bawa Bendera Revolusi* (*Under the Flag of the Revolution*) about Sukarno and Hatta, and I knew Suharto's power was only from the army. I read the whole book. I graduated! That was before the book was banned."[98]

As Rahmat became established, more hill folk opted to join their kin, attracted by the proximity to a road, but there was no land for them. Together with official resettlers whose assigned land was unusable, these would-be settlers took the initiative to find work as wage laborers in neighboring villages, or they sought more fertile land on the sloping, forested, valley edge, where they founded small hamlets and planted swidden rice, coffee, corn, cassava, and vegetables for consumption or sale in the local market. The population on the forest edge was augmented when hundreds of hectares of functioning *sawah* in Rahmat and adjacent sites was washed away in a series of floods in the 1980s and 1990s, leaving the settlers scrambling for replacement land. Forest Department and resettlement officials gave their approval to this informal extension of the resettlement site across the boundary of the state-claimed forest, a compromise that solved the problem of subsistence and enabled them to keep the resettlers from abandoning Rahmat altogether.

Land pressure in Rahmat increased in the mid 1980s, as Bugis migrants from South Sulawesi and Bugis and Chinese investors from Palu began to buy up the dysfunctional *sawah* from resettlers who saw little use for it, and from officials who had assumed control over the land "abandoned" by resettlers who returned to the hills. The Bugis who moved in to Rahmat and the absentee landlords from Palu began planting cacao and prospered, acquiring more land from resettlers whenever the latter ran into debt. The "us and them" divide long familiar to Papa Eli, the Tompi elder in the Kulawi Valley (west of the park), started to emerge also in the Palolo Valley (east of the park). It was intensified by the actions of the Governor of the province, who took over 168 hectares in Rahmat in 1983, stating that the land was needed to resettle victims of a volcanic eruption at Gunung Colo. The new resettlers, however, never arrived. Officials acting on the orders of the Governor forced the resettled hill farmers who were already farming this land to abandon it, in what the reset-tlers later concluded was a deliberate deception. In the late 1990s, the son of the ex-Governor consolidated the private appropriation of this land by selling it off in lots of ten to forty hectares to Bugis land brokers and filling the re-mainder with Bugis sharecroppers. Minor officials also appropriated land. When I conducted a survey of Rahmat in 2001, twenty-five years after the resettlement process began, about 50 percent of the population was Bugis, and a significant number of the original resettlers were landless.[99]

Rahmat resettlers who had cleared and farmed land on the valley slopes beyond the project's original boundary suffered a further exclusion in 1982, when forest boundary markers were placed at the valley edge immediately beside their self-made hamlets, spitting distance, as they put it, from their kitchen doors. The markers designated the boundaries of a timber concession allotted to a private company, PT Kebun Sari. After the markers were placed, forest and company officials told the Rahmat farmers that their hillside farms and coffee groves hitherto condoned by the Forest Department were illegal. The reversal of the previous compromise over the forest boundary resulted in decades of conflict between Rahmat villagers and the Forest Department, a conflict that became even more severe when the forest in question was in-

FIGURE 2 Barren land ruined by flooding in a Depsos site, Palolo
FIGURE 3 The homes of prosperous cacao farmers in Rahmat

cluded as part of the Lore Lindu National Park in 1993. Forest guards stepped up the intensity of coercive measures such as cutting and burning "illegal" crops and farm huts.

EMERGENT POSITIONINGS

For people defined as "estranged" to be properly civilized according to the dictates of the Depsos program, it might be assumed that they must first accept their classification and begin to position themselves as primitive. In practice, this step was not required for the program to proceed. The people who were resettled did not read the program documents and were not much concerned about or even aware of the program's civilizing rationale. Many regarded it, rather, as a straightforward resettlement scheme that provided "free" land and houses. They were insulted by the label *masyarakat terasing* but were more concerned about the way it positioned them as subjects without rights: people who could be forced to move on command and cheated of their entitlements. It did not make them abject or depoliticized. Rather, it awakened their critical sensibilities.

Depsos routinely faulted the settlers for their failure to become "ordinary villagers" securely established on two hectares of land accessible to markets, a road, a school, and a health center. Scores of interviews I conducted with resettlers in Rahmat and other resettlement sites convinced me that they *share* this concept of improvement.[100] In Rahmat, settlers expressed a desire to become modular farmers of the kind the resettlement program proposed. They had no nostalgia for life in the hills. Nor did they voice a desire for modernity simply for my consumption. Their desire was confirmed by the actions of hundreds of hill families who applied to join resettlement schemes or subsequently moved in around the edges, hoping to escape their isolation and improve their lot. Rahmat settlers characterized their former life in the hills very concretely in terms of the number of days and nights it took to carry their coffee to market, and the dismal returns for their labor. They had food, they said, but no money for clothes, batteries, sugar, kerosene, or other modest consumer requirements. There was no education for their children. Thus their critique of resettlement was not focused on what they had lost. It was focused, rather, on what the program promised but failed to deliver—secure tenure of two hectares of fertile land well serviced by roads and other facilities. Their problem, as they saw it, was the acute vulnerability that followed from being taken from one place and deposited in another without adequate provisions.

One evening in his wooden house on the forest edge in Rahmat, lit by the flicker of a tiny oil lamp, with his wife beside him adding comments and corrections, an informal leader, Pak Kunjiro, spoke eloquently about his experience of being subject to force, dubious expertise, and the arbitrary shifting of boundary lines:

> At our place [the hills east of Palu] they burned three huts. They said if we didn't come down, they would bring up the army. They scared us. Even though we refused. We said we have always lived in these hills, we are not new people who just arrived.[101] They said we couldn't live there. So we had to come here to Rahmat. They said it was because of erosion, but there was no erosion. Some people didn't leave, they just moved a short distance . . . and collected fire wood for sale in the market until they could go back home. . . . Forest boundary markers were placed in the hills after we left. The officials said it was so that the hills could become a national park [sic: a protected forest]. The people who went back still plant hill rice up there, and now they have coffee, cacao, candlenut. They are getting an asphalt road. They stayed there, now they are doing better than the people down below. We didn't go back because we were already here in Rahmat, it was too far.
>
> We came here to Rahmat because we were afraid. They had started burning things. We said to the Subdistrict Head, "you know we are not accustomed to sawah, how shall we manage." The Subdistrict Head told us to go try farming there at Vatu Bose [the sloping forest land at the valley edge]. He said, "You can live there as you used to live in the hills before, that place will be for you." . . . The forest official gave us the area up to three kilometers from the valley edge. He said, "Don't exceed that boundary, this part is for the Forest Department, that part is for you." . . . We kept our boundary. We planted hill rice up there and corn, many times, as well as coffee. . . .
>
> Then in 1982 the logging company Kebun Sari came and put a logging road right through our fields [at the valley edge]. We were afraid to see that, you know we are to lare. Then, in 1993, the park boundary was placed down here right beside the road, just because they were too lazy to go up there to our boundary. I

told them don't put it here, put it up there. But they didn't want to. . . . They didn't ask where was the boundary of peoples' farms. They said they were just doing their jobs. They said it was temporary.

I was not afraid of the forest guards. I was called in by the police chief. . . . I said too bad, even if you jail me. Because you are just a newcomer here, but I have been here for a long time. Imagine, they would get mad at us just for taking firewood! They yelled at us as if we were young children. But I didn't go to jail. I just slept there at the police station for two nights. I told them, we were there first before the logging company put the road in the middle of our fields. They got tired of feeding me after a while, and sent me home.

You ask about selling land. Those Bugis, where do you think they bought the land? Do you think they bought it from us? No. They bought it from the officials. As far as I know, here in Palolo it is officials, government people who sell tens of hectares. It does happen that ordinary people sell land, but only half a hectare, and that is only when they are really in trouble. We could answer back to the officials when they blame us for selling, but we don't, because they are big shots [touching his shoulder to signal army stripes].

We keep on being chased out. We were chased out of the hills, we come here and they chase us out again. They just chase us hill people left and right. I'm tired of being chased about. It is better to stay and fight. We come here, and they say it belongs to the Governor. We go there, it is another official. So where are the people supposed to be? I said to the forest guards, "You are making me confused. You forbid us there, then you say here it is the national park. So where is the place that is really for us?[102]

Pak Kunjiro's use of the term *to lare* (hillbilly) in this narrative evoked a collective experience of being bullied, and a well-founded fear of coercion. It did not signify his acceptance of this bullying as a legitimate consequence of being "estranged" from the officials and "ordinary" villagers. On the contrary, he was sharply critical of expert rationales that had no empirical basis (there was no erosion), that failed to recognize legitimate claims (where is the land for us?), or that used the idiom of public good to secure resources for personal enrichment (the Governor). He and other settlers supplied me with ample details about who actually acquired the official resettlement land, knowledge that countered the dominant narrative that blamed them for their own fate (e.g., by selling their land). Their narratives provided an analysis of forces and relations, an accounting of how power worked to shape their landscapes, livelihoods, and possibilities for action that was far more acute than the diagnoses of primitiveness and deficiency supplied by the experts who devised programs to reform them.

CONCLUSION

In this chapter, I explored the first of a series of improvement programs implemented in the hills of Central Sulawesi. Devised by missionaries, scientists, and officials of the colonial regime and the New Order, these were programs to resettle people from hillslopes into valleys, cordon off forests, and intensify production. Their rationale was governmental: the aim was to optimize processes and relations to secure the well-being of the population at large. The strategy was also governmental. They set new conditions from which, they calculated, improved conduct would follow. Their means for setting these conditions were hybrid and included law, force, and the detailed discipline of groups deemed to be especially deficient.

The programs I described were not implemented as planned. Officials made many compromises to take account of floods and diseases, the condition of the land, and the habits and desires of the target population. Incomplete though they were, these programs had consequential effects: they altered the conditions under which the highlanders lived their lives. The compromises and failures produced effects of their own. Resettlement programs did not obliterate the highlanders' claims to their ancestral territories high in the hills, nor did they fix the highlanders securely on two hectares of valley land. Instead, resettlement set people on the move, creating landscapes layered with overlapping claims. Nor did cordoning off forests stabilize their boundaries: under the forest canopy, there is coffee and cacao, a sign of enduring claims. Improved farming techniques did not stabilize the family farm—they stimulated the privatization of land and the formation of capital, with further consequences I will shortly explore.

Most significantly, resettlement did not make the resettled population abject, malleable, or easily bullied.[103] The Rahmat leader Pak Kunjiro's comment that it was "better to stay and fight" for access to farmland at the forest edge was not an empty threat, and I return to it in chapter 5. Before I can explain how he and others mobilized to defend their livelihoods and assert claims, I need to examine the broad processes set in motion by the programs I have described in this chapter, as well as the processes with which they intersected. The key processes already featured in the witches' brew in Rahmat and in Papa Eli's tale about Tompi: the migration of Bugis farmers into the hills, the arrival of cacao, the selling of land, the actions of unruly officials, and the emergence of unequal access to the means of production. These processes are the subject of the next chapter.

FORMATIONS OF CAPITAL AND IDENTITY

In 2003, a friend sent me this e-mail message:

> Hi Tania. I was in Tanah Toraja at the end of January (very beautiful) and met a group of army officers on the road back down to Makassar. They had just finished a tour in Poso and, when I asked them how things were going, one of them replied, "everything is calm on the surface but we are worried because, now that the supply of cacao from the Ivory Coast has been interrupted due to civil war, there will be greater pressure on locals to sell their land to [Bugis] people from Makassar so that the merchants can take advantage of higher cacao prices and new opportunities for Indonesian cacao in the international market. This will inevitably lead to new conflicts." Maybe he had read your book?[1]

Beginning in 1998, there was violent conflict between Muslims and Christians in Poso District, a conflict in which between 500 and 2,500 people were killed, at least 90,000 people displaced, and 4,000 houses burned to the ground.[2] Indonesia's army officers, integral parts of the administrative apparatus in Indonesia since Suharto took control in 1965, did more than patrol. They shared with other authorities a concern to manage processes and relations. The officer quoted above did not need to read my book to stimulate his reflections on ethnic groups and territories, the dynamics set off by new crops and world market trends, and the problem of land transfers. He recognized that the social and economic processes at work in the Poso conflict were complex and difficult to control: "We are worried." The decisions of thousands of smallholders to buy or sell land, the price of cacao routed through the Ivory Coast, the overlapping of ethnic, religious, and class identities—these are not readily managed by calculated schemes.

The officer did propose a solution: prevent highlanders from selling their land. In so doing he identified the highlanders as the authors of their fate and positioned them as deficient wards, unfit to survive in a market economy. The need to protect culturally distinct and especially vulnerable others has been a repetitive theme among trustees from colonial officials of the old school reacting to native dispossession in the late nineteenth century, through Van Vollenhoven and proponents of ethical rule, to contemporary advocates for indigenous rights. Yet, as I showed in chapter 2, a series of governmental interventions has transformed the landscapes, livelihoods, and identities of people living in even the most remote places. Sulawesi highlanders became Christian as the result of a plan. Their vulnerability to the pressures presented by the entrepreneurial, mobile Bugis can also be traced to improvement schemes, albeit indirectly. Once processes are set in motion, there can be no return to the status quo ante.

In this chapter, I examine two key processes articulated together at the tense conjuncture the officer described. First, I explore the formation of capital, integrally linked to the process of agrarian differentiation, defined by Benjamin White as a "cumulative and permanent . . . process of change in the ways in which different groups in rural society—and some outside it—gain access to the products of their own or others' labor, based on their differential control over production resources and often, but not always, on increasing inequalities in access to land."[3] In the Sulawesi hills, as I will show, the conditions under which agrarian differentiation became "cumulative and permanent" were not a natural outcome of market processes. It took intervention, by force and law, to transform land into private property that could be bought, sold, and accumulated, and to transform people into wage laborers available for hire. Yet the mechanisms of transformation were complex, a reflection of situated practices and struggles.

Second, I explore the formation of identities in the highlands, as people positioned themselves in relation to others and drew lines of inclusion and exclusion. More specifically, I explore how the positions migrant and local, Muslim and Christian, haves and have-nots emerged and how they came to coincide in the strongly marked "us and them" manifest in the conflict in

Poso, and in Papa Eli's tale of the body and the ear. The officer was quite right to be worried, as both the effects and the limits of governmental intervention were strikingly exposed.

MAKING LAND INTO PRIVATE PROPERTY

Private ownership of agricultural land is an important route to capital formation in the Sulawesi hills. In principle, there are only two ways in which land can become private property: (1) through the customary understanding that labor investment creates private rights; (2) through the grant of state land. The practice—the way in which land in the highlands has actually been privatized—is much more complex.

The legal status of customary land was left ambiguous in Indonesia's 1960 Basic Agrarian Law, passed under the populist Sukarno, and further undermined by the two Forestry Laws passed in 1967 under Suharto and in 1999 under his successor Habibie. Under these laws, the Forest Department claimed jurisdiction over about 70 percent of Indonesia's total land mass, including most of the hinterland of the major islands.[4] In Central Sulawesi in 1993, the Governor, anxious to maintain the status quo under threat from the donor-supported scheme to strengthen customary land rights I described in the introduction, asserted that in his province there was no customary land at all. In his interpretation all land in Central Sulawesi was former autonomous domain (*bekas tanah swapraja*)—the land of the Rajas recognized or appointed by the Dutch as part of the system of indirect rule. Since rights to this category of land had passed to the nation on independence, it was under state control.[5]

Laws and proclamations such as these provided New Order administrators with the justification to dispossess people and move them about at will. By 2000, at most 20 percent of Indonesia's farmers held formal certificates of title to their land, and titles were especially rare outside Java.[6] Millions of Indonesians continue to access the land and natural resources upon which they depend through customary rights that are locally recognized and respected, but not formally registered, and not acknowledged by the various official agencies responsible for allocating "state" land. Some indication of the vulnerability of smallholders in Central Sulawesi can be gleaned from the data compiled by land rights activists from official reports. They found that land allocated to large-scale plantations was 1.2 million hectares; land allocated to timber concessions and industrial timber plantations was 2.2 million hectares; land under protected forests and wildlife reserves was 2.5 million hectares; and land granted as mining concessions was 1.1 million hectares. Thus the total "state" land officially allocated was 7 million hectares, although the total land area in the province is only 6.8 million hectares.[7] Under these conditions, farmers without title can only hope that the various official agencies that claim to have jurisdiction over their land do not have urgent plans to use it. Small-holders can be robbed of their livelihoods, violently expelled, and sometimes forcibly "resettled," but even under the New Order it was not possible to coerce all the people all the time, and have them starve. There had to be compromise.

In the highlands, villagers continue to argue that their labor invested in land improvements creates enduring rights. Officials responsible for land affairs sometimes recognize this principle. I described in chapter 2 the compromises that were made over resettlement land and coffee inside the Lore Lindu National Park. There are other, more routine examples. Land without title is registered indirectly through the system of land tax. Land sales are documented by the issue of an official letter, an *Akte Jual-Beli*, witnessed and stamped by Subdistrict Heads. By officializing these transactions, Subdistrict Heads effectively acknowledge the customary rights of the land seller. If no customary rights exist, why would the seller be required to sign the sale document? An official who did not recognize the prevailing customary tenure system would be unable to facilitate these routine transactions, resolve local disputes, or collect the attendant fees. Yet the recognition is partial, and it is easily ignored or circumvented when there are more powerful claimants.

On an everyday basis, legal uncertainty gives village Headmen significant scope to recognize the customary rights of villagers *or* to deny those rights. It permits them, in short, to dispossess a landholder when they want to access the land themselves, or favor one party in a dispute, or when they plan to sell the land to a third party. To justify their actions, Headmen in the Sulawesi hills apply various "rules" that purportedly limit the validity of customary rights to swidden land. The list of rules enunciated by one Headman in the Kulawi Valley in 2001 was as follows: customary rights lapse if the land is unused for five years, or if the area exceeds two hectares, or if no permanent improvements (tree crops, terracing, irrigation) are made, or if the land is not registered with the Headman, or taxed, or issued with formal title. The legal standing of these rules is disputed by legal experts on customary land rights, but in the absence of such countervailing knowledge and support, a Headman's bullying along these lines can be sufficient to unsettle villagers who are isolated and unsure of their ground.

The second route to private ownership of land, a grant from the state, turns out to be no more secure. As I explained in chapter 2, customary landowners routinely contest the status of the "state" land allocated to transmigrants or resettled hill farmers. In Palolo and Napu, some of these owners, especially members of the village elite with some connections, attempted to prevent "their" land from being taken for resettlement schemes. Or they permitted the scheme to proceed, then harassed the settlers into giving up or paying for the land. Alternatively, they persuaded resettlement officials to compromise by giving them a share of project benefits (e.g., a house, free rice)—benefits with a cash value.

From the settlers' perspective, well illustrated in the narratives from Tompi and Rahmat quoted in chapter 2, the difficulty with the grant of "state" land was that the state they encountered did not present itself as a coherent entity with a single plan. Both in the colonial period (Tompi's case) and in the New Order (Rahmat), there were officials who made compromises in order to obtain personal advantage, cultivate clients, or simply to make their jobs easier. There were rules that were contradictory. Within this field of uncertainty, settlers I spoke to derived their sense of entitlement to land and resources by reference to *both* of the principal sources I have described. They argued that their land was a gift from the state, their reward for compliance with official instruction, and they argued that their rights derived in the customary way— from their own labor investment. To further explore how they made these claims, and their fragility in the face of countervailing powers, I delve deeper into the specificities of resettlement in Tompi and Rahmat.

The hill farmers from Tompi came to live and work in the Kulawi Valley because they were ordered to do so by the Dutch. But what was the status of that command? Did it amount to a grant of state land? What were the tenure implications of the fact that they labored to construct *sawah*, but their *sawah* failed? What was the status of the compromise in which they stayed close to the valley for several decades as instructed, but survived by swiddening on the valley sides, a prescribed practice? Why did the Raja feel entitled to grant the land they had previously farmed to the Bugis? Did the Raja know the Tompi people were living there? Should the Bugis migrants have recognized that the land granted to them by the Raja was already claimed by the Tompi people? To my knowledge, none of these commands, transactions, claims or assignments were documented. Colonial-era resettlement in Kulawi did not involve the detailed supervision of Kruyt's mission or of the later Depsos scheme. As Papa Eli recalls it, his family and their neighbors were instructed to move, and they complied. Formative as the move was from Papa Eli's perspective, for the presiding officials it was simply part of an ongoing campaign. In view of how matters turned out, retaining the name Tompi for the settlement that emerged in the valley was important to Papa Eli because it was the only sign that the Tompi people were ever there. Perhaps the Bugis who took over the village did pay compensation, buying the valley land from the Tompi farmers as they withdrew back into the hills. Perhaps Papa Eli's bitter sense of exclusion was the outcome of a subsequent process—the growing prosperity of the Bugis whose possession of the place "became concrete" in the form of fine houses complete with satellite television.

In Rahmat, the point of contention was the failure of the resettlement scheme to supply two hectares of viable land per household. The settlers were content with the compromise they were able to negotiate with the officials who agreed they could use the land on the valley edge, outside the official borders of the resettlement site. But what was the legal status of that compromise? On paper, the borders of the state-claimed forest, mapped in the 1970s at the same time as the resettlement scheme, were not changed. The compromise was an ad hoc arrangement that enabled the officials to keep the settlers in Rahmat. It unraveled when forest officials allocated the land the settlers were using to a logging company and later included it in the national park. The compromise was replaced by confrontations, arrests, the burning of huts and crops, and a determination by the settlers to stay and fight.

The difficulty experienced by highland villagers in claiming and holding on to the state-claimed land they had been granted contrasts rather sharply with the experience of more influential individuals and groups. From the perspective of the Tompi leader Papa Eli, the first Bugis migrants to the Kulawi Valley obtained their initial grant of land—the source of the capital with which they

FIGURE 4   Bugis house that "became concrete" with cacao out to dry

later expanded their holdings throughout the valley—by "knowing how" to approach the Raja (a Kulawi aristocrat and Dutch appointee). The Bugis were not rich people—their leader was living in an abandoned warehouse. Yet they dared to approach the Raja, and they brought him cakes. They got what they wanted—small in scale, compared to the concessions granted to European companies in other parts of the archipelago in the colonial period, but significant in relation to the limited land base of the Kulawi Valley.

Under the New Order, Suharto's cronies were granted massive blocks of land as plantations and timber concessions.[8] In the Central Sulawesi highlands, eight plantation companies received land, of which the two largest were Hasfarm with 7,740 hectares, and PT Gimpu Jaya with 5,000.[9] In addition, military foundations colluded with officials to lay claim to state-claimed land up to about one hundred hectares, and individual employees of the agricultural department, the resettlement office, schoolteachers, and even health workers ended up in private possession of land in amounts of ten or more hectares. In Rahmat, as I explained, the Governor appropriated more than one hundred hectares of land that was intended for resettled hill farmers. Many other officials appropriated land in and around all the resettlement schemes in Palolo; Rahmat's story was not unusual.[10] For these officials, power came first, followed by land and capital.

For most of the Bugis who migrated to the highlands, capital came first, followed by land and power. Some bought land with capital accumulated elsewhere; others arrived with nothing, saved money from wages or trade, bought small parcels of land, invested, accumulated, and eventually became people of influence with a chance of holding on to what they had acquired. This was the trajectory described to me by Pak Sulaiman, a Bugis migrant who arrived in the Napu highlands in 1997:

> After my parents brought me here to Central Sulawesi, we sharecropped people's land. We opened a small garden in the hills. Then we moved to Palolo, to some forest land on the edge of a Depsos resettlement site. A person from the village let us open that land and use it for three years, until he wanted it back. We are migrants—we can only borrow. Then we opened some other land and the army came in. They said it was a battalion project. The Headman transferred the land we were farming to the army. They said we had to sign. They brought a big book. But we did not sign, and were chased out. I can't read, but my understanding is, if I sign, it means I give it to you. Those who stayed had to give half their produce to the army. We just moved on and borrowed again. Here [in Napu] I bought three hectares. I thought, I've been too long just borrowing people's land. I paid Rp6 million [to another Bugis migrant]. My wife sold everything, even her clothes, to get the capital.

MAKING LAND A COMMODITY

The land of the highland valleys and hillslopes took on new value in the 1990s with the introduction of a new crop, cacao, and the arrival of thousands of Bugis migrants seeking land to purchase. Many highlanders sold land to incoming migrants. One survey conducted in three villages east of the park in 2002 found that 40 percent of local households had sold land within the last five years.[11] Some village Headmen and other officials took control of the land of their covillagers and sold it to migrants. Echoing colonial arguments about profligate natives, they argued that the land was improperly used and thus fell within their jurisdiction. Fallow swidden land and forest patches with coffee were especially vulnerable to this maneuver, since they failed the test of the various "rules" Headmen started to apply. Such land was also vulnerable to fraudulent claims. In one Napu village, the Headman and his cronies claimed that the land they were selling to migrants belonged to them, as it was cleared by the labor of their ancestors. "Their ancestors must have been superhuman," a village cynic observed, "to clear so much land. That was lots of peoples' ancestors, not just their own. Whoever has the power, they say it is their land."[12] This was one reason for sale: insecure tenure increased the temptation for highlanders to sell their land while they could, before a more powerful party took it from them.

Ironically, the more secure the highlanders' tenure over the land—if they had in fact paid taxes, planted cacao, or made other improvements—the higher the price buyers were willing to pay, increasing the temptation to sell.[13] Would-be purchasers interpreted improvements, tax receipts and, best of all, a paper trail of *Akte Jual Beli* as confirmation of private ownership, and guarantees that the land they had purchased would not be subject to overlapping claims by disgruntled kin or neighbors. The sums offered by migrants were higher than the going rate among highland villagers and disproportionate to other local sources of capital such as the daily agricultural wage. The new land owners quickly planted perennials, communicating to all would-be counterclaimants that the land was under new ownership, and additional capital and labor had been invested. They also sought to generate documents to confirm their purchases.[14] The two Napu village Headmen with whom I stayed in 2001 and 2003 had a steady stream of Bugis visitors seeking signatures on land transactions.

For hill farmers resettled into the valleys under colonial or New Order schemes, there were some additional factors at work in their decisions to sell land. Their experience of resettlement and processes of capital formation intersected in two ways. First, resettlement unsettled them. As I noted in the last chapter, thousands of people who were moved into resettlement sites could not stay where they were placed due to disease, famine, floods, the infertility of the soil, or because the land they were allocated was unusable or claimed by others. Thus they began a trajectory of movement back and forth to their original hamlets, or from one valley location to another in search of land to farm. Johanis Haba's detailed study of resettled hill farmers found that kin and neighbors had become separated by multiple moves. Neither colonial nor Depsos schemes emptied entire hillside hamlets. Some people stayed behind; others left, only to return; others formed new ties in the resettlement sites but retained ties to kin still living in the hills. Thus they became linked into diasporic communities that stretched throughout the region and generated further mobility. As Bugis migrants arrived in the valleys wanting to buy land, this history of mobility had a further, unsettling effect. Resettled households calculated that, if they did not prosper in one place, they could move on, or move back, and try again. Several resettlers explained to me that they were planning to return to their original hillside hamlets, where they intended to reassert claims to ancestral land. Whether or not they succeeded in this venture, the concept of retreating back to an ancestral place was a factor in their decision to sell their valley land.

Second, resettlers I queried on land matters did not express a sense of entitlement to the land and forests surrounding the borders of the resettlement site. They were all too aware—and people of the valleys often reminded them—that they were in someone else's place. Conversely, the resettlers did have a strong sense of individual ownership regarding their officially allocated farm plots, and any additional land they had cleared or purchased since arrival. For this reason, their resettlement land was readily commoditized. In contrast to swidden land in the hills, which in this part of Central Sulawesi is generally subject to overlapping claims of kin, resettlement land has a short and clear history. Thus it can readily be sold to new migrants as a private, individual commodity.[15]

PROCESSES OF ACCUMULATION AND DISPLACEMENT

Uneven ownership of land and capital initiated a cycle of accumulation, but for people to be fully excluded from direct access to the means of production, in this case land, further conditions had to be set. Villagers had long viewed valley land that they had improved by the development of *sawah* or planted with coconuts as private property. By the 1970s good valley land that villagers could claim by improving it was already scarce. Thus many households lacked access to land of this kind. In the isolated Bada Valley, for example, two surveys carried out in the late 1990s found that the *sawah* was monopolized by the hereditary elite, and 30–67 percent of households had no *sawah* at all.[16] Further, since precolonial times large areas of the upland valleys had been converted to pasture for the livestock owned by the local elite, excluding would-be farmers from developing *sawah*. Yet, until the 1970s, absolute landlessness was unknown in the highlands because farmers without *sawah* could access forest land on the hillslopes to use for independent swidden production, and they could plant coffee under the forest canopy. Colonial policies attempted to restrict people's use of the state-claimed forest, as I explained, but they were not effective. The situation changed in the New Order period, when the Forest Department assigned these forests to timber corporations for logging or designated it for conservation and began to police the boundaries. The closing of the forest frontier set the conditions for a landless class to emerge.

A second, endogenous process of exclusion arose in the 1990s as hill farmers began to plant cacao on the hillside land they previously used for swiddens. By planting a perennial crop, they effectively excluded the kin and neighbors who shared customary rights to use this land on a seasonal basis. District statistics confirm the dramatic change in land use. In Poso District, the area dedicated to swidden fell from 11,000 hectares in 1986 to 600 hectares in 2001. Matching this shift almost exactly, the area dedicated to cacao increased from 600 hectares in 1986 to 13,000 hectares in 2001.[17] Once farmers planted their former swidden land with cacao, they treated it as a private, individual commodity that could readily be sold.[18] Thus the shift to cacao signaled the definitive privatization of most of the remaining swidden land in the province. In the 1990s, the combination of land privatization mediated by cacao and the enforcement of forest boundaries spread the class differentiation long present in the valleys into the hills, and to every pocket of land where cacao could be planted.

How have trustees reacted to these processes of class formation? Optimizing "men in their relations with wealth, resources, means of subsistence" and managing the disruptive effects of capitalism's advance is a task assumed by trustees since the nineteenth century. Yet in colonial and postcolonial contexts, trustees' understandings of capitalism have been colored by their views of difference. I have already mentioned the army officer's proposed solution to a problem of displacement he understood as a confrontation between two distinct cultural groups: forbid naive and feckless highlanders from selling up to market-savvy migrants. As I have explained, colonial officials of the ethical period promoted Native economic development, but they expected the conventions of customary law to prevent Native farmers from overreaching themselves. Indeed, colonial experts in customary law set out to embed Native property rights in a concept of communal domain that would keep Natives in their place. Natives were forbidden from selling or mortgaging their land. The trustees' goal was to protect the Natives from agrarian capitalists—not to make them into agrarian capitalists. Colonial scholars such as Boeke elaborated the idea that Native production comprised an entirely distinct, "natural" economy, and the policy was to keep it so.[19] With independence, the difference attributed to "Natives" was realigned along axes of status and spatial location. Depsos set out to normalize primitive others, but the goal was modest. They were to become peasant farmers, securely anchored on two hectares of land. The model did not anticipate that some would become capitalist farmers who expand and accumulate. Thus resettlement sites were wedged between existing villages and along forest boundaries, with no room for expansion in current or future generations.

In these models for development appropriate to cultural "others," some critical processes were excluded. One was the operation of naked power. In Palolo, as I explained, unruly officials robbed many settlers of their due. A second was the operation of market forces—the way that capital, once formed, is accumulated. A third was the way in which planned interventions and market processes intersect. Albert Schrauwers has traced this intersection in Tentena, the headquarters of the missionaries Adriani and Kruyt, where highlanders were forced to develop new *sawah* almost a century ago. By the 1990s Tentena had a highly unequal pattern of land ownership. This was in part the "natural" product of differences in household size and capacity that caused some households to accumulate assets and others to lose them over time. But the process had other components. Schrauwers found that it was at most quasi-autonomous. It reflected the Dutch-imposed design that insisted on *sawah*, for which the suitable land base was small, and forcibly excluded highlanders from access to swidden land on the forest frontier, the usual recourse of ambitious individuals. It reflected the New Order strategy to use resources controlled by the state apparatus to tie local elites to the regime, "betting on the strong" with agricultural subsidies and deliberately sponsoring rural class formation. Finally, it was the product of elite agency, as the hereditary nobility who had been

incorporated into leadership positions by the colonial state and mission apparatus used their privileged position to monopolize the resources needed to maintain and improve their position in the emerging market economy.[20]

In Rahmat, processes of uneven accumulation unfolded in a similarly
hybrid fashion. Not only did the appropriation of resettlement land by officials
make it impossible for the settlers to become modular farmers as planners
proposed. When the officials and Rahmat settlers sold land to Bugis migrants,
they introduced individuals with significant capital resources into the resettlement arena, people whose capacity to buy land only increased over time. A
successful Bugis farmer in Rahmat explained the dynamic to me very clearly:
"Whenever I need money, I run to my boss in Palu. I just bought two more
hectares of land for Rp50 million [5,000 times the daily agricultural wage in
2003]. I say never mind how expensive it is, so long as I can buy it." This
farmer's access to capital routed through particularistic connections, in this
case to a trader he described as his boss. He saw the formation of agrarian
classes in Rahmat as permanent and cumulative. He recognized that it would
be very difficult for the relatively impoverished resettled hill farmers to hold on
to the land that remained to them, and impossible for them to buy land in
Rahmat to establish an economic base for the next generation. Bugis without
capital faced the same predicament. He did not expect more Bugis settlers to
move into Rahmat, because he and other established farmers would buy up
any land that was for sale, even at very high prices. Landless Bugis laborers
would never be able to purchase land with their wages, and he expected the
ambitious ones to continue to fan out across the hills to find cheaper land to
purchase on a new frontier. This process was well under way by 2001 as the
Tompi people, resettled at the end of the Kulawi Valley after the flood, were
once again in the process of selling up their land to Bugis migrants with capital
in hand. Beyond their village there was no road, but migrants prepared to hike
were buying up land deeper and deeper in the hills. The same process was
occurring all over Central Sulawesi.

Agrarian differentiation based in unequal control over land might have
been mitigated by increased labor opportunities and improved wages but cacao, the crop of choice in the 1990s, has limited labor demands. Cacao smallholders depend mainly on family labor.[21] Moreover, in the highland valleys of
Kulawi, Palolo, and Napu, much of the cacao is owned by Bugis migrants who

draw upon the labor of their kin and covillagers from South Sulawesi. By 2001, landless highlanders had become, in effect, a "surplus" population. Observing the riches stemming from cacao, they were desperate to acquire some land on which to establish independent production.

In the 1990s, the process of capital formation and its converse, increasing landlessness, intersected with processes of identity formation in which the various groups of people inhabiting the highlands positioned themselves—and were positioned—on opposite sides of a binary divide. Like the process of capital formation, identity formation was an outcome of expert schemes, but not in a simple, linear fashion. Identities variously ascribed and assigned came to life as they were refracted through situated practices and shaped by contingencies such as the price of cacao.

BUGIS MIGRATION AND CACAO

Cacao arrived in the Central Sulawesi highlands in the 1990s together with a large number of Bugis migrants from the south. The combination of the crop and the migrants it attracted accelerated the processes displacing highlanders from their land, as the army officer I have quoted clearly understood. Bugis migration was not the result of expert design; it was mainly the outcome of the initiative of the migrants themselves, taking steps to improve their own condition. In the Napu highlands, migration was facilitated by the completion in 1997 of the Poso-Palu road, but the road, built in phases beginning in the early 1980s, was intended mainly to service the logging and plantation operations of Suharto cronies. Spontaneous migration of Bugis smallholders was a by-product of other plans.[22]

At the height of the migrant wave in 1998, groups of prospective migrants hired buses to tour the Central Sulawesi highlands in search of suitable land. Their arrival was facilitated by social networks as the Bugis traders and farmers who had been present in the highlands for many decades helped to broker the purchase of land. Some of the new migrants came to the highlands directly from the lowland rice sector in South Sulawesi, where they had worked as sharecroppers or farmed tiny plots of inherited land. Others had already established cacao elsewhere and were looking to expand or to replace diseased or worn-out groves that had reached the end of their profitable life.[23]

By 2000, Indonesia had become the world's third largest producer of cacao, much of it grown by Sulawesi smallholders.[24] In analyzing this phenomenon, agricultural economist Francois Ruf finds that Sulawesi had all the preconditions for a cacao boom, fitting into a pattern of booms previously observed in Africa.[25] The conditions are: (1) the availability of land, typically a forest frontier, where rich forest soils supply an initial subsidy or "forest rent"; (2) proximity to an abundant labor pool in which would-be migrants are seeking new opportunities; (3) knowledge of the crop and its profitability, demonstrated by the success of the first pioneers; (4) space in the world market vacated by former cacao producing regions drifting away from the crop as their boom ends, trees and migrants age, and replanting worn-out groves proves technically difficult and uncompetitive. The trajectory of a boom, according to Ruf, is also well known. Infestation by the pod borer pest sets in after a particular planting density is reached, causing productivity to decline unless controlled by expensive chemical inputs. Thus the need for credit ensures that farmers with more capital will better survive setbacks, embedding agrarian differentiation in cacao's pathway. Cacao is relatively egalitarian at the outset, however, as short-run profits can be made without heavy capital investment, so long as a farmer has access to land.

The question begged by Ruf's analysis is why cacao's potential was recognized and taken up by migrants rather than by the highland farmers already in situ. On this point, differential knowledge was key. Napu highlanders explained to me that they did not know about cacao until the Bugis started to plant it and reap the rewards. Thus they sold their land before they recognized its greatly enhanced value. Some reported a conspiracy: an extension worker had explicitly told them that cacao would not grow in Napu. They later suspected he was in league with Bugis migrants who bought the land and promptly planted cacao. The migrants' ability to purchase land was a phenomenon with its own history. The land they acquired was not free for the taking; it was the land of highlanders who were "unsettled" and unsure of their rights.[26] Also important was land appropriated by officials and sold on to Bugis farmers and land brokers in large contiguous lots. This was the point made by Pak Kunjiro, the leader from the forest edge in Rahmat I quoted in chapter 2: aware of the common accusation that highlanders were feckless and foolish, selling off land for the price of a shiny new tape recorder, he responded that it was "big shots" who were the principal culprits, while he and his neighbors sold only a little, under duress.

The contingent element in the migrant wave was the huge hike in export prices caused by Indonesia's monetary crisis. Between 1997 and 1998, when the Indonesian economy went into abrupt, overall decline, the returns to cacao tied to the U.S. dollar increased sevenfold. Migrants who had cacao already in production sought land in which to invest their unexpected windfall. If they had no cacao, they were determined to position themselves to profit from the brown gold. The rate of conversion to cacao was so marked that the Subdistrict Head of Palolo issued an official letter in 1998 forbidding the conversion of rice fields (mostly dysfunctional, unirrigated *sawah*) to cacao—an echo of colonial concerns about boom crops displacing food production.[27]

REACTING TO THE WAVE

The extent and rapidity of the Bugis influx in 1997–98 took highlanders by surprise. In Rahmat, the Bugis population living on land acquired from the Governor and other officials greatly expanded after 1997. When I interviewed the village secretary in 2001, he told me he had become aware of the extent of the increase only when he conducted the preliminary phase of the national census. The Rahmat population had doubled in the past three years, the newcomers largely Bugis migrants he had not seen before. They had not reported their arrival to the village office. They were living crowded in houses and barracks in the outlying hamlets away from the village center. When he took me to visit one of these hamlets, he seemed uneasy. The Bugis "boss" he knew was not at home, and there was no one else he knew well enough for us to call on. He was also concerned that the newcomers might not speak Indonesian.

In the Napu highlands, Bugis migrants were attracted by the flat land near the new road and enabled by village Headmen willing to sell land. In one Napu village, Watumaeta, Bugis outnumbered highlanders and comprised 63 percent of the total village population by 2001.[28] There, too, the village secretary expressed surprise at these numbers and claimed to be unaware of how many Bugis families had moved into the outlying hamlets. In the 2002 elections for the post of village Headman, the son of the former Headman was elected with the support of the Bugis majority, concerned to ensure that their land dealings with his father did not unravel. In this village, my survey in 2001 found that about half the long-resident households were landless or near landless, surviving on wage labor for Bugis farmers and collecting rattan from the park.

Around 2000, who should be considered "local" in the highland villages of Napu, Palolo, and Kulawi was a matter of intense debate. Most villages are heterogeneous, each with a distinct ethnolinguistic mix that reflects the unique circumstances of its founding and settlement.[29] When I queried them on this topic, villagers made fine distinctions between the group with ancestral ties to the place, the various groups of highlanders who had moved in spontaneously or through resettlement, and the members of different (and sometimes competing) Christian congregations. But in 2001, these differences paled in comparison to the way they described the Bugis/local divide. From the perspective of the self-described locals, the signs of Bugis otherness overlapped: they came from another province, South Sulawesi; they were Muslim; and they were successful. Locals, in this binary scheme, originated from within Central Sulawesi, were Christian, and saw themselves as relatively deprived. Several Napu locals suggested to me that this divide was new. They described their neighborly relations with the few Bugis traders who lived for decades in the village core. They had attended school together, and their children played freely in each other's homes. They had no interactions, however, with the new Bugis migrants who lived out of sight in the monoethnic hamlets that had sprung up on former garden land. In the Kulawi Valley, by contrast, monoethnic Bugis villages and enclaves were well established, some of them (like Tompi Bugis) decades old.[30] In the Palolo village of Rahmat, the Bugis enclave was big enough by 2003 to consider splitting off into a separate village, leaving behind the Christians who were resettled in Rahmat under the original Depsos scheme.

Spatial segregation furnished the conditions for exaggeration, rumor, and envy. In one Napu village where Bugis migrants were struggling to make anything grow on the compacted, infertile, former pasture land far from the village center they had bought from village officials, a Bugis farmer remarked: "If those people in the village core told you we are doing well here, it is a lie. . . . I've been here for five years and not sold one kilo of cacao." Bugis migrants, as I noted earlier, are far from homogeneous.[31] I have already quoted one Bugis farmer's story of hardship and exploitation. Bugis migrants I interviewed told me how they had sold fish, worked for logging companies, and pulled rickshaws. Many had been wage laborers or sharecroppers for decades before finally arriving in the highlands and acquiring some land.

Even as they concurred on Bugis/local as a critical dividing line, highlanders I spoke to in 2001 and 2003 differed in their response to the Bugis advance. The difference related to their class position. For impoverished highlanders without land, it was not the presence of the Bugis but the finality of land sales that they experienced as the critical defeat. Those who sold up their land to Bugis migrants knew it would be impossible to buy it back. Pak Silo, a young man from Napu, put it this way: "Now one hectare costs Rp2 million. . . . The Bugis have capital, fertilizer, insecticides, so they get rich quickly. . . . After the Bugis came in, we saw their cacao and asked for a few seeds. Now we feel jealous, angry, regretful. . . . Soon everywhere will be like this, the locals will all sell up. You have nothing so you sell up. We sold one hectare in 1993 for Rp200,000." Pressed on the point, he acknowledged that not all Bugis had capital. Further, despite his envy and regret, Pak Silo did not hold the Bugis solely responsible for his impoverished condition. His own kin and rich covillagers also played a role, as he explained:

I hardly went to school because I had to help my parents. We survived by processing sago [low-status famine food] to sell and to eat. We had a small swidden plot for corn and cassava. We had very little *sawah* and no buffalos. My family never had any. We got harvest shares in return for our work for rich people. After the road came in, buffalos became even more expensive, and there was no hope of buying one. We had to build fences to keep buffalo out of the *sawah*. There were hundreds of them, and in the forest, too, there were wild ones. Rich people could sell buffalos and horses to pay for school, to build their houses.

After I finished primary school in 1979, I went to do wage work in Palolo. I worked for two years and saved money to help my parents and siblings—eight of them—and I started at junior secondary school, but I couldn't manage. Only in 1991, with the asphalt road, could we sell our corn and other crops. Now I do wage labor, collect rattan, haul timber. Half-day wage work is good, so I have time to go to my garden.

My grandfather had some land, but my uncle sold it to a Bugis in 1998. Six hectares at Rp300,000 per hectare. My father did not get a share. I said, "If you are going to sell, we should get a share," but he didn't give us anything.

We were so late with cacao. If we had known how it would be, we would have asked more for the land. My cacao was burned by someone in the dry season. I'm trying again now. Rice is so expensive here. We sell to the store for Rp1,500 [at harvest time] and buy it back for Rp3,500.[32]

Locals, in Pak Silo's account, were differentiated. His family had always been poor. Their labor was exploited by the village elite, "rich people," as was their chronic lack of cash (having to sell rice cheap and buy expensive). With the arrival of the Bugis, they had sold off the little land they had, unknowingly foreclosing what might have been a brighter future.

For the highlanders who comprised the local elite—those who owned significant amounts of *sawah*, buffalos, and new forms of capital (rice mills, village stores, official positions in the village, a family member with a government job), the arrival of the Bugis had different effects. The elite did not sell off their productive *sawah* land. If they sold land to migrants, it was infertile and compacted pasture, or forest land they had no immediate plans to use. Their concern in relation to the Bugis migration was this: How could they retain their position of leadership in the village and a sense of control over "their" place? They could follow the approach of the Tompi people—withdraw and try to regroup somewhere else. Or they could attempt to reassert control over the incoming migrants. The latter approach was difficult for people who were themselves resettled, or who had moved or been moved multiple times. How could they assert leadership in a place that was not their own? This was the predicament of the Tompi people displaced from the valley decades ago, and also of Rahmat, where Bugis migrants were asserting their own claims to place by splitting the village in two. Reasserting control was more feasible for people who had remained on their ancestral land. The process can be illustrated by the repositionings that emerged through the 1990s around Lake Lindu.

RECLAIMING PLACE

The four villages nestled by the shore of Lake Lindu occupy an official agricultural enclave deep inside the Lore Lindu National Park, eighteen kilometers from the nearest road. In the early 1990s, Lindu villagers threatened with eviction to make way for a hydrodam came to recognize themselves as indige-

nous people and drew strength and legitimacy from the language of the transnational indigenous rights movement, events I described in the introduction.
In the subsequent decade they continued to mobilize under the banner of
indigeneity but shifted their critical attention from an external enemy—an
oppressive state apparatus attempting to evict them—to their covillagers. More
specifically, their critique focused on the conduct of the Bugis and Kulawi
migrants who had moved into the enclave but failed to acknowledge that they
were guests on Lindu land. It also focused on the conduct of the village Headmen who had permitted these outsiders to enter Lindu and acquire land.

By 2001, Lindu villagers had organized a strengthened customary council
that claimed to have jurisdiction over a customary domain covering the four
lakeside villages and the surrounding park land up to the hill peaks. The
council was comprised of elders drawn only from the original Lindu community, although it claimed sovereignty over all the people living within the Lindu
territory, migrants included. The council members prepared a document out-
lining the differential penalties they would apply for failure to respect the
authority of the council, and for infractions of the rules: Lindu people would
be subject to customary fines; migrants would be expelled from the Lindu
domain.[33]

In addition to the new regulations, Lindu leaders devised a set of new
practices to assert their sovereignty over the land and its inhabitants. They
identified migrants with more than two hectares of land and planned to retrieve it from them for reallocation to land-poor Lindu people.[34] "We tell them
we don't want your coffee and cacao, you can keep that, but the land is ours. We
never gave it or sold it to you. You took it and now we're taking it back," said
Papa Gisi, a Lindu elder I interviewed in 2003. He wanted to prevent migrants
from treating Lindu land as commodity. He was deeply frustrated by the fact
that he could not undo the scores of individual land transactions through
which migrants had gained access to Lindu farmland, but he argued that the
migrants had only acquired rights of use. If they no longer used the land,
under the rules he proposed, they would not be permitted to sell it. It would
revert to "the Lindu people." He also planned to prevent new migration by
setting up a checkpoint on the trail to Lindu at which an appointee of the council would inspect identity cards. He proposed that the council would repeat
their census of residents every three months, to check that no newcomers had

arrived. "We have become the manager (*kami jadi manijer*)," Papa Gisi said, using the English term *manager* to signal, perhaps, the hybrid form in which reasserting sovereignty required the customary council to assume functions associated with modern government—listing, surveying, classifying, regulating, and thinking ahead to the resource needs of future generations.

Bugis migrants countered the attempts of Lindu leaders to assert sovereignty and regulate their conduct by arguing that, as citizens of Indonesia, they had the right to live anywhere in the nation and to prosper through their own labor and initiative. The only law they were obliged to recognize was national law. In their view, it was the four village Headmen, not the customary council, who had jurisdiction. The land the migrants acquired did not belong to the Lindu people. It was state land that the profligate Lindu had failed to improve. Migrants made the land productive, and their investment of labor and capital conferred rights. Their energies helped to meet state goals for development. From the migrants' perspective, claims by Lindu people signaled only jealousy and opportunism.[35]

Heightened tensions notwithstanding, by 2003 the highland valleys of Napu, Kulawi, Lindu, and Palolo had not become sites of mass violence pitting migrants against locals, Muslims against Christians, or haves against have-nots. Yet all the preconditions were there. As the army officer said, "We are worried." There were incidents in which quarrels between two individuals over land, theft, damage to property, or some personal insult escalated into violent encounters between massed groups, and other incidents in which—despite the presence of collective grievances, inequalities, frustrations, suspicions, and grudges—escalation did not occur.[36] The most serious and protracted violence in the period 1998–2003 was in Poso Town, the Poso coastal zone, and the Poso hinterland, the sites of the army officer's patrol. In the next section I explore the contours of the conjuncture at which that violence occurred.

RELIGIOUS LINES

The planned intervention with the most obvious and far-reaching effect on the Sulawesi highlands was the creation of Christian communities and the institution of a sharp divide between Muslims and Christians. This divide, as I noted in chapter 2, was no accident. The late-colonial regime encouraged missions in order to halt the progress of a politicized Islam. It aimed to create Christian enclaves in highland areas that would ally with the Dutch. By the end of Dutch rule, long before the processes of migration and class formation I have just described, religion was a prime marker of identity. It was reflected in national elections. In 1955, the last elections before the New Order, Muslims and Christians in the Poso District each voted for their own political parties. Muslim parties received 61 percent of the vote, Christian parties 27 percent, and the secular parties (Nationalist, Communist, Socialist) received a combined total of only 10 percent.[37]

Christian converts came to have a radically altered sense of their place in the social universe. New communities arose not only from new ideas but from new practices. Especially important was the introduction of formal education, opening the door for highlanders to seek white-collar work as teachers, preachers, nurses, and officials. By 1942, in the hills around Palu and the Kulawi Valley there were 140 Salvation Army corps (congregations), 19 schools, 5 medical clinics, and 66 officers, some of them trained in Java.[38] In the Poso area, Kruyt's mission created its own system of schools, hospitals, and churches with trained personnel, an apparatus transferred in 1947 to an indigenous synod with its headquarters in Tentena. By 2000, the indigenized Christian Church of Central Sulawesi (GKST) had some 150,000 members.[39]

Under missionary tutelage, highlanders who had long been stigmatized by coastal Muslims for retaining their heathen, primitive ways not only increased their agricultural production and settled into orderly, law-abiding villages, some of them began to surpass Muslims in literacy and other skills associated with Western modernity. They, too, could claim membership in a recognized world religion. But their standing as mature citizens was still challenged. In the hills around Palu and west of the Kulawi Valley, where Salvation Army Protestantism had become a central feature of identity, New Order functionaries still treated the farmers as primitive and deficient.[40] In Tentena in the 1990s, no longer plausibly primitive, officials seeking "culture" for tourist promotion resurrected animist songs and dances and highlighted headhunting, much to the chagrin of the highly educated, longtime Christian residents.[41] These representations overlooked the involvement of coastal Muslims in headhunting and neglected to note that coastal aristocrats were often its prime sponsors. The primitive other was situated firmly in the highland interior.[42]

In the 1990s, New Order politicians and administrators intensified the connection between Islam and state power. Suharto's response to the urban middle classes angered by the corruption and greed of his family and cronies was to offer support to some of the more strident Islamicist groups in return for their political loyalty. He used state funds to support their missionary efforts (*dakwah*), directed mainly toward secular Muslims and inflected state institutions with a more assertive Islam. There was a change in routines. I noticed, for example, that Muslim blessings began to be used to open and close official events, replacing secular greetings or the combination of a Muslim greeting with another, appropriate to the non-Muslim participants. Habibie, Suharto's successor as president in 1998–99, was head of a prominent Muslim foundation with branches throughout Indonesia, and an especially strong presence in Sulawesi, further diminishing the separation between religion and state. Christians felt marginalized as the neutral stance toward diverse organized religions promised by the official ideology of Pancasila disappeared.[43]

Shifts in national policies toward different religious groups resonated loudly in Poso Town and the surrounding hills. The three major rounds of violence in Central Sulawesi in the period 1998–2001 all began in Poso Town and involved struggles over senior political or administrative positions in which a Christian candidate was displaced by a Muslim.[44] The appointments breached a convention that had been well established under the New Order, balancing senior appointments between Muslims and Christians roughly in proportion to their populations. Educated young Christians saw their chances of jobs in the bureaucracy diminish as a Muslim-dominated district administration reconfigured patronage networks to favor Muslims. The tight links binding Islam, the ruling regime, and the administrative apparatus at every level also affected rural matters such as development contracts, licenses, and land allocation.[45]

Cacao helped to carry urban tensions to rural areas in a rather unique way. With the dollar price so very high in 1997–98, cacao offered for the first time an opportunity for underpaid Christian bureaucrats and their offspring to make serious money and attain a comfortable life in the highland areas educated people routinely left behind. Young people who had been unable to obtain jobs as officials decided to try their hand at agriculture. For some of them, it was quite a stretch: two young men who had moved back to Kulawi told me with self-deprecating humor how they had first planted their cacao seedlings complete with their plastic bags and wondered why they did not grow. In much of the highlands, however, the potential of cacao was discovered by Bugis migrants, who bought up land at low prices before the highlanders caught on. It was not a Malthusian resource crunch but expanding opportunity, combined with unequal access to knowledge and capital, that increased the tensions in the countryside.[46]

Yet the attractions of cacao, growing class inequality, and the struggle for land were not the dimensions of the conflict highlighted by Christian highlanders in Napu when I visited in 2001. At the time, Christian refugees from Poso Town and adjacent coastal villages were streaming into the Napu highlands in trucks. Muslims were exiting the hills in trucks headed in the opposite direction: toward the towns and the coast, where Muslims predominate. Christian highlanders were overwhelmed with worry about kin in Poso, where part of the town was burning, and horrified by tales of violent attacks. Muslims I spoke to were nervously debating whether to leave the highlands or to trust the village officials who assured them that Napu was peaceful, and they would be safe. A Napu Christian with whom I discussed the causes of the mass Bugis migration in 1997–99 did not share my political-economic analysis of the reasons for their arrival, a narrative centered on the price of cacao and the ease of land acquisition in the hills. He interpreted the same events very differently. In 1998, he said, Habibie became president. He began sponsoring Muslim foundations to infiltrate the Christian highlands and take over.[47] "We do not know," he pointed out, "how the Bugis who come here get their money, or who they are, or what they really want."

Many Christians viewed the introduction of Muslim populations into the highlands as a deliberate attempt to marginalize them. They assessed the transmigration program in this light. The Subdistrict of South Pamona, for example, had a Muslim population of 3 percent in 1982 and 35 percent by 2001, of whom the majority were transmigrants.[48] Similarly, many Muslims suspected that the Christians were being manipulated by outside forces. They read the presence of Mission Aviation Fellowship airplanes servicing remote highland locations as a sign of the economic and technological power of an American/Christian/Zionist conspiracy. They questioned the purpose of oversize churches in predominantly Muslim areas. They saw Tentena as the focus of missionary activity designed to convert Muslims.[49]

Critical observers of the conflict argued that it was not only religious zealots and frustrated politicians who had conspired to stimulate and sustain violence in and around Poso Town. They suspected that the military was provoking violent incidents in order to justify their presence. These observers documented the profits made by members of the military who charged "fines" at roadside checkpoints, sold off army rations, ran gambling and prostitution rings, and sold protection services. They linked military entrenchment to the large-scale mining projects planned for the province.[50] For these critics, the "mysterious shootings" in which lone farmers tending their cacao were attacked by masked men, or fire was set to houses at night, were calculated to keep refugees from returning to their homes and maintain a state of tension. Between the Malino declaration in 2001, which was supposed to end the violence, and November 2005, there were fifty-nine "mysterious shootings," forty-seven bombings, and very few arrests.[51]

Christian refugees I interviewed in Napu, Tentena, and Palolo in 2003 expressed the sense of being manipulated by unknown forces. "We always got on fine with our neighbors, there was nothing between us" was one refrain, followed by "We don't know who the perpetrators were, or how this could happen." This kind of statement could be interpreted as a rhetorical device to deflect blame and avoid future reprisals—we are not violent, it was not us, it was others. Yet in the earlier phases of the violence, thousands of "ordinary" people—Christians and Muslims—were involved in confrontations between mobs, enraged at news of atrocities committed by the other side. The militias that were formed subsequently had assistance from outside (Java for the Muslims, Minahasa for the Christians), but they recruited locally and had popular support.[52] Tensions among villagers over land and belonging were among the factors that enabled malevolent manipulation and popular action to become linked.[53]

By 2003 ethnoreligious segregation, long a feature of villages, hamlets, and urban wards, was consolidated at a broader scale.[54] Poso Town and the Poso coastline were Muslim strongholds, while Christian militias and refugees were concentrated in the highlands, especially in Kruyt and Adriani's mission town, Tentena. Muslims moved about in Poso Town with some security, but whenever tension mounted, officials who happened to be Christian could report for work in Poso only by paying armed guards. Some Muslims who feared attack sold the land they had purchased in the highlands and moved back to the coast, to the cities, or to the south. Fewer Bugis migrants arrived— also a sign that cheap land could no longer be found. But tens of thousands of Bugis migrants were securely in place in the highlands, some of them purchasing land deep in the hills, others congregated in established Bugis enclaves and villages were there was safety in numbers. They had a well-deserved reputation as diligent farmers and astute entrepreneurs, and there was every indication that they would continue to prosper and buy land.

To judge by their public statements, few officials shared the astute analysis of the army officer, an analysis that recognized the impact of Bugis migration and the uneven accumulation of land. They classified the conflict in Poso and smaller incidents around the province as "anarchic action" (*aksi anarkis*) or "mass rampage" (*amuk massa*), symptoms of the perennial deficiency of people in need of "mental guidance" (*pembinaan mental*).[55] Mental guidance, as I mentioned earlier, was the key word of trusteeship in the New Order: people with superior knowledge and status must instruct their inferiors on proper conduct. By reasserting their superiority in this way, officials overlooked the part played in the conflict by politicians and military men, who deliberately provoked conflict by setting one group against another. They overlooked the rational assessments that villagers on both side of the conflict made about their situation, the risks they faced, and the initiatives they needed to take to protect their families and their property from attack. They overlooked the processes of class and identity formation stimulated by the expert schemes and unruly practices in which officials were deeply involved. They made sparse reference to conflicts over land, still less to the consequences of landlessness. In this they were not alone—a World Bank program to manage and mitigate conflicts among villagers initiated in 2005 similarly evaded structural inequalities to focus on the deficiencies of villagers and the need to reform them, a point to which I will return.

CONCLUSION

In this chapter I explored processes of capital and identity formation that were stimulated by expert schemes, even as they exceeded their scope. The conditions under which highland land became a commodity and was accumulated by some parties to the exclusion of others were deliberately set. Yet the particular conjuncture at which exclusion from forests intersected with the arrival of Muslim migrants into the highland villages that had been Christianized by the Dutch was not part of any plan. There were further, extraneous processes experts neither anticipated nor contained—floods, the disease cycle of cacao, and a sevenfold increase in the price of cacao, among others. These processes arose at the limit of governmental interventions. Yet the limits were productive. As I will show in the following chapters, they stimulated new rounds of intervention designed to address new or unexpected problems, or long-standing problems that earlier interventions failed to solve.

The improvement programs I have described thus far positioned high-landers as deficient subjects, in need of expert guidance and correction. How highland villagers came to position themselves as political actors challenging the authority of those who presumed to improve them is a matter I will explore further in chapters to follow. By 2001, villagers in Rahmat and other Depsos resettlement sites in Palolo and in the highland valleys of Napu and Kulawi were squeezed between a migrant influx and the park boundaries. Relations between locals and migrants were tense. Informal leaders had moved well beyond the kind of regret expressed by Papa Eli at being left with "the ear" to organize collective action. Being landless, poor, and out of place, the refractory outcome of the array of projects, practices, and processes I have described, became a position—one of those "cramped spaces"—from which incisive critiques could be launched.[56] Yet it was the park—not their covillagers—that was at the focus of the highlanders' critical insights and initiatives. To explain why this was so, I need to examine another round of governmental intervention—1990s programs for "integrated conservation and development." How a new set of experts apprehended highland landscapes and livelihoods and set about trying to optimize them is the subject I turn to next.

RENDERING TECHNICAL?

The governmental interventions described thus far—programs to resettle people, cordon off forests, and intensify agriculture—were followed in the 1990s by further, more detailed and ambitious programs devised by a new set of authorities who claimed to know how best to arrange landscapes and livelihoods in the Central Sulawesi highlands. Indeed, the interest in examining and optimizing the relations between "men and things" reached an extraordinary intensity. The focus of all this attention was the sixty-seven villages in the upland valleys (Kulawi, Lindu, Palolo, Napu, Besoa, and Bada) that border directly upon the Lore Lindu National Park. Proponents of biodiversity protection felt the conduct of villagers in this "border zone" needed to be reformed. Their interventions drew from an assemblage of techniques and calculations that went under the label "integrated conservation and development."

My conceptual focus in this chapter is the operation of "rendering technical." In the first part of the chapter, I explore how this new set of programs identified an arena of intervention, bounded it, dissected it, and devised corrective measures to produce desirable results. I start with a close reading of project documents, which I set in the context of the fraught and messy conjuncture I explored in chapters 2 and 3. This approach enables me to discover what these programs sought to change, and what was excluded from their technical domain. It exposes multiple gaps: gaps between one document and the next, gaps between the world conveyed in the texts and the world to be transformed, and gaps between what the programs proposed and what they delivered. Later in the chapter, I take up the implications of the question mark in the chapter title to argue that the political-economic processes excluded from programs' technical design did not go away. Instead, the experts' technical diagnoses and prescriptions stimulated a political response as the highlanders and their NGO supporters arrived at their own critical analyses of the problems that beset them.

PARK PROTECTION

The park occupies 229,000 hectares, 3 percent of the total land area in the province, but a much higher proportion (13–56 percent) of the land in the surrounding subdistricts.[1] Most of the park comprises precipitous hills and mountains, with 90 percent of the land area above 1,000 meters.[2] The principal zone of contention is the area of the park adjacent to the valleys, which are densely populated and land-scarce. As I explained in chapter 2, residents of the border zone had various claims on the land and resources that fell inside the park boundaries when the park was formed in 1982. It was a site for hunting and rattan collection, the site of well-established coffee groves, fallow swidden plots, and some former hamlets. The park also carries signs of more ancient habitation—megaliths, stone rice mortars, and distinctive clumps of bamboo that signal to border villagers that their ancestors once occupied the land, even though precise genealogies and histories of settlement are lost. By 2003, some border villagers were also making their claims in nationalist terms, arguing that the park belongs to the people of Indonesia, and the benefits that flow from it—incomes, water, livelihoods, patents—should accrue to them rather than to the foreigners promoting biodiversity conservation.

For the experts in conservation who designed the park, the need for biodiversity protection was a self-evident and preeminent goal. Their position was supported by the Conservation Law of 1990 and national park regulations that forbade agriculture and settlement within park boundaries. As I noted earlier, although the commitment to create the Lore Lindu National Park was made at the World Parks Congress in 1982, precise determination of the park boundaries and the positioning of boundary markers did not begin in earnest until 1993, when a park management office was established under the Directorate of Forest Protection and Nature Conservation, in the Ministry of Forests.

In the 1990s, park-based conservation was supported by donors and transnational NGOS, and 50 percent of Indonesia's conservation funding came from these sources, as did the livelihoods of many experts, bureaucrats, and NGO staff.[3] The list of donors and conservation agencies that announced an interest in the Lore Lindu National Park was impressive. The park was said to contain the majority of Sulawesi's unique flora and fauna, biodiversity resources of global significance. Donors that committed funds included the Asian Development Bank (ADB) and the U.S. Agency for International Development (USAID). Concerned transnational organizations included UNESCO, the International Union for the Conservation of Nature, Birdlife International, the World Wildlife Fund, the Nature Conservancy (TNC) and CARE International (CARE). Each of these agencies used a technical term to designate the object of its attention: Man in the Biosphere Reserve, Center of Plant Diversity, Endemic Bird Area, Global 200 Eco-region.[4]

Adding to this list of authorities, each with an agenda, was a major research program funded by the German government: Stability of Rainforest Margins (STORMA). Beginning in 1999, teams of German and Indonesian researchers associated with STORMA were active in park border villages, investigating every dimension of people-park interaction. Although STORMA did not devise its own set of interventions, its research reports often ended with recommendations or highlighted "issues" for further research. When it identified optimal farm practices, the hope was that these would be promoted by agricultural officials and adopted. STORMA's vision of improvement was manifest in the program title: the marked and valued landscape was rainforest, and the goal was stability. That the destabilizing practices of Sulawesi highlanders were of concern to German scientists and funding agencies strengthened the position of the conservation agencies with programs on the ground. TNC, CARE, the ADB, and STORMA with project offices in Palu and expatriate staff were the visible frontline of the global biodiversity agenda.

INTO THE DOCUMENTS

Donor-funded programs for integrated conservation and development around the park were preceded by careful research in the proposed target area. Such detailed and site-specific project planning seems to bear little resemblance to the scenario in Lesotho described by Ferguson in the 1970s, in which ahistorical, generic descriptions were used to characterize "underdeveloped" countries, little was known about the "target group" whose lives were to be improved, and technical solutions were proposed in a vacuum. Yet despite the attention to detail, the programs I discuss in this chapter retained two fundamental features of the development problematic Ferguson identified. First, they reposed political-economic causes of poverty and injustice in terms amenable to a technical solution. Second, they highlighted only those problems for which a technical solution could in fact be proposed—sidelining much of the data so painstakingly collected.

To render a set of processes technical and improvable an arena of intervention must be bounded, mapped, characterized, and documented; the relevant forces and relations must be identified; and a narrative must be devised connecting the proposed intervention to the problem it will solve. Some insight into how this was done in the case at hand can be gleaned from a detailed reading of a series of three documents prepared by consultants for the Asian Development Bank in preparation for its Central Sulawesi Integrated Area Development and Conservation Project (the ADB project). This project was approved in 1998 for a sum of U.S.$53.7 million, of which U.S.$32 million were loan funds. Close reading reveals the shifts that occurred between one document and the next as the planners filtered out the processes they could not render technical or contain. For the sake of clarity I will call these documents the design study, the environmental assessment, and the project plan, the latter being the document approved in a formal memorandum of understanding as part of the loan agreement.

The first document in the sequence was the design study, prepared by a consulting company ANZDEC. This detailed and insightful study examined the history, economy, and social structure of the park border zone. It recognized and documented the processes I have described: (1) the acute shortage of land and growing landlessness in the border villages; (2) very high levels of indebtedness among the indigenous population; (3) the heightened vulnerability of indigenous and previously resettled populations to displacement by more aggressive migrant groups; (4) their tendency to sell land to cover social or ritual expenses, debts to traders and money lenders, and livelihood crises. The design study noted that the process of boundary marking was contested, and villagers insisted on their claims to land and resources within the park.[5] Yet the project plan, the third document in the sequence, proposed optimistically that income-generating projects and improved farming techniques would boost the economy in the border zone sufficiently to protect the park. Villagers would participate in devising and signing "conservation agreements." U.S.$52 million was committed on the basis of the connections drawn between problems and outcomes. How was this done? What happened between documents one and three?

Key to the project rationale was the "integrated" approach that enabled planners to recognize the tension between conservation and livelihoods, while proposing "development" as the solution:

> The Project rationale stems from the Government's recognition that an integrated approach is needed in the Project area to reconcile protection for the ecological functions and unique forest habitats of Park with the economic interests and development needs of the surrounding population. . . . Although gazetted in 1993, the Park lacks a proper management system to manage and protect its biological diversity. Thus, improving protection for the Park is a priority concern. However, the Park is located in the midst of poor farming communities with few alternatives to an agricultural livelihood and with many dependent on the Park's land and forest resources for economic sustenance. About 97 percent of the population are poor, with an average annual income of $250, significantly below the provincial poverty line of $415. About 2000 households living in 60 villages that surround the Park are directly dependent on income from cultivating trees inside the Park and harvesting of forest products to supplement their farm income. Thus, development activities are also required to generate alternative income sources for the nearby population and reduce their economic dependence on the Park's resources.[6]

The need for biodiversity protection through techniques such as zoning and spatial planning was stated in the project plan, citing national laws.[7] Some critical questions might be asked about biodiversity: Who needs this? At what cost? But these questions were not posed, as the "integrated approach" meant that conservation and development could both be achieved. There was no need to choose between them. The plan hedged on the issue of villagers' rights. It labeled their practices "agricultural encroachment and poaching" and asserted the need for "effective law enforcement" but also observed that villagers had a "legitimate claim to some form of compensation to offset their loss of free access to the Park's resources."[8] The question of rights was subsumed by the promise of development: since villagers would benefit, there was no need to clarify whether this was a matter of entitlement, or simply a means to bring unruly villagers onside. The plausibility of this "integrated" solution depended, significantly, on the capacity of the project to improve village livelihoods.

LIVELIHOOD IMPROVEMENTS

Agriculture was to be the ADB project's principal focus. Since the rugged mountainous terrain prevented expansion of arable land use, increasing yields on the extant farmland outside the park would be the key.[9] The plan correctly noted that the average population density in the province was low at 30 people per square kilometer but omitted an important finding of the environmental assessment: already in 1997, actual population densities were as high as 476 per square kilometer in some of the park border villages.[10] Further, the plan did not differentiate villagers by assets, characterizing them as generically poor. It noted that average landholdings were 2.5 hectares per household.[11] By averaging population densities and landholdings, the plan constructed an image of a modest smallholding peasantry, ripe for agricultural improvement. Disruptive information—absolute landlessness among the indigenous population of around 10 percent—was noted in the plan but treated as a static and isolated fact.[12] It was not situated in ongoing processes: the arrival of migrants and the progressive displacement and impoverishment of the indigenous population, processes discussed at length in the design study.

That the project could actually increase agricultural productivity on land outside the park was a major premise. The plan observed that farm yields in the project area were significantly below provincial averages. Abstracting from the average, it proposed that yields could be increased by the addition of more biochemical inputs and improved seeds. The results expected from these modest technical interventions were nothing short of spectacular. The plan stated that 11,000 participating farm households (half of all households in the project area) would experience increased yields of 20 to 180 percent within a few years.[13] There were multiple gaps in this analysis. The plan did not set the proposed income gains against the income that would be lost from existing and future coffee and cacao within the park. The characteristics of the land in the border villages that might prevent it from reaching the provincial average— steep slopes, narrow valleys, pockets of infertile peat and poor soils—were not computed. Although the environmental assessment noted that the project area is highly prone to landslides, erosion, and flooding due to its rugged topography and intense rainfall, the plan made no mention of these ecological risks, or their potential to ruin farmers persuaded to purchase expensive chemical inputs on a credit basis.[14] The proposed technologies, the plan stated, were "known, adequately tested, and well within the capabilities of the technical services and farmers."[15] If that was so, I find myself asking, and the payoff was so substantial and apparently guaranteed, why did farmers not already adopt them?

In the plan ecological concerns sat rather awkwardly with the promised gains in farm productivity. Agrochemicals supplied by the project would be restricted to officially approved brands.[16] The design study reported that "assistance in sustainable intensification methods which may include terracing, contour planting, diversified alley cropping and mixed agro-foresty" was specifically requested by villagers.[17] Conveniently, villagers were interested in precisely the kinds of technical inputs a contemporary conservation and development project was eager to supply.[18] But, as several researchers have shown, these are labor-intensive practices from which spectacular income gains have not been obtained under trial conditions, much less over wide areas.[19]

Not mentioned in the project plan was one farm improvement opportunity of which some farmers in and around the park were already aware in the mid-1990s: monocropped cacao. The project planners cannot be faulted for their failure to anticipate the boom in cacao prices created by the crash of the Indonesian currency in 1997. But they should have recognized that farmers were already experimenting with new tree crops, learning new techniques by observing other farmers, and carrying out their own trials. Many tried cloves and cashews before cacao became the obvious choice. They did not need a U.S.$53 million project to persuade them to attempt to improve their production. They were already doing it. What they were not doing in the 1990s, for good reasons, was planting "economically useful tree species native to the area." This was an activity the project planned to promote, taking precious space away from the lucrative exotics cacao and coffee.[20] Nowhere did the plan offer a realistic calculation of the values circulating in the local economy—the value of the land and resources in the park, or the opportunity cost of diverting agricultural land and labor from higher-value crops to lower-value native species. Nowhere, in short, did it calculate the actual cost of conservation to be borne by the villagers. Hence the proposition that development benefits would offset losses and compensate villagers had no empirical basis.

In addition to the agricultural component of the project, there was a plan to promote alternative sources of income for the landless or near-landless villagers heavily engaged in rattan collection. The plan described rattan collection as being "small but commercial scale" and anticipated a postdevelopment future in which rattan would be collected only for domestic use.[21] Small-scale it may have been, but in the 1990s, as the design study recognized, rattan collection was highly significant for the poorer households, which derived a major part of their incomes from this source.[22] Moreover, as the design study also observed, these rattan collectors were chronically indebted to their rattan bosses, from whom they took advances for daily food supplies. Unable to cover their debts, they sold or forfeited any remaining land they held inside or outside the park.[23] Debts obliged them to continue with rattan. They were, in the graphic idiom of one rattan collector I interviewed, "tied at the throat"—a reference to buffalo or cattle in harness.

As a technical answer to debt, the plan proposed "affordable credit." Yet the details of the project's credit plan cast doubt on the viability of this solution. Credit was to be extended only for new or existing productive enterprises, and subject to scrutiny for its environmental soundness. Moreover, the credit scheme would only be set up in villages that had successfully "mobilized savings." Only savers could become members of credit schemes. And members who borrowed funds would pay market interest rates—3 percent per month, generating funds to pay management costs and to ensure sustainability of the credit program.[24]

In setting the interest rate at its market value, the project plan correctly acknowledged that the interest rates charged to border villagers were not in fact usurious, as often assumed, but accurately attuned to the lending risk. It failed to observe that for people able and willing to pay these rates, credit was already available. Thus it was unclear how the project's credit program would increase access to *affordable* credit, the need identified in the design study.[25]

Further, restricting access to credit to people who were environmentally responsible, entrepreneurial, and able to save effectively ruled out the intended target group: the indebted rattan collectors. Presumably, the loan criteria were intended to encourage the rattan collectors to conform to the desired behavior, but the project offered them no practical means to initiate such a transformation. Thus the credit program could not compensate rattan collectors, relieve poverty, or protect the park.

THE WILL TO CONSERVE?

The plan proposed that project benefits would not only compensate villagers for their losses, they would induce them to sign "conservation agreements." It proposed a trade-off. In order to access project benefits, a household or an entire community must formalize their commitment to abide by the park rules. But what were the benefits? From the project, they were the livelihood improvements outlined above and funding for village infrastructure such as minor roads, irrigation, and flood control. From the park authorities, there were no promises at all. The plan stated: "In return for their compliance with park protection regulations in the buffer areas, it is envisaged that the Park Authority *might consider* granting villagers harvesting rights to areas designated for traditional use according to the Park's 25 year Management Plan; and temporary harvesting rights to their coffee or cocoa trees inside the Park."[26]

The plan proposed to bolster inducement with two further measures: increased enforcement of park exclusion, and the attempt to educate villagers and officials about the value of conservation. For problems not covered by law, the promotion of new ways of thinking and acting would be the primary solution. The design study and the environmental assessment recognized the threat to the park posed by migration into the border zone—a threat that was already evident well before the cacao-related migration of Bugis to the highlands in 1997–98. The problem, accurately reported in the design study, was that spontaneous migrants were "untouched by formal planning processes." There was no law to prevent the free movement of Indonesian citizens anywhere in the archipelago. It noted, further, that migration was encouraged by officials who perceived migrants as a positive example to the locals with their diligence, productivity, and pioneering worldview.[27]

The environmental assessment recast the problem of migration as a matter of inadequate knowledge that could be remedied by technique. The project would institute a new "community planning process, which will enable community members to assess their available resources and development options and to reach consensus on the desirability of local in-migration and the application of available control measures."[28] A fact noted in the design study was omitted from the environmental assessment: by 1997, migrants already made up about 50 percent of the population in many of the border villages.[29] The assessment posited unified, consensual communities, ready to identify the presence of migrants as a problem and act to exclude them. It also ignored the design study's finding that the village officials who would need to implement "control measures" were involved in supplying land to migrants.[30] As backup, perhaps, the assessment proposed to make its own law: like villagers who failed to sign conservation agreements, migrants not registered as "target beneficiaries" at the beginning of the project would be excluded from project largesse.[31]

Through its program for community development, the project proposed to create a new collective subject, a community that would assess, plan, reach consensus, and think of population and natural resources as entities to be managed. The proposed technique for creating this subject was to guide villagers through a carefully crafted sequence of activities: participatory assessment of community resources, problem analysis, preparation of development proposals, application for funding under the official budget planning process, monitoring, and evaluation of outcomes.[32] The plan referred frequently to participation, but how villagers would participate and to what ends was predefined. Like the reconstructed villages of Java in the ethical period I described in chapter 1, Sulawesi's park-border villagers were to be true to themselves while also conforming to new requirements. The contradiction produced sentences that are impossible to decipher, much less to translate into action. Try this: "Participatory mechanisms built to achieve outputs at the community level (savings mobilization, formulation of village proposals, and conservation agreements) are means through which villagers, including women, would decide the types of development assistance that would be appropriate for their circumstances."[33]

The plan also expected officials to learn new practices and become new subjects as a result of educative interventions. While the design study observed that many officials in the provincial bureaucracy, in the Forest Department, and in the police force and army were deeply involved in extracting rattan and timber from the park, this information was omitted from the plan.[34] Instead, unruly practices were attributed to a lack of knowledge: "Park community programs are designed to instill a greater understanding of conservation issues, and increased compliance with Park protection measures. Increased local government involvement from their participation in Park-community programs and buffer zone forums will likely increase their commitment to law enforcement to protect the Park."[35] The plan noted that the public character of the buffer-zone forums would encourage the exposure of corruption and collusion among officials, but it did not elaborate on how such forums would operate, or why officials would support them. Like villagers, officials were expected to change their ways as a result of "increasing public awareness of environmental values and the destructive potential of commercial exploitation."[36] Perhaps recalcitrant officials would also learn something from the army of consultants to be employed by the project under twenty-six separate terms of reference.[37]

The project plan envisaged the state apparatus of Central Sulawesi as a rational legal bureaucracy requiring only the transfer of technologies and skills to acquire environmental perspectives and improve its performance. After all, the design study had observed that the provincial Rural Community Development Office already had programs for "guidance for village improvement," "village community self-resilience," and "village economic effort and village settlement"; it also had programs for data collection, motivation, training, credit, and village institution building.[38] Further, as stated in the project rationale, "the Government of Indonesia" had already declared park protection a priority, so all that remained was to help "the Government" to meet its goal.

Development programs that naively accept a ruling regime's public statements tend to meet the fate memorably described by Ferguson: positioning themselves as craftsmen approaching their raw materials, design in hand, they end up "like a bread crumb thrown into an ants' nest." They are pushed and pulled by forces they did not expect to encounter, then "frustrated and abused by the very 'Government' they imagined they were trying to 'help.' "[39] This was pretty much what happened in this case, as I will explain. But why were the planners so naive—or more accurately, why did they elect to ignore the design study's findings? The reason, I suggest, is still the one Ferguson identified decades ago. Development interventions can proceed only on the basis that "the government" is a neutral vessel dedicated to improvement for "the people." By the 1990s, development experts recognized that bureaucracies were often flawed, but treated this, once again, as a problem that could be rectified by technical interventions: institutional strengthening, capacity building, and instruction in "good governance." Refractory findings suggesting that "the government" is not dedicated to the public good cannot be processed by the development machine.

A final component of the project plan merits scrutiny: the calculation that deemed a total commitment of U.S.$53 million dollars, of which U.S.$32 million were loan funds, a sound financial investment. The project plan calculated the Economic Internal Rate of Return at 18 percent. Bank officials produced this number by assigning monetary values to a range of environmental "benefits" including carbon sequestration and biodiversity protection—global environmental goods for which indebted Indonesians were to pay the price. Other benefits assigned a dollar value were the protection of downstream irrigation facilities for which the park serves as a catchment, and the payback from clean water and improved health services, which would reduce time lost to illness and time spent in water collection.[40] Expert advice was once again ignored as the budget was devised. The environmental assessment stated explicitly that biodiversity and carbon sequestration benefits were "nonquantifiable,"[41] yet they appeared in the balance sheet of the project plan. These two benefits were calculated to comprise a staggering 58 percent of the gross project benefits at year seven, when the project was to end. Without them, benefits minus costs would produce a deficit, and the project loan would not have been approved.

The desire of bank officials to sell a loan and the desire of Indonesian officials to see project funds flow their way were clearly influential in the project approval. Yet I do not regard these interests as sufficient to explain why the project was devised, or why it took the form it did. Interests, as I noted in the introduction, are part of the development enterprise but they are not its master term. In this case they coexisted with the earnest desire of the design team to achieve "integrated conservation and development"—a quite specific, technical, and benevolent end.

The proximate effects of the ADB project were dismal indeed. The agricultural interventions, although backed with huge technical and financial resources, encountered the structural limitations already apparent in the logic—or rather the illogic—of the project plan. The project formed "farmer groups" and handed out gifts such as tools and sacks of fertilizer and pesticide—items of no use, as critics pointed out, to people without land. Not only were there no benefits, there were losses: the media reported an incident in which a number of cattle died after eating sacks of fertilizer stored behind a house because the recipient had no use for them. Needless to say, the project did not deliver the promised gains in farm incomes, not even modest gains among farmers who had land at their disposal. The experts had no new techniques to offer. The community development component of the project was equally ineffective. High-level officials formed their own NGOs to carry out the community activities, aiming to keep the project resources conveniently "in-house." The midterm project evaluation concluded that these NGOs had met none of the obligations stated in their terms of reference and called for a formal compliance audit.[42]

The construction component of the project that was to deliver improved roads, irrigation, and flood control measures was monstrously corrupt, and it too received media scrutiny. The nature of the scrutiny reveals just how wide was the gap between project assumptions about "the government" and vernacular understandings of how development projects actually proceed. According to one media report, the project paid out Rp13 million per kilometer for the construction of a road link from Napu to Bada. From this sum, Rp7 million per kilometer was passed down to the Subdistrict Head. He in turn passed down only Rp3 million per kilometer to the villagers who did the work. Even that sum was not paid to the villagers—they received nothing at all. An unnamed intermediary who had negotiated with them for the work disappeared. A member of the provincial legislature with ties to Bada made a complaint against the project leader for his inhumane (*tidak manusiawi*) treatment of the villagers. To me, the most striking element of this story was the media focus on how the poor villagers were cheated. There was no comment on the apparently normal practice of "cutting" the budget at many steps along the administrative chain. There was, however, a call for the head of provincial planning agency responsible for the project to be held legally accountable for the failure to pay the villagers or to complete the road.[43]

Villagers were appalled at the project's waste and incompetence. Micro-hydro-generators were installed in places with insufficient water; river bunds to prevent flooding were swept away with the first modest flood. A villager I interviewed in Napu expressed his frustration thus: "What's the point of having fish without fish ponds, or building fish ponds without water? It is absurd. Then they want us to follow the Forest Department. We all have to plant teak. So where are we supposed to put our own crops? . . . The community facilitators were being paid Rp400,000 per month but they didn't do anything; they were never in the village. We had to do all the work for them. That's because their pay was supposed to be Rp1 million, but they never received that amount."

By 2003, five years into the project, no community conservation agreements had been developed or signed through the project, and the planned buffer-zone forums were only just being formed, their mandates uncertain. The credit program had not been launched. The official responsible for this component of the project explained to me that credit was not a good idea, because the villagers were "only rattan collectors." They did not have enterprises, nor did they think like entrepreneurs. If they were given money, he suggested, they would only waste it. Thus every gap and contradiction present in the plan was quickly exposed. The outcome, however, was not just a dull thud as another failed development project bit the dust. There were reverberations in many directions, as I will later explain. First, however, I examine two more programs for integrated conservation and development that began work in the 1990s. They too set out to render complex problems technical and manageable, sharing many of ADB's assumptions and flaws and adding a few twists of their own.

CARE'S PROGRESSIVE FARMERS

CARE's projects were titled Protection of Tropical Forest through Environmental Conservation on Marginal Lands, and Biodiversity Conservation for Lore Lindu National Park. The principal focus was again agriculture. CARE promoted fruit trees and techniques for sustainable agriculture such as bench terraces, shade trees, alley cropping, green manures, and integrated pest management. It, too, set an ambitious target—to improve the farming practices of 2,250 households in twenty-two villages around the park. An evaluation report for phase one of the project recognized, however, that adoption of new techniques such as row cropping was low because they showed no "real success." So too with integrated pest control: farmers reported that they still preferred to use chemical insecticides if they could afford them, because they were "practical."[44] Thus the CARE program ran into the same problem as the ADB. The theory elaborated in terms of contour lines and nutrient cycling did not translate into practices farmers willingly adopted, because they did not pay.[45]

CARE was more consistent than the ADB with its agricultural program and its free farm inputs, and extension services did benefit some farmers. This modest success revealed two further flaws in the program logic. First, the "target group" CARE deemed most likely to encroach on the park—poor villagers—were not able to take advantage of CARE's inputs because they had no farms. If they had some cacao, they wanted it to produce maximum incomes as soon as possible. They did not have the luxury or incentive to prioritize long-term ecological stability. Thus CARE's agricultural interventions were captured by the village elite. Excluded villagers saw CARE as yet another vehicle of patronage operating in their name but not for their benefit. Second, farmers who benefited from CARE's attentions acquired new resources and an added incentive to expand their holdings outside the park, where they bought up the land of their impoverished neighbors. They also expanded their holdings *inside* the park.[46] Thus agricultural improvement did not promote conservation, it undermined it.

The illogic of CARE's farm improvement program seems so obvious, I find myself curious, again, as to how this program came to be. CARE, like the ADB, devised its program for integrated conservation and development by drawing upon elements from a broad assemblage of knowledge and technique current at the time. It found the integrated concept attractive, I suggest, because it was consistent with CARE's vision of the type of improvement proper to highland villages. CARE aimed to secure a balance between subsistence and cash-oriented production in a stable, orderly, cooperative village setting. Like the colonial and New Order programs that preceded it, CARE's agricultural improvement program did not anticipate changing needs or aspirations. It was especially partial to traditional forms of village cooperation. In its programs around the park, it encouraged villagers to make use of the traditional practice of labor exchange (*mapalus*), in which farmers take turns to work each other's fields, reciprocating a day for a day.[47] But why did this traditional practice need to be encouraged? It was already familiar to highland villagers. If they did not use it for tasks such as planting and tending cacao, presumably its benefits were not compelling.[48] Thus CARE's promotion of *mapalus* was less about economically efficient farming than about restoring the capacity of Indonesian villagers to live a culturally appropriate, moral life. Rendered technical by the project, dissected and instrumentalized, CARE's *mapalus* went the way of the neat rows of alley crops that failed to take hold.

Despite the problematic assumptions of the agricultural component of the project noted in the evaluation of phase one, CARE proceeded in 2000 to design a further phase of the project with more of the same. There was some new technical terminology. CARE proposed that "Low External Input Sustainable Agriculture" (LEISA) combined with "Participatory Technology Development" would blend science with local knowledge to arrive at "improved and integrated farming systems that yield stable and sustainable production levels." CARE described LEISA as a principle and process rather than a fixed technology. Its virtue was to combine the livelihood needs of small farmers with conservation. It would increase on-farm biodiversity by mimicking nature and maintaining living soil and nutrient flows. It would also improve farmer incomes, an intervention that CARE still expected would reduce the incentive to expand production inside the park.[49]

Unsurprisingly, a midterm evaluation of phase two reported that CARE's agriculture experts had not been able to identify sustainable technologies of interest to farmers, since the farmers were fixated on cacao. The experts confessed to the evaluator that they did not believe they had the capacity to improve livelihoods for anyone around the park. At best, they saw their work as a "door-opener" for conservation activities and other project components.[50] Belatedly attending to the situation of the landless, phase two proposed to organize the poorest villagers into self-help groups for "livelihood activities." Yet despite a series of participatory planning exercises, by the time of the midterm evaluation CARE staff had not been able to identify any activities that would actually improve livelihoods for this particular "target group."[51]

More problematic for park border villagers than the failure to deliver on promised livelihood improvements was CARE's stance on park protection. Like the ADB, CARE's program aimed to produce new subjects who would adopt ecofriendly practices on their own land and respect park rules. Specifically, CARE expected villagers to devise regulations committing them to police each other and report on individuals who infringed park rules. The outcome in phase one was disappointing. The evaluation reported that only two villages prepared regulations, and only one reported an infraction. The constraints reported were the lack of fit between park regulations and local needs, and "social jealousy" resulting from the perception that the park authorities were inconsistent in enforcing park rules.[52] The formal conservation agreements CARE sponsored in some of its target villages clearly prioritized a park protection agenda. They did not acknowledge villagers' rights to resources within the park.[53] As a result, villagers angered by their exclusion from the park positioned CARE together with TNC, the ADB, and STORMA as foreigners' organizations concerned more about flora and fauna than about people.

THE NATURE CONSERVANCY'S DISTRACTION

TNC billed its activities in Central Sulawesi in the 1990s as pioneering integrated conservation and development, a "brave experiment to apply the philosophy that long-term conservation of protected areas can only occur with the involvement and active participation and empowerment of the local people most closely associated with and affecting the protected area itself."[54] Yet for TNC's project planners, empowerment of park-border villagers did not mean recognition of their rights to land and resources within the park. TNC denied the existence of ancestral rights to park land, stating boldly that the border villagers "use natural resources in the forest for trade and cash, but do not have any cultural or spiritual attachment to the park."[55] A TNC design study conducted in 1991 described the villagers as "subsistence farmers" who lacked stable production systems and made poor use of their land due to improper management. Their profligate ways made them doubly culpable when they encroached on the park for agriculture, hunting, and the harvesting of timber and rattan.[56]

Like the design study for the ADB project, the design study for TNC's Lore Lindu program was detailed. The TNC team visited every village around the park. Amid its generalized statements about village profligacy, it recorded a set of much more specific processes: migration into the park border zone (organized and spontaneous), lack of enforcement of park boundaries, resource conflicts, legal uncertainty, lack of economic alternatives to agriculture, lack of appropriate land use plans, lack of administrative capacity, and lack of a conservation ethic. But in its plan TNC, like the ADB, screened out the issues of migration, resource conflict, and legal uncertainty to devise interventions of a technical kind. TNC would improve official planning systems, raise conservation awareness, increase economically sustainable sources of income, and link project benefits to conservation performance through conservation contracts.

Limited funds obliged TNC to focus its efforts. Unlike the ADB, it could not contemplate an overall development benefit. Instead, it set out to target its interventions very precisely. The design study suggested that "specific groups in the community rather than the community as a whole are responsible for encroachment, and development activities should be targeted directly at these groups." It rejected poverty as a motive: "Some of the threats to the park are not poverty-related, but stem from economic opportunism among residents of boundary villages and outsiders."[57] Young men, the study claimed, filled idle periods in the annual rice-harvest cycle "opportunistically" by rattan collection. To address this problem, it proposed two approaches: "strict enforcement" and diversion—shifting the attention of young men away from the park by occupying them in new labor-intensive activities.[58]

One plan to divert villagers' attention was to intensify agriculture on what TNC described as "communal lands which are currently underutilized or poorly managed." Much of this was former swidden fields on which tree crops could be grown. It called for "the establishment of village-level organizations" to manage these "community lands."[59] This plan overlooked the fact that the fallow swidden land in question was not communal, it was subject to private rights. Thus it was not at the disposal of village or TNC planners, nor was it accessible to a newly isolated and pathologized subject, the idle young man. The second plan was to devise "micro-enterprise" projects carefully crafted to achieve several goals at once: distraction, alternative incomes, and popular awareness of the need to conserve biodiversity. The planners researched twenty possible micro-enterprise projects and presented the results in a matrix, ranking the candidate projects according to their economic, physical, and institutional sustainability, their ability "to provide high conservation returns quickly for a small amount of investment," and their potentially high "public relations value for the Sulawesi Parks Program and potential donors."[60]

The micro-enterprises eventually selected were marketing support for wild-honey collection, white-water rafting, butterfly farming, and beekeeping. All four were dismal failures from the perspective of incomes and sustainability. TNC claimed that its support for wild-honey marketing had some success in boosting incomes, but the claim was hard to sustain because the villagers were already collecting and selling wild honey before TNC made a project of it. TNC inputs, by its own admission, were "negligible."[61] The other interventions proved to be expensive to launch, required expert assistance, were taken up by a tiny number of households, and did not produce sustainable incomes. More important, as TNC acknowledged, they did not come close to matching the profits to be made from existing economic activities in the park, namely, rattan collection and "illegal" cacao and coffee farming. Like the ADB and CARE, TNC micro-enterprise experts seriously underestimated the opportunity costs of land and labor in the border villages, as well as the desires and capacities of the villagers.[62] This is the classic failing of the approach Michael Dove labels "rainforest crunch": consigning relatively poor and powerless people to the least profitable "development" alternatives.[63] So long as they had better options, park villagers stayed away.

If the income effect of TNC's micro-enterprise projects was neutral, their effect on public relations was disastrous. They undermined the credibility of TNC in the eyes of border villagers, who accused TNC of playing about with butterflies and bees while the people for whom it professed to have a concern still lacked secure access to land and livelihoods. As one villager from Rahmat put it, "their projects were like chicken shit, a little bit of steam at first but it quickly fizzles out." The former TNC cadre I interviewed shared this critique, describing their involvement with TNC as a waste of their time. TNC expected them to attend frequent meetings and training sessions, organize villagers, and facilitate the visits of TNC staff, all this as volunteers acting on behalf of their "community." As one ex-cadre observed, "We got a certificate from those trainings, but what can you do with a TNC certificate? It is not accepted at the bank."

In the late 1990s, opposition to the park intensified. Frustration with the ADB, CARE, and TNC for their failures in "integrated conservation and development" were part of this conjuncture, but there were other elements: (1) intensified, coercive exclusion from the park, as crops and huts were burned and villagers were arrested; (2) increasing landlessness and marginalization among the local population in the context of Bugis migration and the arrival of cacao; (3) increased freedom to express grievances and mobilize to claim entitlements with the end of the New Order and the beginning of *reformasi*; and (4) the emergence of a strong NGO movement in Palu closely engaged with the fate of highland villagers.

For the "targets" of the governmental programs I have discussed thus far— resettlement of highlanders from hills to valleys, agricultural improvement, integrated conservation and development—critique did not develop from a close reading of the project documents, identifying the gaps and contradic- tions internal to program design—the strategy of a scholar like myself. Rather, highland villagers derived their critiques from their experience of what these projects did, as one governmental intervention layered upon another and in- tersected with the other processes shaping their lives. Park enforcement had an especially dramatic and visceral effect, amplified by the association villagers made between enforcement and the presence of foreigners excessively inter- ested in park affairs. Mama Yonas, an articulate woman with grown children, told me of her experience with tears, anger, and indignation:

> We didn't have land in Palolo. We were sharecropping *sawah*. To get somewhere, you need to have land. So in 2000 we decided to try in the park. We came in with twenty people, to clear two hectares. The usual pay was Rp5,000 but I offered my workers Rp10,000 because the work was hard, they had to cut big trees.
>
> Then a party of forest guards came by, fifteen of them. They came to my hut. I was getting the food ready for the workers. The workers ran to hide. They thought I had been arrested. So I gave the guards coffee and food. They stayed for one hour to eat. Then they said, "It's time for us to go. Do you know this is inside the park?" I said I know, but I need to eat. They asked me what I planned to plant. I told them candlenuts, cacao, durian, to replace the trees. I said I have

nothing in Palolo. They said, "Excuse us now" [i.e., they politely took their leave]. Then they started hacking at my hut and everything I had planted, cut it all to pieces, burned it down.

I cried. I said, "God will see you. You have no pity." They just smiled. My cacao, coffee, chili peppers, they pulled it all up. I asked them, "Don't you eat chilis too? We are just going to grow crops, not take the land." They said, "You can't do that here, this place belongs to lots of nations" (*banyak Negara yang pegang in*). So I thought, does this land belong to Indonesia or to some other country? If it belongs to Indonesia, it belongs to me, too. Then they left. My workers came back and went right back to work, because I had already paid them. They went back to work, clearing the forest, brave. Until it was all done. It was cleared, but we hadn't planted yet.[64]

The attempt by Mama Yonas and her husband to clear land in the park was one of many. A prime site for these incursions was the Dongi-Dongi valley, where the main road transects the park between Palolo and Napu, offering easy access to good potential farmland left and right. There had been small-scale, surreptitious clearing for agriculture at Dongi-Dongi since the road opened in the 1980s. Palolo villagers working for the logging enterprise Kebun Sari, or hunting and collecting rattan in the forest, had planted coffee there. In the mid-1990s a group of about thirty households led by Papa Lili, an elder from one of the resettlement villages in Palolo, began clearing on a larger scale. It was a game of cat and mouse (*kucing kucingan*). The farmers planted their crops one day, and the guards uprooted them the next.

One evening, as a group of men and women sat with me enjoying a treat of fresh corn on the cob, the men described their experiences attempting to claim land at Dongi-Dongi with bitterness, but also with pride: "We took it in turns, plant-uproot, plant-uproot (*bergantian, tanam-cabut*); we got used to it, we just kept replacing, we didn't retreat." Another noted humorously that the guards "just pruned the trees [cacao and coffee] for us, so they became young again!" Humor was mixed with anger at the guards' hypocrisy: "They got tired cutting, we got tired planting, but they were more tired. They said 'don't,' but they also used to hunt, and they harvested our cucumbers before they cut them down. They brought bags to carry home the food. We said to the guards, 'We just want our children to be able to read, to be like you!'"

FIGURE 5
Rahmat farmer carrying
home an edible rattan tip
from the forest edge

The game of cat and mouse had a price. Papa Lili was arrested and spent three months in jail. Other members of the group were transported back to their home villages and threatened. Guards confiscated knives and cooking pots. But some members of the group persisted. "We would come up here on Sundays and work, then we'd go back to the village on Friday. We ate cassava, sweet potato [food that can be planted in small clearings], and rattan tips. On Saturdays we did wage work back in Palolo. We'd get up very early to start clearing the small trees and bushes. Then we'd wait in the huts. We didn't light a fire. We didn't dare to cut the big trees. It continued like that; we didn't get bored." There were larger scale attempts to occupy Dongi-Dongi in 1998 and 1999, rebuffed by the authorities with the promise of action on the land problem, but the promise was not kept. TNC was involved in the eviction of would-be settlers and further implicated in the failure to find land.

In Rahmat, confrontations with the forest guards became very heated in 2001, as people protested the cutting and burning of their crops by park guards. There were violent incidents in which massed villagers physically threatened the park guards. At one point villagers destroyed a wooden bridge, trapping the guards on the road at the forest edge without a means of escape. Eventually the park guards abandoned all their guard posts in Palolo, and by 2003 they had not returned. Most of the guard posts were burned to the ground.[65] In one Palolo village, the Headman built himself a house on the concrete base of one of the burned guard huts, some distance from the village center, where he lived in relative isolation. Like his covillagers, he farmed inside the park boundary. The siting of his house was a powerful metaphor for the compromised condition in which he found himself. What could a Headman do, caught between the livelihood needs of his covillagers and his responsibility to uphold the law and please his superiors? In every village around the park, coffee inside the park boundary continued to be tended, and cacao was introduced.

THE CASE OF KATU

One particular struggle served to sharpen critiques of park-based conservation and forge links between highlanders and Palu-based NGOs. The struggle was over Katu, a village situated within the park that was slated for resettlement as part of the ADB project. Katu people facing eviction swore an oath to reject resettlement and remain in the park come what may. They contacted a Palu-based NGO, Yayasan Tanah Merdeka (YTM), to ask for help. YTM had made its name a few years earlier when it helped people at the Lindu Lake resist eviction and oppose the building of the hydrodam. In Katu, YTM used some of the same techniques, offering paralegal training to educate the Katu people about their rights and helping them to map their customary land and document their traditional land-use practices. Evidence in place, the Katu people made the argument that they were an indigenous community with the right to use and manage their customary domain. They described their land use and tenure practices as a sustainable, traditional resource management system that inflicted minimal damage on the park. They also documented their move from the Besoa enclave to Katu in the colonial period, noting that officials had approved the settlement of Katu because it enabled the people to grow coffee to pay their taxes.[66]

Faced with the challenge presented by the Katu people and their allies, officials responsible for the ADB project rejected the Katu peoples' claim to be indigenous. Although a decade earlier Indonesian officials routinely denied that Indonesia had any indigenous people, by the late 1990s officials recognized that such people exist. The senior official responsible for the resettlement of Katu argued, however, that the Katu people did not qualify, since Katu was settled only in 1908 by "migrants" from Besoa. The Katu people had not been in place since time immemorial. In addition to rejecting the argument about indigeneity, officials determined to resettle Katu repeated the well-worn arguments of the colonial and New Order regimes: swidden cultivation destroys the forest, and there was insufficient land in the vicinity of Katu for the development of orderly production, namely *sawah*. They insisted that the Katu people would not progress until they were moved away from their isolated locale and put in contact with more open and progressive people. They used, in short, the language of the Depsos program for estranged communities, positioning Katu people as backward and deficient, in need of official tutelage. The officials did not accept the Katu people's assertion that they were satisfied with their lives. They countered that Depsos had a responsibility to change aspirations and make static people dynamic.[67]

The argument made by officials that Katu was isolated and its people lacked familiarity with the modern world was problematic, given the evident success of the Katu people in identifying NGO allies, and the organizational skills and dedication they displayed in preparing their documents and maps (complete with global positioning). Katu people attending a Palu forum organized by the NGOs to debate the forced resettlement of Katu made the point: if they were isolated, it was the government's fault for failing to provide them with an access road and other routine village services. The threat posed by articulate Katu voices must have been significant, because a group of Katu people was arrested en route to the forum and thus prevented from demonstrating their competence to the attending media.[68]

Faced with a critical, mobilized, and informed village population, officials sought to reverse the signs. They read the mobilization as evidence that the Katu people were victims of NGO manipulation.[69] In this way the officials sought to restore the positioning of the Katu people as backward and needy subjects who did not know what was good for them. As it turned out, there was a reversal—a dramatic rearticulation of positions and the forging of new alliances. But it went against the officials supporting resettlement. Katu people, armed with their maps, documents, arguments, and supporters, successfully persuaded the park Director that they could manage park resources in a sustainable fashion according to their traditional, indigenous techniques, and should therefore be permitted to remain in their village inside the park. In an exceptional move, the park Director issued a letter recognizing the existence of Katu as an indigenous community whose livelihood activities covering 1,178 hectares of the park were "an integral part of the Park management system." For Katu people and their supporters, and for the larger NGO movement arguing for the recognition of indigenous rights and traditional wisdom, it was a nationally celebrated breakthrough.[70] The innovative park Director, Banjar Yulianto Laban, gained national acclaim as an ecopopulist, a philosophy he later elaborated in a series of articles published in the national press and presented at NGO meetings on Java and abroad, where he was invited to speak. He received an award from the national environmental NGO umbrella organization WALHI. He emerged as a champion of indigenous rights, a humanist who recognized that conservation agendas should not trump livelihood needs. He also emerged as an opponent of corrupt and wasteful megaprojects such as the ADB's integrated conservation and development project at Lore Lindu, funded by a loan that the Indonesian people would have to repay.

NGO CONNECTIONS

In helping the people of Lake Lindu and of Katu to resist eviction, the NGOS YTM and WALHI contributed to the work of articulation in the dual sense explored by Stuart Hall: they helped people to articulate their grievances and to make explicit the critiques embedded in practices such as tending swiddens and coffee groves; and they helped to connect people's struggles to globally circulating concepts, such as the right of indigenous people to their customary land, a right supported by international conventions. They also helped to situate particular struggles on a broader canvas of national and transnational activism. YTM in particular used the struggle of Katu as a window through which to expose and critique the array of official policies, programs, and practices negatively affecting landscapes and livelihoods in the Central Sulawesi highlands.

In a series of news articles and pamphlets, YTM's director Arianto Sangaji took up "integrated conservation and development" not to dismiss it, but to turn it around.[71] He argued that the proper means to accomplish this integration were radically different from those adopted by the park authorities and foreign donors. Katu's land use practices, he argued, were significantly more effective at maintaining biodiversity within the park than state-led conservation, and much less damaging than state- or donor-led "development."[72] Specifically, Sangaji argued that the regime's claim to a technoscientific expertise capable of optimizing relations between people and resources was hollow. The claim to rational land-use planning was especially thin. Officials claimed to prioritize park protection while building roads and bringing transmigrants from outside Sulawesi into the park border zone. Adding to the land pressure, officials had allocated about 15,000 hectares in the vicinity of the park to private corporations for large-scale plantations. They had granted a gold mining concession *within* the park—a concession that would have massive impacts on landscape and livelihoods when it went into production. They had approved a plan to build a hydrodam at Lake Lindu in the center of the park, a plan that would have required new roads and forest destruction. It would already have been built, if not for the vigorous resistance of the Lindu people with NGO support.

Sangaji argued that the incapacity of the state apparatus to manage processes and relations in a rational or fair manner undermined both its right to rule and its claim to govern. Thus sovereignty should be returned to the communities that had proven their competence in resource management over hundreds of years. This sovereignty was anyway usurped without legal justification when land under customary jurisdiction was unilaterally declared state forest. The unruly practices of officials only added to the insult. Farmers were attacked for taking rattan or making small clearings to farm, while officials were complicit in destruction on a much larger scale, supplying licenses and using park guard posts as toll booths, collecting "fines" from passing timber trucks laden with illegal rattan and timber. To untangle the morass of contradictory plans, unfair rules, and unruly practices, YTM together with WALHI and other NGOs called for a moratorium on the park: the cancellation of all existing licenses and development plans, including the gold-mining permit; a revision of the boundaries based on a consultative process and recognition of customary rights; and a redistribution of land stolen by officials to the landless. The park authorities, they argued, should not discriminate: if the claims of Katu could be recognized, the same treatment should be given to the remaining sixty or so park-border villages that also had legitimate claims to land within the park boundaries.

Responding to the allegation that NGOs provoked the masses to challenge the authorities, Sangaji pointed out that popular opposition to the park had been continuous since 1992. Farmers in several villages had protested against park guards who confiscated their rattan or destroyed cacao and coffee, and they asked for the boundaries to be moved; church officials in Poso had taken the case to the Minister of Environment; customary leaders had approached the Governor; park guard posts had been burned down. Thus a critical community was already present and active, in word and deed, years before the NGOs began to assemble the various voices, connect the issues, and articulate them with broader concerns about democracy and justice.

Sangaji's critique extended beyond the park to what he called the "ecofascist" practices and assumptions of park-based nature conservation modeled on the Yellowstone Park in the United States and imported into Indonesia by international conservation organizations. In Yellowstone, too, indigenous people were expelled and livelihoods sacrificed to protect flora and fauna. He argued that the Indonesian conservation legislation of the New Order was more damaging to local livelihoods than the Dutch conservation ordinance of 1941, which recognized customary rights and required the agreement of affected parties before use rights could be changed. In contrast, the Indonesian Conservation Law, following the Yellowstone model, envisaged only activities such as ecotourism as legitimate use of park resources.

ROUTES TO DONGI-DONGI

For international agencies committed to park-based conservation-by-exclusion—TNC, CARE, and the ADB—the park Director's recognition of Katu's right to remain in the park and use park resources was a defeat and an embarrassment.

It undermined their efforts to defend the park by painstaking development activities and conservation education in border villages. Their fears of a flood-gate effect and the loss of control over the park boundaries were justified. For the thousands of villagers surrounding the park, Katu's success was a stimulus to take action. If Katu people could reclaim their customary land from the park, so could others. Border villagers rejected the argument made by the Katu people that they were especially indigenous or had unique wisdom in forest management. This was an argument the ecopopulist park Director accepted, but border villagers pointed out that the swidden system of Katu was standard for the area. As I noted earlier, even transmigrants who were supposed to teach the locals superior farming techniques quickly adopted local practices such as rattan collection and planting coffee in the forest understory, their best options in the light of inadequate land allocation and failed *sawah*. One Napu villager suggested to me that "the only difference between the Katu people and us is that they are clever talkers."

Inspired by ideas about ecopopulist park management, and recognizing that his park guards were not safe in and around Rahmat, where the anger generated by park enforcement activities was intense, the park Director made a further concession in 2001. He gave the farmers on the forest edge in Rahmat permission to maintain their coffee groves within the park. He proposed that they should develop a social forestry system, by which he meant a landscape designed by experts comprising optimal combinations of natural forest and useful, indigenous species. He was out of touch: the farmers of Rahmat and the adjacent villages had long since replaced their old coffee with cacao, planted surreptitiously beneath the forest canopy. The farmers interpreted the park Director's words to mean that they could remove the forest canopy, enabling their cacao to flourish. By 2003, there was a belt of cacao, coffee, candlenut, and fruit trees along the edge of the park, extending between one and three kilometers inland, back to the old boundary the Rahmat farmers had negotiated with the Forest Department in the 1970s.

The outcome the park-based conservation lobby most feared was a large-scale occupation of the Dongi-Dongi Valley, site of the earlier incursions I described above. This did indeed come to pass in 2001, when 1,050 families calling themselves the Free Farmers Forum laid claim to about 4,000 hectares of the park alongside the road and began clearing it. In the next chapter I examine the case in detail. Here I want to trace the links between "integrated conservation and development" and the politicization of the border population. Not only did CARE, TNC, and the ADB fail to meet their goals, they stimulated new practices and the formation of critical communities in ways the planners certainly did not intend. From the perspective of park border villagers, the failure of "development" to bring any benefits was bad enough, but the failure of so many experts to take the land problem seriously was worse. The involvement of foreigners in park protection added insult to injury. Further, the practices the foreigners introduced—village meetings and discussions with development experts—had a perverse effect: they clarified to the villagers that this set of experts could not help them solve their problems.

The midterm evaluation of CARE's project made the links explicit. It observed that CARE had been active

> in communities where Dongi-Dongi occupants-to-be were living. Facilitation by the project brought them together to discuss their predicament and it became very clear that their options were extremely limited. Indeed, CARE's project itself had nothing to offer because, being agriculturally driven, it only assisted those who had land, and primarily the so-called progressive farmers. It is said that CARE staff promised to look into the possibility of land being available elsewhere, but never reported back on this. . . . The great irony of the case, then, is that CARE appears, unwittingly, to have been an important facilitator of the Dongi-Dongi land occupation. To the extent that this is so, the case holds an exemplary lesson about the unintended consequences of project action.[73]

TNC did not acknowledge the adverse effects of its failed small projects and their role as a stimulus to the occupation, tending to blame backlash on the failures of the ADB project, which raised expectations it failed to meet.[74] But forum leaders did make the connection. Many of them were former TNC cadre. One of the younger forum leaders explained to me the very difficult personal predicament in which he found himself as a result of his involvement with these projects. In 2001, as a cadre for TNC and a village monitor for the ADB project, he tried to dissuade fellow villagers from expanding their farms inside the park, assuring them that gifts from the project would soon arrive. He asked them to be patient. His task as village cadre was to form groups in Rahmat and other Palolo villages, registering people to receive project inputs for farming, fish ponds, handicrafts, and so on. This was a time-consuming task, and it raised expectations. When the promised inputs failed to arrive, his covillagers accused him of corruption.[75]

> The Subdistrict Head got his new car, and the forest guards got theirs, but we got nothing. People said I had lied. They threatened me, they accused me of taking the money. I was very embarrassed (*malu*). They came at midnight, yelling and threatening. So I brought my people here to Dongi-Dongi. I recovered my good name. I know what we are doing here is wrong (*haram*). We [names Forum leaders] were all TNC cadre. Now we are their enemies. We just need this flat land . . . We are the young generation. We have to criticize policies and projects that are not correct.

An even more direct route to Dongi-Dongi was forged, inadvertently, by the ADB. In the more open political climate of *reformasi*, national NGOs such as WALHI highlighted the massive debts accumulated by the Suharto regime for corrupt or ineffective development loans. The Asian Development Bank's Central Sulawesi Integrated Development and Conservation Project, designed in the last years of Suharto's rule and coming on stream in the reform era, was a prime target for such scrutiny. It was not difficult to identify the acute irony of accepting a large U.S.-dollar debt for a conservation project when the interest and principal must be repaid with foreign exchange earned from the export of timber or plantation crops, neither of them ecofriendly.[76]

It was in the context of monitoring the ADB project in 2001 that WALHI staff working with another Palu-based NGO went to visit Palolo. Their visit was part of the national WALHI antidebt campaign that needed field data about ADB projects to confirm anecdotal evidence that the projects were poorly designed and the funds misspent. In Palolo, they found plenty of problems with the ADB project, and much more besides.[77] They made note of the deficiencies of the project's construction component, the failure to pay the village facilitators their full wages, and the lack of consultation and transparency. Then the discussion progressed to the issue most pressing to the people of Rahmat and the other resettlement villages: the acute shortage of agricultural land as a result of misappropriation and flooding. The villagers told the NGOs that they had repeatedly raised the land problem with officials and with all the other experts who had come to ask them about village livelihoods, land uses, and development needs.

In one resettlement village, an informal leader showed the NGO visitors a map he had obtained. It was the original map of the planned boundaries of the Depsos resettlement sites. According to a witness, he had grabbed the map from the hands of an official a few months earlier and refused to give it back. His was a politics of practice, tactile and violent, with a map—prime instrument of sovereign authority and expert design—situated at its core. From the map, the visiting NGOs could see how much of the land promised to the settlers had been enclosed by the park or taken by officials. These were grounds not only for critique, but for gathering a community and planning action. In Rahmat, discussion at the time of the NGO visit focused on the 168 hectares appropriated by the former Governor, and how it could be reclaimed. Informal leaders in Rahmat felt direct action to reclaim the land would be difficult because some of it had been sold to Bugis brokers and migrants, or was being farmed by Bugis sharecroppers. They feared igniting conflict between Christian locals and Muslim migrants, especially in the context of the violence in and around Poso that was still ongoing. Besides, 168 hectares reclaimed from the Governor would not be enough land to meet the need of hundreds of landless or near landless families in Rahmat.[78] They turned their eyes on the park. It was better, they argued, to take the land of one (the Forest Department) than the land of many—their covillagers.

In the months following the NGO visit, there were many meetings and discussions between Palolo villagers, WALHI, and its affiliates. There was a series of mass demonstrations in Palu in which the villagers demanded a response to the problem of landlessness. The Free Farmers Forum took shape through these rallies and established a leadership structure to supply organization, present petitions and demands at the parliament building, and liaise with the NGOs. The demonstrations produced only empty promises from politicians and officials, who did nothing to follow up on the problem of land. Frustrated at the lack of response, the forum and several NGOs agreed to use the Dongi-Dongi Valley as a bargaining tool. The forum would threaten to occupy Dongi-Dongi if the demand for land was not met. After the third major demonstration in Palu on August 24, 2001, the forum went straight into

FIGURE 6   Protest banner on land stolen by the Governor in Rahmat

Dongi-Dongi en masse and began the occupation. Soon thereafter, members of the forum began clearing land to farm.

CONCLUSION

In this chapter I examined a second set of interventions designed to direct highland lives and livelihoods, specifically in the area bordering the Lore Lindu National Park. I explored how the planners of "integrated conservation and development" constructed a boundary around a knowable, improvable, technical domain. Their approach to knowledge was partial—both skewed and incomplete. Although the design studies clearly identified processes such as increasing landlessness, impoverishment, debt, accumulation, and migration, and practices such as corruption, illegal logging, stealing with impunity, incompetent planning, and villagers' ongoing challenge of the park boundaries, much of this knowledge was excluded from the plans that were devised by the Nature Conservancy, CARE, and the Asian Development Bank. Based as they were on faulty premises, their plans did not achieve the outcomes they sought. Nevertheless they had significant, unexpected effects. Villagers who experienced these projects as one among other forces shaping and constraining their lives took stock. They developed a critique that was embedded in their actions and increasingly articulate. In chapter 5, I examine how their mobilization unfolded, and how it was received by the many authorities who continued to position themselves as trustees and guides.

POLITICS IN CONTENTION

The occupation of the Dongi-Dongi Valley inside the Lore Lindu National Park by the Free Farmers Forum in 2001 caused a huge controversy among NGOs in Central Sulawesi and beyond. For activists, it fractured the wish-laden "middle ground" in which conservation, indigenous rights, and economic justice can all be achieved simultaneously.[1] Conservationists were naturally upset: Dongi-Dongi was inside a park. Indigenous rights advocates had a different problem. It was common for them to be in conflict with a park-based conservation model that did not accommodate indigenous peoples' needs, but in this case there was a catch: members of the Free Farmers Forum were not obvious candidates for the indigenous slot—they came from the hills around Palu and Kulawi and were resettled in Palolo by Depsos. For land-rights activists, the problem was different again. Their usual practice was to help villagers reclaim land assigned to corporations for logging, mining, or plantations by the New Order regime. To take over land inside a conservation area pushed at the limits of their social justice agenda.

At the heart of the Dongi-Dongi controversy were some deep questions about how best to govern. Which ends should be pursued? By what means? For which social groups? At whose expense? Under what authority? Under what regime of truth? For a few years (2001–3) when the controversy was at its height, scores of people inside and outside the state apparatus were involved in debating these questions both in the abstract, and in terms of the details of this very particular case. Much of the debate was committed to text. My collection of printed e-mails, news articles, and reports about Dongi-Dongi is at least four hundred pages.[2] Two collations were published as books, one of them complete with an ISBN. Each of the parties was anxious to explain its perspective. Among them were some that took up the position of trustees, anxious to assess the deficiencies of the Farmers and correct them. Others were concerned to amplify and respond to what they understood as the Farmers' legitimate political demands. But the line separating improvement from political challenge was far from clear. It too was the subject of debate.

This chapter's exploration of the contentious politics of Dongi-Dongi embraces its complexity. In so doing, I hope to avoid the problem of "ethnographic refusal" Sherry Ortner identified in studies of resistance that position subalterns as monochrome heroes dedicated to a struggle against power. "Resistance studies are thin," she writes, "because they are ethnographically thin: thin on the internal politics of dominated groups, thin on the cultural richness of those groups, thin on the subjectivity—the intentions, desires, fears, projects—of the actors involved in these dramas."[3] Thus without claiming to supply a complete description or to have access to the innermost thoughts of the actors I describe, my account highlights specificity, locatedness, ambivalence, contradiction, dissent, errors, disasters, regrets, and the hierarchies of gender, class, and brute force operating within the Farmers Forum as well as without. I attend not only to the discourses of the various parties but to their practices—what they were doing, and how their practices were interpreted and judged. My own practices were also judged in relation to this case. The Farmers at Dongi-Dongi hesitated to let me stay at their settlement when I visited in 2003. They wanted to know whether I supported them or not. They were unhappy with my response: that I would not judge them on hearsay, as others had done, but listen to them with an open mind. They accepted my presence, in the end, because I reminded them that they had used my data on landlessness in Rahmat to help justify the occupation. I was already implicated in their story. Further, I told them that I had once been employed as a consultant to conduct a formal evaluation of the Depsos resettlement program. My visits to numerous resettlement sites in Kalimantan and Sulawesi in 1997–98 confirmed that problems over land allocation and land quality were routine.[4] This was not the guarantee they sought, but it was common ground.

I begin with a summary of the reasons for the occupation from the perspective of the Dongi-Dongi Farmers. Next I examine how the Farmers' positions and practices were interpreted by allies and opponents, how the NGOs involved in the debate positioned each other, and how they positioned themselves. The NGOs differed not only in the substance of the actions they supported or opposed but also in their understanding of the proper relationship between themselves and the villagers they aimed to educate or support. Then I take a closer look at practices inside Dongi-Dongi. In a final section, I examine how and why the political agency of the Farmers was denied and trusteeship reasserted.

YOU ARE ENTERING THE SOVEREIGN DOMAIN OF
THE FREE FARMERS FORUM

"You Are Entering the Sovereign Domain of the Free Farmers Forum":[5] so stated the banner over the road, mimicking the official banners that demarcate space at the entry to every officially recognized village in Indonesia. Sovereignty is not part of everyday vocabulary. The banner bespoke the support farmers had received from Palu-based NGOs in June 2001 when the Free Farmers Forum occupied the Dongi-Dongi Valley.

The banner's claim was exceptional on many counts. It shocked the head of provincial parliament when he visited Dongi-Dongi in 2003 to meet with the Farmers.[6] "It seems we have independent nations inside Indonesia now," he said.[7] Seeing me in the crowd, a member of the politician's entourage whom I had known for some years asked me, "Don't you think it is strange for these people to be living here, without government?" By inhabiting a space that was not a recognized village, indeed a space in a park where a village cannot be, the Farmers put themselves outside the administrative grid in which every Indonesian citizen is supposed to be enmeshed. They also put themselves beyond the reach of paternalistic guidance—a requisite of village life. Since forest demarcation began in the colonial period, many forest villagers have found themselves in this position, living "illegally" inside state-claimed forest land. What was unusual at Dongi-Dongi was the boldness of the declaration.

More ominously, the District Head had reportedly referred to the Farmers as "like GAM" (Gerakan Aceh Merdeka), the armed separatist movement in Aceh against which the Indonesian army was waging all-out war at the time, reported daily complete with gory footage on the television news.[8] Yet the Farmers were still in Dongi-Dongi when this book went to press in 2006 five

FIGURE 7   "You Are Entering the Sovereign Realm of the Free Farmers Forum"

years after the occupation. Despite numerous ultimatums and threats, they had not been evicted.[9] Their continued occupation of land inside the park exposed the incapacity of the ruling regime to assert its sovereign authority over the state-claimed forest. To use force, however, would expose its incapacity to govern wisely and enhance life. This was the dilemma Dongi-Dongi presented for the many officials with jurisdiction in matters of law and order, village administration, conservation, and the resettlement of unruly populations.

Exceptionally, the banner's claim to a sovereign subnational space did not coincide with the indigenous territory of an ethnolinguistic group. The Farmers hailed from diverse hillside hamlets and were resettled in Palolo by Depsos. Their claim to Dongi-Dongi was articulated in terms of their need for land and livelihood, and the failure of the many authorities who had intervened in their lives to deliver on their promises. Specifically, the Farmers stressed the failure of Depsos to furnish them with the two hectares of land to which they were entitled under the resettlement scheme; the failure of donor-funded "integrated conservation and development" programs to address their needs; and the illegitimacy of a national park that cordoned off fertile, accessible farmland so badly needed by the landless poor. "Over there is the park," an elderly woman told me, pointing to the steep mountains at the center of the park, "that is no good for farming. We understand that. Don't put boundary markers here on this flat land by the road. This here is for us." I was struck by the class idioms the Farmers used to describe the implications of their landlessness: "We work on other peoples' cacao so they get to be happy, but we don't have anything," commented one Farmer. Another Farmer added an ethnic twist: "Working for wages means becoming a slave to the Bugis."

The Farmers I spoke to saw themselves as indigenous but situated their claim to indigeneity on a territorial canvas broader than the occupation of a particular patch of land since time immemorial. As "children of the province" (*anak daerah*), they argued their claims trumped those of migrant Bugis and the Javanese who were placed in the province under official transmigration schemes. In the words of one Farmer, "If the government can give land to the Javanese, then why not to us?" As citizens of Indonesia, the Farmers argued their claims trumped the conservationists' argument that the park was "the property of the world," a "global biodiversity resource." Some Farmers took the concept of global property quite literally. They informed me that the park had been sold or mortgaged and divided up between "nine nations," as payment or guarantee for Indonesia's foreign debts. They were convinced the foreigners wanted to profit from the park's genetic resources or to mine there for gold. They saw the occupation as reclaiming the park for the nation. "We are true to the constitution," argued Pak Ratu, one of the most articulate forum leaders I interviewed. He continued:

> The constitution says the land and water belong to the people, for their well-being. . . . It is the officials who are breaking the law. . . . If we are wrong, they are more wrong. They say, "Masyarakat sejaterah, taman nasional lestari" (the people will be prosperous and the park secure), but how can that be if we have no land? . . . They have taken tens of thousands of hectares, we are just asking for 4,000. . . . We can manage this park if they will recognize us. We would study each species, see where they go, what they like to eat, where they like to drink, and we'll have our gardens too. We can do a land-use plan. The logging companies steal timber on a big scale (*pencurian besar*), they don't cut where

they are supposed to, they never pay taxes. Why are only the small people faulted? It should be fair.

Pak Ratu had traveled to Bali to attend Indonesia's preparatory meeting for the Johannesburg environment conference (a decade after Rio). He and Mama Rani, also a Farmer from Dongi-Dongi, were selected by Palu-based NGOs as authentic representatives of a people's movement struggling for environmental justice. The experience broadened his critical vocabulary. "Political ecology," he informed me, "means who is it *for*."

Farmers pointed out that Dongi-Dongi, although classified as part of the park's core zone because of its watershed function, was the site of a logging concession assigned to the timber company PT Kebun Sari in the 1970s. "If Kebun Sari can receive a twenty-five-year lease," a Farmer observed, "why not us?" Forum leaders were eager to show me the evidence of this former land use: old truck tires, industrial debris, a helicopter pad used when logs were airlifted out of the hills to Dongi-Dongi for transfer to the trucks transporting them to Palu. In their understanding of national park regulations, the core zone was supposed to be pristine nature, with unique biodiversity resources. Thus the logged-over forest at Dongi-Dongi did not qualify. The Farmers did not challenge the right of the state apparatus to define who should live where but judged their practices inept, inefficient, corrupt, and biased against "small people." This was treatment they were no longer willing to tolerate. An older man whose story I told earlier—the one whose land in a Palolo resettlement site was appropriated and sold by an official—had joined the Farmers at Dongi-Dongi. Reflecting on those events, he commented, "That was before *reformasi*; in those days, even low-level officials thought they were really big, powerful, and they oppressed us."

During the New Order, it was common to hear critiques of corruption and greed, but rare to hear such explicit critiques of class relations and of governmental programs gone awry. In a decade of research in Central Sulawesi I had not previously heard such a clear articulation of the just claim of "small people" to a share of the very best land in an ideal location so that they too could prosper. I heard this language not only from forum leaders whose encounters with officials and NGOs had yielded a well-rehearsed, consistent set of arguments.[10] It showed through the details of the narratives recounted to me by two dozen Farmers about the insults and injuries, the experiences of exploitation and exclusion, and the series of inept interventions that promised improvement but produced nothing. It also showed through in the high hopes aroused by the possession of two hectares of good farmland at Dongi-Dongi. The combination of injury and hope was compelling enough for the Farmers to risk positioning themselves outside the normal apparatus of rule and inside the park, vulnerable to punishment or violent eviction.

In a group discussion one afternoon, I asked some Farmers what they understood by the word *sovereignty*. "It means we can organize ourselves according to our own customary laws," they answered. "We can work together; we are not organized by the government." Or, more simply, "It means we have our own rules." Despite the brave words, the forum leaders were finding it quite difficult to organize more than a thousand families and enforce "their own" rules. They thought it would be much easier if the authorities recognized them and made Dongi-Dongi an official village. "We want to be under the order of the government" *(mao diatur oleh pemerintah)* was a phrase I heard several times, followed by the caveat "made orderly here in Dongi-Dongi, nowhere else." Forum leaders had prepared a large white board, complete with the headings for standard village data collection (number of households, gender, age, occupation, religion, number of hectares of *sawah*, and so on). "We are civilized people," one leader stressed, "we understand the need for rules." There was no celebration of the position of rebel or bandit. They found their positioning outside the normal system of village administration awkward but necessary.

That night when I was sleeping over at the house of Mama Lot, a thoughtful, quiet spoken mother of six, we stayed up late to talk after everyone else was in bed. She showed me the copy of one of YTM's pamphlets about the park: "I've been trying to read it," she said, "but the language is hard." I decided to test out the challenge leveled by opponents of the occupation: "People say you were provoked [encouraged, led] to come to Dongi-Dongi by the NGOs." This was her reply:

> There is no way that those young people from the NGO could gather so many people. They are just helping with the peoples' struggle. It is our will, not theirs. . . . Even when the authorities threatened us, saying if we did not leave in

twenty-four hours, they would attack, we stayed here. We were afraid. Some people left, but those like us who have nothing in Palolo stayed here. We don't have enough to eat there. We'll stay here come what may. We have already buried our heads here [i.e., we are prepared to die].

The next day Mama Lot's neighbor, an older woman living alone, echoed the sentiment. "Even if the government is angry with us and beats us," she said, "we will stay here. We are seeking life, not death."

RESETTLEMENT REDUX

Soon after the occupation in 2001, the provincial authorities decided the Farmers must be removed from Dongi-Dongi and placed in an official resettlement site. To soften the deal, they promised to find a location acceptable to the Farmers. But two years later, such a site had not been found. The failure of the authorities to provide a viable resettlement alternative exposed some of the core contradictions in the resettlement program. According to the forum leaders and NGO supporters who inspected the two potential resettlement sites the authorities proposed, they were inaccessible. They could be reached only on foot, one of them requiring more than a days' walk and the fording of eighteen rivers, some of them deep. Further, the land was already settled and farmed by other people. "If the authorities put us up there," one Farmer explained to me, "there would be war. Those people also need the land." Residents at one of the candidate sites had already sent a strong message to Dongi-Dongi that newcomers would not be welcome.

The irony was intense. It was the inaccessibility of their ancestral hillside hamlets that had caused the Farmers to be resettled into the Palolo Valley in the first place. "Why," a Farmer asked, "would they take people from the mountains then send them back to mountains again? It makes no sense."[11] Other Farmers recalled the coercive dimension of their original resettlement. "We were projectized (kami diproyekkan)," said an elder from Kulawi, "we had to move down and have sawah." According to one Farmer from the hills west of Palu, "They told our parents don't just stay there and be hill people. They called us to lare because we had never seen cars. From our place down to Palu was a full day's walk, leaving at 4 a.m., arriving at 9 p.m. But in Palolo, the family got only one hectare and we were four siblings." When I asked some Farmers whether they thought the authorities were responsible for providing land for everyone, one replied, "Not if you stay in your own place, but they brought us here (*kami didatangkan*), so yes, they must provide."

A few dozen families moved to Dongi-Dongi directly from the hills around Palu, one group walking for a week, carrying children and cooking pots, because they had no bus fare. They were monolingual speakers of Da'a, the Kaili variant spoken in the hills. They knew no Indonesian, because in their hillside hamlet there was no school. "We are so happy here," said a member of this group. "Our happiness is ten times greater than before, because now we get to see cars passing by in front of our houses." It seems the Depsos resettlement program accurately read the desire of isolated highlanders to be integrated into the Indonesian mainstream, but it failed to deliver the goods. These people described to me their experience of being abandoned in the remote hills, excluded from the action. "They kept promising us a road up there but it never came, even though we voted for Golkar [the ruling party]. It is much better here at Dongi-Dongi."

The main argument used by park and provincial authorities to justify eviction was the forest's catchment function, a technoscientific rationale the Farmers disputed. The park Director accused them of jeopardizing the lives and livelihoods of 300,000 people at risk of siltation and flooding downstream in the Palolo and Palu Valleys.[12] To the experts' claims, the Farmers counterposed their own situated knowledge. "They say we can't stay here because of erosion, but this land is flat for three kilometers." "We know all about erosion. There are lots of natural landslides around here. We know where to farm, and where to avoid. Our ancestors in Kulawi have been farming on steep slopes for generations, and they are still there." More poignantly still, one Farmer remarked: "If the government is worried about erosion, why did they build a resettlement site on steep land at Lemban Tongoa? It was floods from Lemban Tongoa that destroyed our land downstream in Palolo." Layered effects in this case were quite literal: earth and sand flowing down the river from one resettlement site had rendered the one below unusable. The land at both of the candidate alternative resettlement sites was steeply sloped. Experts sent from Jakarta to inspect the proposed sites agreed with the Farmers that the land was indeed too steep to farm. Thus the solution to the Farmer occupation proposed by Palu officials was deeply flawed, and flawed precisely on the technoscientific grounds usually arrayed to justify programs to reorder landscapes and move people around.

Further, the Farmers noted the corruption and misappropriation associated with the resettlement schemes in Palolo, the details of which they knew all too well. Having been misled by promises of security and improvement once before, the Farmers insisted that any alternative resettlement site the officials proposed must be at least as accessible, fertile, and promising as Dongi-Dongi. If they did not receive a full two hectares of good land beside a road free of competing claims, they would not move. By 2003, as the occupation entered its third year, they were unwilling to move under any conditions. Their cacao seedlings were growing, and they had no desire to start again from zero. During my visit, there was an announcement that the authorities would begin moving people out "by stages," fifty households per year, on a "voluntary" basis. This proposition made the savvy Mama Rani—the woman who had represented the Farmers in Bali—chuckle. It was one of those compromises that attempted to save face but instead exposed the incapacity of the authorities to direct and plan. Mama Rani and friends calculated that it would take twenty years to empty a thousand families from Dongi-Dongi at that rate, and by then their occupation would surely be regularized, and their cacao in full production, or indeed, past its prime. Even if they were forced out, they said they would keep coming back to harvest their cacao or to replant if it was destroyed, "unless," as an older man mused, "they send us across the sea to Kalimantan, or they take away the road through the park."

The economics favoring Dongi-Dongi were compelling. Mama Lot, the mother of six, recounted to me her experiences as a young woman forced to move from one place to another seeking wage work on people's *sawah* and as a laborer on a tea plantation. She left her older children with relatives and kept only the youngest by her side. She worked long hours in the attempt to make enough money for them all. Despite the threat of eviction and uncertainty about the future of Dongi-Dongi, she considered her life there more secure and more hopeful than it had ever been before. She was able to feed her family from her own garden produce and the steady cash she made from selling vegetables to traders who passed daily along the road. Mama Lot's husband

FIGURE 8   Hut and garden, Dongi-Dongi

helped little with household provisioning. She was the one adept at calculation, and she planned ahead. She had kin in the proposed alternative resettlement sites, and she knew for sure the economics did not add up:

> To get to Lemban Tongoa is just eight kilometers, but it costs Rp10,000 by jeep,
> because there is still no proper road, twenty years after the people were resettled
> there. From Lemban Tongoa to Manggalapi [one of the candidate sites], you
> leave on foot at 3 a.m. to arrive at 2 p.m. You get Rp7000/kg for cacao at
> Lemban Tongoa, and Rp2000 at Manggalapi, because of the cost of paying
> porters. In Palolo you get Rp14,000 for cacao, and we will get the same here at
> Dongi-Dongi since we are on the road.

Dongi-Dongi had everything, in short, that the Depsos programs promised
the "estranged" hill farmers but failed to deliver—land, market access, a bright
future. The Farmers did not need to be guided and cajoled into entrepreneurial
roles. "Instead of criticizing us," observed Mama Rani, "the authorities should
see that Dongi-Dongi will be a production center for the province, and we'll
pay taxes. Why don't they ever think of that?"

From 2001 to 2003, as debate over Dongi-Dongi raged among Palu NGOs and extended to advocacy networks in Java and beyond, arguments for and against the occupation were articulated, described in "position papers," and widely discussed in the media and activist newsgroups.[13] Whatever qualms an ethnographer might have about revealing the hidden transcripts, the internal conflicts, the confusions, ambiguities, or deficiencies of a political struggle— good reasons, perhaps, for ethnographic refusal—such qualms were mute in the orbit of Dongi-Dongi. Every action taken or not taken by the NGO protagonists, every observation about what the Farmers at Dongi-Dongi were doing or saying, every debate, critique, and autocritique was committed to text and circulated. There were several attempts at synthesis. These were requested by members of NGO networks on Java who were confused by the claims and counterclaims from Sulawesi flitting across their computer screens and disoriented by the difficulty of fitting Dongi-Dongi into their usual advocacy niche.

In this debate the Farmers' capacity to gain allies and support depended upon their ability to fit the places of recognition that others supplied. Many of the arguments made for or against the occupation of Dongi-Dongi hinged upon how the practices and positions of the Farmers were interpreted. Were they victims of misguided policies? Heroes of democracy? Model farmers bent on modest, equitable, sustainable, community-based livelihoods? Cunning pretenders exploiting the gullibility of their NGO supporters? Greedy profit-seeking opportunists? Forest destroyers? Illegal squatters? Criminals? Ignorant folk vulnerable to the persuasions of timber merchants? Dependent wards mislead by enthusiastic but irresponsible tutors? Or several of the above?

Unfortunately but perhaps inevitably, binary labels were applied to the Farmers and also to the officials and NGOs who took sides in the debate: pro- or anticonservation, populist or fascist, corrupt or sincere, effective or inept, consistent or opportunist. The NGOs divided into two clusters. Those supporting the occupation formed an alliance called Aliansi Katavua (the profarmer alliance). It included WALHI and a legal aid NGO in leading roles, a student organization, a farmers' union, and WALHI affiliates, including YTM. This alliance accepted the argument that the Farmers were landless people, victims of misguided policies and other injustices. Core themes for the profarmer alliance were social justice and agrarian reform. The group opposed to the occupation was focused on park-based conservation and clustered around TNC. The NGOS in this group were members of the Partnership Forum for Lore Lindu (the propark alliance). These two sets of NGOS had distinct intellectual formations, networks, and institutional trajectories. Members of the propark alliance tended to spend their student days in nature lovers' clubs, while the profarmer group spent their time in student unions with links to farmers and workers' unions. The controversy became more complex when a third group emerged, waving the banner of indigenous rights and linking itself with the propark alliance on the grounds that the Farmers had invaded the ancestral land of the indigenous people of Napu, who had the rightful claim to the Dongi-Dongi Valley.

Besides these major groupings, the controversy stimulated the formation of further, sometimes instant coalitions, fronts, and alliances issuing statements and claiming to represent one constituency or another. *Who are you, and who do you represent?* was a frequent refrain of the e-mail correspondence. The question was not new. Since the emergence of Indonesia's NGO movement in the 1980s, it has been common for critics to challenge someone who speaks "in the name of" someone else (*mengatasnamakan*), claiming a constituency that cannot be verified. In this case, the question became urgent. There was a maverick e-mailer who commented continuously on the ecological damage at Dongi-Dongi, the complicity of the Farmers and supporting NGOS in illegal logging, and their seizure of land from the legitimate indigenous claimants. This e-mailer refused when challenged to reveal his or her identity or meet for a discussion. The controversy within the NGO network was so heated at one stage that the NGOS agreed to a moratorium on Internet communications and on contact between themselves and "their" villagers. All the NGOS were to stay away from Dongi-Dongi and Napu while the Farmers and surrounding villagers worked out their own agreements.[14] Arianto Sangaji, director of YTM, proposed that the NGOS and other experts so busy debating peoples' identities, interests and futures should print out all the e-mails, photocopy them, and distribute them to the villagers so that they would know about the claims made on their behalf, and clarify their own positions. His proposal was not taken up.

The high degree of scrutiny to which the Farmers at Dongi-Dongi and their supporters were subjected put a premium on communicating clear positions, especially concerning the claim to sovereignty and the capacity for self-government. The Farmers announced plans for a sustainable and equitable regime. They would organize themselves into groups to work collectively on clearing blocks of land that would then be distributed among the families, two hectares per household. They would formulate their own rules, enforced by strict sanctions derived from the customs of the constituent ethnolinguistic groups. These would include a sanction on anyone who attempted to sell land or timber for profit. Cut timber would be used only for houses and public buildings such as a meeting hall and places of worship. To dramatize their commitments, they held a ritual land blessing celebrated with a feast shortly after they arrived en masse at Dongi-Dongi. The feast included the sacrifice of four head of cattle. They took an oath to stay at Dongi-Dongi come what may. At one of their demonstrations in Palu, they brought bundles of freshly harvested corn and cassava to the parliament building, emphasizing the link between land and livelihood. At another demonstration they sacrificed two chickens at the parliament building, one red, one white. As one of the participants recounted, "We cut the red one's head off—that means only cut up like this will we leave Dongi-Dongi. That was our blood. The white one means accept us, this is as white as our hearts, asking for land." In these ways they tapped into the symbolic fields associated not only with the life of a farmer but with traditions many Indonesians view as indigenous: a commitment to collective action, mutual well-being, democratically agreed and community-enforced discipline, an orientation to subsistence and careful use of resources, and a link to the spirit world signaled through ritual.

WHO IS INDIGENOUS HERE?

The self-positioning of the Farmers in the niche of indigenous people and responsible managers of natural resources was rejected by opponents of the occupation. They countered the claim to indigeneity with the argument that the Farmers were out of place. For parties committed to park-based conservation, any human presence in the park was problematic. The park Director made an exception for Katu, because Katu residents and their supporters successfully convinced him that they were indigenous people living in harmony with nature on their ancestral land. Katu's argument was one TNC and others committed to park-based conservation could grudgingly accept—so long as the indigenous claim was confined to Katu. But in their view the Farmers occupying Dongi-Dongi were an entirely different case. They were newcomers, resettled in Palolo by Depsos. They had no ancestral claim to the land at Dongi-Dongi. It wasn't even inside their district, Donggala—it straddled the border of the next district, Poso. If there were ancestral claims to be made, opponents of the occupation argued, they pertained to the Napu people, especially the residents of Sedoa, the nearest village to the south. The occupation at Dongi-Dongi confirmed to supporters of park-based conservation that villagers' designs on the park could not be satisfied and must be stopped if conservation was to have a future. A line must be drawn—not just a physical boundary around the park, but a delimitation of the groups and spaces to which indigenous rights would apply.[15]

Supporters of the occupation took a different position. For them the fact that the Farmers at Dongi-Dongi were previously resettled by Depsos did not render their livelihood struggle and its attendant politics illegitimate. On the contrary, their struggle highlighted the situation of all poor farmers lacking adequate farmland. It served to broaden the debate. YTM's director Sangaji repeated the argument that the park Director should not discriminate on the basis of histories and identities. Whether or not they qualified as indigenous, all sixty villages surrounding the park had problems with the unilateral way the park was established and contested its boundaries. The park-based conservation model needed a radical overhaul to make it compatible with rural livelihoods, not just a concession to accommodate a few, apparently unique villages like Katu. YTM and WALHI argued that the Farmers at Dongi-Dongi had an especially strong claim precisely because they had been multiply victimized: forced out of their ancestral territories in the hills by Depsos, resettled on inadequate land, and then excluded from viable farmland on the grounds of conservation.[16]

In the eyes of the ecopopulist park Director, the indigenous position carved out by Katu was definitely not one the Farmers at Dongi-Dongi could fill. Not only were they out of place, they could supply no evidence of ecofriendly traditions. He argued, more specifically, that they had lost their indigenous customs and culture as a result of resettlement and become rather ordinary farmers, fixated on land, cacao, and timber profits.[17] In Dongi-Dongi, they were behaving like capitalists. They were not "interacting" with the forest as proper indigenous people do—they were cutting it down.[18] The sight of fallen trees on both sides of the road in the occupation zone was a dramatic provocation: a statement that conservation had lost and the Farmers had won. This scene was captured on video by a member of the propark alliance and circulated through the activist network in Java. The park Director was infuriated by WALHI's support of the Farmers at Dongi-Dongi and publicly tore up the award he received from WALHI for his ecopopulist stance when he recognized Katu as an indigenous community with the right to participate in park management.[19] This was one of many alliances shattered by the occupation.

The issue of indigeneity became extremely heated shortly after the occupation when opponents accused the Farmers of trespassing on the ancestral terrain of the indigenous community of Sedoa (in one version) or of Napu more broadly (another version). They accused the Farmers of neglecting to ask permission from the true indigenous owners of the land whose claims long preceded the establishment of the park. They had added insult to injury by seeking to legitimate their occupation with a ritualized feast calling upon their ancestors for blessing. The argument was articulated by a Palu-based NGO emphasizing indigenous rights. It created another bitter divide within the NGO movement in Palu and beyond. Some of the NGOs supporting the occupation, especially WALHI and YTM, had been deeply involved in promoting the indigenous cause in Central Sulawesi and remained committed to it. They were key players supporting the people of Lake Lindu to resist eviction for the proposed hydrodam in the early 1990s, and key in the struggle of Katu to remain within the park. They envisaged the occupation of Dongi-Dongi as a protest against the authorities and the park. They did not anticipate that it would become a conflict between one impoverished group, landless farmers, and the people of Sedoa asserting customary jurisdiction. Dongi-Dongi lies technically within the village boundaries of Sedoa, but twenty kilometers from the Sedoa village center, and about sixteen kilometers from the last roadside house in the Sedoa Valley heading north up into the Park. Sedoa's control over the Dongi-Dongi Valley had already been severely attenuated, if not abrogated, when it was enclosed within the park boundary.

Faced with Sedoa's unexpected claim, the Farmers in Dongi-Dongi and their

FIGURE 9   The Sedoa Valley

supporters acknowledged Sedoa's legitimate standing as the group closest to Dongi-Dongi who should have been consulted. But they questioned the timing and spatial logic of Sedoa's protest against the occupation. They suspected that the indigenous claim had been "provoked" or engineered by members of the propark alliance to undermine the settlement at Dongi-Dongi. In turn, the NGOS promoting Sedoa's case accused the NGOS supporting Dongi-Dongi of bad faith and opportunism: supporting conservation and indigenous rights strategically, as vehicles for political activism, rather than for their intrinsic merit. The case these NGOS had made at Lake Lindu and at Katu had emphasized conservation values. How could they now support wholesale land clearing at Dongi-Dongi, and the trampling of Sedoa's indigenous rights? Land occupations, the pro-Sedoa NGO argued, should be directed toward other targets—officials and corporations that had appropriated land, for example—not the land of indigenous people, a group whose land rights were already precarious.[20]

Reports soon after the occupation in 2001 were that leaders from Dongi-Dongi had approached leaders in Sedoa, who had given them permission to settle on the land. Critics argued that this agreement was coerced. On a radio talk show in 2002, the Headman of Sedoa stated clearly that he opposed the settlement of Dongi-Dongi.[21] By 2003, when I visited both Dongi-Dongi and Sedoa, positions had hardened further. In Dongi-Dongi elders elaborated on their indigenous positioning. They used the term *masyarakat adat*, devised by the Indonesian indigenous rights movement as a translation for the transnational concept of indigenous people. Literally translated, *masyarakat adat* means "customary communities." This is indeed how the Dongi-Dongi elders explained themselves, when I asked them what the term meant for them. It meant (1) that they adhere to unique cultural precepts inherited from their ancestors; (2) they follow customary ritual practices surrounding life-crisis events (birth, death, marriage); (3) they refer disputes to elders with experience in matters of custom, whether or not the elders are formally organized as a customary council; and (4) they use rituals to mark important public events. From their perspective, a positioning as *masyarakat adat* was constant and portable—it endured even when people found themselves outside their ancestral domain as a result of migration and resettlement. They did not share, that is, in the "sedentarist metaphysic" of the transnational indigenous rights movement that considers indigenous identities whole only when attached to fixed territories since time immemorial.[22] Nor did they associate a positioning as *masyarakat adat* with especially ecofriendly forms of farming and forest use. To make farms they must cut trees, a fact of life they share with other highlanders, whether or not they happen to be living on ancestral land. In their view, labor investment in cutting forests did not signal the absence of indigenous values—it was the normal, customary basis for making a living *and* for claiming land.

Rather than a simple binary, indigenous/not indigenous, the Farmers situated themselves in a nested hierarchy of belonging. Together with the people of Napu and Palolo, they saw themselves as indigenous or "local" in contrast to the people they defined as migrants, namely the Bugis and the Javanese. In making finer distinctions among "locals," time was a relevant factor. As I noted in previous chapters, the population around the park has been mobile. In every village there are clusters of households that arrived in different migrant waves. The Farmers recognized that people who were there first had some precedence over those who came later. For them, being *asli* (native, indigenous, belonging to a place) or *pendatang* (migrant) were relative positionings both spatially and temporally. Again the concept *asli* accords poorly with the concept of indigenous people as a fixed group that can be protected by international legal instruments such as the International Labor Organization's Convention 169.

In relation to Sedoa's claim to Dongi-Dongi as ancestral terrain, Farmer leaders brought both spatial and temporal criteria to bear. They argued that the customary lore common to the region divides sovereign domains according to watersheds. The water from Dongi-Dongi drains toward Palolo and Palu, placing it within the historical domain of Sigi, hence of the Kaili people, legitimizing the occupation of Dongi-Dongi by the Da'a, a Kaili subgroup. They recounted the story of a Kaili princess with a magical white buffalo who once inhabited the Dongi-Dongi Valley during a severe drought, a story that further confirmed the Kaili claim to the land. Further, they suggested that her marriage to a noble from Sedoa provided grounds for reconciliation between the two parties and an agreement to share space. They acknowledged that there were ancient rice terraces and stone rice mortars at Dongi-Dongi, but they argued there was no evidence to indicate they belonged to the ancestors of Sedoa people. The history of population movements in ancient times could not be recovered. They also noted that the imprint of the labor of Sedoa people on the land at Dongi-Dongi, if any, was less prominent than the imprint of people from Palolo, who began clearing land for farming and settlement at Dongi-Dongi when Kebun Sari operated there in the early 1980s.

In Sedoa in 2003, village elders explained to me their reasons for opposing the settlement at Dongi-Dongi in terms quite different from those enunciated by the NGOs supporting Sedoa's side two years before. They mentioned nothing about living in harmony with nature, nor did they emphasize ancestral ties to Dongi-Dongi. Instead, they made their argument in administrative terms. Dongi-Dongi falls within their official village boundary, which is also the official border between the districts of Poso and Donggala. They recounted the story of how they helped to fix the border in 1973. On the appointed day, one group of village Headmen and other officials set out walking along the trail from the last village in Palolo and another group set out from Sedoa. The boundary marker was placed where the two groups met. The presence of a trail through Dongi-Dongi reflected a much older history. It was used by the people of Sedoa to take offerings to the Raja of Sigi in precolonial times and to trade for salt. The path fell into disuse when the Dutch incorporated Sedoa and Napu under the Raja in Poso, reorienting directions of travel toward the south. The route north began to be used again in the mid-1970s, when Palolo was opened up for logging and resettlement and people from Napu and Sedoa went there to find wage work. Administrative practices also shaped the Sedoa peoples' sense of their boundaries to the south, which date from colonial times. The Dutch required villagers to mark their *damar* trees for the purpose of tax collection. Each tree bore a tin plate stamped with the identity of the tree owner. The boundary between *damar* areas was usually placed along a ridge and came to be regarded as the boundary between villages. As one elder recalled, "The Dutch made the boundaries so we wouldn't fight over the *damar* and we would all pay our taxes."

The principal complaint of Sedoa village leaders in 2003 was that their forest—recognized as theirs by the Dutch through the *damar* marking system—had been taken from them. They recounted the arrival of a forestry official from Java in the 1970s bearing a Dutch map with red crosses marked on it. They asked the official what the crosses meant, but he did not reply. A few years later, Kebun Sari arrived to start logging their *damar* trees. Then the park cut them off from the forest to the west and the north. To cap it all, the Farmers went into Dongi-Dongi, an area Sedoa people had also eyed for its agricultural potential and hoped one day to reclaim for their use. As one elder explained, "We are annoyed because everyone takes our wealth from us. . . . We are like animals in a pen. This land we are using here was just meant as pasture; our gardens were in the forest, and now we have none. . . . Those people in Dongi-Dongi are brave [*berani*, which also means fierce, determined]. . . . We feel bound by the regulations." The main goal of Sedoa leaders in 2003 was to recover their ancestral land from the park. If there were to be revenues from timber, they wanted a fair share of those, too. When I asked Sedoa leaders what they would do with their land if they were successful in regaining control over it, one replied, "We will cut the forest and sell the timber, then plant cacao and some candlenut, but mainly cacao, because cacao sells for Rp8000/kg, while candlenut is only Rp1000/kg."

The many activists involved in debating the merits of the occupation at Dongi-Dongi in 2001–3 shared in the will to improve. They each had their own ideas about how others should live, and more or less explicit programs for bringing their versions of improvement to fruition. None of them were empty vessels. They differed, however, in the balance they struck between responding to villagers' aspirations, which meant taking them seriously as political agents with their own concepts of justice and attempting to reform their aspirations. For the propark alliance, the need to change the Farmers' aspirations was uppermost. The Farmers must be made to understand the importance of conservation and the damage they would cause downstream by their irresponsible forest destruction. For the activists who supported the Farmers, the key concern was to improve the capacity of the Farmers to engage in a political struggle, to formulate their own critiques, and to advance their claims.

To help others learn how to conduct a political struggle, Indonesian activists have devised various techniques. I earlier described the use of such techniques at Lindu Lake and in Katu, where activists offered legal training and taught villagers how to draft platforms and press releases. They taught mapping as a tool for claims making, and as a vehicle to stimulate new forms of consciousness and capacity for collective action. They helped the villagers to assess the merits of different strategies and proffered advice. In devising strategies, these activists drew on their own stocks of knowledge and analysis. For example, members of the profarmer alliance associated with the national Consortium for Agrarian Reform argued for the occupation on the grounds that benevolent bureaucrats and politicians would not attend to their demands without leverage.[23] Other members of the profarmer alliance were concerned to guide the Farmers' conduct in other spheres, instructing them in how to organize themselves in democratic and accountable ways, be environmentally responsible, and offer help and solidarity to other groups in need.

In the *reformasi* period, the dual positioning of some Indonesian NGOS as stimulants of a critical, justice-oriented politics *and* as the educators of deficient subjects in need of improvement was often an awkward one. It was subject to debate both within and outside the NGO movement. Bureaucrats and politicians argued that NGOS should stay out of "politics," and desist from a practice they label *provokasi*: provoking normally quiescent villagers to protest. NGOs should confine themselves to guiding villagers in practical matters such as income generation and conservation. In the case of Dongi-Dongi, the contending clusters of NGOs also scrutinized each other, asking questions usually posed by the regime. Were the political goals and platforms of the NGOs actually shared by their subjects or imposed upon them? Did the NGOs reflect and amplify the authentic voice of the people or put words into their mouths? Did the NGOs guide their respective sets of villagers too little, too much, or inappropriately? In a debate between NGOs about proper NGO practice, the political agency of the subjects—the Farmers of Dongi-Dongi and the leaders of Sedoa in particular—was implicitly called into question.

The propark alliance accused WALHI and associates of creating the Free Farmers Forum and using it for their own purposes. In this critique the propark alliance echoed the official line, popular in the Suharto era and since, that NGOs manipulate gullible, uneducated masses, provoking and exaggerating conflicts for media effect and to present themselves as heroic champions of the poor. This argument had arisen before in the struggles over eviction at the Lindu Lake and in Katu when critics suggested that the NGOs who claimed to be on the side of the people were actually pursuing economic gain. In the case of the Dongi-Dongi occupation, some members of the propark alliance suggested that the Farmers Forum and its supporters were in league with timber barons seeking to rob the park for profit. Alternatively they suggested that WALHI and affiliates deliberately created a "case" that they could sell to justice-oriented donors to keep project funds flowing into their organizations and their pockets. A further accusation associated the members of the profarmer alliance with left-leaning political parties seeking to cultivate a popular following in preparation for the 2004 elections. A more pernicious suggestion was that the supporting NGOs were not only left, but pro-Christian, since several of the groups supported by these NGOs over the years were Christian.[24]

The profarmer alliance responded that it had not provoked the Farmers but merely supported and "accompanied" them in a struggle the Farmers themselves both led and initiated. The practice of *pendampingan* (accompanying, offering assistance as a colleague, standing beside someone in solidarity) is key to NGOs' self-positioning as part of the politically engaged component of Indonesia's NGO movement. The term pendampingan asserts that NGOs are not the vanguard leading and educating the people, but merely their associates, ready to offer assistance with technical matters such as mapping, organizing demonstrations, and negotiating with officials. A contrasting term is *pembinaan* (guiding, educating, leading)—a keyword of the New Order, as I earlier explained. Yet in the case of Dongi-Dongi, the distinction between accompanying, educating, and leading was not clear-cut.

The propark alliance took the position that NGOs *should* be educators. The problem was that the profarmer alliance had taught the Farmers the wrong things—how to break the law and destroy a conservation area. When it transpired that timber from Dongi-Dongi was being sold, and that prominent leaders of the Farmers Forum who had made brave statements about equitable and environmentally responsible self-government were implicated, the propark alliance accused the profarmer alliance of failing as tutors of their dependent wards, their *masyarakat binaan*.[25] The term *warga binaan* is used by Despos to refer to the waifs, strays, prostitutes, and estranged communities under its paternal care and tutelage. Recall that the majority of the Farmers at Dongi-Dongi were once classified as estranged people and subject to the Despos program to civilize them. By using this term, the propark alliance implied that the Farmers were still backward, still delinquent, and the NGOs that had set themselves up as guides had failed to do their jobs. They further implied that the Farmers were not mature, not fully adult, so they could not possibly be autonomous political agents, capable of analyzing their own situation and figuring out that much of what passed for improvement was inept and unjust.

In contrast to accounts that positioned the Farmers, especially the Da'a, as instruments of others, some members of the propark alliance held the Farmers fully responsible as agents—cunning and effective ones—who used the claim of landlessness as an excuse to invade the park for profit. They described this move as selling poverty, treating it as a commodity with which to garner support or deflect criticism. According to this perspective, the profarmer alliance, if not complicit, was duped. These critics disputed the Farmers' claim to be farmers, rather than loggers. They argued that the Farmers had provided no evidence that 1,050 families were actually living at Dongi-Dongi, nor had they confirmed the claim that these families were landless. One critic stated that he was sympathetic to the plight of the impoverished farmers until he noticed that there were motorbikes outside some of the houses at Dongi-

Dongi. Another observed that a year after the initial occupation, there were at most five hundred households still living at the site, implying that the other half had moved on after realizing their timber profits.[26] Despite various attempts, no definitive data about the background or economic situation of the Farmers was collected by the authorities or made available by the supporting NGOs, making it difficult to evaluate sporadic observations.

A variation on the argument that the Farmers were indeed autonomous agents made a distinction between the leaders of the forum, who were both savvy and fiendish, and the ordinary Farmers at Dongi-Dongi, who had been used. Members of the propark alliance argued that the forum leaders were working closely with illegal logging syndicates, backed by the army, police, and Forest Department.[27] Logging the park was always their intent, but they used populist rhetoric and the genuine poverty of some of the Farmers to mask their nefarious schemes. This argument positioned the Dongi-Dongi occupation in series with other cases in which poor people are used by illegal logging syndicates who profit from their labor and the cover they provide. When the poor villagers who actually cut the timber and haul it out to the roadside are caught, they claim to be impoverished folk seeking only some timber to repair their houses, or a small patch of land to plant some crops. They take the risk because they are indeed poor, and the returns from logging are significantly higher than the local agricultural wage.

Yet another argument held the Farmers, especially the Da'a, responsible for their actions and their fate. It positioned them as agents of their own defeat. Critics of the occupation argued that Da'a people have the incorrigible habit of acquiring land and promptly selling it. Within a few years, Bugis migrants and officials would own all of the land at Dongi-Dongi, and the Da'a would be landless again, possibly repeating the cycle in another part of the park. These critics attributed the Da'a practice of land selling variously to their cultural values, primitiveness, laziness, preference for short-run returns, or innate nature as forest destroyers. They suspected that the Da'a had in fact received their full land allocation of two hectares from Depsos at the Palolo resettlement sites but sold the land, then looked to the authorities for a further handout, instead of learning to take care of themselves. Since experience showed that the Da'a could not be reformed, however hard the authorities tried, giving land to them at Dongi-Dongi would not solve anything. By reading Da'a prac-

FIGURE 10   Dongi-Dongi huts and cut timber

tices in this light, these critics positioned the Da'a both as agents *and* as
deficient subjects incapable of managing resources or acting autonomously in
their own interests. They needed to be protected and guided in the name of
their vulnerability, or abandoned to their fate. The last thing they needed was to
be provoked. The implication was that Da'a could not be political actors.

One of the most cynical interpretations circulating among the NGOs in Palu
by 2003 was that the authorities had allowed logging at Dongi-Dongi to continue unchecked for the past year not only because many of them profited
from it but also because it would destroy the reputation of WALHI and thereby
further another agenda: the building of the hydrodam inside the park at Lindu
Lake, a project WALHI, YTM, and others had helped the Lindu people to oppose a
decade earlier. In this version, the political agency and even the relevance of
the Farmers at Dongi-Dongi disappeared from view. The focus was on how
WALHI and YTM had been "played" by scheming officials. Taking this line of
argument further, the propark alliance including TNC had also been "played":
their alliance with WALHI forged over the campaign to oppose the dam at Lindu

was torn to shreds and the dam, brought back onto the table while the Dongi-Dongi controversy raged, would proceed.

Whoever was blamed—the Farmers, the forum leaders, the supporting NGOS, scheming entrepreneurs, or officials—what was clearly visible from the road passing through Dongi-Dongi in 2003 was the fallen forest, piles of cut timber waiting to be picked up by trucks, some tiny huts, some more substantial wooden houses, and banners such as the one announcing the sovereignty of the Free Farmers Forum. At one point the Farmers put up roadblocks, vetting vehicles passing along the road, demonstrating their seriousness about controlling sovereign space—a move that alarmed a foreign bird watcher, who filed a report on the Web.[28] Some Farmers jeered young people passing by on motorbikes, identifying them by their long hair, bandannas, patched jeans, and backpacks as university students and members of nature lovers' clubs. These clubs had participated in a propark, antifarmer rally in Palu. Another banner at Dongi-Dongi stated, "If You Give Us Land, There Will Be Peace in the National Park" (*Beri Kami Lahan, Taman Nasional Aman*). This is a highly ambiguous phrase. The park will be safe if you give us land? Or if you give us land, there will be no violence—implicitly, a threat. Opponents of the occupation said they feared to pass through Dongi-Dongi because of roadblocks and threats. The Farmers countered that their presence had made travel much safer for people passing along between Palolo and Napu, where the thirty-kilometer stretch of road that traversed the park was previously dark and quiet (*sepi*). With this comment, they referenced the fear of ghosts and brigands that Indonesian villagers commonly associate with forests, reversing the city-dwelling nature lovers' valuation of the forest as a place of tranquillity.

INSIDE DONGI-DONGI

The model proposed by the Farmers for how they would construct their brave new community at Dongi-Dongi envisaged a modest agrarian utopia, a return to the traditions and practices some populist, urban intellectuals and many Sulawesi villagers consider to be authentic, wholesome, and just.[29] The model certainly did not reject market relations—cacao was always the goal—but it did reject the corruption and greed embodied in practices such as the monopoly of land and the destruction of forest for the purpose of profit. Undoubtedly the model appealed to members of the profarmer alliance, some of whom assumed rather naively that a responsible, self-governing farming community would form itself naturally, once the Farmers had the land. Other supporters and forum leaders understood how much work—guidance, education, monitoring, planning, policing, punishing—would be needed to put principles into practice on a consistent basis.

Not surprisingly there was a gap between the principles that were announced by the Farmers and the practices that emerged inside Dongi-Dongi. Not all the Farmers remained true to the ideals expressed in the model. Yet talking to Farmers in 2003 I found that many held fast to the idea that they came to Dongi-Dongi for the land, not the timber. Women such as Mama Rani, Mama Lot, and Mama Yonas—who told the story of how her hut was burned by guards, and who later became a leader in Dongi-Dongi—were determined never to sell land but to stay, farm, and prosper responsibly on the land they had claimed. They argued that the limit on landholding of two hectares per household was fair, and sufficient for their needs. The ban on clearing steep slopes and riverbanks and the importance of reestablishing tree cover made perfect sense to them. They had no interest in losing the fruits of their labor to a flood. The ban on land selling and, more poignantly, the explicit ban on selling land to Bugis or to officials resonated with their own, very bitter experience in the Palolo villages from which they were displaced. Nevertheless, there were serious contraventions.

The Free Farmers Forum, formed at a point of crisis, did not develop as a democratic body with a mass base, a common ideology, and a capacity to make and enforce rules that were collectively agreed. Forum leaders were not consistently rule-abiding, much less heroic. Several of them were autocratic and unaccountable. Some were heavily involved in logging and selling timber. Among the Farmers there were also differences. Some were permanent residents at Dongi-Dongi, active in forum meetings, and determined to stay. Others hedged, waiting to see if the occupation would receive official recognition before they invested labor and funds in establishing gardens at Dongi-Dongi. Their stance infuriated the determined full-time settlers, who felt that these "speculators" were undermining both the solidarity and the credibility of the forum. Yet not all cases were black and white. Some families were staying in Palolo so that their children would not miss school, working their land in

Dongi-Dongi on the weekends. Families without capital were obliged to continue working as day laborers in Palolo and could spend time at Dongi-Dongi only when they had accumulated sufficient cash.

Forum rules about land disposition were generally upheld. A few Farmers who were part of the original occupation subsequently sold their land, though not as many as critics supposed. By 2003, half a dozen Bugis families and the same number of Poso refugees had acquired land at Dongi-Dongi against the forum rules. No officials had been able to gain access to land at the site, although several had tried. The great bulk of the land was still in the hands of the original Farmers. The modest huts, sparse possessions, and the Farmers' detailed accounts of their livelihood struggles before they came to Dongi-Dongi attested to the fact that most of the Farmers—though not all—really were very poor. When I compare these outcomes to the rampant misallocation of land I observed in Depsos resettlement schemes in Sulawesi and Kalimantan, schemes conducted in the name of the landless and poor but principally benefiting officials and local elites, I conclude that the self-organized settlement of Dongi-Dongi was more effective at reaching its target.

Many of the Farmers, together with the supporting NGOs, were acutely aware of the weaknesses in organization at Dongi-Dongi. During a series of forum meetings I attended, Farmers spoke with spirit about the need to improve the conduct of themselves and others—most of all, the leaders who had betrayed the principles of the forum. As it became clear that I was aware of their misdeeds, which were common knowledge anyway, some of the leaders discussed with me at length their regrets, recognizing how their participation in timber selling had confirmed the public perception of Dongi-Dongi as a timber grab. They were looking for ways to make amends, to use their influence as leaders to turn the situation around and bring it back into line with the original goals. Several leaders commented on what they perceived to be a circular bind: without recognition, it was difficult to be serious about organizing themselves for the long term, but their own errors and failings had contributed to the reluctance of the authorities to grant recognition.

I was struck by the contrast between the active engagement of forum leaders and Farmers in the ongoing project of determining their own fate, and the desultory, elite-dominated, formulaic, official development planning meetings I had attended in many Sulawesi villages and administrative offices over the past decade. The topics discussed at the Farmers' meetings were substantive, the debates and the tensions real. A core debate concerned whether or not to retrieve land from the half-hearted settlers who were not running the risks or undertaking the collective labor demanded by the occupation. There was a consensus that, after due warning, their land would be reassigned—easier to say than to accomplish, given the tenuous authority of the forum and the likelihood that stern moves would result in violence. On a more mundane matter, in a forum meeting to discuss how to celebrate the second anniversary of the Dongi-Dongi occupation, the participants decided not to organize volleyball matches because the nets and balls were too expensive. Even though they thought a trader willing to sponsor the event could probably be found, they were concerned that they would incur a debt that would be called in with a demand for timber. There was much discussion over how to handle the celebration funds transparently and responsibly. The young man who told the story about how he was accused for corruption when he worked for TNC made the point: "We better not try to reform others when we ourselves are corrupt." In these public discussions and individual interviews, I found the depth of political mobilization impressive: many people, not just leaders, had arrived at an analysis that connected the circumstances of their own lives with their subjection to powers of various kinds, yielding a sense of entitlement and a will to act to secure a better future for their families.

Critics of the occupation made a great deal of the practice of timber selling, arguing that the theft of timber from the park had been the Farmers' motivation all along, or that the Farmers had been deflected from their original goals by illegal logging syndicates. From inside Dongi-Dongi the practice looked rather different. If the land in question was not classified as state forest, and the Farmers had not promised to use the timber only for their own needs and refuse the cash offered to them by the timber merchants daily prowling the site, the practice of selling timber would not have occasioned any comment. Selling timber is part of the normal process of clearing land to farm. The owner of a chain saw negotiates with a farmer to cut the timber on the intended farm plot. The farmer gets the land cleared free of charge and half to a third of the timber for personal use, or the equivalent in cash. The cash helps the farm family sustain itself until the first food crop, usually corn, can be harvested. The timber is used for building a dwelling. Establishing a new farm plot and timber harvesting are symbiotic practices. But Dongi-Dongi is inside a park, and the Farmers' actions were severely scrutinized. They had to present themselves as pure subjects, desiring only land to farm and exempt from the need or temptation of ready cash. Further, continued uncertainty about the future of the occupation made it entirely sensible to sell off timber during the open season and not invest too much in building houses or planting cacao that could very well be bulldozed by the army.

The divergent class positions among the Farmers were also relevant to the logging scenario, and to the matter of social justice at Dongi-Dongi more broadly. The poorest Farmers, the Da'a who had come directly from the isolated hills around Palu, brought with them only a lantern, a cooking pot, a bush knife, and an ax. Together with those who had been working for daily wages as landless laborers in Palolo, they had to find ways to support themselves while clearing the land and waiting for their first corn harvest at Dongi-Dongi. They had no capital at all. Thus they worked for the better-off Farmers by helping to clear their gardens, and they worked for loggers by hauling timber out from the forest to the roadside. One group of Da'a told me that they worked for half a day for their logging boss in return for payment of fifteen cacao seeds—their hope for the future. These were the relations of production that exploited the labor of the poorer Farmers at Dongi-Dongi but also enabled them to begin to establish themselves as independent farmers on prime land next to a road—a dream repeatedly promised but in practice denied to marginalized people such as themselves. They were without exception optimistic about the future they were building through their own initiative.

There were other status differences at Dongi-Dongi. Some of the Farmers originating from the hills of Kulawi considered themselves superior to the Da'a, often dismissed as primitive and feckless. Yet at Dongi-Dongi even the most "backward" Da'a fresh from the hills had the protection of their charismatic patron Papa Lili, the veteran who had organized the early, surreptitious land clearing, and was jailed for his efforts. Papa Lili was reputed to have magic powers, powers feared and respected by Da'a and non-Da'a alike. The Da'a had strength in numbers: they were the majority ethnic group at Dongi-Dongi, and the majority population in Palolo as a result of Depsos resettlement and the subsequent diaspora.[30] The Da'a could make their presence felt in Palu City, too, when they descended from the surrounding hills en masse to join demonstrations. Da'a capacity for collective action made it risky to cross them. There was a report in the local papers that thousands of Da'a from the hills would create havoc if their kin and co-ethnics at Dongi-Dongi were attacked by the police.[31] The authorities took this threat seriously in view of the high degree of antagonism between Da'a and Bugis in Palu, and the ongoing conflict in Poso. It might in part explain why the police and army did not evict the Farmers from Dongi-Dongi despite several ultimatums.

Intimidation and force were also present among the Farmers. The land was not distributed equitably through a calm and measured process, as announced. Some forum leaders staked large areas and then allocated them to the people who had participated in the demonstrations or otherwise registered for a share of land. In some cases there was a scramble: whoever arrived first selected and staked their two hectares, then defended their claim from others who tried to intimidate them into giving it up. A few farm huts were burned down. Some found the frontier atmosphere at Dongi-Dongi too rough and withdrew back to Palolo. Some exceeded the two-hectare limit, but a survey conducted by one of the supporting NGOs confirmed that there were no large landowners and the excess that a few had claimed was modest. The charismatic Da'a leader Papa Lili claimed a large area thinking of his family still isolated in the hills west of Palu to whom he had promised land and hope at Dongi-Dongi. He distributed the land as promised, and kept only one hectare for his own use.

Some forum leaders and members, backed by the supporting NGOs, attempted to replace the delinquent leaders whose logging activities had brought the occupation into disrepute. Their efforts to institute a democratic process with an election were rebuffed with intimidation, betraying the combination of charisma and coercion that had made these men leaders in the first place. As I noted earlier, several of the forum leaders were recruited by TNC and the ADB as village organizers and facilitators because of their leadership skills and ability to get things done. These qualities, combined with a willingness to act coercively, were also recognized by the park forest guards who relied upon these same leaders to help organize illegal timber extraction. Some of them had helped the guards to police the park, and they participated in the burning of huts and crops, the confiscation of pots and knives, and the threats and arrests of their fellow villagers. At Dongi-Dongi they became leaders of the very people they previously tyrannized. The character of their leadership qualities had not changed. They were articulate, brave, and forthright in talking to outsiders. They took decisive action, for better or worse. It was risky to cross them. Critics of the occupation claimed that one forum leader, the one who had grabbed the map of the resettlement borders from the hands of an official, was so dangerous he had terrorized all the village Headmen in Palolo.[32]

When women at Dongi-Dongi organized to protest against the recalcitrant forum leaders who were selling timber from Dongi-Dongi, the leaders responded with the threat of violence. The women's group, formed with help from an NGO supporter, put up a banner: "The Women of Dongi-Dongi Oppose Illegal Logging." They went to the parliament building in Palu to demonstrate and publicize their stance. They made a vow to stop the practice that was destroying the good name of Dongi-Dongi, impeding its chances of official recognition, and undermining their interests as farmers, finally in possession of land. They planned to put up a roadblock at the exit from Dongi-Dongi heading toward Palu to stop the logging trucks. Leaders of the forum active in the logging business accused the women of trying to take over the leadership of Dongi-Dongi. They taunted the women's husbands for being weak, ruled by their wives. They threatened to strip the women naked and beat them if they proceeded with the roadblock. Knowing that their husbands would be obliged to defend their honor and there would be violence, the women gave up their plan. They vowed instead to work quietly and individually to persuade their husbands to withdraw from any involvement in logging. This was not easy: the men profited directly from the logging money, often used to buy alcohol. Some women said their husbands gave them no share. Their main income source was farming, especially the vegetables they sold by the roadside to pay for food, school fees, and other costs. Gendered interests and struggles shaped the constellation of practices that emerged inside Dongi-Dongi.

POLITICS DENIED

Challenged in an open letter by YTM director Arianto Sangaji to make its position on the Dongi-Dongi occupation clear, TNC argued that its role in relation to the park was purely technical. As a foreign organization operating under a memorandum of understanding with the Forest Department, TNC had no mandate to become involved in politics. Sangaji countered: "You should recognize that conservation is politics. When the boundaries were placed without consultation with villagers, that was politics. When the guards confiscate timber and rattan extracted by villagers, that is politics. When the people of Katu were to be evicted from the Park, that was politics. When you prepared the zonation of the Park, that was politics. The presence of TNC in Lore Lindu is also a matter of (international) politics." He reminded TNC that the Palolo villages collectively opposing the park were those in which TNC had invested most of its efforts in the failed micro-enterprise projects and the training of cadre, among them the leaders now at Dongi-Dongi. He challenged TNC to take its share of responsibility for failing to correctly diagnose or address the land crisis, and for unresolved conflicts over park boundaries that alienated the villagers.[33]

By highlighting its technical role and deferring political matters to the Indonesian authorities, TNC denied the political charge of its own activities. When I interviewed an international consultant on the ADB project, he took a similar approach. "ADB is mainly a development organization," he said, "conservation comes second. But the Indonesian government has to decide what it wants to do. Our project is technical." He was mystified by the tale of nine nations owning the park and by the claim of some officials that they could not regularize the settlement of Dongi-Dongi because the foreigners would come to collect on their debts.[34] He resented the way his "technical" project was being used as a vehicle for different parties, each with their own agendas—in this case, as an opportunity for officials to shore up their populist credentials by deflecting responsibility for the Farmers' problems onto foreigners.

A staff member of CARE in Palu with whom I discussed Dongi-Dongi had firm views on what should be done to resolve the problem, none of them engaging with the political critique made by the villagers or the profarmer alliance. He argued that the Farmers should be evicted; park rules should be enforced; the park Director should stick to conservation and avoid associating with the "radical" NGOs who made him confused. He argued, further, that villagers around the park should democratize their customary practices and share land fairly among themselves, putting their own house in order instead of turning to the park. CARE proposed to use satellite images to identify unused or underutilized lands in park border villages. The idea was to use this information—proof of the profligacy of villagers and their neglect of the communal ways assumed to be proper to them—to rebut the claim of landlessness, and hence to rebut claims on the park.[35] Superior information, literally, information from the sky, would help to contain a political challenge.

Anthropologist Oyvind Sandbukt, who conducted an evaluation of CARE's program, came to a different conclusion. He drew attention to "the seemingly inexorable progress of this marginalization of indigenous local populations," which rendered them landless and contained "an extremely potent mechanism for encroachment on forest." He predicted that "large proportions of the indigenous populations may end up as an utterly impoverished underclass," with those in the lowest strata of indigenous society most at risk. He urged CARE to recognize these processes and start thinking about ways to address them. Minimally CARE should recognize that the occupation of Dongi-Dongi was permanent. If the Farmers were evicted, others would take their place. CARE should be working with the NGOs trusted by the villagers to help mitigate the obvious risks of land selling, logging, and further expansion into the park.[36]

Yet this was not the approach adopted by members of the propark alliance I talked to in 2003. Instead of examining the processes that were creating pressure on park land and taking seriously the political challenge presented by the Farmers and their supporters, they still looked for people to blame and behaviors to correct. They did not engage with park border villagers as political actors capable of autonomous analysis and action. They continued to read the occupation of Dongi-Dongi as the outcome of provocation.[37] They dismissed other villagers in the border zone who were reasserting claims to park land in the same way: These villagers were simply following the path blazed by irresponsible NGOs at Katu and Dongi-Dongi. The propark alliance did not recognize that the practice of reclaiming land from the park and using it to redress the economic marginalization of the indigenous people of the province (however defined) had caught on in scores of highland villages not because of a single model promoted by provocateurs but because it emerged from the villagers' own critical reflections on the conditions of their lives—a point to which I will return.

CONCLUSION

Dongi-Dongi was an unusually contentious site of struggle. There were at least three dimensions to its complexity. First was the tricky switch between the practice of government and the practice of politics that I teased out not once but repeatedly: failed improvement programs provoked the Farmers into a political response; NGOs in the profarmer alliance used technical means to enhance Farmer capacities to act politically; the involvement of profarmer NGOS permitted the propark alliance to deny that the Farmers were autonomous political actors with their own agenda; experts of various persuasions, watching these events unfold, identified new problems and deficient conduct that needed to be improved. The position of political actor was not fixed—it was claimed, fought over, ascribed, and denied.

Second was the problem of fit. The Farmers fit the place of recognition reserved for the landless, but their chosen site—a national park—was problematic. They did not readily fit the place of recognition supplied by advocates for indigenous rights or community-based conservation, although they laid claim to this position. Sitting in an NGO office in Java, or even in the office of the eco-populist park Director in Palu, it was possible to imagine a world clearly divided into people who are indigenous, and people who are not. Yet after a century of more or less forced mobility few communities in the Central Sulawesi highlands are unambiguous candidates for the indigenous slot. Nevertheless, by 2003 the language of indigeneity had taken hold.[38] The Farmers deployed a concept of indigeneity to advance their claim, just as their opponents used a different concept of indigeneity to oppose it. Living in heterogeneous villages, long engaged in market relations, and wanting economic security and advance, the Farmers found themselves on uncertain ground. Similarly, the misfit at Dongi-Dongi put many activists in awkward positions—allied with enemies, opposed to friends, their practices challenged, and their integrity in doubt.

Third, the case did not fit the familiar binary memorably characterized by Henry Bernstein as "virtuous peasants" versus "vicious states."[39] The Farmers were far from virtuous. The state was not vicious. The occupation was indeed opposed by the authorities because it challenged their right to configure landscapes and determine where people should live, but no eviction took place. The incapacity of resettlement officials to identify a viable alternative was surely one reason for this, but there were others. During the course of the meeting between the head of the provincial parliament and the Farmers of Dongi-Dongi that I attended in 2003, the politician shifted his ground. Although he started the meeting with a firm statement that the Farmers must leave Dongi-Dongi because of the negative impact on the watershed, he ended the meeting stating that if the matter was his to decide, they could stay where they were, but they should not extend the cleared area or let themselves be manipulated. It was definitely a compromise, and the Farmers, reflecting later on this shift, regarded it as a triumph. They believed they had convinced the politician that their critical analysis was accurate—they were indeed victims of programs that, in the name of improvement, had thrown their lives and livelihoods into disarray. Further, in the era of *reformasi*, some politicians and officials were willing to acknowledge the injustice of land seizures and misallocations and understood that victims of these practices had the right to protest.

During the height of the controversy, attempts by the propark alliance to reassert a position as trustees lacked focus and conviction. In relation to the Farmers, they had no solution to propose except persuasion or eviction, neither of which made any headway. Yet the disarray of governmental intervention in the park border zone turned out to be temporary. Faced with the fact of the Dongi-Dongi occupation, which was expected to stimulate further park encroachments; the rising tide of monocropped cacao pressing in on the park in all directions; the continuing land pressure caused by migration; the political mobilization of the post-Suharto years; and the instability caused by the conflict in Poso, the Nature Conservancy could well have decided to abandon the attempt to protect the park. Indeed, this course was contemplated. A senior manager for TNC told me when I met him in his office in Jakarta in September 2002 that he could not raise funds for projects when "conservation outcomes" could not be guaranteed. A breakthrough in the form of a new approach to park management persuaded TNC to stay. TNC's new program, a carefully crafted attempt to contain the political challenge presented by park border villagers and their allies, is the subject of chapter 6.

PROVOCATION AND REVERSAL

In this chapter, I explore how the Nature Conservancy tried to contain the challenge to park-based conservation presented by park border villagers and their activist allies. TNC's new management model was a significant departure from the integrated conservation and development model of the 1990s. It did not attempt to alleviate poverty in park border villages, or to provide economic compensation for the loss of access to park resources. Nor did it rely on intensified policing and coercion. Rather, it attempted to alter practices and desires so that communities would elect to participate in park protection. TNC called the approach collaborative management, an apt term for the uneasy blend of cooperation and betrayal demanded of its participants.

In the context of the Lore Lindu National Park in 2001, the project of constituting compliant communities that agreed to stay out of the park so that its biodiversity could be preserved seems extraordinarily ambitious, almost quixotic. How did it come about? To account for it, I will read TNC's new set of program documents through the prism of the set of relations articulated together at this particular place—relations I have described in the preceding chapters. This approach enables me to examine TNC's novel governmental strategy not only in its programmatic mode, as captured in its discourse and procedures, but also in its tactical mode, as it responded to particular challenges. My aim is to account for power—to explain why it takes on these forms, how it works positively to create new conditions, and how it is in turn shaped by the "strategies of struggle" with which it is engaged in permanent relations of provocation and reversal.

As I will show, there were multiple tensions in TNC's new program. Often, a technoscientific or legal rule was boldly asserted, only to be followed by a compromise to accommodate a challenge. The attempt to make the categories enshrined in the documents "real" was a further exercise in compromise. Compromise enabled an engagement to take place, even as it compromised the moral and coercive authority of the rule makers. It facilitated the production of new subjects that recognized the value of conservation, even as it opened up new fronts of struggle in which conservation values were disputed. It implicated both parties and tied them into a new relationship of antagonistic complicity.

I begin by examining the rationale of TNC's collaborative approach, situating it in relation to the problems it sought to solve. Then I conduct a close reading of the microstrategies devised by TNC to elicit participation in park management and to contain political challenge. Finally, in iterative mode, I return once again to the park border villages to examine how people responded to the invitation to devise "community conservation agreements," critically engaging the nexus of knowledge and power presented by conservation and the presence of the park.

CONSERVATION BY DESIGN

The Nature Conservancy characterized its new approach to park management in Indonesia as results-oriented and nonconfrontational. *Community* and *partnership* were the key words. The TNC country program director Ian Dutton argued in May 2001 that TNC had come to recognize the importance of conflict management and the need for microplanning: "Each solution needs to be expertly tailored to individual community needs." Management must also be firm, he argued, because "simple appeasement of populist demands is bound to fail." Between too much and too little community engagement in conservation and development lay, he suggested, the "right balance."[1] Dutton did not question the technoscientific necessity of conservation, or the right of conservation organizations to intervene in peoples' lives. He presented the issue as a matter of correct technique, backed by the requisite information. He explained that a GIS collage would soon show "where villagers' needs and conservation priorities can be accommodated, and where potential conflicts exist."[2] He was optimistic about the future: "We are close to being able to prescribe best-practice guidelines on what types of community partnerships work best in certain circumstances and to quantify the risks and damages of not engaging communities in all stages of the development process."[3]

At Lore Lindu, the shift in TNC's approach was directly related to its recognition that TNC could not manage the economic processes affecting the park, nor could it count on enforcement of the law. This problem was made doubly evident by the occupation of Dongi-Dongi in June 2001. TNC labeled its response "Conservation by Design."[4] It was a carefully calculated attempt to set conditions and direct conduct. The governing philosophy of "collaborative management" was accepted by the park authority and embedded in the draft twenty-five-year management plan for the park prepared by TNC in cooperation with the park office.[5] Work on the draft plan was funded by USAID and involved a large number of consultants, both Indonesian and foreign. It resulted in a document of three volumes totaling about six hundred single-spaced pages, plus supplements and related reports.[6]

By 2001, TNC had acknowledged the sound economic logic of village protest against the exclusionary boundaries of the park: "These impoverished communities find it very difficult to bear the full opportunity costs of setting aside the lands for conservation that they depend on for a portion of their livelihood."[7] Specifically, TNC noted that the "lure of cash crops and harvests for export promote agricultural encroachment and excessive harvesting of forest resources by local people living at subsistence levels," with coffee and cacao "the biggest threat" to the park because they "deliver the largest incomes in the shortest time."[8] Yet TNC no longer proposed to improve the livelihoods of park border villages, or to divert them from their park-based activities. As the bitter experience of failed income generating projects in the 1990s demonstrated, TNC had no real means of relieving poverty, and there was ample evidence that inadequate projects would backfire. The Asian Development Bank, with far greater financial resources, failed even more miserably with its income improvement schemes, and the backlash embodied in the occupation of Dongi-Dongi was catastrophic.[9] From these lessons, TNC drew the conclusion that poverty alleviation was not the task of a conservation organization, nor was it the purpose of a national park.[10] The mandate was biodiversity conservation. Economic development initiatives, if any, should serve only to "demonstrate goodwill on the part of the conservation implementing agencies."[11]

TNC made no promise that biodiversity protection would provide economic returns to the villagers, or to anyone else for that matter. It recognized that no one had shown any interest in commoditizing the park's genetic resources, nor did the prospect seem likely.[12] TNC deferred the problem of economic development in the border villages to CARE, which, it argued, had more experience with people; TNC would recover its focus on the park itself.[13] However, CARE staff had no confidence in their capacity to improve livelihoods in these villages, and park villagers were alert to empty promises. So how would this work? Why would villagers buy into a conservation regime that directly countered their economic interest? TNC argued that the payback to villagers would take the form of better relations with the park authority, and their repositioning on the right side of the law. This, a TNC survey found, was what villagers wanted: "A lifting of communal guilt over accusations of forest destruction. They were willing to accept community agreements with the Park, as long as these were mutually beneficial, simple, and sure. . . . villagers in general want an ordered and understandable relation with the National Park."[14] This interpretation of villagers' desires sat awkwardly with the second set of forces TNC also acknowledged: the capacity of the park border villagers to exert their will and the lack of enforcement.

Although the park authority had the formal power to control and exclude human activity, TNC recognized that villagers also had powers: "[A] villager's power is informal, largely deriving from his or her ability to affect the situation practically, be it to sustainably manage a resource or to occupy and slash and burn protected forest."[15] For TNC, Katu's success in resisting eviction and the Farmers' occupation of Dongi-Dongi were only the more blatant examples of this capacity.[16] TNC's vegetation and land use studies of the park confirmed the extensive presence of cacao and coffee in the understory, evidence of a much broader human challenge.[17] Faced with this array of powers and practices, TNC recognized that exclusion by force would not work. In the era of *reformasi*, forest officials were not enforcing forest boundaries, widely regarded as illegitimate. Popular protests and claims gained a more sympathetic hearing than they did under the New Order. Moreover previous attempts at strong enforcement around the park had backfired just as badly as failed development, increasing peoples' sense of anger and entitlement. In 1998 and 2001 in Palolo the use of force in the context of a dispute over land and confiscated timber had caused rather direct and immediate backlash in the form of arson, riot, and attacks on park staff and facilities.[18] Most of the guard posts had been burned down and abandoned. Thus, despite its professed preference for conservation by enforcement, TNC acknowledged the reality that " 'top-down' control measures" were failing to operate.[19] TNC was also aware that any move it made to become directly involved in enforcement would jeopardize its ability to work in park border villages.[20] TNC and CARE facilities had been attacked and staff threatened and refused entry to particular villages, especially in Palolo.[21] In the context of this particular park, TNC concluded, "enforcement can only be carried out with community acceptance."[22]

TNC's challenge was to bring about a reversal—to recapture the initiative, shifting from a defensive position in which peoples' critiques, demands, and actions drove the conservation agenda to one in which TNC and the park office would once again set conditions.[23] It proposed the collaborative approach as a way to reassert the authority of experts, and the authority of "the state" as the maker of laws. Law and participatory procedures would become tactics of government, tools to educate the desires of villagers and reform their practices. The concrete outcome TNC expected to achieve from collaborative management was effective, binding community conservation agreements.

TNC declared its new approach "a major breakthrough in integrating scientific knowledge with community aspirations."[24] Yet, as my account has revealed, community aspirations suitable for "integration" by TNC were not easy to find in the border villages. Nowhere in its voluminous documentation, still less in its design, did TNC directly address the most obvious aspiration in park border villages—for the park boundaries to be moved, or for agriculture to be permitted within the park. Thus the participatory process TNC devised has to be understood as an attempt to *produce* sets of aspirations appropriate to the project of biodiversity protection.

LAW, LIMITS, AND COMPROMISE

In the TNC documents, reference to the law served to set limits to what could be accepted within arrangements for collaborative management. The reason the park could not adopt comanagement, according to TNC, was that comanagement implied coequal powers, whereas the Indonesian Conservation Law clearly assigned the right to manage the park to the Forest Department. The law granted communities a supporting role as collaborators or participants in management, but the state, through the Forest Department, was sovereign. The park, stated TNC unequivocally, "lies on state-owned forest land, and is within the sole planning jurisdiction of the PKA, a Directorate of the Department of Forestry."[25] The critical tactical move of collaborative management, for TNC, was to incorporate "input and buy-in from communities," while firmly situating "final decision making authority with the park management."[26]

The draft management plan contained a preface by the Director General of Forest Protection and Nature Conservation that drew attention to the exceptional character of the conjuncture at which lawmakers must reassert the legitimacy of the rule of law, even as they acknowledged that the law was being challenged, and indeed could not be enforced:

> In writing of the Management Plan national guidelines were adhered to. This gave basic structure to the document. Importantly, nothing was included in the Management Plan that was contrary to Indonesian law. This may appear an obvious point but national laws are being questioned as never before, and with them the right of the national park authority to implement conservation-related laws. Some groups are exerting pressure on park managers to allow activities that are counter to planning laws. A case in point is the pressure to allow commercial harvesting of wood and rattan in the traditional use zone of the Park. The plan resists the temptation to deem legal illegal activities that cannot at present be stopped. Instead a flexible approach has been sought that finds new ways to manage the Park which is inclusive of all stakeholders. . . . The plan has in its mission statement the guiding concept of collaborative management, which embraces the idea of people and staff working together to bring about conservation.[27]

The preeminence of the law set the "structure" for the draft management plan and the limits of collaboration, defining the parameters of what could and could not be tolerated. The task of stakeholders included in park management was preset. It was to "bring about conservation." Yet the plan promised a "flexible approach" inclusive of all stakeholders. What did this mean?

Flexibility signaled compromise, or room for maneuver. The law, as the preface stated, must not be contravened. Throughout the document, the preeminence of law and technoscientific authority were reasserted. But since some rules could not at present be enforced, there had to be compromise. There were two tactics for compromise in the draft management plan. First was a compromise on time, the tactic of the old Coffee Agreement. Forbidden activities such as coffee and cacao farming should be phased out gradually, with "the consensus of local people" and "in such a way as to cause least social unrest."[28] Second was a compromise on space, but this was severely limited. The chapter of the plan devoted to park borders recognized that borders were contested in some locations but did not recommend that their location should be reviewed or moved to accommodate ancestral land claims or the need for farmland.[29] The boundaries and the total area of the park were located outside the realm of flexibility. They were established by law, as the set of official decrees concerning the establishment of the park included in the plan confirmed. The main discussion of boundary revision was a proposal to extend the park by the enclosure of additional land.[30] Thus the principal complaint of border villagers, that the park boundaries cut them off from valuable farmland, was not addressed. Tactical room for maneuver in the dimension of space came from the system of park zoning, the division of the park into core and wilderness zones, and a zone for activity or use.

In TNC's collaborative approach, the use zone of the park took on extraordinary importance. A clause in the Conservation Law that allows some human activities within the use zone of a national park (in this case, 13 percent of the total park area) enabled TNC to invite villagers to collaborate. Setting aside basic questions about the existence of the park and its external boundaries, TNC would engage the community in providing "input" on who could use the use zone and what they could do there. Thus positioning villagers as collaborators, TNC expected them to "buy in" to the park as a whole and stop contesting the park managers' technolegal authority to mark boundaries, limit livelihoods, and regulate lives.[31] Villagers would also submit their unruly practices within the park to a whole new level of scrutiny and supervision.

According to TNC's analysis, lack of participation in the past was the cause of conflict between park and villagers, and participation, correctly arranged, would guarantee acceptance:[32] "Active community participation in all zone identification, boundary revision, regulation development and field demarcation is the basis for all co-management and land-use planning. . . . This process must be allowed to proceed in the target villages adjacent to the national park and its enclaves and will take considerable time. The end result, however, will be boundaries, zones and regulations that are accepted, respected and maintained by the Park authorities, local government and communities who are affected by National Park establishment."[33]

This, then, was TNC's design. It was a calculated attempt to respond to provocation and reverse it. Yet classificatory schemes, as Timothy Mitchell points out, are not models of the world, they are models for it.[34] Mapping spaces and identifying people and activities appropriate for the use zone was not simply a matter of reflecting what was there. Truths had to be produced. But the *success* of this production was not guaranteed. If appropriate subjects could not be identified, or their activities did not conform to requirements, there would be further compromises, instabilities, and reversals. As it turned out, matrices were filled but awkwardly, as the operation of classifying opened up new fronts of contestation.

MAKING CATEGORIES REAL

In practice, programming for the use zone was almost as difficult as policing the external park boundaries. The draft plan recognized that the zone system threatened established interests and practices. Not only would activities in the use zone be closely monitored, all illegal economic activities would be eliminated from the nonuse zones. Opposition to increased enforcement was to be offset by the process of participation: "It is imperative that stakeholder ideas are incorporated into the zonation model. Zonation must reflect the reality of village use patterns which remaining [sic] within national park laws and regulations."[35] The instability of this compromise was palpable. What would be done about village use patterns that contravened the regulations, not least the hundreds of hectares of cacao and coffee inside the park? The problem of nonconforming uses was not addressed in the draft plan, which acknowledged only "misunderstandings" and the need to avoid them: "Stakeholder participation will reduce potential misunderstandings by helping to assure people that zonation implementation is a long-term process, offering no immediate threat to livelihoods."[36]

The draft plan vacillated between using the label "use zone," and the more restrictive label found in the loan agreement for the ADB project: "traditional use zone."[37] The latter more clearly reflected the purpose of the use zone in the Conservation Law, which was to allow "limited resource extraction of locally occurring species."[38] The use zone's imagined subject was the traditional villager gathering indigenous resources for use in traditional, noncommercial ways. This concept fit uneasily with the reality of resource use inside the park. One obvious problem was that many of the resources present in the park and valued by villagers were not actually indigenous, they were exotic. Ecologists advising TNC produced a long list of exotics that should ideally be eliminated both from the park and, even more contentiously, from surrounding villages. The list included coffee, cacao, dogs, cats, chilies, carp, deer, tilapia, and water buffalo.[39] A second major problem was that the use zone provision prohibited commercial extraction of resources.[40] It assumed that traditional systems of resource extraction prioritized subsistence use. This was incorrect. From around 1870, commerce has driven the ebbs and flows of resource extraction from the forests of Indonesia.[41] *Damar* (resin) from the trees enclosed by the park was collected and exported for at least a century (1870–1970), and rattan was a major export in the 1980s and 1990s. A third problem was identifying an appropriate subject to fill the niche of the "traditional" community. In this matter, Katu reemerged in the draft plan in a prominent but troubled role.

TNC had opposed the park director's decision to let the village of Katu remain inside the park. Nevertheless, the presence of Katu presented opportunities for a tactical advance. Katu helped to make the category of traditional resource use real. It served as a placeholder for the concept of traditional management anticipated in the use zone. It also served to mark a boundary, to explain why the rights and privileges of Katu did not apply to other, more ordinary park border villages. Recall that this was precisely the argument used by the park director to explain why Katu could stay in the park, while the Farmers at Dongi-Dongi must be evicted. Katu was used, that is, to contain a much broader political challenge. But the containment was precarious. Park border villagers disputed Katu's specialness, as I mentioned earlier, and they emphasized the need of all the park border villagers for access to agricultural land. TNC's experts were also concerned that Katu might be ordinary, and they worked hard to define and maintain the grounds of distinction.

The draft plan noted the disjuncture between concepts of tradition and existing practice. To qualify for the use zone, villagers—including Katu villagers—would have to demonstrate that they were indeed traditional. Put differently, concepts of tradition would serve to limit what villagers could do in the park. Thus, according to the draft plan, "application of adat or customary practice would, presumably, restrict hunting to indigenous communities who have traditional hunting grounds. Techniques would, presumably, have to be traditional, thus ruling out the use of guns and wire snares."[42] Katu's practices were disjunctive. Although the ecopopulist park director applauded the interest that Katu people showed in restoring their old rice terraces and planting them with biodiverse strains of local rice, he was disappointed when his exemplary indigenous subjects joined the rush to plant cacao.[43] Less inclined to trust the wisdom of tradition, the TNC experts writing the draft plan argued that managers, not villagers, must decide which practices would be forbidden or permitted in Katu, guiding the villagers on an appropriate path.[44]

Making distinctions between social groups and allocating rights according to those distinctions was a central feature of the draft plan. In addition to the axis of indigenous/nonindigenous and traditional/nontraditional, the plan emphasized the distinction subsistence/commercial, sometimes amalgamated with a concept of scale (small/large). In relation to agriculture, for example, enforcement efforts were to distinguish between a subsistence farmer and a "commercial coffee planter."[45] This might seem quite an appropriate distinction, appealingly populist, but it was disrupted by the actual pattern of livelihoods around the park. Almost all the coffee grown in the park in 2001 was sold, and no farmers in the vicinity of the park had coffee groves bigger than about four hectares. There was no distinct practice of subsistence coffee growing, nor was there a distinct class of "commercial coffee planters." Yet on the basis of this and related distinctions, the draft plan developed a scheme for classifying land users and determining the kinds of "action" that should be taken to control, reduce, or eliminate their activities. These sets of distinctions are set out in figure 11.[46]

The classificatory grid formalized in the chart proposed a set of distinctions through which park authorities could apprehend, redirect, and manage extractive and agricultural activities within the park. Yet, as I have explained, there was a gap between the reality of the grid, and reality in and around the park. This gap could not be left unfilled. The plan called for "precise mapping," the

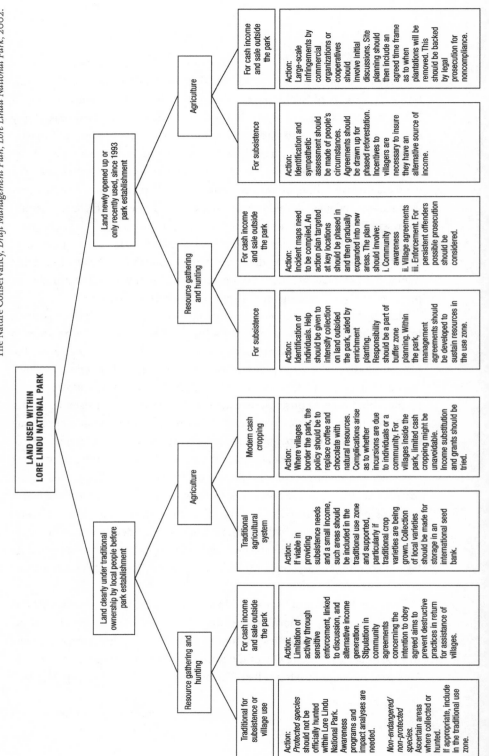

FIGURE 11 Indicating types of areas utilized within the park and possible actions to be taken. The Nature Conservancy, *Draft Management Plan, Lore Lindu National Park*, 2002.

LAND USED WITHIN LORE LINDU NATIONAL PARK

Land clearly under traditional ownership by local people before park establishment

Resource gathering and hunting

Traditional for subsistence or village use

Action:
Protected species should not be officially hunted within Lore Lindu National Park. Awareness programs and impact analyses are needed.

Non-endangered/ non-protected species. Ascertain areas where collected or hunted. If appropriate, include in the traditional use zone.

For cash income and sale outside the park

Action:
Limitation of activity through sensitive enforcement, linked to discussion, and alternative income generation. Stipulation in community agreements concerning the intention to obey agreed aims to prevent destructive practices in return for assistance of villages.

Agriculture

Traditional agricultural system

Action:
If viable in providing subsistence needs and a small income, such areas should be included in the traditional use zone and supported, particularly if traditional crop varieties are being grown. Collection of local varieties should be made for storage in an international seed bank.

Modern cash cropping

Action:
Where villages border the park, the policy should be to replace coffee and chocolate with natural resources. Complications arise as to whether incursions are due to individuals or a community. For villages inside the park, limited cash cropping might be unavoidable. Income substitution and grants should be tried.

Land newly opened up or only recently used, since 1993 park establishment

Resource gathering and hunting

For subsistence

Action:
Identification of individuals. Help should be given to intensify collection on land outside the park, aided by enrichment planting. Responsibility should be a part of buffer zone planning. Within the park, management agreements should be developed to sustain resources in the use zone.

For cash income and sale outside the park

Action:
Incident maps need to be compiled. An action plan targeted at key locations should be phased in and then gradually expanded into new areas. The plan should involve:
i. Community awareness
ii. Village agreements
iii. Enforcement. For persistent offenders possible prosecution should be considered.

Agriculture

For subsistence

Action:
Identification and sympathetic assessment should be made of people's circumstances. Agreements should be drawn up for phased reforestation. Incentives to villagers are necessary to insure they have an alternative source of income.

For cash income and sale outside the park

Action:
Large-scale infringements by commercial organizations or cooperatives should involve initial discussions. Site planning should then include an agreed time frame as to when plantations will be removed. This should be backed by legal prosecution for noncompliance.

listing of "those people certified to exploit resources within the zone," and the preparation of protocols "specifying the type of community activities" that were permitted.[47] The boxes on the grid had to be filled with actual people and places that met the criteria. These maps, lists, and protocols had to stand up to scientific, legal, and bureaucratic scrutiny, since they must be approved in Jakarta and then circulated to numerous officials.[48] How could this be done? In the effort to fill the grid, scientists proved to be just as awkward as villagers, as I will demonstrate with three examples: the case of rattan "management," the matter of maps, and collaborative monitoring.

RATTAN REGIMES

Rattan extraction was one activity potentially permitted in the traditional use zone. To qualify, it had to be sustainable and "traditional." The draft plan proposed that rattan collection, which was "claimed as a traditional activity but in the last twenty years has become a major local business," should be subject to "tight control measures, including codes of practice" if, indeed, it was to be allowed at all.[49] To help fill the grid, TNC sponsored a scientific study of rattan ecology, collection, and use. But the findings of the study, conducted by Stephen Siebert in the late 1990s, did not support the preferred management strategy. Siebert's report cited critiques of the concept of sustainable harvesting as an "ecological fallacy" based in "utopian thinking." He was skeptical that technical criteria and practices for "sustainable harvesting" from forests could be devised. Despite widespread interest there were, he wrote, "few, if any, documented examples." Even if guidelines for sustainable rattan extraction could be devised, he pointed out that there was no scientific basis for predicting the sustainability of the park ecosystem as a whole. He also argued that the concept of sustainable extraction assumed that ecosystems, property regimes, and markets were stable, and that extraction could in fact be controlled.[50] His study demonstrated that none of these conditions were present in relation to rattan in the park.

The idea that subsistence could be separated from commerce was a non-starter in Moa and Au, Siebert's two study villages in Kulawi. In Moa in the 1990s, 85 percent of households were highly dependent on rattan incomes to meet subsistence needs, and in Au the number was 58 percent. The search for rattan income, further, had attracted landless households to move into these rather remote villages—mainly Kulawi "locals" who had sold up their land to incoming migrants. But by around 2000 he found that interest in rattan collection was declining because there were no more suitable canes within ten kilometers of the villages, and alternative, more lucrative opportunities had become available.[51] Given the "phenomenal increase in the value of cacao," he argued, "it is unclear whether rattan will continue to be as economically important to area households at it has been in the recent past, and thus whether [villagers] will invest capital and labor in its management."[52]

Siebert also questioned the concept of customary rattan *management*. Minimally, management requires territorial exclusion. He found that the village head of Moa had attempted to declare an exclusive harvesting zone reserved for villagers. Outsiders could access the rattan only with permission. His study showed, however, that the Headman's rules were not familiar to Moa's longtime residents nor to outside rattan collectors, much less were they enforced. Without tenurial security vis-à-vis the park and other collectors, the incentive for "sustainable management" was effectively zero.[53] Thus, Siebert argued, in the case of the park, a rattan tenure and management system would have to be devised and implemented from scratch. It could not simply build on "tradition" or "custom" as proponents of sustainable management assumed. The connection between village and territory was also precarious. A catastrophic flood in Au had cut the village in half, destroyed rice fields, and caused residents to relocate two kilometers downstream, far from the zone that would have been carefully mapped, classified, and monitored for their "traditional use," under the TNC's draft plan. After the flood he found the people of Au "so busy rebuilding homes and rice fields, and planting cacao, that no one appears to be gathering rattan."[54]

Based on this research, Siebert concluded that programs for the community management of wild rattan should *not* be developed. Instead he recommended interventions to increase the productivity and sustainability of cacao and coffee on privately owned and managed lands outside the park, and the addition of cultivated rattan to the repertoire of farm-based perennials where farmers showed an interest.[55] Rattan, in short, was not a resource that villagers had an interest in managing in the use zone of the park. Nor, argued Siebert, were there any other forest products of sufficient value to compete with cacao.

Although Siebert's report was included in the draft plan, complete with its dissident conclusions, TNC opted to ignore the scientist's advice. The TNC plan for the design of the traditional use zone was premised on the concept of sustainable gathering of forest products according to traditional norms and new monitoring protocols that would bring expert knowledge, conservation requirements, and village interests into alignment. Thus the draft plan stated that Siebert's recommendations were "not in keeping with the general approach to resource issues within the Park. The way forward is generally perceived to be through Community Agreements."[56]

THE MATTER OF MAPS

My second example, the matter of maps, also reveals the complex character of TNC's containment strategy, and the difficulty of making categories real. TNC stated that maps were to be generated in collaborative workshops, with the goal of "empowering villagers within a formalized framework of regulated zonation."[57] This contorted phrase meant that villagers should help to map the areas where they undertook traditional activities appropriate to the use zone. In these areas (and not elsewhere), they would be permitted to make use of some resources, subject to criteria of sustainability, and close monitoring by experts. The benefit to villagers was that their use of the use zone would be formally recorded, recognized, and regulated, rather than treated as criminal. But what of village empowerment? This turned out to be double-edged.

Mapping in and around the park was a tool of struggle as well as regulation.[58] Recall that Katu's production of detailed maps persuaded the park director to recognize Katu's presence as "an integral part of the park's management system." Legibility was dangerous, even when TNC was directly involved. A TNC staff member informed me in 2003 that TNC had stopped participatory mapping of customary resource use inside the park because villagers believed that once their uses had been documented on an official map, their claim to the resources was legitimized.[59] Maps did actually empower villagers in ways that exceeded the "formalized framework of regulated zonation" that TNC was attempting to make real through its draft management plan. I will return to this point when I discuss the impact of TNC mapping in Sedoa.

The data shown on park vegetation maps was equally tricky. TNC's scientific advisers found that hundreds of hectares of park land, in some places extending ten kilometers inside the borders, were underplanted with coffee and cacao.[60] They also confirmed, more contentiously, the long history of agrarian land use. Up to 26 percent of the park area, they reported, was under light or heavy anthropogenic forest, mainly former swidden land. Further, it was difficult to distinguish natural from anthropogenic forest, or to confirm whether or not human activity was the cause of forest damage. On lower montane forest, they found, "forest structure and composition under poorly-drained conditions, predominantly in the internal watersheds, suggest a much higher rate of natural disturbance and appears to undergo seasonal flooding. The canopy in these areas is often quite ragged, with large isolated individual trees and the lowest strata of the canopy densely closed with small trees. Distinguishing human disturbance from natural disturbance in this forest type is quite difficult."[61] The defensive posture of park science was also implicit in the detailed land studies included in the draft plan. They document the suitability of park land for agriculture, anticipating the risk that they would be taken over for that purpose.[62]

COLLABORATIVE MONITORING

My third example, collaborative monitoring, was intended to fill the space on the grid reserved for self-managing, conservation-oriented villagers. According to the plan, monitoring was to be conducted jointly by forest guards and villagers. A report on a monitoring exercise sponsored by TNC in Rahmat reveals the difficulty of making this category real. The exercise was designed to measure the extent of damage to the forest on the village edge by means of transects. The results would be compiled in a database entered into a GIS system for long-term comparison and decision making by people—villagers as well as experts—with a shared concern to protect the park. But who were these imagined villagers? Why would villagers want to help supply the park authorities with details of the "damage" their farming and extractive activities caused to the park? What interest, if any, did they have in biodiversity monitoring?[63] CARE had also built a significant part of its revised conservation program at the park around "biodiversity monitoring systems." It envisaged the practice of monitoring as an educational tool to "precondition" the border population toward regulated resource use. It was a technique designed not so much to produce data, as to produce new, environmental subjects.[64] But as the midterm evaluation of the CARE project observed, a similar initiative in a CARE project in Southeast Sulawesi had already been abandoned because of the "lack of clear legal basis . . . and misgivings among locals about utility of system."[65]

The park Director who recognized the villagers of Katu as "an integral part of the Park Management system" was an enthusiastic promoter of village monitoring to detect and expel illegal loggers and rattan collectors. In his plans, monitoring by villagers would be backed by customary councils who would arrest the culprits and impose heavy fines. It would also be backed by a strengthened forest police supplied with more guns.[66] This plan took no account of the way that some villagers gain from logging. He assumed that logging was a net minus for villagers—the source of damage to their water supply, and the accusation that *they* were the ones engaged in illegal activity. Thus he overlooked the complicity of village officials and park guards in the logging, their role in organizing village labor and providing local "security" for logging syndicates. He overlooked the ways village leaders compete over the spoils, factionalizing their own villages, and compete with outsiders who try to log village lands (inside or outside the park) without making the proper financial arrangements. Under these conditions, the Director's plan to "empower" villagers to monitor forests did not amount to support for their self-regulating, conservation-oriented, "customary" ways. It did not engage a unified community of people who cared about the park, and who together with park staff would challenge greedy and irresponsible outsiders. It amounted to a requirement that villagers should confront their covillagers, village elites, and powerful outsiders, including officials—a recipe for vigilantism and violence.[67]

SECURING "INPUT AND BUY IN"

To secure "input and buy in,"[68] TNC needed to do more than construct a grid. It needed to act on actions by the application of calculated techniques. Intervention was necessary because communities did not naturally do what they ought: Katu went into cacao; the landless went into Dongi-Dongi; everywhere, park border villagers wanted to access park land for agriculture. It was, as TNC observed, the villagers' capacity to act that made its own action necessary:

FIGURE 12   Outline of the Nature Conservancy Site Conservation Planning Model: Compiled from the Five-S Framework for Site Conservation.
The Nature Conservancy, *Draft Management Plan, Lore Lindu National Park,* 2002.

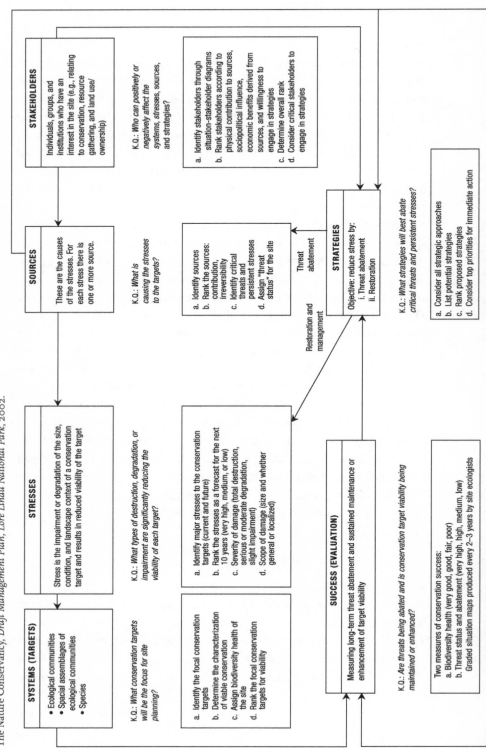

"Communities and certain individuals interacting either legally, or illegally, with the Park have *de facto* power to disrupt the implementation of plans and planning processes. The development of agreements with such people is a practical necessity."[69] But how could "such people" be engaged in making agreements? More specifically, how could they be brought to a new awareness of the importance of biodiversity conservation and formalize their buy-in by signing on to agreements that listed their rights and responsibilities, specified a monitoring regime, and included enforceable penalties for transgression? TNC's answer to this question was technical. It consisted in a carefully designed strategy spelled out in detail in TNC documents and manuals.

TNC was very clear about the objective of collaborative management. It was to "improve the willingness of people living around the park to commit to its long-term survival."[70] Thus the purpose of "input" was not to learn about villagers' aspirations or engage in debate. It was to reform their aspirations and alter their conduct. The intended outcome—park survival—was determined in advance. For this reason, not all the villagers' concerns could be taken up in the consultation process. Crucially, there must be no misunderstanding about issues such as moving park boundaries or approving illegal activities. The community conservation agreements forged through the consultation process must conform to the law and promote biodiversity conservation. They should cover "such issues as removing exotic species, controlling commercial logging, sustaining rattan collection, preventing encroachment, and stopping illegal hunting and trapping."[71] TNC put it this way: "The most important factor in designing *successful* management strategies is community support and acceptance; the early identification of acceptable strategies, and the elimination of unacceptable ones, is a valuable management objective."[72]

For insight into how TNC planned to manage participation en route to community conservation agreements, I turn to the TNC "Participatory Conservation Planning Manual," which I read in relation to TNC's reports of the results obtained from seven iterations of the exercise carried out in various locations around the park in 2001. Figure 12 summarizes the steps. The key questions are italicized.[73]

Site conservation planning as it was implemented around the park was a highly directed activity. The manual included notes on the kind of atmosphere facilitators should establish, one focused on "joint learning" rather than enforcement or conflict, although it was mainly the villagers who were expected to learn. The exercise used participatory formats such as mapping, listing, and ranking, and was conducted by means of workshops attended by selected participants who were set to work with colored paper, markers, circles, and arrows. Yet facilitators were warned not to call the exercise "participatory rural appraisal," since there were signs that park border villagers were jaded with exercises of this kind, conducted repeatedly by different agencies without benefit to them.[74]

The first step in site conservation planning was to "identify eight biological or ecological systems that represent community priorities," elicited through asking the question: "What is most important to you in the reserve?"[75] Note that attention was directed firmly toward assets *within* the reserve, not to the existence of the reserve or its borders. When TNC carried out this exercise in seven different locations around the park, the following list of "priorities" was produced (with the number of mentions in brackets). Rattan (7), timber for household use (7), water sources (4), rare birds (4), rare animals (4), forest/protected forest (3), medicinal plants (3), hunted animals (3), traditional land (3), plants for weaving (3), megaliths (2), pastures (2), *damar* (2), and others—bamboo, butterflies, bat caves, bees, community gardens, recreation sites, *anoa*, lake (1).[76] Note that rattan and timber, the anticipated focus of the use zone agreements, came to the fore, rare fauna and flora of little or no practical benefit to villagers became priorities, and hundreds of hectares of coffee and cacao within the park all but disappeared from this list.

The second step involved identifying the status of the relevant ecological "systems." In all seven iterations, the participants concluded that these systems were in decline. Having achieved consensus that resources valued by the community were under threat, the next exercise in the consultation sequence was designed to identify the source of threats.[77] It produced a list of "critical threats, ranked by score," including tree felling (909), land clearing (780), rattan collection (546), hunting and snares (454), population growth (446), lack of alternative employment (290), pollution (219), irresponsible harvesting techniques (94), natural processes (84), and increased prices for forest commodities (71).[78] By this point, villagers had been led to identify their own economic activities (cutting trees, developing gardens, and collecting rattan) as the primary causes of the destruction of the ecological systems they themselves had just defined as valuable (step one).

The third step in the exercise moved toward buy-in. Participants were asked to "formulate strategies aimed to mitigate the critical threats," determining which parties should be involved and target outcomes.[79] The Indonesian version of the manual used a matrix: to every threat was attached a strategy, and for every strategy, a set of activities.[80] The participants were then asked to assess probable support for implementation, quantifying the likelihood of buy-in taking into account expected opposition from various "stakeholders." This exercise tapped participants' knowledge of the social forces at work in their villages. The results were translated into numbers, rendered in a table. The summary listed the following set of strategies, ranked according to their frequency (how often they were mentioned) and "support score" (likelihood of implementation). Enforcement of regulations with participatory monitoring systems was the strategy most frequently mentioned, but participants were skeptical that it could be implemented. They anticipated opposition from parties who would lose out. Developing human resources and developing alternative/compatible economic activities were frequently mentioned, with good support, presumably because they implied a net benefit, with no losers. District spatial planning, market development, and forest rehabilitation were also mentioned, though less frequently.[81]

Note that despite the rather accurate reality check supplied by the villagers—their assessment that "participatory monitoring" would be difficult to implement—community conservation agreements complete with participatory monitoring were already fixed as TNC's goal. Economic activities had already been rejected by TNC due to their unhappy history of failure and backlash. No change in the management plan was actually to be made through site conservation planning, which moved along to the identification of indicators for success and programs for monitoring these indicators.[82] The indicators selected by participants through the seven iterations were an improvement in the health of the important park ecosystems; a reduction in destructive activities (logging, rattan extraction outside the use zone, hunting); a complete stop to agricultural land clearance; and an increase in local capacities for conservation, with popular support, organized groups, and a functioning system of customary and village regulations.[83] The exercise thus arrived at an apparent consensus on the necessity of the conservation goals that were pre-set: buy in.

Further insight into how site conservation planning was conducted, and the presence of dissonant "inputs" that did not find their way into the sum-marized "outputs," can be gleaned from TNC's detailed documentation about the consultations at each of the seven sites. This document, included as vol-ume 3 of the draft plan, was a candid reflection of the messiness the TNC facilitators encountered in villages around the park. It indicates how seriously the parties must have talked past each other as they filled boxes and arranged arrows to produce the results I summarized above.

At the first site conservation planning exercise held in Kulawi in 2001, participants voiced their problems with the park at the beginning of the meet-ing. The facilitators duly recorded the villagers' concerns.[84] Participants from the villages that abut directly on the park reported their acute shortage of land as a result of the park border, absentee landowners, and the size of their village populations. They stated that their best land, including their gardens and ancestral village sites, was enclosed by the park. Discussion of conservation then focused on the activities of powerful elites who degraded the forest by organizing logging and rattan extraction, a situation the villagers stated they would like to see controlled to restore ecological health. Emphasizing the role of outsiders, the participants occluded their own involvement in these extrac-tive activities. The strategies they then devised to abate "threats" to the park included control of logging, strengthening of customary law, measures to limit population growth (birth control, refusal of new migrants), prevention of land selling, intensification of production on land outside the park, and the ban-ning of new gardens inside the park. From TNC's account, by the end of the meeting a reversal had occurred: the challenge to park legitimacy voiced at the beginning was replaced by a discourse in which Kulawi villagers absorbed responsibility for limiting and rearranging their own activities and agreed to police themselves and others to protect the park. It appears that the consulta-tion process produced similar results at Lake Lindu and in Bada, where vil-lagers ended up emphasizing the need for an orderly system of resource management involving strengthened customary and village regulations, coop-eration with park staff, and enforcement.[85]

In Palolo, TNC again reported that participants made their problems very clear at the outset of the meeting. They had a shortage of agricultural land caused by poorly planned resettlement. The villagers were serious: "If this problem is not solved there is a strong likelihood that the people will cut the forest and convert land in the LLNP."[86] This was no idle threat, as it turned out, since the occupation of Dongi-Dongi followed a few months later. Despite their combative stance, the priority "systems" that the Palolo participants identified through the planning process were bamboo, water, traditional medicines, forest, timber, rattan, butterflies, hunted meat, caves, and honeybees. Their list, as recorded by the TNC facilitators, did not include actual or potential agricultural land. Indeed, the participants identified clearing of land for gardens as a major threat to the park, together with poor resource management, problems that should be rectified through the development of village regulations. The solutions proposed by the participants from Palolo included the identification of alternative land for resettlement; the intensification of land use outside the park; increased understanding of the importance of conservation; and enforcement of the law.

In Napu, too, the land problem was "voiced," loud and clear, at the beginning of the consultation exercise. Participants reported that almost all the park border villages in Napu had ancestral land inside the park, cut off by the park boundary. This claim was recorded by the TNC facilitators: "The people are very concerned to reclaim their garden land, or want some other solution to solve the problem."[87] Ancestral land (tanah adat) appeared first on the participants' list of "systems" they valued within the park. It appeared first on their list of strategies: "review the park boundaries," and later "recognize and return ancestral land to the people."[88] But the strategies voiced in Napu did not appear on TNC's summary of results from the seven sites I reviewed above. The summary announced a consensus among park border villagers on the need to devise regulations to prevent encroachment on the park.[89]

COMMUNITY CONSERVATION AGREEMENTS

After site conservation planning, the next step was to negotiate the community conservation agreements (CCAS). The purpose of the CCA, according to TNC documents, was to specify the principles regulating the relationship between people and park. Agreements would be operationalized by the formation of a village conservation board (Lembaga Konservasi Desa) mandated to devise and enforce regulations, negotiate specific access rights with the park office, and participate with park staff in monitoring the outcomes. Satisfactory performance (on the part of villagers) would be a condition for renewal of the CCA.[90]

TNC's legal adviser proposed that a CCA should specify the territory covered by the agreement, the parties to have access, the activities permitted, provisions for transfer of rights (by sale, rental, inheritance), penalties for infringement, the time period of the agreement, and the organizations involved.[91] Thus the activities required were technical—listing, mapping, delimiting, and identifying. Yet the formulation of these agreements also required boundary work of a different kind: the careful management of unruly or disruptive social forces, and the containment of political challenge. This was a difficult task. It was assigned to community conservation facilitators who were to enable villagers to conduct "their own" process while guiding them toward the desired result.

TNC specified the facilitator role in a report compiled after TNC had completed community conservation agreements in five villages in Napu in 2001–2. Ambiguously an account of what had happened and a recommendation for the future, the report highlighted the need to prevent the village-level CCA committee from being dominated by elite villagers who might be excessively paternalistic, or who might attempt to use the committee for their own advantage.[92] It recommended that the formation of the CCA committee, though nominally an autonomous, democratic process, should be guided by the facilitator. Once the committee was in place, the facilitator had to educate its members about their function, which was to explain the CCA to villagers and garner their support. To do this job, CCA committee members must acquire an appropriate understanding of conservation, the importance of biodiversity, the function of the park, and the Conservation Law. The report was very explicit about the role of the facilitators in containment. The facilitators should:

> direct, as far as possible, the villagers' proposals so they remain within the corridors of conservation, to prevent a direct confrontation between their proposals and the purpose of having a CCA. Also, to prevent the people from becoming disappointed. Because, once their proposals have been formulated as clauses in the draft agreement, their expectation for recognition of their claims

will increase. For this reason, the CCA facilitator must understand the Conservation Law and regulations, and must be able to explain them to people using analogies from the natural world, ecology, biology and sociology, avoiding direct reference to the juridical aspect. At present, people are resistant to the formal juridical aspect of the LLNP [the park], mainly because the law is only weakly upheld, not because of peoples' inclination to disobedience.[93]

This extraordinary statement both acknowledged the existence of a challenge to the park in the form of peoples' struggle for the recognition of land rights, and denied that their struggle was properly political. It suggested that with better explanation and more consistency from the authorities people could be guided toward making conservation their own. Confrontation and an explicit discussion of contested legal limits were to be avoided.

When the time came to call a village meeting to present the draft agreement, the report recommended against extending a broad invitation. The reason for restricting attendance was "to prevent a misunderstanding that the management of the Park has been decentralized to the people, as has happened before."[94] An enthusiastic crowd that expected something must be avoided at all costs. The ominous "before" probably referred to the occasion I mentioned earlier, when the ecopopulist park Director made a public statement about social forestry that villagers in Rahmat interpreted as a lifting of limits, a return of their sovereignty, leaving TNC and other members of the propark alliance gasping in horror as villagers began to clear the forest canopy and plant more and more cacao.

TNC's original idea for the CCAS was that each would be unique, a product of village-level consultations. The legal adviser proposed, however, that the main issues were generic and could be covered by a standard agreement. There would be three appendices to the standard agreement: (1) the specific management plan negotiated between the village and the park office; (2) a village history describing the places and resources named in the management plan, an account of tenurial relations, and a description of the relevant traditional knowledge; and (3) a map compiled by GIS at a very detailed scale.[95] With so much documentation, it was clear that a CCA would not simply devolve authority to villagers, restoring their right to use park resources as they saw fit. Their actions were to be directed and intensively monitored.

The standard agreement, consisting of thirty-two clauses, was eventually drawn up by a legal adviser after a two-day workshop involving representatives of the village CCA committees and the park office. TNC, by its account, played a mediating role. Its facilitators had to persuade skeptical villagers that their problems could indeed be resolved by means of a CCA, while keeping their demands within the law. TNC facilitators also positioned themselves as advocates of the villagers, helping them to obtain approval from the park authorities for their plans—so long as those plans fell within the "conservation threshold."[96]

The standardized CCA that emerged from this process began with paragraphs on the importance of biodiversity and species interdependence, and the looming crisis to life on earth caused by species loss. Next, it made a direct statement about the land problem, noting that the unilateral placement of boundaries that infringed peoples' rights caused conflict between people and the Forest Department, putting conservation at risk. There was a statement that some of the park overlapped ancestral land, rights to which should be respected, but no discussion of what this would mean. Nonancestral rights, the rights of the thousands of people who had moved into the park border villages voluntarily or under duress, were not discussed. The goal of the CCA, stated vaguely, was to balance the needs of conservation and of people living in and around the park. Specific clauses imposed limits on use: timber from the park could be cut for collective or ritual use, or for house building, but not for sale. Rattan was to be managed collectively with a system of rotation and replanting, and the edible rattan tips may not be sold. Implicitly, rattan canes could be sold. Hunting of "protected animals" was forbidden, leaving open the possibility of hunting species that were not protected. *Damar* could be collected. Most significantly, there was no resolution of the farming issue. "In principle," the agreement stated, "no farming, grazing, or settlement inside the Park is permitted; to meet peoples' needs, there will be participatory planning with the Park office; this planning will take into account the function of the Park, the ecosystem, historical facts and customary rights." What this clause would actually mean for village livelihoods was deferred to future "participatory planning," although the "principle" was not encouraging. Other clauses specified the composition and role of the Village Conservation Committee, and the role of customary authorities in setting and enforcing sanctions for infractions.

TNC reported that in the five villages where CCAs had been completed in 2001, they were greeted with enthusiasm.[97] It attributed its success to the site conservation planning exercise that had established "community priorities for management" and served "to switch participants on to resource use issues."[98] It had, in TNC's view, constituted new environmental subjects who understood conservation not as a burden imposed by others, but as a shared goal for which they should take some responsibility. Through the exercise, villagers were repositioned as "collaborators" or "partners" who thought and acted in new ways. I was not present to witness the TNC procedures in operation in 2001, so I cannot comment on whether this effect was actually produced at the time. I can report that when I visited the Napu village of Sedoa two years after they signed a CCA, there was little sign of it.

In 2003, leaders of Sedoa were still waiting for confirmation that the CCA they had worked on with TNC had been signed by the requisite authorities. Their plan for managing their customary land within the park, they informed me, was to reclaim it for agriculture—their objective all along. They felt they had been very cooperative throughout the long and time-consuming process of mapping, listing, and consulting. They had also participated in unpaid patrolling exercises to challenge illegal loggers on their territory. They thought it was unfair that the park office had not supplied them with boots or equipment, still less the salary that park guards received for doing the same job. Frustration was setting in.[99] They needed to see some payback. If not, they said they would consider direct action to reclaim their territory from the park.

Despite TNC's strategy for containment, what I heard in Sedoa was not a discourse of conservation but a discourse of rights. "We want to move the boundaries of the Park, so we get back our *adat* land," said one leader. From the perspective of a conservation committee member, "The purpose of the Agreement is so that customary communities are restored their rights within the Park." It was not the limited right to subsistence rattan collection he had in mind. "We will cut the forest to plant cacao and candlenut. The land will be jointly owned, but the produce will belong to individuals. We won't disturb the forest function because cacao is a tree crop. Of course [to plant cacao] we need the cut the forest first." Other Sedoa leaders were equally clear: "If we do not get what we want from the Park authorities, we will not give up, because this is our ancestral land."

According to one village leader, the process of preparing the maps of ancestral land enclosed within the park and the other planning activities he and other Sedoa leaders conducted with TNC had awakened in them a sense of entitlement. They came to recognize that their customary rights were real and they should assert them. Indeed, the detailed history of the parcels of ancestral land enclosed by the park prepared by Sedoa leaders as part of TNC's process in November 2001 ended with a bold statement to this effect: "So this is why the people of Sedoa request and propose to the park office and the government that these locations be given to the people of Sedoa as land that can be used by [us] so long as we do not change their function so they can benefit the people." Further, the TNC process gave the customary council a new role. Previously, issues related to forest access were handled by the village Headman and forestry officials. Stimulated by the concept of village-based resource management, they formulated new village rules that clarified the jurisdiction of the village committee.[100] Thus political challenge was not contained by TNC's process—inadvertently, it was provoked.

Reacting to the claims being made in Sedoa and other Napu villages, TNC again blamed provocateurs. It argued that "the occupation of Dongi-Dongi has cast a large cloud over the Community Conservation Agreement process. Understandably many villagers ask the legitimate question 'If they can take Park lands without punishment, why shouldn't we do the same?' "[101] In TNC's view, the villagers' impulse to seek the lifting of park controls was being stoked by "irresponsible groups," and the "agrarian movement building amongst NGOS in Palu" with its calls for a moratorium that would annul the park or renegotiate its borders.[102] TNC did not take seriously the possibility that park border villagers were reaching their own, dissident conclusions. The Napu village of Watumaeta was another case in point.

When I visited in 2003 Watumaeta village leaders expressed no sympathy for the plight of the Farmers at Dongi-Dongi. They opposed the occupation on the grounds that the Farmers had no ancestral claim. They had no respect for the NGOS TNC labeled irresponsible. They firmly believed, however, that Watumaeta had ancestral land enclosed by the park that should be restored. The dissidence of Watumaeta was not new. It was recorded during a TNC consultation in 2000, in the form of a threat: "If the park office returns the land in question to the people of Watumaeta, the customary council will vouch for security but if not, there is a likelihood of clashes between the people and the forest police."[103] The leaders were very wary of conservation agreements. The analysis they shared with me was acute. "They open up a discussion about the park, then close it down again. . . . You can participate, then there is some new restriction." They had attended a meeting in the village of Toro in Kulawi, where there was a fanfare about a new conservation agreement. Yet they realized, on inspection, that the only benefit Toro villagers obtained under the agreement was the right to collect forest products. Only access to agricultural land, they argued, was relevant in Watumaeta. All the conservation meetings they had attended, every seminar and workshop related to the park, with all their elaborate language and talk of management and participation came down, in their view, to one word: *jangan* (don't). "Their principle is just *jangan*," one leader said; "there is no other solution from the government. There is all kinds of forest classification, but there is no forest designated for the people. . . . They just invite village leaders, but the people who really need the land are not there. So people just listen and say yes yes, but nothing happens." So long as "don't" dominated, Watumaeta would have no interest in a CCA. For some time the Watumaeta customary council had been distributing land "reclaimed" from the park in two-hectare lots, with priority to Napu "locals." The goal was cacao.[104] During my visit the Headman received another letter from the District Head instructing him to stop his people from clearing land inside the park, another "don't" he could not concede.

WHO REPRESENTS?

Collaboration, in English at least, has the connotation of betrayal—of elites or other individuals selling out their covillagers for their own advantage. The "communities" that TNC worked on so intensively in 2001, the imagined subjects of its conservation agreements, are not homogenous. They are divided by class, ethnicity, and gender. Elites in the park border villages do not obtain their incomes by collecting rattan in the park. Thus when they agree to control this activity, they agree to limit the livelihoods of their poorest covillagers.[105] Elite villagers generally have sufficient land outside the park, and no need to encroach. If their land is irrigated, the water-catchment function of

FIGURE 13   Village Headman and family, with the author

the forest may indeed be their priority. Interests in the park are also gendered, as women gain their incomes from agriculture, while men are more involved in rattan collection and logging. Further, village elites often blame the poor for their own poverty, accusing them of a lack of work ethic, an inability to plan, and an addiction to short-run returns from daily wages or land sales. The poor, they often told me, are not patient. They do not want to invest for deferred rewards. I heard this language run through an ethnic lens, when the Bugis were described as hardworking and the "natives" as lazy, but village elites also deployed it to describe their own class inferiors. Local "knowledge" of this kind was voiced in TNC's "participatory" planning exercises in Napu and reported uncritically in a TNC document.[106]

TNC recognized the problem of village-level heterogeneity: "One of the major steps in reaching conservation agreements is the formation of active groups that represent communities in the consultation and negotiation process. There is a real risk of conflict between loggers and rattan collectors and other villagers within the communities should this process fail."[107] It proposed to solve the problem by means of formal representation through a stakeholder approach. Participants in planning exercises and committees should include all social groups—women, youth, rattan collectors. TNC had no way to guarantee, however, that each group's interests would be taken equally seriously. Indeed, as I have just noted, CCAs weighed in on the side of the landowning elite. TNC's model did not stress substantive equality, but rather the need for formal structures which specified who had the authority to make decisions and enforce rules: "True collaboration requires formalized, democratic decision-making structures to be set up based on transparency and effective representation."[108] Finally, and most problematically, TNC described representation as a matter of voice: "If the concerns of local people are not presented adequately by those chosen to represent them, then the future of the Park cannot be regarded in any way as secure."[109] This statement reads strangely when set in the context of the procedures for formulating conservation agreements I have described: TNC instructed its facilitators to engineer "democratic selection" of village conservation committees and direct the consultation process toward conservation, making it difficult for the committee to "adequately" represent local concerns—access to agricultural land foremost among them. In TNC's approach, selected representatives were tasked with covering the gap between people's actual concerns and what a CCA could deliver.

TNC envisaged the constitution of formal "representative" committees not only at the village level but also at the level of subdistricts, districts, and the province as a whole. These committees would each have terms of reference that specified their jurisdiction over a delimited set of "issues." To make this happen, both "issues" and the process of issue identification had to be rendered technical and contained. Yet TNC was fully aware that the identification of issues was political through and through:

> How management issues are identified, and by whom, crucially affects the park planning process. The reason being that the "determinants" of issues are not impartial. They not only identify what the main issues are, but how they are defined, perceived and dealt with. . . . Within each determinant there are different agents or stakeholders and they emphasize different issues. Hence, it is necessary to assess the degree of influence that such agents have on how issues are brought to the attention of the Park Authorities whose responsibility it is to implement measures to address issues.[110]

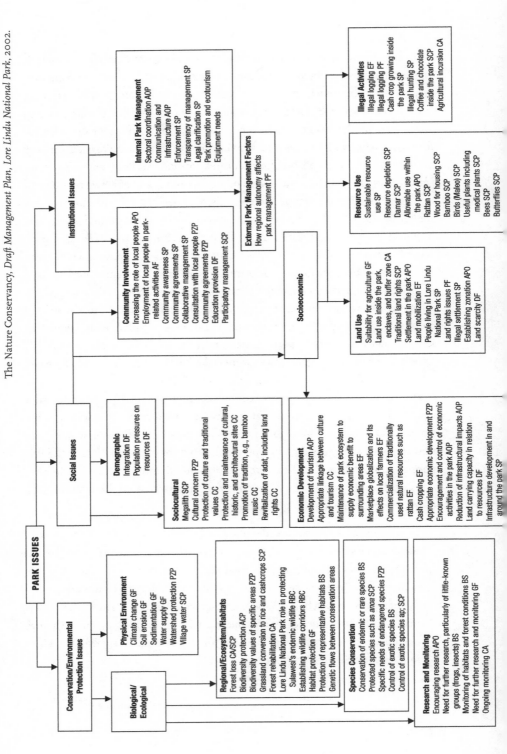

FIGURE 14 The main issues of Lore Lindu Park Management.
The Nature Conservancy, *Draft Management Plan, Lore Lindu National Park*, 2002.

In this passage, TNC acknowledged that the identification of issues was a political process—the outcome of relative powers to determine what was or was not an "issue" and for whom. It simultaneously positioned the park office as the expert authority that would map, list, circumscribe, select, and rank the "issues," and be responsible for addressing them. The will to govern was reasserted by rendering the vectors, relations, and forces affecting the park technical, but the rendering was awkward and incomplete. Consider the diagram that appeared in the draft management plan, reproduced here as figure 14.[111]

In the diagram, issues were listed and grouped in boxes. Flora, fauna, problems, and solutions were oddly juxtaposed. The interconnections between "issues" were indicated by means of arrows. The determinants of issues were identified by a coding system that positioned park staff as agents with objectives, policies, and perceptions, but ascribed no parallel position to park border villagers. Determinants were listed as: Aims, Objectives and Policies of the Park (AOP); Geophysical Factors (GF); Regional Biological Contexts (RBC), Change Analysis (CA), Park Zonation Process (PZP), Lore Lindu Staff Perceptions (SP), Demographic Factors (DF), Cultural Concerns (CC), Political Factors (PF), Economic Factors (EF), and Site Conservation Planning (SCP). Political and economic "factors" were not located by address. Hence the depth and extent of the political challenge to the park posed by the occupation of Dongi-Dongi and the protest of scores of other park border villages was absent from the diagram. This politics was, one could say, present by its absence: it was the "permanent provocation" that brought the diagram into being but could not be admitted into its representation, except as mediated by arrows, boxes, lists, and acronyms. Calculation and technique obscured, or attempted to obscure, the political stakes.

It is instructive to compare TNC's rendering of "issues" in figure 14 with the set of eight problems or "issues" identified by representatives of sixty park border villages assembled by YTM to discuss problems with the park in 2000, a year before the Dongi-Dongi occupation.[112] The problems identified at this meeting were: (1) the boundary markers, (2) abrogation of rights to forest products, (3) enclosure of gardens within the park, (4) illegal logging without notice to the village authorities, (5) nonrecognition of customary rights, (6) poverty that makes the park a necessary livelihood source, (7) in-migration, (8) nonprovision of roads because of the park. For each of these problems, the assembled group identified the root cause, who caused the problem, and who paid the price. They assigned blame to the authorities, but in relation to points 6 and 8, also to villagers who sold land, the village elite, and people with capital who exploited the labor of others. It was an accurate "presentation of local concerns" to use TNC's terminology, but it pointed away from a managed process of "input and buy in" toward a political struggle.[113]

PROVOCATION IS MUTUAL

Not only did political challenge to the park limit and configure governmental interventions, the reverse was also true. Rather than reject conservation outright, there were signs in the decade 1993–2003 that park border villagers were attempting to position themselves within its logic. They acknowledged the legitimacy of conservation goals while challenging the limits conservation placed on their livelihood activities. To varying degrees, they did become environmental subjects, absorbing responsibility for governing their own conduct, and making their future under conditions that were not of their choosing. Several border villages devised their own conservation agreements, some with the help of NGOs but others without. Their agreements contained none of the passages about biodiversity elaborated in TNC's version, but they recognized that some of their own practices were destructive and should be forbidden.

Residents of the Besoa enclave (also known as Behoa) crafted a conservation agreement in 2000 that began with a bold political statement: "We the customary community of Behoa will continue to fight to retain our customary rights to land, especially to our customary land that now falls within the park, including our gardens and our *damar*." The maps they prepared with the help of NGOs showed the extent of their customary land appropriated by the park to total 68,476 hectares. Such a clause could not have appeared in an agreement crafted through TNC's process. Many of the other clauses, however, would be applauded by TNC and the park authority as evidence of an appropriate conservation consciousness: absolutely no selling of land or timber; forest product collection limited to village residents, duly regulated and taxed by the village authorities; no use of guns, snares, or electric current (used to stun fish); no land clearing in the vicinity of rivers and streams; and cooperation with the park office to apprehend illegal loggers on village territory.[114]

The intractable issue was agricultural use of park land, as villagers continued to contest the unilateral declaration of the state-claimed political forest. Park border villagers pointed to their traditional swidden systems as evidence of forest conservation. During a dialogue session with park officials facilitated by YTM, one villager stated: "We move our farms in order to retain soil fertility; we return to the land later; we don't exhaust the soil; we do clear the forest (membongkar) but we don't destroy it (tidak merusak). Our question is, will the Park authorities ever agree to that? . . . We doubt it. We want our customary land back and we will use it our way. We can't be accused of invading the Park when we are just taking back what belongs to us."[115] From the perspective of park border villagers, cutting trees—"ordinary trees," (pohon biasa)—was not destruction. It was the normal and necessary practice of people who farm.

The park border villagers' lack of concern with the conservation of forests led a STORMA researcher to conclude that these Sulawesi highlanders lack systems for customary forest management. "Traditional rules on forest resource use are almost absent," wrote Gunter Burkard, "little restrictions on forest use were developed and no well defined traditional mechanisms to regulate resource use among community members have been created."[116] Villagers in the park border area, he found, also lacked a concept of collective benefit or responsibility. They had no local cohesion and little sense of community or mutual assistance in livelihood matters. Each family took care of itself, and theft of perennials, plants, and harvests was common.[117] They did not fit, that is, with Burkard's model of indigenous people living in harmonious communities deeply in tune with nature.

Yet from the perspective of border villagers I encountered, nature loving was an urban predilection, and biodiversity protection an imported concern. They valued useful species and protected them when they were scarce, but they viewed many tree species as "ordinary."[118] The key scarcity of pressing concern to them was not the scarcity of forests, but the scarcity of agricultural land. As I explained earlier, this scarcity had several causes: the increased population, the closure of the forest frontier by state regulation, and the privatization of significant areas of swidden land planted with cacao. It was access to agricultural land, not forest conservation, that held the key to the improvement they wanted to bring about for themselves.

By the standard of scholars such as Burkard, looking for customary systems of forest management, Sulawesi highlanders were judged to be deficient. Even when they formulated conservation agreements, experts suspected that their motives were not pure. A TNC report noted, for example, that "traditional leaders are attempting to develop Community Conservation Agreements at Lindu, but it is difficult to say if this is a response to environmental issues, or an attempt to influence actions of newcomers/immigrants to the area."[119] Indeed, the conservation agreement formulated at Lindu in 2001 was a mixed bag. It forbade the clearing, owning, or selling of land without the knowledge of the customary council, a response to the bitter experience of land alienation to the Bugis, mediated by village Headmen. It rejected new migrants or the extension or breaking off of villages, in response to the land crisis. It proposed strong sanctions for anyone who tried to stir up trouble between ethnic or religious groups. It rejected the use of poisons, guns, and traps for hunting. It rejected all selling of rattan, *damar*, and timber—a severe limitation on poorer villagers dependent on forest resources. It emphasized that the prime fishing spots by the lake were reserved for the use of Lindu people descended from the aristocratic stratum.[120] The agreement asserted, in effect, the right of Lindu villagers, represented by the aristocratic elite, to act as sovereigns in their domain and to manage resources according to their own priorities.

One important finding from STORMA research was the variable depth of knowledge about conservation agreements in different villages. Researchers found that in villages where the agreements were facilitated by CARE, few people knew that these agreements existed, and they knew nothing of the provisions regulating their conduct agreed by the village elite on their behalf. TNC had a similar problem. Recall that TNC's process for devising community conservation agreements sought to *avoid* large gatherings in which many people would hear about—and possibly reject—the agreement. In contrast, for the agreements that were the outcome of a political struggle in which villagers faced the threat of eviction (Katu) or were desperate to end harassment by park guards for using their customary lands (the case in Besoa), awareness was much higher.[121] Mobilized communities demanding rights, in short, understood the concessions they would need to make in order to secure those rights.

In Dongi-Dongi, many settlers spoke to me of the need to reestablish tree cover and avoid steep slopes and stream edges as a matter of their own personal awareness (*kesadaran sendiri*), and also a matter of public profile: they wanted to be viewed as responsible subjects, able to govern themselves with respect for the environment and the rights of others downstream. Rules the Farmers made against accepting Bugis people or officials into the settlement were equally significant to them. Conservation took its place among other concerns. In Rahmat, after the confrontation in which the forest guards were expelled and the park manager agreed to relax control over "maintaining the coffee" inside the park, villagers formed two groups to manage the reclaimed land. Each group had a leader responsible for distributing unclaimed plots to landless farmers resident in the village, two hectares per household. Like the forum at Dongi-Dongi, they made rules against clearing steep slopes or stream banks, adopting the conservation measures that seemed sensible in the context. They too refused to allocate land to Bugis. Pak Kunjiro—the man who had described how tired he was of being chased about—was one of the organizers of the land occupation in Rahmat. As he explained, "the Bugis already own all the land below the road, they own most of Rahmat, this up here is for us, for the local people, so we can also plant cacao." Restoration of forest cover was under way: "Candlenut grows very fast; in three years it will be twenty meters tall. We plant it every ten meters between the cacao." The Rahmat farmer groups were eager to register the land reclaimed from the park for taxation "so the government will get its share."

By 2003, biodiversity talk had also arrived in Rahmat, in a modest fashion. "You see," said one farmer, who took me and companions from YTM for a hike three kilometers inside the park to see the gardens, "we know how to look after the animals here in the park. We plant something for all of them. Whatever their preference, whether they like to eat coffee berries, or cacao, or fruit, or rattan tips, or corn, or something else—we make sure they have a continuous supply of their favorite foods! Before when the park guards kept cutting down our fruit trees and food crops, it was a bit limited, there was only the coffee that kept seeding itself, but now we can give them a real feast."

CONCLUSION

In 2001, TNC had an opportunity to form conservation agreements with mobilized communities, turning a political reversal into a governmental advance. But it did not seize this opportunity. Bound by its conviction that it alone knew the proper way for villagers to live, and bound also by the provisions of the Conservation Law, itself a U.S. import, TNC devised a collaborative management program that was intended to counter a political challenge. It did not engage with park border villagers as political actors, only as targets of governmental strategies. It interpreted the agency of park border villagers—their capacity for action and critique—as a problem to be contained. Despite the language of consultation and agreement, TNC sought only acceptance of its plans.

In highlighting villagers' agency, my purpose is not to reinscribe a concept of the pure subject, resisting power from the outside. On the contrary, through these chapters on Sulawesi I have explored how subjects were formed within power's matrices. Highlanders were Christianized, educated by missions, moved out of the hills and forests, labeled primitive, made to farm in new ways, intimidated by officials, faced with "choices" about whether or not to sell their land, made to feel poor as they watched others advance, told to be grateful for development assistance, informed about conservation, and invited to "participate" in a micromanaged process designed to consolidate their own dispossession. Much of this transpired, moreover, in the name of their well-being.

My point in drawing up such a list is not to emphasize the highlanders' position as victims, but to stress that their capacity for agency was the *product* of all this history. No one program fully shaped the highlanders according to plan, but all of them left traces on livelihoods, landscapes, and ways of thinking. The forms in which highlanders' agency was expressed were also shaped within these matrices. Thus farmers reclaiming land from the park positioned themselves in relation to multiple fields of power: they asserted a claim on behalf of the indigenous people of the province; they excluded Bugis migrants but they did not confront or expel them; they excluded officials even as they wanted their children to *be* officials; they recognized the legitimacy of some conservation practices and rejected others; they wanted to share in the riches promised by cacao; they promised to fill the provincial treasury with taxes; they wanted be "made orderly by the government," so long as rule was just.

TNC's prospects for achieving buy-in were limited by its governmental stance. It refused to engage in participation in its political sense, as a "process involving contestation and conflict among different people with different interests and claims."[122] It recognized the political-economic processes configuring the claims made by the border villagers for land and livelihoods. It even recognized the legitimacy of their claims: conservation imposed a burden that was unjust. Yet TNC deliberately excluded this injustice from its technical arena and proposed procedural measures to manage dissent. This exclusion was no accident, nor was it confined to the Nature Conservancy. In chapter 7, I step back from Sulawesi to examine a national program of the World Bank in which participation, community, and empowerment became tools for extending the will to improve, and further provocation to the practice of politics.

DEVELOPMENT IN THE AGE OF NEOLIBERALISM

In this chapter I examine a governmental program that came, at the turn of the millennium, to occupy a prominent place in the World Bank's strategy to improve Indonesia. The program went under the heading "Social Development."[1] It drew from the assemblage of knowledge and practice glossed as neoliberalism in which concepts of competition and accountability loom large. It combined these elements with concepts of participation and empowerment drawn from an earlier assemblage promoted by NGOs. It emphasized the restoration of community and had striking continuities with the late colonial programs for village reconstruction and the perfection of tradition that I described in chapter 1. Its aim was to transform "society" or, as one expert put it, to "get the social relations right."[2] Social relations, in this program, were treated as distinct from political-economic relations, too difficult, the experts claimed, to render technical or redesign.

The scope of the program the World Bank's social development team devised for Indonesia was enormous. In phases one and two (1998–2003), it was implemented in tens of thousands of villages across the archipelago, one in three. With its offshoots, it absorbed U.S.$1 billion of loan funds and accounted for more than half of the World Bank lending to Indonesia in 2001–3.[3] Its principal point of intervention was "communities" that had, the team argued, natural capacities for self-management that were damaged by New Order rule and should be restored. Empowered communities, they proposed, would be able to plan their own projects, manage conflicts, and reform the state apparatus from below.

The program's chief architect, anthropologist Scott Guggenheim, was self-conscious in promoting the use of social science. The Indonesia program, he stated, was "among the first large development projects funded by the World Bank to draw directly on social theory."[4] More specifically, he argued that the program was "substantively different" from others because it saw "community-state relationships through the glasses of an anthropologist rather than those of a development economist, rural planner, or an irrigation engineer."[5] Its novel contribution, in his view, was that it did not aim to deliver predefined products—so many bridges, or kilometers of road. It offered, rather, a carefully designed process for planning and managing projects, and placed that process in the hands of villagers. From the perspective of its designers, the program supported "development plans made and approved by communities."[6] This did not mean that the program merely responded to villagers' desires. Rather, like the other governmental interventions I have described, the village level planning process devised by the bank, backed by its rule books, monitors, and auditing devices, was designed to *shape* desires and act on actions, setting the conditions so that people would behave as they ought.

My goal in this chapter is not to evaluate the program in terms of its effects. To do this would require the empirical examination of what happened as the program intersected with diverse forces across the archipelago—a significant research project beyond my current scope. My focus is on the program's rationale, its diagnoses, its calculations, and its tactics. I set this rationale in relation to the program's constitutive exclusions—the political-economic relations that were excluded from the program's knowable, technical domain, yet shaped what the program became. What, I ask, was the chain of reasoning by which the bank's social development team came to link poverty reduction to improved transparency in village level planning? How did they conclude that the violence currently besetting the Indonesian countryside could be averted by analyzing conflict pathways and instituting new "rules of the game"? These are questions that merit critical scrutiny, not least because the program pioneered by the bank in Indonesia was quickly declared "best practice" and replicated.[7] By 2005, there were clones of the program in the Philippines, East Timor, and Afghanistan.[8] Indeed, this eventuality was anticipated by the program designers in 2001, who spotted its potential to become a "Golden Arches" or "franchise" model.[9] In Aceh after the 2004 tsunami, the bank's program was one of the primary vehicles for aid delivery not only by the bank, but by several bilateral donor agencies that contributed their own funds.[10] How, then, did this program come to be?

I start my analysis by situating the program in the assemblage I call, following Nikolas Rose, "government through community." I explain its surprising affinities with neoliberalism. Then I describe the conjuncture in Indonesia post-Suharto when donor attention was focused on deficiencies in civil society, failures of governance, and the search for interventions to correct them. I outline the neoliberal strategy adopted by the bank, one that sought to foster responsibility and competition. In later sections I examine the World Bank social development program in detail. To end, I return to the world this program attempted to transform, in order to reflect on the program's exclusions and its limits.

GOVERNMENT THROUGH COMMUNITY

"In the institution of community," writes Nikolas Rose, "a sector is brought into existence whose vectors and forces can be mobilized, enrolled, deployed in novel programmes and techniques which encourage and harness active practices of self-management and identity construction, of personal ethics and collective allegiances."[11] Government through community, Rose stresses, creates something new. It is not concerned simply with imposing state control over a given sociospatial arena such as a remote village or urban slum, in the manner explored by James Scott.[12] Rather, community becomes a way of making collective existence "intelligible and calculable." Issues are "problematized *in terms of* features of communities and their strengths, cultures, pathologies." Solutions take the form of acting upon community dynamics.[13]

At the heart of government through community is a paradox. Rose puts it thus: "community is to be achieved, yet the achievement is nothing more than the birth-to-presence of a form of being which pre-exists."[14] Community is assumed to be natural, yet it needs to be improved. Communities are said to have the secret to the good life (equitable, sustainable, authentic, democratic— however the good is being defined), yet experts must intervene to secure that goodness and enhance it. To contain the paradox, attempts to govern through community often elide what currently exists with the improved versions being proposed, making it unclear whether talk of community refers to present or future forms. They locate the model for the perfected community in an imagined past to be recovered, so that intervention merely restores community to its natural state. Or they argue that they are not introducing something new, merely optimizing what is naturally present. Even when the object of desire—the authentic, natural community—is found to be intact, experts on community argue that it is vulnerable to degeneration because it lacks the capacity to manage change. It is the paradox of community that makes it an exemplary site for governmental intervention: trustees do not direct or dominate, yet they always have work to do.

Elements of this governmental assemblage, and this paradox, were already operative in the colonial period. In Indonesia, as I explained, officials attempted to reconstruct the Javanese village and preserve customary communities while also perfecting them in ways that experts prescribed. In both these cases the attempt was made to build upon existing social forms rather than replace them in toto. Innovation was presented—and indeed imagined—as restoration of a natural or ancient state. The objective was to optimize social relations for their intrinsic worth, and as vehicles for meeting other goals.

Although the theme of loss of community and the need to remake it appeared repeatedly in both metropoles and colonies from the nineteenth century onward, Rose cautions that "the community appealed to is different in different cases: differently spatialized and differently temporized."[15] In the governmentalization of community under neoliberalism in Euro-America at the turn of the millennium, he argues, the community referred to is "not primarily a geographic space, a social space, a sociological space or a space of services, although it may attach itself to any or all such spatializations. It is a moral field binding persons into durable relations. It is a space of *emotional relationships* through which *individual identities* are constructed through their bonds to *micro-cultures* of values and meanings."[16] It emerged as neoliberal regimes moved away from the idea that they had the responsibility or the capacity to define the good life and shape the citizenry according to an overall plan.[17] Instead, populations were reimagined as forming so many natural communities—ethnic, religious, linguistic, territorial, professional, ideological, gendered, aged, and lifestyle-based. Such communities were assumed to regulate the behavior of their members according to their own values. Thus the task of government shifted. It was no longer to plan but to enable, animate, and facilitate. It was to devise appropriate constitutional frameworks for recognizing diverse communities, then set them free to find their own destiny within a strategic field Rose describes as autonomization and responsibilization.[18]

In the same period, development regimes in the global South shared the frustrations of the Euro-American regimes described by Rose: the perceived failure of state planning, social engineering, and the comprehensive management of political and economic life. This conjuncture stimulated interest in community as a self-generating formation capable of governing itself. Communities of various kinds were made up, autonomized, and responsibilized.[19] In the distinctly neoliberal formulation of the World Bank, communities of poor people were encouraged to take on responsibility for their own improvement by engaging with markets, learning how to conduct themselves in competitive arenas, and making appropriate choices.

To govern through community requires that community be rendered technical. It must be "investigated, mapped, classified, documented, interpreted."[20] It takes expertise to reveal a community's characteristics through specialized techniques. In the global North, favored techniques in the 1990s were attitude surveys and focus groups, the latter used initially as a tool for market research. In the global South, beginning in the 1980s, the arch-technique for knowing "local" communities and rendering them technical was participatory rural appraisal (PRA). This technique both assumed and constructed communities as bounded units. It invited communities to reveal their geographies, histories, livelihood strategies, and institutions in the form of maps, diagrams, charts, and lists, using templates experts supplied. The technique screened out the role of prices, laws, and militaries. If these forces appeared at all, it was in the surreal and disembodied form of arrows pointing in from the edges of the village maps or diagrams taped to the walls of meeting halls after a participatory planning meeting. They could not take center stage. Instead, PRA directed people to turn to their own communities to solve their own problems, presumed to be preeminently local in origin. Its premise was that people who were stimulated to reflect on the (containerized, local) conditions of their lives would arrive at new understandings that "*empower* the poor as social actors to embark on locally managed change."[21] Through the same exercise officials, development consultants and other high-status outsiders were expected "to gain satisfaction, fulfillment and even fun, from disempowering themselves and empowering others."[22] In PRA the process of consultation was itself the principal intervention. It was designed to foster new desires from which new conduct would follow. It simultaneously made up communities, responsibilized them, and emphasized their autonomy.

Groups were another form of community in the global South rendered technical in the 1990s. The exchange between two people chatting informally about a water distribution problem as they walk home from the fields, approaching the topic indirectly and in a joking manner because they are kin and want to avoid a fight, may be critical to the management of water in their village. But informal practices of this kind, embedded as they are in finally calibrated and intimate relationships, can barely be described, let alone improved. To construct an arena of intervention, experts had to identify or create groups that could hold meetings and prepare plans. Only then could social forces be enrolled and calculations applied. In this spirit, groups were made visible, formalized, and improved where they already existed, crafted where they were absent, or resuscitated where they were disappearing.[23] They could then be funded, counted, evaluated, licensed, legitimated, and replicated on an industrial scale. In 2001, development experts enthusiastically announced "remarkable advances in group formation" resulting in "some 408,000 to 478,000 groups emerging with 8.2–14.3 million members in watershed, irrigation, microfinance, forest, and integrated pest management, and for farmers' research."[24] They proposed a "new typology" to describe the evolution of groups through three stages, and a scheme through which they could be evaluated and ranked according to their "degree of maturity." The latter was defined "in terms of their potential for self-defining and self-sustaining activity." This was a state to be brought about by combining the existing capacities of communities with "inputs from government and voluntary agencies." Thus groups were envisaged as natural, but "institution building" and "local participation" were matters for experts to arrange.[25]

Not all communities that caught expert attention in the 1990s were spatially contained. Networks also became technical. Development experts examined transnational networks linking NGOs north and south, social movements and donors. They dissected the components of these networks, investigated their effectiveness, their communications, hierarchies, and tensions. They worried over how networking could be instrumentalized, accountability increased, and the "social learning" engendered through networks captured and replicated.[26]

Following the collapse of the Soviet bloc in 1989 and the demise of some of the military regimes in the global South that had been backed by the United States in cold war mode, civil society at large became the community of concern. Although critics of this approach argued that "successful civil societies develop their own systems and structures, norms and sanctions, over hundreds of years: by and large, they take care of their own strengthening,"[27] civil society strengthening became a domain of expertise.[28] The deficit of civil society, its putative absence, distortion or immaturity, had to be rectified. Civil society became a thing to be designed and promoted, "grown from 'the outside,' "[29] a project to be accomplished by training and capacity building. As civil society was rendered technical, it was bounded and defined. Its components were listed and prioritized according to both moral criteria (what was to be supported or rejected) and instrumental ones—which components of civil society had the capacity to be effective in pursuit of specified ends.[30] Experts devised techniques for improvement and set them out in detail, manual-style, complete with diagrams, lists, classificatory schemes, alternate strategies, and instructions.[31]

Donor programs to improve civil society were extraordinarily ambitious. Their target was not just delinquent components of the population (farmers, women, the poor, for example) but "society" imagined as a whole. Experts constructed a model of society made up of three sectors—state, market, and civil society—and set about reforming each of these "sectors" internally and brokering the relations between them. They made plans to create enabling environments, devise appropriate laws and regulations, facilitate dialogue, and foster processes of consultation. They monitored the performance of the state apparatus and they monitored "civil society organizations" to ensure they were accountable to their members, especially given the risk that donor funding would attract unscrupulous leaders.[32] Yet in the attempt to optimize what was naturally present, the paradox of government through community reemerged. There was a risk of governing too much—a tension amply reflected in donor attempts to rebuild civil society in Indonesia after Suharto's resignation in 1998.

In the era of *reformasi*, as donors initiated programs to strengthen civil society, they stepped up their sponsorship of NGOs, renamed "civil society organizations." Yet they soon became aware of the limitations of the "NGO sector" as a vehicle for reform. New Order practices and perceptions proved intransigent, as did New Order officials, many of whom still held key positions. Hans Antlöv, civil society specialist at the Ford Foundation in Jakarta, pointed to a further problem: the risk that donor support for civil society would undermine its authenticity. Donor money brought with it the power to set agendas, create new practices, and decide whose causes would be supported. NGOs, Antlöv noted, were "subject to training modules from a long string of donors, seeing this as a means to amplify public voice and encourage democratization."[33] Yet they still lacked the characteristics he attributed to a *genuine* civil society: "A critical consciousness to act politically: to build constituencies, engage the public in debates, formulate and disseminate alternative public policies, discuss ideologies, search for broader consensus, find middle grounds, compromise, innovate."[34]

The paradox of government through community ran deep. Even as Antlöv argued that political engagement had to come from within society, he identified lists of deficiencies and offered expert advice. NGOs, he wrote, needed "internal governance structures," their "own accountability" and "self-certification." The "pattern between NGOs and mass organizations must change. And what must happen is that autonomous mass organizations must be created, and be let to operate independently from NGOs" but only after they have been "trained and thoroughly facilitated." They "must focus their attention more explicitly on pluralism and tolerance."[35] Thus he outlined techniques for creating a civil society that would be autonomous, self-limiting, critical, constructive, virtuous, and politically engaged, while arguing that in a genuine civil society, these qualities were naturally present.[36]

The Ford Foundation and other donors promoted stakeholder forums and worked toward strengthening the village development councils that were given a prominent role in the context of legislation for administrative and fiscal decentralization that went into effect in 2001. Donors saw these forums and village councils as vehicles to promote political engagement among citizens at the local level. The goal of "deliberative processes," according to Antlöv, was to "redress basic power relations within society by giving the poor and disadvantaged a voice."[37] But Antlöv did not explain how formal equality—voice—would relate to substantive equality or how it could "redress basic power relations." According to one expert in stakeholder techniques, their purpose is to define "how a society composed of formally equal citizens could be ordered so that those having access to more political resources, luck or talent would not use their advantages to exploit others weaker than themselves."[38] Where, I have to ask, can we find this world of "formally equal citizens" in which exploitation stems from variable luck or talent? I have yet to encounter such a world in Indonesia, or anywhere else for that matter. Antlöv admitted as much. Indonesia's elites, he wrote, were "not willing to empower and trust the citizens" and were not ready to "abolish state patronage and give up their privileged access to power and resources."[39] "Local politics," he further observed, was saturated by the "political economy of global-state-local relations," and "contentious issues of power, class, gender and ethnicity."[40]

It was in this context that the program designed by the World Bank's social development team took up the challenge confronting donors who wanted to empower the poor and create a vibrant civil society. The bank team took a different approach. It did not focus on "civil society organizations" (NGOS, social movements) already diagnosed as inauthentic, but on society at large, especially the rural poor in tens of thousands of villages. Further, the bank program linked the empowerment of villagers directly to the bank's mandate of poverty reduction. It did so, however, in a way that excluded the saturated sites of political-economic contention Antlöv had observed and reposed the matter of poverty in technical terms.

Poverty, the bank team argued, was "actively maintained by the difficult and almost non-existent access that communities have to higher level decision-making on development priorities and resources; the formal bottom up planning mechanism is ineffective and non-responsive to community needs; government gives neither incentives nor rewards for communities with good organizing performance."[41] Although the team did not suggest that inadequate planning and failures of governance were the *only* source of poverty, they were the only sources taken up in the team's very large and expensive anti-poverty program. The screening out of refractory relations—unequal relations of production and appropriation foremost among them—was intrinsic to the construction of communities as sites of improvement. Village welfare, the team declared, was linked to the "ability to influence investment decisions and set community priorities" through "deliberative institutions—public discussion and exchange," which enabled people to evaluate alternatives and make choices.[42] One bank study noted that villagers were relatively successful in solving problems of a social nature, especially those within their local arena, but "economic factors are largely beyond villagers' control."[43] Taking the lead, it would seem, from villagers, the bank team set unsolvable economic problems aside and focused on planning.

The team conducted detailed ethnographic studies of village life and came to the conclusion that the corruption, greed, and paternalism of the New Order regime had been deeply damaging. The New Order's imposed consensus, backed by a rhetoric of family, had made contestation illegitimate. It caused previously cohesive, capable, creative rural communities to become disorganized. Villagers had become passive, ignorant of their rights, accustomed to corruption, and diminished in their capacity to mobilize their own resources. Yet, according to the team, the villagers' still-extant cultural norms and the natural cohesion that stems from physical proximity and smallness of scale offered the prospect that self-managing communities could be restored. Further they could, in Rose's words, be "mobilized, enrolled, deployed in novel programmes and techniques." Specifically, the team proposed that restored rural communities could provide the backbone of an invigorated civil society that would exemplify good governance in autonomous local institutions and practices.[44] The discursive framing of rural communities as capable but impaired renewed the attempt to govern through community initiated in the late colonial period. The distinctive feature of the bank's approach to community, a century on, was the neoliberal stress on competition and choice, key themes of the bank's "Country Assistance Strategy."

THE COUNTRY ASSISTANCE STRATEGY

The World Bank's Country Assistance Strategy (CAS) for Indonesia (2001–3) was phrased in a very different language from the CAS of the New Order. It explicitly engaged with the problem of governance and discussed the many past and present failures of the ruling regime.[45] These were topics generally avoided in previous decades, when donors applauded Indonesia's steadily increasing gross domestic product and improved health and education indicators, and turned a blind eye on regime-sponsored violence, corruption, and authoritarian rule.[46] The CAS discussed various causes of poverty. No longer was the focus on deficient farming techniques or the lack of infrastructure. Yet critical scrutiny of relations of production and appropriation were still excluded from its analysis. The CAS identified only problems and deficiencies that could be rectified by technical interventions of the kind bank experts might be prepared to supply.

Governance, stated the CAS, was "Indonesia's key medium-term development challenge."[47] Hence governance had to be rendered technical: parsed into its components (corruption, lack of accountability, transparency and rule of law), each of which could be rectified by design. To emphasize that the focus on governance was not an imposed bank agenda, the CAS referred to development partners, including civil society organizations, who had requested bank support in this area.[48] It thus constructed a discursive terrain that positioned the bank not as a coercive force, attempting to use its control over funds to dictate how people should live, but rather as a reservoir of expertise to assist indigenous reformers who had set their own agenda.

The techniques through which the bank proposed to achieve good governance were neoliberal. Specifically, the CAS argued that good governance could best be promoted in a climate of competition that rewards performance. Its approach conformed rather closely to the governmental assemblage in Euro-America that Rose labels advanced liberal, which is

> not a matter of "freeing" an existing set of market relations from their social shackles, but of organizing all features of one's national policy to enable a market to exist, and to provide what it needs to function. . . . All aspects of *social* behavior are now reconceptualized along economic lines—as calculative actions undertaken through the universal faculty of choice. Choice is to be seen as dependent upon a relative assessment of costs and benefits of "investment" in the light of environmental contingencies. . . . And the paths chosen by rational and enterprising individuals can be shaped by acting upon the external contingencies that are factored into calculations.[49]

Indonesia's decentralization program that went into effect in 2001 presented an opportunity for the bank to insinuate calculation and choice at multiple spatial scales. In place of standardized national programs evenly spread, a hallmark of the New Order, Indonesia's provinces, districts, sub-districts, and villages would have to compete for bank support. The competition was designed to direct conduct in quite specific ways. At the provincial level, the bank would "seek to support reform-minded, pro-poor leaders and performing governments, through on-going supervision, project preparation, and sub-national dialogue. Selection criteria and a short-list of areas would be reviewed with the central government, to seek agreements on 2–4 provinces in which the Bank could initiate deeper engagement through consultations with local governments and civil society, and through provincial public expenditure reviews."[50] To receive bank support, that is, candidate provinces must first demonstrate that they had absorbed appropriate values or, better still, had autonomously arrived at a position that was reform minded and propoor. They must be "performing" according to bank standards. Selected provinces would then become eligible for a further intensity of World Bank expert supervision, including scrutiny of their accounts.

Why would a province's senior officials volunteer to submit to World Bank tutelage, or indeed, compete for the role of tutee? Access to bank money was the "external contingency" that enterprising leaders would learn to factor into their calculations. The cas did not stress the persuasive power of cash, however, perhaps because money might complicate the idea that being propoor is a characteristic of authentic leaders, a group needing only to be encouraged and supported by the bank and other propoor reformers in collegial partnerships. It hints at bad faith, dancing to the donor's tune, a problem integral to the project of building civil society. Through the cas, the bank sought merely to assist in the birth-to-presence of responsible, autonomous, self-governing communities.

The attempt to foster competition between provinces, restated and intensified in the 2004–7 cas, was in tension with the bank's "overarching goal . . . to reduce poverty and vulnerability."[51] It was markedly at odds with the rights-based approach to development strongly advocated by the undp in the same period, which argued for higher public spending to meet the health, education, and other basic needs of the poor, with a priority to the poorest.[52] Caught in this contradiction, the bank could not support only a few "performing" provinces. In the CAS, neoliberalism and poverty reduction were brought into alignment by deflecting the principles of autonomization and responsibilization downward. Through its "community-driven development" programs, the World Bank would "empower communities so that poor everywhere have an opportunity" even if they happened to live in districts or provinces where authorities were "reluctant to undertake reform."[53] What was proposed, in this neoliberal vision, was equal opportunity to compete for funds, not equality of outcomes. Moreover, access to this opportunity required conforming to strict conditions—structural adjustment, in effect, all the way down to village level.

Empowering communities fell within the social development team's remit. Before the CAS was written, the team had already devised a program that would give "teeth to the reform agenda laid out in the CAS and Indonesia's decentralization program by turning broad principle into a program of action."[54] The team saw the program, called the Kecamatan (subdistrict) Development Project (KDP), as both a program of action and a policy argument. Their goal was to use " 'facts on the ground' to show that properly designed community empowerment programs lead to higher returns, greater benefits for the poor, and more sustainable outcomes."[55] The team would demonstrate how to do development better. To accomplish this goal, they bypassed Indonesia's existing bureaucratic systems for project planning and delivery. They also bypassed government officials, with the exception of the top level officials in the Central Planning Agency, KDP's official sponsor. KDP was delivered by up to 4,200 consultants supplied through private-sector contracts. These consultants, almost all of them Indonesian, operated as a loyal, parallel bureaucracy, answerable in the last instance to the bank.

The team justified the bypass model in these terms: "Initially," stated one report, "KDP did not allow local governments to meddle much in the project. The risks of misguided government takeovers were too high."[56] Further, the report noted, contract workers were more flexible and could be hired without inflating the civil service payroll.[57] Not until phase three of KDP (2005–8) after the virtues of its approach had been confirmed did the team attempt to integrate KDP delivery and normalize its rules as part of the regular administrative system.[58] The phasing was also shaped by the changing context—very different when phase one was being designed in 1997, with Suharto still in power, than the situation that emerged after 2001 when decentralization mandated a stronger role for local government. In the following sections, I explore the history, goals, and modus operandi of this project in some detail.

OPTIMIZING SOCIAL CAPITAL, OR GETTING THE SOCIAL RELATIONS RIGHT

The nexus of research and programming that became KDP was initiated in 1996 when Indonesia was selected as one of several sites in which to study social capital and test its impact on development.[59] Members of the social development team in Jakarta were involved in promoting the concept of social capital at the bank throughout the 1990s. For them, social capital was a means to engage the attention of bank economists and open a space for researching the social dimensions of development thus far neglected. Responding to the work of Ferguson and other critics who had stressed development's closed discourse and structure of knowledge, they were concerned to show that development discourse could be changed by reformers working within development institutions. Further, a change in discourse could produce new policies and projects with better, propoor outcomes.[60] They argued that their position "in the belly of the beast" allowed them to translate new concepts into project design in ways that were not possible for outsiders.[61] Significantly, from the perspective of an analytics of government, the concept of social capital enabled them to constitute community as a terrain of technical intervention.

Drawing upon Robert Putnam's definition of social capital as the "features of social organization, such as trust, norms, and networks, that can improve the efficiency of society by facilitating coordinated actions," bank social experts used the concept of social capital to identify the social relations that animate communities—relations otherwise intangible and amorphous. These relations, they argued, could be measured according to various indices, correlated with desirable ends such as good governance and economic growth, and subject to econometric analysis.[62] Social capital, in their version, had a feature consistent with the strategy of government through community I described earlier: it was naturally present, yet potentially deficient. Analysis of social capital thus enabled social development experts to identify a new task. They should create social capital where it was lacking, protect residual pockets of social capital from unwitting destruction, and experiment with deploying social capital to new ends.

In the early stage of World Bank thinking about social capital, the emphasis was on quantity. Social capital became "yet another 'thing' or 'resource' that unsuccessful individuals, families, communities or neighbourhoods lack."[63] In later work, bank social experts identified different kinds of social capital, tracked their distribution within and between social groups, and sought ways to promote the optimal balance. Social capital was parsed. It became linking, bonding and bridging capital. Some social groups were found to have too much of one, not enough of another. Too much bonding and not enough linking made social groups too tight—crime families, clans, and ethnic enclaves were often-cited examples. Bridging capital named the vertical links between poor people and the patrons, experts, and officials who, the experts proposed, could be invited to help them.[64] The recognition that social capital in the wrong quantities and combinations had "downsides" opened the terrain of social relations to ever more refined analysis and intervention.

For Putnam social capital promoted "the efficiency of society." But efficient for what, and for whom? Critics of the bank approach to social capital argued that bank experts defined efficiency primarily in relation to commerce. Improved social capital meant more trust and transparency, and better links between villagers and the markets from which they were purportedly disconnected.[65] John Harriss, for example, argued that bank deployment of social capital served as a "very convenient screen" for neoliberal market agendas, appearing to address social issues while leaving power relations and inequality intact.[66] I concur with Harriss that the bank's approach left fundamental power relations intact. Yet I want to take this observation further to explore the terrain of governmental intervention social capital opened up. In Indonesia, members of the social development team were not conspirators, pursuing a covert but dogmatic goal. They sought a number of "specific finalities." By optimizing social capital or "getting the social relations right," they thought they could supply village infrastructure more efficiently, alleviate poverty, promote economic growth, foster good governance, and enhance local capacities for conflict management—diverse ends that, separately and in combination, they thought would benefit the nation overall, and the poor in particular. Theirs was a multifaceted agenda that took them deep into the minutiae of village life. It required the bank to go ethnographic.

THE ETHNOGRAPHIC TURN

The bank team's empirical investigation of social capital in Indonesia proceeded through two studies, Local Level Institutions phase one (1996–97) and phase two (1998–99). The principal finding of these studies was that top down development under the New Order had caused a "lamentable loss of traditional mechanisms of social control," especially at the village level.[67] The studies confirmed, however, that autonomous local institutions continued to exist in Indonesian villages, and these institutions had the capacity to mobilize village resources for collective purposes. The strongest capacity was situated at hamlet level, where physical proximity, relative social homogeneity, and kin ties created "natural" communities. In contrast, capacities were weak at the village level, since the village was a standardized administrative unit that had been imposed under the New Order. Villages were often physically dispersed and socially fractured. Their administrators were oriented toward implementing top-down policies and pleasing their superiors, New Order habits that continued to be intact in many rural areas in the period of *reformasi*.[68]

According to the studies, the main groups active at the hamlet level were formed for religious purposes, social service, or credit. Within their customary fields of operation, these groups "set up special committees to plan out and implement projects and events, and often make regular workplans with their respective groups. They also raise funds, mobilize labor, carry out collaborations and mediate conflicts."[69] These natural communities already had instituted "nearly the same range and scope of projects that government and development agencies" pursued. Further, these communities had "mechanisms that would allow members to challenge leaders and to call for reflective "breaks" should disputes remain unsettled."[70] Thus Indonesia's communities already had—or could have, with appropriate facilitation and incentives—everything good governance and village development required. To rectify deficiencies, the studies proposed, best practices already present in some villages could serve as models for authentic, endogenous improvement.

The studies paid significant attention to the relationship between villagers and the state apparatus. They found this relationship troubled. They diagnosed that local capacity was undermined by distrust, a disconnect between community and state, and the limited space for civil society involvement in the provision of services.[71] In particular, the routine procedures for vetting annual applications for village development funds were inept and unresponsive. Yet the studies discovered positive examples, confirming that "effective groups could take advantage of project schemes that provided them with funds, clear accountability rules and the space to implement their own projects without interference." Strong groups had strong leaders, and they formed alliances with civil society groups operating at the district level. They were assisted by officials, the best of whom already played "roles of conflict mediation, coordination, facilitation, and problem solving together with community leaders and village-based extension workers."[72] The improved model, that is to say, already existed. All the experts had to do was to document it, replicate it, and make some adjustments.

The bank's Local Level Institution studies should be read in relation to the discursive formation of which they were a part. They were part of a development discourse that is, as Ferguson pointed out, sui generis. Their purpose was not to increase the stock of scholarly knowledge. It was to diagnose deficiencies and delineate a technical field. The findings had a project telos. They were simultaneously the product of empirical research and blueprints for KDP. Indeed, the first phase of KDP was well into the planning stage before the findings of the first study were compiled, so the writing was in part a retrospective justification for interventions already under way. The problems identified were those for which the social development team had, or was attempting to devise, technical solutions. More specifically, as I noted earlier, the governmental strategy that works through community requires that authentic, capable communities still exist, or can be restored. This feature enables experts to position themselves as midwives, assisting in the birth-to-presence of natural communities, rather than as ethnocentric outsiders imposing their views about how Indonesian villagers should live. For this reason, the studies had to confirm the presence of actually existing community capacity. This finding, from the team's perspective, also set their initiative apart from standard rural development projects that failed to respect village ways.[73]

The tight relation between what the studies researched and the kinds of solutions they anticipated yielded the conclusion that the way for villagers to improve their condition was by reforming local-level governance, beginning with improved planning and control of projects and resources close to home. The fact that villagers were indeed dissatisfied with the existing project planning system was duly confirmed through focus group discussions.[74] The policy argument embedded in KDP, neoliberal through and through, was that improved well-being was within the grasp of responsible communities that made appropriate choices.

THE KECAMATAN DEVELOPMENT PROJECT (KDP)

The design for KDP responded to the problems identified by, and indeed already implicit in, the Local Level Institution studies. Its objective was not only to alleviate poverty but also to inculcate habits of transparency, accountability, and efficiency. These were the habits empowered rural communities should adopt to govern themselves and should also demand of officials at supralocal levels. Yet popular demand for accountability, the team recognized, had to be created. Their ethnographic studies showed that too many rural Indonesians passively maintained New Order routines. They opted for stability, loyalty, and customary standards of acceptable behavior, including the diversion of a share of project resources to officials.[75] Their resistance to the abuse of power was indirect. It took the form of avoiding contact with official programs and refusing to hold village office or pay village fees.[76] Yet according to the team's studies, villagers behaved differently when they had contributed their own labor and resources to hamlet-based collective endeavors, or when they were given clear control over funds and the right to decide on their own priorities.[77] The desire for accountability, the experts concluded, could be stimulated by project design and clear "rules of the game," a central feature of KDP.[78]

The template for KDP was simple. It provided block grants of U.S.$60,000 to U.S.$110,000 to subdistricts where a committee adjudicated between competing proposals for infrastructure projects (local roads, water, irrigation) or for small enterprise credit proposed by groups of villagers.[79] A quota of the projects had to come from groups of women. Poorer subdistricts were given priority on principle and because the relative neglect of these subdistricts meant that modest infrastructure investments would yield high returns. The team considered the emphasis on common facilities to be propoor because the poor would capture benefits in improved transportation, time saving, and water quality. The poor would also benefit from millions of days of paid labor in construction projects, especially significant at a time of economic crisis. The evaluation of KDP in phase one showed that it exceeded its material targets: 31,000 rural construction projects selected and managed by villagers were completed at costs up to 23 percent below the average for state-managed projects, and 25 million work days were generated.[80] Targeting credit programs to the poorest proved more problematic because KDP, following the practice of other microcredit programs, insisted on lending only to viable enterprises with limited credit risk who could pay market interest rates. Repayment of loans was also low (45 percent).[81]

As the social development team stressed, the innovations of KDP lay not in its activities, rural infrastructure and credit, which were conventional, but in the mechanisms of project planning and delivery. Indeed, one observer who studied the project in 2002 concluded that the objective to raise rural incomes had actually been dropped due to the difficulty of measurement and "the primacy of the overarching objective—creating participatory institutions and processes."[82] Every technical feature of KDP was designed for a transformative purpose. Project funds were to act as leverage. In order to access these funds, villagers had to subscribe to a very detailed set of rules that obliged them to form committees, hold consultations, and interact with each other in new forums and new ways.[83] The rules were elaborated in manuals, checklists, information sheets, and other documents. They were also presented verbally and reiterated constantly by the army of consultants and facilitators (over four thousand) hired by the project to work at village or subdistrict level, and by selected residents, a man and a woman from each village who received training and stipends for their work on project implementation.[84]

There was a tension between KDP's claim to be building on the social capital naturally present in Indonesian communities and the detailed specification of nationally standardized KDP rules. As Guggenheim observed, "KDP could not function without its operational manual, disbursement system, poverty targeting criteria, and innumerable 'coordination teams' . . . KDP villages twenty kilometers from Jakarta use the same formats, planning cycle, and facilitator structure that villages in the jungles of Papua do."[85] How then did KDP support "local forms of organizing" and "local adaptation and ownership"?[86] The claim came down to the way KDP granted villagers responsibility and choice *within* the project framework.

KDP's structures were designed to direct conduct. Neither the ends they sought to achieve nor the means were up for debate. The social development team argued that KDP's detailed rules and constant monitoring were necessary because of the complexity of the social terrain they aimed to transform. Their ethnographic studies showed that villages had the potential "to become self-managing actors in development programs" but warned against overly romantic assessments. "Most villages are not egalitarian, harmonious units, but conflictive and highly stratified entities with internal problems of exclusion, corruption, and conflict of their own." In view of the high risk of elite capture, procedures must be designed to prevent it. KDP set out to correct the deficiencies of past projects that "simply 'gave' resources to villages with no planning structure for negotiating through these problems" and watched "their funds slip through village fingers with little return for the investment."[87]

The routing of funds was key to KDP's reversal of New Order–style development routines. The block grant funds were sent directly to a bank account in the subdistrict, cutting out the many layers of bureaucracy through which "leakage" normally occurred. Villagers were informed about the exact funds potentially available to them, and they were encouraged to select projects from a menu of options. This procedure gave them autonomy, responsibility, and choice.[88] Each village that elected to apply for project funds had to present its proposal in the appropriate format and explain how it met KDP criteria of being propoor. The subdistrict committee that adjudicated between competing proposals was comprised of villagers, facilitators, and officials. Its task was to select the best proposals, those with the best plan, thereby rewarding "performance."

Once a proposal was accepted, villagers had to monitor to ensure that contracts for construction were awarded competitively, and materials met quality specifications. Transparency rules required project implementers at the village level to hold open public meetings to account for how the money was spent and answer questions.[89] There was a complaints procedure to handle breaches of the project rules. KDP contracted independent NGOs and journalists to monitor the project and publicize its successes and failures. Their job was to draw attention to cases of corruption and to the efforts of villagers to get corrupt individuals convicted.[90] Sanctions were built into the project cycle, well publicized, and followed through. Corrupt facilitators were fired, some officials went to jail, and "nonperforming" subdistricts were cut from the program.[91] Through micropractices such as these, KDP set out to "chip away at the fortresses of monopoly power and impunity."[92]

TECHNIQUES FOR CORRUPTION-REDUCTION

The anticorruption strategy of KDP was not an add-on. It was integral to the objective of the project.[93] Every step in the project process was designed to prevent corruption within the project, and to establish new habits that would carry over into other arenas. The anticorruption strategy occupied a seven-page annex in the KDP phase two project appraisal document.[94] Corruption was also the subject of special ethnographic studies, case reports, and experiments. It too was rendered technical, parsed into components for remedial intervention.

Two approaches to corruption can be discerned in KDP. One approach treated corruption as a problem of culture. The bank's ethnographic studies showed that corruption was accepted as normal. Funds were routinely siphoned as a reward for public office.[95] Villagers were driven to complain only when they deemed the balance inappropriate—when too much money was extracted from a project budget, and not enough shared with other claimants. This cultural norm, the experts argued, emerged historically in the distorted context of the New Order, when development assistance was understood as a gift. Villagers were told they should be grateful for gifts, however small, and not ask too many questions.[96] When corrupt parties were confronted, KDP studies showed that villagers were mainly interested in having the money returned so the project could be completed. They were not interested in prosecution or other forms of punishment.[97]

To the bank's social development team, the finding that corruption was accepted by villagers flagged a problem in need of correction. They proposed that KDP village facilitators should attempt to change defective cultural precepts through moral argument, explaining to villagers why corruption should not be tolerated. They should discuss corruption openly and consistently, and "shine a bright light" wherever it occurred.[98] Nikolas Rose describes this strategy as "throwing a web of visibilities, or public codes and private embarrassments over personal conduct," adding "we might term this *government through the calculated administration of shame*."[99] For the strategy to work in Indonesia's villages, it was necessary to create the conditions in which perpetrators did in fact experience shame. Such conditions, the bank experts thought, might already exist in embryonic form. They tasked ethnographic researchers to identify "key opinion makers, channels of information, and the forums where communities discuss among themselves local forms of anti-corruption action."[100] Once these makers, channels, and forums were identified, they could be optimized to achieve the results—transparency, empowerment—desired not only by outsiders, in this case the bank, but also by communities already engaged in anticorruption action of their own. Ethnographic thick description of corruption cases could also be used to reveal how social norms entered into incentive structures.[101]

In addition to researching norms and practices related to corruption, bank corruption experts recommended teaching villagers techniques to reformat their local knowledge as a tool of surveillance. KDP's village facilitators should be trained to map local power structures, record the names of key players such as village office holders and elite families, and list their kinship and other links. In this way, the practice of tracking power and making networks explicit—a standard research tool of anthropologists—would be devolved. Responsible villagers would learn to reveal to themselves the workings of power in their own communities, and would be able to devise preemptive measures finely tuned to local details. They should also forward information of this kind to subdistrict level facilitators, who could use it to reduce opportunities for elite manipulation and capture.[102]

The second approach to corruption in KDP treated it as a problem of rational choice. From this perspective, corruption is not a personal failing. It is a rational response to a given structure of incentives and disincentives.[103] It occurs wherever the benefits of corruption outweigh the costs, or, from the victims' perspective, the costs of protest outweigh the benefits. In this spirit, a bank social research expert analyzed the cost-benefit equations for each step of the KDP process for the different parties involved. Based on the findings, the consultant proposed adjustments to the reward structure to close loopholes, increase the risks, and reduce the benefits from corrupt behavior to the point where such behavior would no longer be rational.[104]

Bank experts also worked on changing the cost-benefit equation from the perspective of the victims. Their studies showed that the victims of corruption often had quite complete knowledge about how, when, and by whom project resources were stolen, but the costs of protest were too high for them to use the information. Costs included harassment or intimidation by the perpetrators or by police and other officials; being accused of giving the village a bad name, reducing the prospect of receiving development funds in future; the cost of transportation to make repeated visits to the city to present information to the police and prosecutors; and time and energy spent in a legal process that few villagers believed would produce any result. To change this equation, the bank team experimented with the use of informal or customary settlement procedures, which they thought might be more effective and less costly for the complainant, both socially and financially.[105] Researchers also documented cases where "poor people have been able to use the justice system successfully to defend their interests and rights." From this analysis, they identified the enabling conditions for successful village action and devised schemes to replicate them.[106] KDP also piloted a program of legal assistance to support village groups wishing to take a corruption case to court. In its usual comprehensive fashion, the team set guidelines for legal aid lawyers, who should be volunteers committed to public service, not individuals seeking private gain. They should abide by agreed "rules of the game," which included breaking from the customary practice of paying off the judges.[107]

An experiment designed to test the cost-effectiveness of alternative techniques to reduce corruption within KDP was perhaps the most explicit example of the social development team's commitment to honing techniques to reform society with economy and efficiency. The experiment posed this question: if good governance is to be the product, what is the most efficient way to produce it? To answer the question, the team proposed controlled tests of four anticorruption methods, to be run in 2,500 to 3,000 villages, the results to be measured by statistical analysis. The methods were: (1) generating more attendance at project meetings, to test whether more participation resulted in better projects; (2) an anonymous complaint system, to reduce the social costs of complaint and risk of intimidation; (3) offering incentives for high-quality, low-budget projects; and (4) undertaking superintensive audits, to see whether the costs of auditing were balanced by better outcomes.[108]

BRAVE NEW WORLDS?

KDP's design was unabashedly governmental. It set conditions to reform desires and act on actions. It exemplified not just the will to improve but the will to empower, and a highly developed strategy for bringing its version of empowerment to millions of rural Indonesians. In terms of reformed desires, it claimed some evidence of success, as villagers started to demand efficiency, effectiveness, and accountability from the state apparatus, augmenting transformation through a "multiplier effect."[109] Yet the "true test of KDP's success or failure," according to team leader Scott Guggenheim, would be the carryover of changes introduced by the project "into other areas of community decision making."[110] Since KDP was designed to transform society, the uptake of its practices and ideas, rather than the number of bridges built or funds dispersed, would be the crucial criterion.

As a quantitative measure of uptake, KDP anticipated that project procedures that had proven effective would be packaged and sold. The goal—becoming a reality by phase three—was for KDP to become a "Golden Arches" or "franchise" model in which "participating districts would 'buy' the rule book and staff training/management procedures . . . with the project funding the full cost of the technical assistance, but a decreasing share of the kecamatan grants."[111] A second measure of uptake was qualitative. Bank social experts envisaged their intervention as a vast experiment. Despite their calculations, they did not claim to know in advance exactly what the effects would be. Thus they monitored the changes seeded by KDP through village studies and field visits and used this data to make changes in the program design.

To dramatize the ways in which KDP transformed people's understandings and practices, Guggenheim told a story recorded by a KDP researcher. The events transpired, coincidentally, in Central Sulawesi where, on "a brilliantly clear morning," a group of villagers spied a pile of lumber delivered for the construction of a bridge by the Public Works Department. They asked about the quantity and price, insisting that KDP rules about transparency and accountability be followed. Unsatisfied with the response, village elders met. The next morning, a "quiet delegation of villagers standing atop a large pile of wood wrapped in an enormous white cloth" protested at the district parliament. They were led by the village head, who explained to the bemused parliamentarians: "This is the cloth we use to wrap our dead . . . and dead is what this project is. We would rather have no bridge and no wood than go back to the corrupt ways of the New Order. From now on we only want projects that involve us in decisions. If KDP can do it, other projects can do it too." And with those words, the story goes, "the villagers got back on their trucks and went home."[112]

I find this tale telling on many counts. For the KDP team, it served to confirm their mandate: rural Indonesians appreciated the project and what it had done for them. Further, the mandate was direct—more direct than a consultation with "civil society" as represented by NGOs or approval by a vote in parliament. For Guggenheim and other members of the team, villagers' satisfaction with the project was KDP's main raison d'etre. Then there was the cultural authenticity conveyed by the symbolism of the white cloth—evidence that Indonesian villagers had absorbed a better way of living and made it their own. There was the meeting of elders that led to considered, responsible action. There was the presence of the village head at the protest, signaling that he was not colluding with the contractor, the typical New Order scenario. The delegation was quiet and orderly. It conducted a protest directed at the appropriate authority. These were the characteristics of the kind of empowerment KDP sought to produce. The villagers in Guggenheim's narrative made their point, then went home. They acted autonomously and responsibly *within* the limits experts had prescribed. They were good villagers—unlike the Farmers of Dongi-Dongi, who stayed stubbornly inside a national park and created multiple rifts between activists, donors, politicians, and villagers because their problem—land—was much more intractable than accountable procedures for building a bridge.

Reactions to KDP from the Indonesian state apparatus, and its willingness to take on a debt of U.S.$1 billion to finance the project, indicated KDP's regime-friendly character. Although the bypass model caused some officials to avoid involvement in KDP because it cut them out from their customary share of project resources, others reportedly welcomed it.[113] Supporters claimed to understand and value the participatory, bottom-up process, and wanted to replicate it.[114] Perhaps the officials who spoke in these terms knew how to please the donor. Perhaps KDP provided sufficient benefits for officials to offset the frustration of lost income. Villagers who received high-quality infrastructure projects that met their needs were a satisfied constituency. In the early years of *reformasi*, the repeated failure of state-sponsored development projects was a problem for administrators and politicians alike. Their job security depended upon being able to lay claim to at least some success, especially success of the measurable, visible kind KDP-funded roads and bridges provided. Despite its bypass procedures, KDP was still a project of the government of Indonesia, one that strengthened the claim of the regime to govern in the interest of the people and promote their well-being. Further, as I explained earlier, donors operating in a decentralized environment could choose their "partners," cutting off troubled or nonperforming provinces, districts, and subdistricts. Officials who cooperated with the consultants hired to deliver KDP acted within a field of possible actions that was structured in calculated ways.

According to Guggenheim, KDP in its early phases operated "below the radar screen" of officials, who saw it as a rather ordinary infrastructure project and did not understand the social transformation it aimed to provoke.[115] Alternatively, they might have believed that KDP's transformations would not run very deep, or could be reversed. Thus the threat to entrenched interests posed by KDP was insignificant. After the project ended and its huge and intrusive monitoring apparatus was disbanded, old practices would resume as the brave new world the project aimed to create disappeared from view. The social development team was all too aware of the fragility of its interventions. "It remains an open question," stated Guggenheim, whether reformed village and subdistrict councils "can avoid slipping back into the authoritarian traditions of rural politics."[116]

The architects of KDP were also aware of the limits posed by its standing as a "development" program financed and managed by a bank. It did not, they stated, "replace in any way the need for a more fundamental restructuring of state-society relationships in Indonesia."[117] Yet they proposed no strategies to accomplish that "more fundamental" goal. Instead they focused on the conduct of villagers and their capacities to plan and demand better "development." They continued, that is, to repose problems of poverty and powerlessness as "technical 'problems' responsive to the technical 'development' intervention."[118] KDP's constitutive exclusions were evident in the documents—in the diagnosis of problems and solutions—and also from what was *not* in the documents. The voluminous documentation of KDP included no discussion of how empowered rural subjects might come to demand not only better infrastructure projects, or better governance, but access to land, fair prices, and fair wages. Despite its promising title, a KDP study titled *Village Justice in Indonesia* did not discuss how the poor might change the structures of inequality that surround them. It focused, rather, on procedural matters—on villagers' access to "the justice system" and, more specifically, the measures needed to help poor people prevent corrupt officials from stealing project funds.[119] The exclusions of "social development" also shaped the team's approach to conflict management, a program that developed as an extension of KDP.

CONFLICT MANAGEMENT

In the late Suharto years and into the period of *reformasi*, Indonesia was beset with conflict, often violent, over valued resources—land, forest, jobs, and many others. This conflict took the form of struggles between communities differently positioned through waves of migration, and through processes of class and identity formation—struggles of the kind I described in the Central Sulawesi highlands, which were far from unique.[120] It took the form of struggles between villagers and state agencies or state-backed corporations over state-claimed land. Often it involved unruly officials and the military intent on plunder. Violent conflict of these kinds highlighted the failure of governmental strategies to optimize the welfare of populations. It suggested to trustees that there was more work to do. Yet conflict—especially violent conflict in which the ruling regime was implicated—was awkward terrain for donors. State complicity was difficult to discuss with the "host" regime, still less to address. This was so whether the violence was direct, as in the all-out attack of the Indonesian military against separatists in Aceh, or indirect, when officials, political parties, and corporations protected their interests by employing thugs and arming militias.

State-sponsored violence challenged the positioning of Indonesia's ruling regimes (the New Order and its successors) as development "partners" committed to govern according to law and expert prescription. It reminded donors that the ruling apparatus as a whole, or some members of it, had an interest in defending the status quo. Donors who protested against abuses risked expulsion. This was the fate of the Dutch aid agency in the 1980s, when it criticized the New Order's human rights record. Large multilaterals such as the World Bank, Asian Development Bank, and the IMF could not easily be expelled, but they nevertheless avoided head-on confrontations. Criticism of the regime, if any, was framed diplomatically as policy dialogue. To continue to make loans, the donors had to assume that their "partner" was dedicated to the public good. When the regime's deficiencies were obvious, the key was that officials expressed the desire to change.

The end of Suharto's rule made it possible for both officials and donors to recognize that all was not well under the New Order and to renew commitments to improvement. Eruptions of violent conflict were described diplomatically as symptoms of the transition from an authoritarian to a democratic system, arising in the vacuum between the collapse of the New Order, with its centralized control over the apparatus of coercion and administration, and the emergence of institutions to support the rule of law.[121] In addition to diplomacy, donor involvement in conflict management was limited by another requirement. Donors could intervene only in arenas they could effectively frame in technical terms, and for which they could identify deficits they were equipped to fill. Officials, military men, militia bosses, and gangsters operating as knowledgeable agents but seeking unacceptable goals—plunder, domination, revenge, or execution—were difficult to position as deficient subjects. But villagers experiencing the confusion of rapid change could be so positioned, making rural communities a prime site for donor attention.

In conflict management, it was again the social development team of the World Bank associated with KDP that led the field with careful studies of the causes and contexts of violence, and the identification of entry points for technical interventions. "Conflict," the social experts declared, was "a necessary catalyst to, and an inevitable by-product of, development," especially where "poverty and lack of opportunity underscore the need for change, and where, conversely, otherwise desirable periods of economic growth themselves become a force for realigning class structures and (potentially) re-imagining the basis for group identity." Inheriting the mantle of trusteeship from the nineteenth century, the team's task, as they understood it, was not to eliminate the source of conflict—economic growth that realigns class structures. It was to devise techniques to manage conflict "in constructive ways."[122] Since they viewed conflict as a normal social process, they focused their attention on social relations, especially the everyday social relations connecting and dividing groups of villagers. Their goal was to set conditions under which rational actors would be encouraged to channel collective energies into development activities and eschew violent mobilizations that undermined both security and economic progress.

The team initiated its work on conflict with another series of ethnographic studies. These studies set out to examine conflict in a new way. Rather than focus only on the large-scale violence in places such as Kalimantan, Maluku, and Sulawesi, where thousands died and tens of thousands were displaced from 1998 to 2002, they set out to examine what was happening in "non-conflict" or low-intensity-conflict areas. One of the provinces selected to represent this category was Lampung in southern Sumatra. The studies found that conflict in "nonconflict" Lampung was pervasive, taking the form of vigilantism, banditry, lynching, extortion by armed militias, and cycles of vengeance. They found that the outcome of violence in both the high-intensity and low-intensity cases was similar: conflict deepened ethnoreligious segregation, caused the withdrawal of police, government services, and development programs, and created no-go zones in which there was no investment or economic growth. Unemployed youths, their studies showed, were prime candidates for recruitment into gangs and militias. A vicious cycle linked violence to economic stagnation. They also found that the triggers and pathways of violence were essentially the same in the low- and high-intensity provinces. Only the specifics of the conjunctures and levels of escalation varied. For the team, this finding pointed away from a focus on the unique causes of exceptionally serious violence toward a focus on endemic problems within rural society, problems of a kind that social development experts could diagnose and resolve.

A second key finding of the bank ethnographies was that structural factors alone did not account for violent outbreaks. Ethnic diversity and economic inequality were present everywhere in Indonesia, the bank researchers argued, but they did not always result in violence. Some conflicts escalated while others did not, for reasons that should be explored. Further, they proposed, explanations of violence that focused on structural factors such as ethnicity were out of touch with contemporary social theories that treated identities as constructed and dynamic. Through careful examination of the perceptions of parties involved in violent conflict as victims, perpetrators, or potential mediators, they tracked how group boundaries were realigned as a conflict escalated. It was a finding that suggested a point of intervention: if escalation could be prevented, so could the hardening of boundaries.

Third, the bank studies described violent incidents in ways that helped to pinpoint when and how intervention to prevent the escalation of conflict might be effective. As they explored violent incidents through case studies, they parsed their elements and framed them in technical terms. There were contexts, components, triggers, sequences, and pathways. There were matters of leadership and recruitment. There were alternate outcomes—resolution, stalemate, escalation. This template of factors, derived inductively from case studies, was used to test variables and correlations through econometric analysis.[123]

Finally, the bank conflict studies built on the earlier research on Local Level Institutions and the experience of KDP. They identified existing social capital and local mechanisms for dispute resolution that could be supported, enhanced, and replicated. They studied innovative practices that villagers had devised for themselves. The research was intimately linked to the proposed governmental strategy, to work through community. Once again, the approach seems counterintuitive: if communities already held the secrets to overcoming violence (or poverty, for that matter), why did they need bank assistance? Yet community, as I pointed out earlier, has uniquely inviting qualities as a governmental terrain. Its virtues are inherent, but located in a past to be recovered, or a future to be achieved through expert intervention.

To explain why communities were both capable and deficient, the studies introduced a temporal before New Order/after New Order distinction. They argued that communities were previously less prone to conflict because customary norms were agreed, rules were enforced, and there were respected leaders capable of mediation.[124] These conditions no longer existed due to the mixture of populations and attenuation of custom brought about by migration, and by the New Order's deliberate displacement of customary institutions in favor of standardized, national ones. Yet the New Order's standardized national institutions had not taken hold. There was no functioning, impartial justice system (police, courts) to which aggrieved parties could turn. The result, the studies found, was confusion. There were formal and informal rule systems that overlapped and conflicted. Rules were differently interpreted, poorly enforced, and easily manipulated. For the bank experts, confusion emerged as a significant cause of conflict. The solution they proposed was to craft coherent rules to restore what was naturally present, and supply something new to meet the needs of the time.

CRAFTING INTERVENTIONS

Inevitably, since the World Bank is in the business of lending funds, there was a project telos to bank-sponsored research on conflict. The research was intended to provide "a concrete platform from which to identify a range of possible entry points for crafting more effective local level conflict resolution mechanisms."[125] The strategy, drawing implicitly on game theory, was to establish institutional conditions and provide incentives to encourage individuals to make peace their choice.[126] The language of the bank ethnographies anticipated a strategy of this kind. The studies explored the "rules of the game"—the laws and norms of engagement between individuals and groups; the "dynamics of difference"—how ethnic and other differences were constructed, mobilized, and strategically deployed; and the "efficacy of intermediaries"—their capacity to resolve conflicts, make decisions, and enforce rules.

As research moved into project-design mode, the claim to be merely assisting in the birth-to-presence of that which already existed was revealed, once again, to be contradictory. Local knowledge and practice should be nurtured, the experts argued, but also adjusted through the "application of general democratic principles of conduct."[127] "Outside technocrats" should not be the ones to determine new rules or resolve disputes. Instead, "spaces, incentives, and resources need to be created and sustained by a range of actors that make it possible for disputants to craft resolutions that all sides can own, uphold and enforce."[128] The role of the bank would be to supply the "mediating institutions" and the "meta-rules," or at least the "minimum standards" for meta-rules that villagers would craft within the space the bank's program would provide.[129] The initiative to alter patterns of conduct, the experts stressed, must come from below. Where opposing sides desired to settle their differences, they needed "the resources—human, financial, and administrative—to seek a resolution." The human resources might already exist within communities, or there might be a need for outside facilitators of "high moral and professional repute," fully trained in the latest conflict mediation methods.[130] Mediators must earn legitimacy by "demonstrated evidence of incrementally more significant accomplishments." All parties must uphold agreements and be accountable for their actions.[131] In social life as in the marketplace, the experts insisted, only good performance should reap rewards.

In tension with the stress on initiative from below, the team proposed to use material incentives to "encourage different communities to participate in the process and agree to certain baseline rules." Minimally, they must outlaw violence as a way of solving problems.[132] The proposed incentive package was the standard KDP fund for small infrastructure projects. Of equal value, according to the team, was the KDP process that provided "relatively neutral intergroup forums within which villagers are potentially . . . able to more peacefully mediate conflicts of certain types."[133] The proposition, in short, was that hostile groups would choose to set aside their differences because they wanted access to resources such as new roads and bridges, which they could obtain only if they agreed to abide by bank rules. Bank-supplied incentives would add weight to the protagonists' own cost-benefit analysis. Rational actors would desire to stop fighting when the costs of conflict outweighed the benefits.[134] At that point, all that was needed was the appropriate mechanism.

Grafting conflict resolution onto KDP had risks, as bank experts acknowledged. Competition between groups over scarce resources was the source of many conflicts, yet they proposed to use more competition—well-crafted, managed, and "facilitated" competition—as the solution.[135] Nevertheless, the chain of reasoning linking diagnosis to remedy was persuasive enough for the team's proposals to be turned into a project funded with millions of dollars in loans. The bank approved the Support for Poor and Disadvantaged Areas Project (SPADA) running from 2005–10 with a loan of U.S.$104 million. SPADA's aim was to help break the conflict cycle by improving relations between different groups and communities, engaging villagers in KDP-style participatory project planning and providing incentives to cooperate. It aimed to strengthen local governance and responsive leadership through institutions such as school and health committees, business forums, and subdistrict and district forums involving various stakeholders. It also aimed to relieve poverty and high levels of unemployment, especially among young men, by supporting the private sector and providing an investment-friendly regulatory climate. Success would be signaled by "increases in trust, and the growth of belief that formal and informal social institutions can provide 'fair' resolutions to problems."[136]

BOUNDARY WORK

The bank social development team's capacity to translate violent conflict into a technical problem capable of technical solution was impressive. Yet the team's awareness of the fragility of the boundaries it sought to draw around its knowable, improvable, technical domain seeped into its documents. The processes that were excluded from SPADA—left relatively opaque, if not invisible—shaped what the project became. This is a feature of all governmental programs, as I have noted. What was unusual in this case was the team's explicit discussion of these limits unlike in KDP where causes of poverty unconnected with village-level planning were simply set aside.

In the formal appraisal document for SPADA, boundaries were crossed, then reasserted. There was a frank acknowledgment of the World Bank's role in creating the conditions in which violence had erupted. The bank had supported transmigration and private investment in mining and plantations in the context of the New Order when rural land rights were insecure, legal institutions weak, and coercion ubiquitous.[137] Thus the bank's best practices of the past were firmly repudiated. But the processes the bank helped to set in motion—the displacement and dispossession of countless villagers, the "empowerment" of unruly officials and militias—were factored out of the highly localized solutions proposed by SPADA. The limits were noted: "The bank is not in a position to influence directly the two immediate causes of conflict: organizational and resource grabs by national and regional elites, and the active or passive role of the armed forces in promoting and resolving conflict."[138] Poverty alleviation, good governance, and conflict resolution were the "realistic entry point" for SPADA.[139]

Localism in SPADA's approach to violent conflict was not only pragmatic. The team justified this approach with reference to its ethnographic research, which had demonstrated that conflicts were rooted in the specifics of diverse localities. Conflict reached into, as it was generated by, the everyday practices of village life. The SPADA appraisal document observed that there was no "revolutionary solidarity" in the Indonesian countryside—hence, presumably, no point in thinking about revolution. Instead, "conflicting loyalties divide local groups into violently opposed factions, thus creating fertile ground for the resumption of conflict at what often appears to be minor provocation."[140] For the design team, the important triggers of violence and the ways to forestall it were located inside rural society. While recognizing that feelings of social injustice were widespread, they had no proposal to transform the material roots of those feelings. Rather, the proposal was that SPADA would transform the feelings themselves, replacing them with feelings of trust, cooperation, healthy competition, and empowerment. Monitoring in SPADA would include the use of "tracer methodologies" to track the effects of training interventions on "changes in knowledge, attitude, and performance at periodic intervals." Household surveys would evaluate impacts on social capital and attitudes toward conflict and violence, together with economic and other indicators.[141]

The SPADA appraisal document acknowledged the widespread and serious problem of conflict over land but reposed it in technical terms. It observed that the "land titling situation" was complex, characterized by "overlapping systems of land entitlements." These could not be resolved by SPADA, however, because of the lack of an appropriate national legal and administrative framework. Indeed, as the SPADA document observed, a "more ambitious reform agenda explicitly linked to conflict . . . [which] would primarily have included greater involvement in resolving land disputes" was rejected on these grounds.[142] Consider, however, what was excluded from SPADA's technical diagnosis. The complexity of Indonesia's land system observed by SPADA is no accident. It reflects (1) the ability of unruly elites to plunder resources with impunity, sometimes using law to legitimate their actions, sometimes ignoring it; and (2) a notion of improvement, present since the colonial period and invigorated by neoliberalism, that assigns resources to the party best able to "optimize" their use according to criteria of efficiency and productivity. Further, the bank continues to be deeply involved in promoting "efficiencies" of precisely this kind. The 2004 Land Administration Program for Indonesia proposed to accelerate individual land titling to make land markets more efficient. The program was opposed by activists because of its potential to further dispossession.[143] Bank support for capital-accumulating and growth-producing ventures in forestry, mining, and plantation agriculture was a key part of SPADA's strategy to reduce violence by creating jobs, and keeping idle young men out of trouble. Yet ventures of this kind are often the source of violence, not the cure. They are routinely associated with appropriation of village land. Indeed, the prospect that rural people would be displaced from their land as a consequence of investment was implicitly acknowledged in the World Bank's Country Assistance Strategy of 2004, which recommended the expansion of "export oriented resource based industries" such as oil palm and proposed to support this expansion by assisting with "resettlement issues."[144]

Just as the SPADA document set aside the disruptive effects of capitalism's advance, and the World Bank's own role in setting conditions and selecting victims, it also had a bifocal vision of the state apparatus. It noted the problem presented by "unruly army and police forces" with "commercial interests in natural resource extraction and other deals with regional power holders."[145] Nevertheless, it advocated "a strong state presence to restore and maintain peace in areas of natural resource grabbing."[146] It did not specify the desired character of the "strong state presence." In SPADA, as in KDP more generally, measures to prevent corrupt officials from grabbing project resources were elaborate, but resource grabs that involved collusion between officials, the military, and investors were excluded from the calculus. So, too, was their violence.

REALITY CHECK

Violent conflicts between villagers and state or state-protected mining, logging, and plantation operations were frequent and widespread in Indonesia under Suharto. In Kalimantan alone, between 1990 and 1999 the environmental NGO LATIN recorded 8,741 cases of violence and intimidation related to logging concessions, 5,757 related to pulpwood and timber plantations, 3,907 related to state-owned plantations, and 405 concerning oil palm and other estates. The era of *reformasi* brought little change. The Consortium for Agrarian Reform (KPA) compiled reports on land-related conflicts from various provinces in 1998–99 and documented 18 deaths, 190 beatings, 44 shootings, 12 kidnappings, 775 arrests, 275 houses burned, 307,109 hectares of local gardens and rice fields destroyed, 2,578 people terrorized or intimidated, 14 disappearances, and 1 rape.[147] In just the first two weeks of January 2004, according to a WALHI report, hundreds of people were subjected to "violence and gross human rights violations." In one incident, police mobile brigades hired by an Australian-owned mine attacked a "peaceful demonstration" of indigenous people protesting appropriation of their land leaving one dead, many arrested and beaten, and hundreds threatened and violently dispersed. The police reportedly "singled out six community activists for charges of 'provocation' at the request of the mining company."[148] The main change post-Suharto was not in the level of violence but in the openness, determination, and scope of land-reclaiming movements, and their relatively sympathetic coverage by the press.[149]

In the southern Sumatra province of Riau, a devastating report by Human Rights Watch (HRW) documented the tight link between corporations, officials, and the police who protect investor interests in the pulp and paper industry. In 2000 and 2001, the giant corporation Asia Pulp and Paper (APP) launched violent attacks on protestors attempting to reclaim village land granted to the corporation.[150] Officials interviewed by HRW argued that these attacks were not an abuse of rights. Villagers were simply lazy and opposed to progress.[151] Officials concurred with corporate spokesmen that the villagers, lacking paper title, had "no rights at all" to the disputed land, even the land adjacent to their houses planted with their fruit and rubber trees.[152] HRW disagreed. It stated unequivocally that the land was "unlawfully seized from indigenous Malay and Sakai communities, without due process and with little or no compensation . . . under intimidation by armed police and military agents."[153]

Driving the conflict between villagers and Asia Pulp and Paper was pressure from the industry's foreign creditors. The industry owed U.S.$20 billion, of which a staggering sum—U.S.$13.9 billion—was owed by APP and affiliates. Some of the funds were used to construct a giant paper mill, one of the largest in the world.[154] In 2001, APP defaulted but avoided liquidation by proposing to expand its area of operation. APP's access to "an unlimited supply of cheap wood from Sumatra's natural forests and pulp wood plantations" was previously guaranteed by New Order intimidation. After 1998, that access was jeopardized by protests.[155] Villagers blockaded company trucks and cut timber on company-claimed land, practices defined by officials as criminal and assimilated to the category of "illegal logging." Protestors were met "with violent attacks by organized mobs of hundreds of club-wielding company enforcers, trained by and sometimes accompanied by state police."[156] APP had a private security force on the regular payroll and reportedly paid for the construction of new barracks for the mobile police brigades that supported its operations.[157]

Despite the appalling social and environmental record of the forest industry throughout the 1990s, the European Union, World Bank, and other donors continued to make loans to the forestry sector. They were silent when APP announced that it would double the size of its plantations, as if ignorant of the rights abuses that would follow as villagers were dispossessed.[158] In the case of APP and many others, impunity for the perpetrators of attacks against villagers and the involvement of police, army, and civil authorities left the victims without recourse. It set off a cycle of vigilante justice, lawlessness, and the emergence of protection rackets. Lives, livelihoods, and forests were placed at risk. So, too, was the forest industry: the Indonesian Forest Industry Association reported in 2000 that fifty-three logging concessions in various provinces had been forced to cease their operations due to conflict with villagers.[159] Impunity also damaged the credibility of activists supporting villagers or attempting to mediate. They were accused of being provocateurs inciting people to protest in order to extort money from companies, accusations that permitted authorities to dismiss village claims.[160] Most importantly, impunity drove a wedge between villagers. Militias and private security forces were ethnicized. APP, for example, recruited laborers among migrants, who were more dependent on company jobs and could be mobilized against indigenous landowners.[161]

Thus conflicts that, according to the social development team, arise "naturally" among (idle) villagers are not separate from the kinds of investment that SPADA's planners envisaged as an important part of the solution. Conflicts over land and other resources blur distinctions between state and capital. They divide villagers and draw them into hostile blocks.[162] They are not simply a natural and inevitable counterpart to economic progress, as the bank's conflict studies maintained. Nor do they result from confusion of the kind that can be resolved by recrafting the "rules of the game." They are indeed local and specific but they are also structural. They reflect gross inequalities in access to the means of production, the means of appropriation, and the means of violence, relations excluded from bank diagnoses and prescriptions.

In this chapter, I examined neoliberal strategies to govern through community, a striking echo of colonial interventions a century ago. Bank social developed experts envisaged community as a bounded domain of social relations to be optimized by the application of calculated technique. Through community they would build civil society, alleviate poverty, and manage conflict. They proposed a social transformation that was simultaneously the return to authentic, Indonesian ways and the realization of expert design. Natural communities, they argued, required expert attention to make them complete.

The desirability of the ends sought by the bank's social development programs is simple common sense: Who would not prefer a well-built bridge to an inferior one, washed away at the first flood? Which villagers would prefer to remain ignorant about what happens to budget lines designated for the poor when given the opportunity to hold authorities accountable? Isn't it reasonable to reward performance? Shouldn't rules be clearly laid out and followed? Even if the social experiment were to fail, a tried and tested mechanism to supply village infrastructure at 25 percent below the cost of equivalent infrastructure built through the routine planning mechanisms is surely worth having. If there might be a way to prevent small conflicts from escalating into big ones, why not try?

Putting the questions this way, within the logic of the program, I would be among those offering applause. Yet the benevolence of a program does not excise the element of power. Even when they set out to learn from the best practices of Indonesian villagers, members of the World Bank team positioned themselves as experts who knew the optimal forms that empowerment should take. Alert to what could and could not be included in a "development" program, they focused upon conducting the conduct of villagers, while leaving the conduct of senior officials, investors, and the military unexamined and unimproved. Capitalist enterprise and the search for profit appeared in their narratives only as a solution to poverty, not as a cause. On the basis of their diagnoses and prescriptions, their diagram connecting inputs to outcomes, they set out to transform social relations in tens of thousands of Indonesian villages.[163]

The bank's grid "for the perception and evaluation of things"[164] set out in the CAS and in KDP was backed by formidable intellectual and financial resources. Nevertheless, its traction for differently situated subjects—who, for example, came to understand the problem of justice as a matter of a defective "justice system"—is a matter for empirical examination. The transformations stimulated by the social development program should be the subject of ethnographic study—many studies, in view of its enormous scope. These transformations doubtless include shifts in political-economic relations, as powers and resources are reconfigured in ways that may or may not conform to the programmers' plans. Since KDP was just being introduced into the hills of Central Sulawesi during my last visit in 2003, I can describe only one brief encounter.

In a Napu village, the Headman decided to take advantage of the presence of an anthropologist staying in his house to ask for my help. He had just returned from an information session to introduce KDP and explain how it works. He wanted to brainstorm ideas for a proposal that would be considered propoor. He was, that is to say, conducting himself in a new way, responding to new conditions. But he was struggling to identify the right kind of intervention. "How about irrigation?" the Headman proposed. "It would not help the landless," I replied. "But the landowners are also poor," he argued. "Perhaps not poor enough," I suggested. "How about giving rights to the irrigation water to the landless, or distributing some land to them, so that the benefits from higher productivity would be shared?" A preposterous idea, he thought: no landowners would ever agree to such a thing. I readily concurred. He had already anticipated arguments the committee might make against a proposal for a road to connect the more distant hamlets to the village center—"they would say that would only benefit the cocoa farmers, most of them migrants." And so it went on. He had already concluded that the project was not worth too much of his attention. It required "a lot of training," he observed, which meant many days of his unpaid labor without any promise that a proposal from his village would succeed. He doubted that proposals would be judged on their merit rather than on the "normal" basis of patronage and favors—a conclusion he may or may not revise, based on experience. What struck me was the disconnect between our rather abstract discussion of propoor interventions and the actuality of what was happening in his village—one of many in which villagers were taking over park land for agriculture, a propoor intervention they had devised for themselves. Land was definitely not on the KDP menu, nor on the menu of the Nature Conservancy, also attempting to direct conduct through the procedures I described.

KDP approached economic development as a matter of addition—add a road, a bridge, or some microcredit to make peoples' lives easier and to stimulate growth. Altering the existing set of political-economic relations was, the planners suggested, beyond their purview. Like colonial authorities and other trustees, the social development team had no prescription for eliminating the contradiction between capitalist accumulation and the dispossession that follows in its wake. They supported economic growth, aiming only to manage and mitigate the fallout. Justice became a matter of distinguishing the legal from the illegal, the accountable from the corrupt, the plan that was propoor from a plan that would benefit the rich, the deserving poor from those whose failure to perform made them ineligible for assistance. Liberal ideas about formal inclusion in institutional procedures and the opportunity to compete took center stage. Structural deformities, and the bank's role in maintaining them, fell outside their programmable domain.

In pointing out the limits of the bank's social development program, I am not suggesting that there was a hidden agenda for which the program's rationale was merely a mask. The bank's social development team was very explicit about what it aimed to achieve, and I take the team at its word. The limits of the program did not stem from deficits in their research capacity or understanding. They stemmed, rather, from the governmental stance that envisaged empowerment as a product that could be manufactured by technique. As Indonesian critic Vedi Hadiz pointed out, experts intent on devising optimal institutional arrangements "overlook the fact that democracy, public participation, accountability and social and economic rights are all historically tied to the outcome of struggles of social forces and interests, . . . the product of grinding social change over centuries, colored by often violent and bloody confrontations, not least between social classes."[165] From the way processes excluded from the arena of intervention infiltrated their reports and shaped their interventions, it is evident that the social development team did not overlook these facts. Nor, however, did they act on them.

The will to improve, and more specifically the attempt to secure the "welfare of the population, the improvement of its condition, the increase of its wealth, longevity, health, etc."[1] has been operative in Indonesia for almost two centuries. Practices of government, calculated programs of intervention, have shaped landscapes, livelihoods, and identities across the archipelago. Experts deploying what Foucault called a governmental rationality have sought to manage process and relations, balance diverse objectives, and conduct the conduct of individuals and groups, all in the name of improvement.

My study has focused on the rationale of improvement programs, and the practices through which programmers draw boundaries around a knowable, manageable, technical domain. I have also attended to the limits of government. These are the limits posed by the coexistence of the will to improve with the sovereign's power to plunder and punish; the limits posed by the dynamic nature of the relations to be optimized—men in their relations to floods, diseases, the quality of the soil, customs and beliefs, wealth, resources, means of subsistence; and the limit posed by the practice of politics—critical scrutiny, in word and deed, of the truths of government, opening them up for contestation and debate between people with different interests and claims. To examine these limits I argued for combining attention to the rationale of improving schemes with the investigation of what happens when these schemes entangle the world they would regulate and transform. I complemented the analytic of governmentality with a conceptual repertoire drawn from Marx and Gramsci.

Finally, I took an ethnographic stance that embraced the witches' brew of situated processes and relations not only as a means of describing what happened but also in order to examine the "how" of government and politics as practice.

My exploration of the will to improve began in chapter 1 with a broad sweep through Indonesia's colonial and postcolonial history to examine how different authorities attempted to balance diverse goals—accumulation and welfare, freedom and order. I traced the varying ways they constituted the boundary that separated trustees from the subjects whose conduct was to be conducted. Then I narrowed my focus to the highlands of Central Sulawesi, where, in the past century, a series of improvement programs have been devised by authorities seeking diverse ends. My exposition of government in Central Sulawesi took the form of a temporal sequence that explored how one intervention layered upon another, sometimes triggered by its unintended effects. Each chapter also had a distinct conceptual focus as theory and ethnography intertwined.

In chapter 2, I examined colonial and New Order programs to resettle populations and draw boundaries separating forest from farm. I highlighted the use of violence as a means to secure improving ends and showed how improvement met its limit in another actant, nature. Forcibly resettled populations died of disease. They resumed farming in forests when their assigned farmland proved to be barren, or disappeared in a flood. I balanced attention to violence with discussion of the compromises made by the officials charged with carrying out orders and realizing plans, compromises that created room for maneuver and contestation.

In chapter 3, I explored processes of capital and identity formation that arose at the intersection of improvement programs, the arrival of land-seeking migrants, and a boom crop, cacao. In that intersection, landscapes, livelihoods, and identities were reconfigured in ways no one had planned. The violence that erupted in the Poso area in 1998–2001 can be traced to calculated programs of improvement. Most obviously, it can be traced to the colonial policy that encouraged missionaries to Christianize the highlanders as a means to extend rule, bring improvement, and restrict the anticolonial forces mobilizing under the banner of Islam. Resettlement was also a factor: it unsettled the highland population and made them vulnerable to further displacement. The closure of the forest boundary intensified processes of class formation by

excluding thousands of highlanders from access to the means of the production. Yet my purpose in this chapter was not to attribute blame. It was to show,
rather, how interventions designed for one purpose had effects that were contingent and diverse.

In chapter 4, I examined a new program of improvement that went under
the label integrated conservation and development. I paid particular attention
to the question of how this program rendered its arena of intervention technical. In rather similar ways the Asian Development Bank, CARE, and the Nature
Conservancy screened out the political-economic processes marginalizing the
highland population—processes their own studies had brought to light. They
had a diagnosis, but no corresponding prescription. The outcome was not only
a failure to bring development benefits to the population excluded from the
park. It was to assemble a critical community and radicalize the highlanders,
alert to the defects of yet another round of interventions that promised improvement but failed to deliver.

In chapter 5, my focus was the Free Farmers Forum and their occupation of
the Dongi-Dongi valley, a corner of the Lore Lindu National Park. I recounted
their narratives of the injuries, the broken promises, the desperation, and the
hope that persuaded them to take control of good farmland and attempt to
build a better future for their families. Conceptually, the key theme of chapter 5
was the practice of politics. I explored how the Farmers came to articulate a
collective, critical position and act on it; I explored how they were attacked or
defended by activists and authorities who had their own ideas about proper
conduct; and I explained why it was so difficult for the Farmers to establish a
positioning as legitimate political actors, not merely victims or dupes. The
imperfections of their own conduct—their failure to obey the rules they had set
for themselves—was part of the problem. The other part, however, was their
inability to fit the niche of the "middle ground" in which land rights, indigenous rights, and conservation agendas can be pursued in one felicitous package. The irony was intense. The Farmers' awkward position was no accident: it
was the outcome of a century of "improvement" that had displaced them from
their original land, instilled habits of calculation, and formed desires for education and a home near a road with good access to markets. Caught between
contradictory models, they devised an improvement program of their own.

In chapter 6, the sequel to chapter 5, I explored the Nature Conservancy's calculated attempt to contain the political challenge posed by highland villagers who rejected the legitimacy of the park and its borders and insisted upon their rights to land and livelihood. Through a close reading of program documents, I explored the discursive and practical strategies the Nature Conservancy deployed in its attempt to reshape the desires and actions of park border villagers. The objective was to have them sign and uphold conservation agreements that would consolidate their exclusion from the use of park land for the commercially viable crops, coffee and cacao, and restrict them to traditional but unproductive options. My conceptual focus was the permanent provocation between the will to govern and strategies of struggle, the points at which an opening became a closure, before the next reversal. Further, the ethnographic density of my account, accumulated from previous chapters, enabled me to explain these reversals not in mechanical terms, like the operation of a switch, but as the outcome of situated practices and the agency of variously positioned subjects.

Finally, in chapter 7, I examined a new wave of programs spearheaded by the World Bank designed to govern through community, manage conflict, and set conditions in which an empowered civil society could reform its own conduct and that of the state apparatus. The conceptual focus was twofold. I sought to expose the power relations embedded in governmental interventions that seem, at first glance, to operate in a different register—respect for local institutions, building on the social capital already present in communities, and deliberately seeking the participation of villagers thus far excluded from decision making. I also emphasized the role of "constitutive exclusions" in shaping and limiting what the program became. The bank's social development experts were fully aware of the problems presented by unruly officials, transnational corporations, and ethnicized militias that dispossess villagers and wreak havoc with impunity. They knew something about capitalism's contradictions, and the role of the bank in setting the conditions under which some would prosper while others lost out. But they devised no programs to act on them. What they did, rather, was attempt to improve the conduct of villagers, a task they set about on a massive scale through minutely calibrated calculations.

Conceivably, the interventions I described in this book could be aligned into a narrative about improvement schemes becoming more effective, more people-friendly, and more participatory. It would go something like this. Colonial interventions—the Culture System on Java, resettlement in Sulawesi—were coercive and inept. They caused death, destruction, and impoverishment because they ignored local ecologies, livelihoods, and cultures. New Order interventions were little better. They were standardized, narrowly sectoral, and they failed to plan ahead.

Alert to the critiques of clumsy top-down interventions, the Asian Development Bank's massive Central Sulawesi Integrated Development and Conservation Project was very thoroughly researched by anthropologists, ecologists, agronomists, and other experts. It included components for community development, participation, and microcredit—the leading edge of 1990s development thinking. It failed, one might argue, because it was not executed according to plan. Problems of landlessness and marginalization could have been mitigated if the agricultural improvement and microcredit schemes had been properly implemented, and officials, technical consultants, and community organizers had done their jobs.

The Nature Conservancy's latest iteration, its detailed attempt to consult with park "stakeholders," especially the border communities, could be interpreted as further evidence of progress toward people-friendly development. TNC had moved a long way from the days of coercing conservation and should be applauded for its innovative efforts to secure input from villagers.[2] Their micromanaged consultation process might even work to secure the kinds of compliance conservation requires. If not, then the experts should examine its deficiencies and come up with a better plan.

In the post-Suharto era of *reformasi*, the World Bank embraced participation and empowerment, allocating U.S.$1 billion to a program designed by the social development team in Indonesia. These were loan funds, but loans are necessary to stimulate growth, and the willingness of senior Indonesian officials to take on this debt could be read as confirmation of their support for the program's transformatory ambitions. The program deliberately set conditions to empower local people to exercise responsibility and choice. Trained facilitators were hired to support them, and NGOS and journalists were encouraged to monitor and expose any problems that arose. The program was systematic about eradicating corruption and unaccountable, top-down schemes—fixing the problems that beset the ADB project in the Sulawesi highlands and caused the villagers to take matters into their own hands. It had initiatives to manage the conflicts that inevitably arise in the context of change.

Although I understand the temptation of a narrative that traces the improvement of improvement, I am not convinced by it. New programs routinely retain the limitations of the programs they replace. Critics have already begun to argue that community-based development has failed to live up to its promise. It has not solved the problems of poverty and exclusion it was supposed to correct. Some critics argue that participatory approaches are tyrannical, embodying the illegitimate or unjust use of power to control, co-opt, contain, and manipulate people. The conclusion these critics reach, however, is not that participatory approaches should be abandoned, but that they should be improved by a more "sophisticated and genuinely reflexive understanding of power"[3] or by "more responsive development agencies . . . promoting more effective and equitable forms of involvement."[4]

Despite the promising language, contemporary development interventions emphasizing community, participation, and empowerment still have crucial limitations. First, they pay astonishingly little attention to the character of ruling regimes, which they continue to treat as development partners desiring only the best for their citizens. In Indonesia, despite the evidence of widespread state-sponsored violence and the trampling of rights, donors continue to assume that the state apparatus operates, or can be made to operate, in a coherent and accountable manner in the public interest. Second, they pay very little attention to the power relations implicit in their own self-positioning. The will to empower others hinges upon positioning oneself as an expert with the power to diagnose and correct a deficit of power in someone else. Rahnema puts the point starkly: "When A considers it essential for B to be empowered, A assumes not only that B has no power—or does not have the right kind of power—but also that A has the secret formula of a power to which B has to be initiated."[5] Empowerment is still, in short, a relationship of power. Third, these interventions continue to exclude structural sources of inequality from their technical domain and focus upon an incarcerated "local" in which properly guided villagers are expected to improve their own conditions by their own efforts.

In the 1990s, programs of participation and empowerment pioneered by NGOs became thoroughly mainstream, not only in international agencies but also in national development bureaucracies. In 1997, when I was employed in Indonesia as a consultant to evaluate the Depsos program for estranged communities, I found officials secure in their paternalistic assumption that they knew what was good for isolated tribes and other deficient subjects, even as they clutched their handbooks on participatory rural appraisal and prepared to "go down" to the villages for a development encounter. In Central Sulawesi in 2001, the Governor issued an edict directing heads of departments to encourage "public participation in managing, using, maintaining and developing natural resources" and to make use of the expertise of the recently created Regional Office for Peoples' Empowerment.[6] Optimal development outcomes, he asserted, could be obtained by drawing effectively on human resources, working through customary councils and NGOs, and supporting creativity and initiative. Yet his concern to strengthen communities, empower the poor, and develop their capacities was calculated to produce communities, powers, and capacities of a particular, limited kind. It was not designed to mobilize critical, multiethnic communities speaking a language of class such as the Farmers at Dongi-Dongi. Like the new participatory program of the Nature Conservancy, it was an attempt to switch from reaction after the event to a reassertion of the will to govern. It was concerned with resource management, but not with the diverse ends "resource managers" might seek, or how the costs and benefits should be distributed. It was not an invitation to participate in a political process.

The prodigious capacity of the national and transnational development apparatus to absorb critiques is part of what makes it operate—more or less effectively—as an "antipolitics machine." Although improvement seldom lives up to the billing, the will to improve persists. The endless deferral of the promise of development to the time when the ultimate strategy is devised and implementation perfected does more than enable the development apparatus to sustain itself. It maintains the divide that separates trustees from their wards. It keeps the attention of many critics focused on the deficiencies of such schemes and how to correct them. Meanwhile, changing the conditions that position some social groups to accumulate while others are impoverished remains firmly off-limits.

In the case of participation and empowerment, as with other governmental interventions, the attempt to constitute a terrain of technical intervention and deflect a political challenge is only that—an attempt. My examples from Central Sulawesi amply demonstrate that participatory projects that stimulated discussion but did not take seriously the problems these discussions revealed had the effect of focusing and intensifying critique. Villagers resented being required to spend long hours and days in meetings drawing pictures and making themselves attractive to patrons, for which they received minimal material payback and no serious response to the fundamental problem of access to land. Participatory planning exercises developed a bad reputation. Villagers concluded that experts had nothing to offer. Participation did in fact empower them, although not in the ways the experts prescribed. Communities envisaged as sites for improvement became sites from which claims were made and struggles advanced.

Yet, as I have argued, analysis of what empowerment programs and participatory initiatives *fail* to do—empower people, alleviate poverty, achieve "genuine" consultation, or even contain and depoliticize—does not exhaust the topic. The emergence of this new assemblage is itself a historical event. As Foucault insisted, programs of intervention are not "abortive schemas for the creation of reality. They are fragments of reality which induce . . . particular effects in the real."[7] They signal new ways in which social forces can be bounded and dissected. They make certain kinds of intervention thinkable and suggest new tactics. This is the line of inquiry I pursued in chapter 6 on the Nature Conservancy and chapter 7 on the World Bank. In both cases, though in different ways, *participation* and *empowerment* were the master terms.

The Nature Conservancy declared the model of collaborative management it tried and tested in Sulawesi a new best practice, suitable for deployment elsewhere. The strategy to govern through community devised by bank experts in Indonesia was taken up as a model to be deployed in postconflict or postdisaster situations. These situations present possibilities for radical restructuring that remind me of the high modern schemes described by James Scott.[8] Experts imagine building upon a clean slate not just physically but socially—constructing a new society in which the delinquent structures of the old order will not intrude. The designers of bank programs for postconflict "Community-Driven Reconstruction" propose to use the vacuum in state capacity to instill new practices in communities and in state-administrative systems that, in normal times, officials might oppose. From Indonesia to East Timor and Afghanistan, bank social experts envisage an "opportunity to re-define the social and institutional relationships that led to the conflict in the first place."[9] Note that redefining political-economic relationships is not on their agenda. The incentives that can be offered through bank programs—rapid and tangible reconstruction—are unusually persuasive to needy populations, and also to a weakened state apparatus that needs to demonstrate returns from peace. Under these conditions, ruling regimes lose their capacity to dictate the terms of donor assistance, enabling experts to rebuild society according to their own prescriptions.[10] Yet there is a limit to this approach, as the experts recognize. In a project designed as "an island of integrity outside state structures, there is a risk of low government ownership undermining sustainability in the long term."[11] I was struck by a passage in a World Bank bulletin concerning reconstruction in Aceh: "Don't forget the Government."[12]

TROUBLES WITH TRUSTEESHIP

The many trustees and types of program I have discussed in this book are not all the same. They are variably open to critical commentary by other experts, to observations about the effects of their programs, and to the reactions and demands of the people they intend to help. Yet they all depend on, as they confirm, a hierarchy that separates trustees from the people whose capacities need to be enhanced, or behaviors corrected. This stance is obvious enough in official programs and in development agencies. It is still present, and more troubling, in social movements where vanguards, advocates, and advisers with definite ideas about the proper way to live seek to conduct the conduct of the rank-and-file. Some vanguards argue, for example, that rural people should not strive for inclusion in markets, or seek a closer relation with ruling regimes, or their share of the material benefits of "development," which, structurally speaking, are impossible for them to obtain. They should lead the way in autonomous, authentic, postdevelopment thinking that is anticapitalist, antistate, and grounded in local traditions and cultural diversity—a view shared, awkwardly enough, by trustees of the colonial period.[13]

The ease with which vanguard-activists can drift from conceptualizing utopias to prescribing and enforcing particular programs upon designated groups was brought home to me by a comment made by an activist who has been prominent in the Indonesian land reform movement. He informed me that he and his colleagues were debating whether landless people who have reclaimed land from corporations through mass land occupations organized by a peasant union should be permitted to own it individually or obliged to farm it on a collective basis. I understand why this debate was taking place. It was stimulated, in part, by the finding that some of the people who reclaimed land later sold it and moved on.[14] Nevertheless I was struck by the presumption that movement activists who were not landless farmers had the authority to prescribe the proper relation between farmers and land. Activists in the indigenous peoples' movement have devised similar strictures. They argue that the bond between indigenous people and their ancestral terrain is sacred. Indigenous people who sell their land or fail to prioritize conservation no longer qualify for the indigenous slot. The consequence of transgression, as I showed in Sulawesi, was heated debate among activists promoting utopias of different kinds and the withdrawal of support from delinquent subjects who failed to conform.

Dogmatism in activists, as in other experts, pushes relations of trusteeship toward the authoritarian pole. Ethnographic engagement, exposure to the "witches' brew" of actual processes and relations, can help to alleviate this problem. Many activists recognize that advocacy not grounded in real-world complexities—action in a vacuum—is not only dogmatic but dangerous. I have found the scholar-activists of Yayasan Tanah Merdeka in Palu exemplary in this regard. They conduct ethnographic research, sometimes in cooperation with outside researchers such as me, and they continually evaluate the politics of their own positioning in relation to the Sulawesi highlanders they aim to support. In my experience of conducting joint research with them and discussions over several years, they do not expect to find heroes in the highlands, nor do they search for authentic communities. However sad and dull the facts, however messy the actualities, they are prepared to embrace them. Their impulse is democratic. When faced with questions about highlanders' desires or priorities, or possible solutions to the problems that confront them, they consistently refer to the highlanders themselves. Let's ask. Their way of asking, unlike the managed participation of the Nature Conservancy or the World Bank, is not constrained by the need to devise technical interventions. Their primary mode of engagement is political: asking questions, provoking debate, and conducting analysis that helps to expose unfair rules, greed, and destruction. They focus on issues of substantive injustice, the litmus they use for deciding when and where to intervene. Their media campaigns, their ways of mobilizing people and assembling critical communities, are highly effective. When they helped to bring farmers, fishers, urban poor, unions, and students together in a Poor Peoples' Forum and held mass rallies in the provincial capital Palu protesting land appropriations and the damage caused by mines, the Governor began to pay attention, even as the forces of reaction regrouped.[15]

Vanguards who espouse a generalized antistate, antidevelopment, or antimarket position run into various contradictions. The antistate position is compromised by the fact that social movements call upon states to guarantee rights and benefits, to recognize groups, and to offer various kinds of support and assistance.[16] Where the state apparatus collapses or withdraws, or its functions are privatized, the usual outcome is not peace and prosperity; it is anarchy, poverty, and despair.[17] Most of the villagers I have encountered in the highlands of Sulawesi seek more involvement with the state apparatus, not less—so long as the terms of that involvement are advantageous. In relation to development, they reject interventions that extract their land and labor without an appropriate return. They do not reject interventions that benefit them. When I ask about the interventions they have found helpful, they often mention the major roads that opened up the highlands and enabled them to sell their produce for a decent price. Yet these roads, as I explained, were not built with the needs of smallholders in mind—they were built to service timber and plantation corporations. The benefit to the highlanders was a byproduct of other plans. When I remind them that these roads also brought in migrants, they respond that they welcome migrants and can learn from them, so long as there is enough land for everyone to prosper. They are unimpressed when I try to explain the processes of accumulation and displacement that follow from agriculture organized on capitalist lines. They are quite prepared to embrace capitalism, so long as the conditions are fair. This has not been their experience thus far, as the conditions for secure access to land and other means of production have consistently been set to favor "big people" at the expense of "small people" such as themselves. They reject the recommendations of experts who promote biodiverse, subsistence-oriented agroforestry systems and an ethic of conservation that leaves them impoverished while others prosper. Like it or not, even in the most remote highland areas, I find that the calculus villagers apply is market-based. Experiments with alternative development in other parts of the world have met with a similar response. What trustees deem appropriate for poor people does not necessarily match their own assessments of what is possible, desirable, and fair.[18]

The idiom of partnership that purports to reduce the hierarchical divide between experts and those subject to expert direction does not resolve the problem. Nor does the strategy of government through community, which begs a key question: If communities already have the secret to productive, sustainable, and healthy lives, what is it that outsiders need to improve or fix? The problem has become more acute since experts began to recognize the value of indigenous knowledge and promote self-help. If outsiders are not to supply money or technology, why *are* they there? I find this question routinely asked by the "targets" of development interventions. Patronage makes obvious sense in many parts of the world, and its varying forms are easily recognized, but the endless concern with participatory processes can be mystifying and frustrating. The question posed by villagers—"*Why* are you here?"—and echoed by the more thoughtful members of the development apparatus—"Why *are* we here?"—is answered in diverse ways, but in every case if outsiders are busy doing things in communities, trusteeship is still in play. It is deeply embedded in the will to improve.

SUMMARY

To sum up the critical interventions I have made in this book, I would like to emphasize four points. First, I have argued that *practices of government* limit the possibilities for engaging with the targets of improving schemes as political actors, fully capable of contestation and debate. They do this by inscribing a boundary that separates those who claim to know how others should live from those whose conduct is to be conducted. Across such a divide, it is difficult to have a conversation. When the boundary is crossed, expertise challenged, and a program forced open by critical scrutiny, the response of trustees is to look for ways to reassert the authority of their own calculations. In its structural positioning, trusteeship has changed little from its colonial to its neoliberal iterations.

Second, I have argued for reclaiming the *practice of politics* and its cognate, *provokasi*, and giving them a positive inflection. In these pages I have engaged in my own form of provocation, a challenge to the conceit of a will to improve that directs the conduct of "small people" while leaving radical political-economic inequalities unaddressed. My provocation aims to work in solidarity with Indonesians struggling for justice, and in critical engagement with fellow scholars and trustees. Scholarship that is not constrained by the *telos* of programming offers different insights to programmers than they receive from scholars-as-consultants. In Indonesia, anthropologists have been prominent in the consultant role for at least a century—among them the missionary-ethnographers Adriani and Kruyt, Van Vollenhoven's *adat* scholars, the experts designing the reconstruction of village Java, the university researchers invoked by Depsos to improve its resettlement schemes, and members of the social development team of the World Bank. At a time when the institutions that fund social science research are being required to demonstrate their relevance, their "real world" applications, I argue that studies that take programming seriously but do not try to program still make a contribution. Their *provokasi* is open ended and can be taken up by differently situated subjects with projects of their own.

Third, I have demonstrated the critical potential of an *ethnography of government*. Contra scholars who separate the study of governmental rationalities from the study of situated practices, I have shown that close attention to the "witches' brew" offers insight into how governmental programs are configured by the very forces they would contain. Reading authoritative texts through an ethnographic lens gave me critical purchase on their rationales and their forms of knowledge. Tracking the effects of governmental interventions revealed not only whether the desires and actions of target populations had been redirected according to plan—predictably, they had not. An ethnographic stance enabled me to explore how subjectivities were produced in the complex conjunctures where multiple powers coincide, how critical practices emerged, and how they provoked new attempts to govern. By expanding the study of government to incorporate the rich insights of people at the receiving end of governmental schemes, I avoided attributing to these schemes a coherence they do not have, and was able to position my critique as one among others, differently grounded. I argue that engaging with the "messy actualities" of rule in practice is not merely an adjunct to the study of government—it is intrinsic to it.

Finally, *the will to improve*. This will, as I stated in the introduction, is both benevolent and stubborn. My tracking of the working out of this will from its colonial to neoliberal iterations reveals some profound limits to what it has accomplished. For vast numbers of people, it falls short of the promise to make the world better than it is. Yet, as my study has shown, it deeply shapes the conditions of their lives. It is not as if the processes intrinsic to the population have been left to take their natural course. For two centuries, conditions have been set, and they could be set quite differently.

INTRODUCTION

1   McClure, "Taking Liberties," 188.

2   In total I have spent about a year in the hills of Central Sulawesi in eight visits beginning in 1990, some of that time in the areas I describe in chapters 2–6. Since the area is large and the period I discuss spans a century, I draw on my fieldwork as only one of many sources. In the text I use the real names of villages, all of which are shown on map 2. I use pseudonyms for individuals. I am responsible for the translation from Indonesian of interviews and texts.

3   See Roe, "Development Narratives," and Hoben, "Paradigms and Politics in Ethiopia."

4   Cowen and Shenton, *Doctrines of Development*, x. Cowen and Shenton track trusteeship through British metropolitan and imperial routes, and the work of political philosophers such as Saint Simon, Compte, and J. S. Mill. The Saint-Simonian concept of trusteeship maintained that "only those who had the 'capacity' to utilise land, labour and capital in the interests of society as a whole should be 'entrusted' with them" (25).

    In *Nature's Government*, Richard Drayton provides a masterful account of the role of science in legitimating the role of trustees charged with "the improvement of the world," again with a British inflection. Foucault and scholars who have drawn on his ideas, working through a different archive, picked up other threads woven into the term *government* and gave the concept an explicit theorization.

5 See Foucault, "Afterword: The Subject and Power," 220–21. See O'Malley, "Indigenous Governance," 313, on common sense. See Rose, *Powers of Freedom*, on uses of coercion (10), and on government at a distance (49).

6 For discussions of governmentality that situate it historically and in relation to other forms of power, see Foucault's essay "Governmentality," and see Burchell, "Peculiar Interests"; Dean, *Governmentality*; Dillon, "Sovereignty and Governmentality"; Gordon, "Governmental Rationality"; Rose, *Powers of Freedom*). Michael Watts ("Development and Governmentality") and Donald Moore (*Suffering for Territory*) discuss governmentality in relation to development, violence, and contested territorializations of colonial and contemporary rule.

7 Foucault, "Governmentality," 100.

8 Scott, "Colonial Governmentality," 202, citing the "preeminent governmentalist" Jeremy Bentham.

9 Foucault, "Governmentality," 93.

10 Ibid., 95.

11 See also Foucault, "Right of Death and Power over Life," 266.

12 Rose, *Powers of Freedom*, 52. See also Foucault, *Power/Knowledge*, 194.

13 In *Seeing Like a State*, James Scott outlines the combinations of utopic dreams and concentrated powers under which high modern schemes emerged. I situate Scott's approach in relation to studies of governmentality in "Beyond 'the State' and Failed Schemes." Compare Cruikshank, *The Will to Empower*, 42, on government as an accretion of "small things" rather than totalizing systems. Karl Polanyi neatly captured the contrast when he argued that the creation of an unfettered market for land and labor in the nineteenth century was a grand utopian scheme—ideologically driven then as it is in its contemporary neoliberal guise. Yet the array of interventions needed to keep populations alive and productive under market conditions emerged in piecemeal and pragmatic fashion: "*Laissez-faire* was planned," he argued, "planning was not" (Polanyi, *The Great Transformation*, 141).

14 Rose, *Powers of Freedom*, 33. I adapt the phrase "rendering technical" from Rose, who glosses it as making something—his example is bonds of solidarity—"amenable to a technique" 79. See also Timothy Mitchell's discussion in *Colonizing Egypt* and *Rule of Experts* of enframing as a practice that produces an apparently exterior object world susceptible to management.

15 Ferguson, *The Anti-Politics Machine*.

16 Ibid., 270.

17 Francois Felix De La Farelle (1847), quoted in Procacci, "Social Economy and the Government of Poverty," 158.

18 Firmin Marbeau (1847), quoted in ibid., 151.

19 Schrauwers, "The 'Benevolent' Colonies of Johannes van den Bosch," 311–12.

20 Rostow, *The Stages of Growth*, 1960. See also Escobar, *Encountering Development*, 32–34; Esteva, "Development," 11.

21 Anderson, "Old State, New Society," 490; MacDougall, "The Technocratic Model," 1176. See also Feit, "Repressive-Developmentalist Regimes in Asia"; Langenberg, "The New Order State"; Pemberton, *On the Subject of "Java."*

22 I find concepts of conspiracy implicit in prominent critiques of development, including Arturo Escobar's *Encountering Development*. The germinal contribution of Escobar's work, from my perspective, is his exposure of the powers at work in constructing an arena of technical intervention (the third world) and planning for its improvement. Ferguson rejects conspiracy but nevertheless insists that the development apparatus has consistent, strategic effects—the depoliticization of poverty, and the expansion of state bureaucratic power. The extent of such effects is an empirical matter, variable across place and time. Where we differ, I think, is in understandings of causality. He explains the existence of an apparatus in terms of its unintended effects, neglecting the possibility that actors might take note of these effects and build them into their plans. As Dupont and Pearce point out in "Foucault contra Foucault" (143), much work in a Foucauldian vein is implicitly functionalist, as it leaves the mechanisms for procuring "strategic effects" obscure. In his later work (see, e.g., *Power/Knowledge*, 194–96) Foucault addressed this problem. Dupont and Pearce argue for including in social explanations "reference to agents who are capable of making calculations" and agents "who *react* to, capitalize upon and rationalize their responses to whatever circumstances they find themselves caught in" (144). See Briggs, "Empowering NGOs," for a careful discussion of how the development *dispositif* can result in the "greater penetration of power" through its regime of practices, but without imputing a strategy.

23 See Michael Goldman's *Imperial Nature* for a contrasting analysis that carefully traces the link between World Bank knowledge production and the profit

motives of the corporations earning billions of dollars from World Bank contracts and from loan conditions that require, among others, the privatization of water. In *The Great Transformation*, Polanyi stressed the pragmatic way that interventionism emerged in the nineteenth century in diverse European milieus where regimes espousing radically different ideologies, and representing distinct class interests, encountered similar practical problems in the management of populations (139–56).

24 Dreyfus and Rabinow, *Michel Foucault*, 196.

25 Mitchell, *Rule of Experts*, 38–42, 52–53, 226, 230.

26 Ferguson, *The Anti-Politics Machine*, 270. Ferguson's "Paradoxes of Sovereignty and Independence" examines the variable depoliticization of discourses of poverty in the 1970s by contrasting the sovereign nation of Lesotho, where poverty was framed exclusively in terms of "development," with the South African "homeland" of the Transkei, in which there was vigorous public debate on the political and economic causes of poverty—debate that experts could not ignore. Defenders of apartheid devised numerous technical rationales for their schemes, but it was all too obvious that the victims were not simply unfortunates left behind by the march of progress—they had been deliberately selected.

27 Rose, *Powers of Freedom*, 192. O'Malley, Lorna Weir, and Clifford Shearing ("Governmentality, Criticism, Politics," 513) and John Clarke (*Changing Welfare, Changing States*) discuss the exaggerated closure of expert schemes. In *Colonialism's Culture*, Nicholas Thomas examines colonial government as situated practices that are heterogeneous, partial, and prone to distortion (4). See also the discussion of the resurgence of disqualified and subjugated knowledges within and around expert discourse in Stoler, *Carnal Knowledge and Imperial Power*, 159–60.

28 Foucault, "Afterword: The Subject and Power," 222. Elsewhere, Foucault writes that the "theme of struggle only really becomes operative if one establishes concretely—in each particular case—who is engaged in struggle, what the struggle is about, and how, where, by what means and according to what rationality it evolves" (*Power/Knowledge*, 164). This approach seems to invite analyses that bring power and struggle into a single frame, yet he recommends keeping them separate, rendering each intelligible in its own terms ("Afterword: The Subject and Power," 226).

29 Foucault, "Afterword: The Subject and Power," 225–26.

30 For example, Mouffe uses the term "the political" to refer to the antagonistic dimension of social life, possibilities of subversion, questioning, opposition, refusal, resistance, the activation of instability—a usage similar to my "practice of politics." She defines "politics" as the attempt to order, pacify, govern, or contain the political—making the term equivalent to my "practice of government." David Slater argues that politics and the political are inseparable since "the political—the possibilities of subversion, questioning, opposition, refusal, resistance . . . constitute a reactivation of the instability that 'order' sought to pacify" ("Rethinking the Spatialities of Social Movements," 388–89). He compares his use of terms to Foucault's—politics as attempted pacification is akin to Foucault's governmentality, and Foucault's "reverse discourses" are equivalent to "the political."

31 Rose, *Powers of Freedom*, 51.

32 Foucault, "Governmentality,"95.

33 Rose, *Powers of Freedom*, 27.

34 Ludden, "India's Development Regime," 253. For precolonial Indonesia, the writings of Clifford Geertz and Benedict Anderson suggest a different model—one in which the well-being of the sovereign was taken as a sign that all was well in the realm, but calculated intervention to secure popular prosperity was not routine (Anderson, "The Idea of Power"; Geertz, *Negara*). There was violence, slavery, and plunder, but the difficulty of holding a mobile population imposed limits on systematic domination. See Elson, "International Commerce"; Henley, *Jealousy and Justice*; Reid, "Political 'Tradition' in Indonesia"; Robinson, *The Dark Side of Paradise*.

35 Mbembe, *On the Postcolony*, 26.

36 Grove, *Green Imperialism*. See also Drayton, *Nature's Government*.

37 For studies of colonial rule explicitly engaged with the concept of governmentality, see Dirks, *Castes of Mind*; Mbembe, *On the Postcolony*; Moore, *Suffering for Territory*; Pels, "The Anthropology of Colonialism"; Pels and Salemink, *Colonial Subjects*; D. Scott, "Colonial Governmentality"; Thomas, *Colonialism's Culture*; and Wilder, "Practicing Citizenship in Imperial Paris." The division of colonial populations and their differential treatment is especially well described in Hindess, "The Liberal Government of Unfreedom." On links between governmental strategies used in metropoles and colonies, see Co-

maroff and Comaroff, *Ethnography and the Historical Imagination*; Drayton, *Nature's Government*, 221–29; Mitchell, *Colonizing Egypt*; Rose, *Powers of Freedom*, 71, 107; and Stoler and Cooper, "Between Metropole and Colony."

38 D. Scott, "Colonial Governmentality," 204.

39 See discussion in Moore, *Suffering for Territory*, 13, 158–65.

40 Drayton, *Nature's Government*, xv.

41 Ibid., 229.

42 Cited in ibid., 227.

43 Rose, *Powers of Freedom*, 22.

44 The despotic underside of liberalism and its constitutive exclusions are discussed in Dean, " 'Demonic Societies' "; Hindess, "The Liberal Government of Unfreedom"; Mehta, "Liberal Strategies of Exclusion"; and Valverde, " 'Despotism' and Ethical Liberal Goverance."

45 Sider, "When Parrots Learn to Talk, and Why They Can't," 7.

46 The "tensions of empire" and debates among colonial officials and metropolitan publics are discussed in Stoler and Cooper, "Between Metropole and Colony." Christian missionaries often argued that natives were improvable, since converts would be judged by the same God, but they tempered this position when their dependence on public donations required them to exaggerate difference (Pels and Salemink, *Colonial Subjects*, 29; Thomas, *Colonialism's Culture*, 73, 89–104). In *Colonialism's Culture* (142), Thomas discusses the contradictions between hierarchizing and assimilating colonialisms, as well as their parasitic interconnections and instabilities. Partha Chatterjee discusses colonialisms' founding in a "rule of difference" and the consequent impossibility of the civilizing mission in *The Nation and Its Fragments*. In "Shades of Wildness," Ajay Skaria, distinguishes between difference posited as an essence and difference as anachronism, in which social groups are situated in a single comparative hierarchy (728).

47 Wilder, "Practicing Citizenship in Imperial Paris," 46, 45, 47.

48 Chakrabarty, *Provincializing Europe*, 8.

49 See Hindess, "The Liberal Government of Unfreedom."

50 Bhabha, "Of Mimicry and Man"; Stoler, "Rethinking Colonial Categories."

51 Hindess, "The Liberal Government of Unfreedom," 102–4.

52 See Cooper and Packard, *International Development and the Social Sciences*, 7; Thomas, *Colonialism's Culture*, 15, 144. In *Citizen and Subject*, Mahmood

Mamdani explores the simultaneous constitution of ethnic subjects and modern citizens in colonial and postcolonial Africa and its rural-urban spatialization.

53 Pigg, "Inventing Social Categories through Place," 507.

54 Ludden, "India's Development Regime," 252.

55 Mbembe, *On the Postcolony*; Watts, "Development and Governmentality."

56 See Foucault, "Afterword: The Subject and Power," 220.

57 Latour, *We Have Never Been Modern*; Mitchell, *Rule of Experts*, 23, 28, 30.

58 See Burchell, "Peculiar Interests."

59 Hannah, *Governmentality and Mastery of Territory in Nineteenth-Century America*, 24.

60 See Hindess, "The Liberal Government of Unfreedom," 97.

61 Burchell, "Peculiar Interests," 137. See also Gordon, "Governmental Rationality."

62 J. Scott, *Seeing Like a State*.

63 See Dean, *Governmentality*, 1999.

64 Williams, *Keywords*, 133. See also Drayton, *Nature's Government*, 51.

65 Hindess, "The Liberal Government of Unfreedom," 99–100.

66 The coercion involved in creating private property and the interventions that constitute and sustain capitalism as we know it are examined in Mitchell, *Rule of Experts*.

67 Polanyi, *The Great Transformation*, 131. See also Gillian Hart, "Development Critiques in the 1990s," 650. Hart has a cogent discussion of the relationship between capitalism (lowercase-*d* development) and capital-*D* Development as an intentional practice.

68 Cowen and Shenton, *Doctrines of Development*, 10, 456.

69 Crush, "Introduction: Imagining Development," 10. See also Mitchell, *Rule of Experts*; and Watts, " 'A New Deal In Emotions.' "

70 Drayton, *Nature's Government*, 55.

71 Ibid., 232. On native profligacy, see also Fairhead and Leach, *Misreading the African Landscape*; Leach and Mearns, *The Lie of the Land*; and McAfee, "Selling Nature to Save It?" 139.

72 Rose, *Powers of Freedom*, 277.

73 For an elucidation of Gramsci's focus on conjunctures, see Crehan, *Gramsci, Culture, and Anthropology*, and Moore, *Suffering for Territory*.

74 Pemberton, *On the Subject of "Java,"* 4, 6. See also Antlöv, "Not Enough Politics!" 75.

75 I examined this conjuncture in "Articulating Indigenous Identity in Indonesia," drawing upon Stuart Hall's concept of articulation as the contingent connection between ideas that challenge the status quo and the social forces that might—or might not—mobilize to pursue them. See Hall, "On Postmodernism and Articulation."

76 Hall, "Cultural Identity and Diaspora," 225–26.

77 *The Will to Empower* is the title of a book by Barbara Cruikshank, in which she offers a striking analysis of this assemblage in a North American context. See also Rose, *Powers of Freedom*, 268.

78 Crehan, *Gramsci, Culture, and Anthropology*, 104.

79 Ibid., 200.

80 For an instructive discussion of compatible theorizations of Gramsci and Foucault, see Moore, *Suffering for Territory*.

81 Allen, *Lost Geographies of Power*, 195–96.

82 On politics in Foucault, see Dean, *Governmentality*, 36–37; and O'Malley, Weir, and Shearing, "Governmentality, Criticism, Politics."

83 Gavin Smith, in *Confronting the Present*, and Donald Moore, in "Clear Waters and Muddied Histories" and "Subaltern Struggles and the Politics of Place," show how the process of political mobilization defines interests and forms communities.

84 Gordon, "Governmental Rationality," 5; Rose, *Powers of Freedom*, 92.

85 This point has been made by O'Malley, in "Indigenous Governance," and O'Malley, Weir, and Shearing, in "Governmentality, Criticism, Politics," 509. They argue that the critical, political edge in Foucault is submerged in the literature on governmentality. It needs to be reaffirmed and linked to the study of sociologies as well as mentalities, in order to expose and expand the arena of contestation. See also McClure, "Taking Liberties," and Valverde, " 'Despotism' and Ethical Liberal Goverance."

86 Rose, *Powers of Freedom*, 279.

87 Ibid., 19.

88 Ibid., 20.

89 Foucault, "Questions of Method," 81–82.

90 Ibid.

91 In *No Condition Is Permanent*, Sara Berry provides a rich analysis of the contestations surrounding colonial attempts to rule Africa through tribal custom but is rather quick to dismiss the study of the programs that stimulated these contestations. In *Rule of Experts*, Mitchell explains how the very appearance of a world divided into thoughts and actions, plans and consequences, is an effect of power.

92 Massey, "Power Geometry," 66. The fecundity of such a concept of place as grounds for critical ethnography is amply demonstrated in Moore, *Suffering for Territory*; see also Bebbington, "Reencountering Development."

93 See O'Malley, "Indigenous Governance," 311.

94 James Scott describes the nonconforming practices necessary to sustain "the pretense of and insistence on officially decreed micro-order" (*Seeing Like a State*, 261). See my ethnographic account of such practices in "Compromising Power" and the extensive treatment of this issue in Mosse, "Is Good Policy Unimplementable?"

95 Ortner, "Resistance," 174.

1. CONTRADICTORY POSITIONS

1 Native was a legal category in the Netherlands East Indies after 1800. I capitalize the term to signal its official status, alongside the category European.

2 Kahin, *Nationalism and Revolution*, 4–10.

3 The voc did conduct some research and by the end of the eighteenth century had experts on Native affairs. See Ellen, "The Development of Anthropology."

4 On the voc's territorial conquests, see Anderson, "Old State, New Society"; Henley, *Jealousy and Justice*; Kahin, *Nationalism and Revolution*; and Reid, "Political 'Tradition' in Indonesia."

5 Kahin, *Nationalism and Revolution*, 10.

6 Kuitenbrouwer, *The Netherlands*; Locher-Scholten, "Dutch Expansion in the Indonesian Archipelago around 1900," 95, 101; Wesseling, "The Giant That Was a Dwarf," 66.

7 The relative importance of profit and prestige as motives for territorial expansion is discussed in Black, "The 'Lastposten' "; Boomgaard, "Introducing Environmental Histories of Indonesia"; Lindblad, "The Contribution of Foreign Trade"; Locher-Scholten, "Dutch Expansion in the Indonesian Archipelago

around 1900"; Robinson, *The Dark Side of Paradise*; and Schoffer, "Dutch 'Expansion' and Indonesian Reactions."

8   Anderson, "Old State, New Society," 479.

9   Houben, "Profit versus Ethics"; Kuitenbrouwer, *The Netherlands*, 278.

10 Locher-Scholten, "Dutch Expansion in the Indonesian Archipelago around 1900," 95.

11 Anderson, "Old State, New Society," 479.

12 Elson, "International Commerce," 155.

13 Locher-Scholten, "Dutch Expansion in the Indonesian Archipelago around 1900," 100.

14 Ibid., 107.

15 Ibid., 110.

16 Kuitenbrouwer, *The Netherlands*, 323–24; Locher-Scholten, "Dutch Expansion in the Indonesian Archipelago around 1900," 106–7.

17 Foucault, "Governmentality," 95.

18 W. Colbrooke, August 4, 1815, cited in Drayton, *Nature's Government*, 93.

19 Furnivall, *Netherlands India*, 69. See also Ellen, "The Development of Anthropology"; Hugenholtz, "The Land Rent Question"; and Schrauwers, "The 'Benevolent' Colonies of Johannes van den Bosch."

20 Hugenholtz, "The Land Rent Question," 149.

21 Rose, *Powers of Freedom*, 33.

22 Furnivall, *Netherlands India*, 70, 78.

23 Ibid., 72–75; Schrauwers, "The 'Benevolent' Colonies of Johannes van den Bosch," 314.

24 Schrauwers, "The 'Benevolent' Colonies of Johannes van den Bosch," 324.

25 Elson, "International Commerce," 137. Elson and Schrauwers translate *Cultuurstelsel* as "Cultivation System." I have retained the alternate translation because of its intriguing resonance with Van den Bosch's technique of governing through what he understood to be Javanese culture.

26 Henley, *Nationalism and Regionalism*, 38.

27 Elson, "International Commerce," 137.

28 Schrauwers, "The 'Benevolent' Colonies of Johannes van den Bosch." I draw heavily on the arguments developed by Schrauwers as well as the information he supplies.

29 Breman, *The Village on Java and the Early-Colonial State*; Elson, "International Commerce," 166.

30 Schrauwers, "The 'Benevolent' Colonies of Johannes van den Bosch," 319, 322–25.

31 Schrauwers does not explain whether Van den Bosch carried ideas about the indelibility of native difference with him to the Indies, or developed them in situ as he reflected upon the practicalities of how to extend the intensive disciplinary regime of the parapenal labor camp for paupers of the Netherlands to the population of the colony as a whole.

32 Fasseur, "Cornerstone and Stumbling Block," 33–35; Lev, "Colonial Law," 61.

33 Lev, "Colonial Law," 58.

34 Baud cited in Fasseur, "Cornerstone and Stumbling Block," 33.

35 Breman, *The Village on Java and the Early-Colonial State*, 27; Kahin, *Nationalism and Revolution*, 2–3, 10–13.

36 Elson, "International Commerce," 184.

37 Kahin, *Nationalism and Revolution*, 12.

38 Elson, "International Commerce," 185; Lindblad, "The Contribution of Foreign Trade," 101, 108.

39 Kahin, *Nationalism and Revolution*, 15; Wesseling, "The Giant That Was a Dwarf," 61–62.

40 Boomgaard, "Colonial Forest Policy in Java in Transition," 117; Furnivall, *Netherlands India*, 217.

41 Furnivall, *Netherlands India*, 180; Kahn, *Constituting the Minangkabau*; Peluso, "A History of State Forest Management in Java."

42 Throughout the archipelago, managed forests are deliberately enhanced with fruit, rubber, resin, sago, sugar palm, building poles, rattan, and other useful crops. Swidden cultivation, also known as shifting cultivation or "slash and burn," is the preferred farming technique wherever land is relatively abundant, labor scarce, and the terrain unsuited to intensive use (Dove, "The Agroecological Mythology"). A forest plot is cleared, farmed, then left fallow for a few years before repeating the cycle. Ownership rights vary. In some areas, clearing a plot in primary forest bestows private rights on the land pioneer and his descendants; in others, pioneer's rights revert to community control if the land is not reused within a certain period.

43 Moniaga, "Toward Community-Based Forestry"; Peluso and Vandergeest, "Genealogies of the Political Forest," 776. See also Vandergeest and Peluso, "Territorialization and State Power."

44 Boomgaard, "Colonial Forest Policy in Java in Transition," 128, 134; Furnivall, *Netherlands India*, 180; Peluso and Vandergeest, "Genealogies of the Political Forest."

45 Peluso and Vandergeest, "Genealogies of the Political Forest," 776.

46 Peluso, "A History of State Forest Management in Java," 33–35.

47 Elson, "International Commerce," 149; Kahn, *Constituting the Minangkabau*.

48 Breman, *Taming the Coolie Beast*; Elson, "International Commerce," 161, 177; Furnivall, *Netherlands India*, 353–57; Lindblad, "The Contribution of Foreign Trade," 98. The indentured labor system devised in the "liberal" decades continued to operate in the "ethical" period. Between 1913 and 1925, 327,000 contract coolies left Java for Sumatra under very harsh conditions. See Elson, "International Commerce," 160; and see Houben, "Profit versus Ethics."

49 Furnivall, *Netherlands India*, 216, 223.

50 Ibid., 225.

51 Conrad Theodor van Deventer was the politician credited with convincing fellow Dutchmen that the Netherlands had a debt of honor to the people of the colony that should be repaid. See Deventer, "A Welfare Policy for the Indies"; Furnivall, *Netherlands India*, 176, 228–32; and Schoffer, "Dutch 'Expansion' and Indonesian Reactions," 87.

52 Wertheim, *Indonesian Economics*, 7.

53 Furnivall, *Netherlands India*, 229.

54 Schoffer, "Dutch 'Expansion' and Indonesian Reactions," 87.

55 Officials stood awkwardly outside the Culture System, for example, to critique excesses of greed and exploitation by factory owners and the decline in rice production without questioning its fundamentals. See Hüsken, "Declining Welfare in Java," 218.

56 The list is drawn from Furnivall, *Netherlands India*, 190. The attention Native Regents were to give to agricultural improvement is detailed in Boeke, "Objective and Personal Elements," 290. From the 1870s, the Residents mainly serviced the needs of European investors, and responsibility for Natives devolved to the Native Regents. The latter were increasingly viewed as officials rather than nobles and deprived of the appanages that had made them, in

Dutch eyes, oppressors of their people (Boeke, "Objective and Personal Elements," 289–92; Furnivall, *Netherlands India*, 192–93).

57 Anderson, "Old State, New Society," 479; Elson, "International Commerce"; J. Scott, *Seeing Like a State*. Specialization was matched by a desire for totalizing knowledge. The Diminished Welfare Inquiry initiated in 1902 covered 544 topics. "It aimed at a complete survey of native life: food, land tenure, methods of cultivation, irrigation and indebtedness; the state of the fisheries, and of industry and commerce; and the influence of European enterprise and Foreign Orientals on native life and welfare" (Furnivall, *Netherlands India*, 393; cited in Hüsken, "Declining Welfare in Java," 216). In "The Development of Anthropology," Roy Ellen traces the kinds of knowledge about Native society required by colonial authorities at different periods.

58 Furnivall, *Netherlands India*, 294.

59 Ibid., 294–95, 365, 383–88.

60 Furnivall, *Netherlands India*, 388–89.

61 Kahin, *Nationalism and Revolution*, 43–44.

62 Boomgaard, "Colonial Forest Policy in Java in Transition," 134.

63 Elson, "International Commerce," 156.

64 Kahin, *Nationalism and Revolution*, 26.

65 Anderson, "Old State, New Society," 479–80.

66 Elson, "International Commerce," 158.

67 Furnivall, *Netherlands India*, 401.

68 Kahin, *Nationalism and Revolution*, 15–18.

69 Elson, "*International Commerce*," 167.

70 Fasseur, "Cornerstone and Stumbling Block," 32.

71 Ibid., 31. The racial boundary was consolidated by the Nationality Law of 1892 that declared Natives and Foreign Orientals residing in the Indies "foreigners," Dutch subjects, but non-Dutch, and excluded them from the exercise of political rights then or in the future. In the 1920s an election bill used the nationality concept to maintain what was, in effect, a racial distinction separating three corps of voters (38, 49). Formal legal and administrative apartheid in South Africa only emerged in 1948. See James and Schrauwers, "An Apartheid of Souls," for a discussion of connections between Dutch-designed apartheids in Indonesia and South Africa. In contrast to the Dutch, the British adopted a unified legal system for India under the East India

Company in 1833, confirmed in 1858 when government passed to the British crown. There was a unified Indian Civil Service and unified judiciary (Fasseur, "Cornerstone and Stumbling Block," 36).

72 Sonius, introduction to *Van Vollenhoven*, liii. An exception was made for Javanese aristocrats and high-level officials given the privilege of access to Dutch courts (Lev, "Colonial Law," 62).

73 Lev, "Colonial Law," 61n7.

74 Ibid., 60.

75 Ibid., 59.

76 Stoler, "Rethinking Colonial Categories," 637–39. See also Schoffer, "Dutch 'Expansion' and Indonesian Reactions," 82–83.

77 Stoler, "Sexual Affronts and Racial Frontiers," 515. People classified as European numbered 40,000 in 1870, 91,000 in 1900, and 250,000 by 1940. The Native population increased from roughly 20 to 60 million in the same period, and Foreign Orientals from about 200,000 to 1.2 million (Furnivall, *Netherlands India*, 347; Schoffer, "Dutch 'Expansion' and Indonesian Reactions," 82, 84).

78 Stoler, "Rethinking Colonial Categories," 644.

79 Stoler, "Rethinking Colonial Categories," 645. Elson notes the role of bureaucratic codes and paperwork in establishing social distance between rulers and ruled ("*International Commerce*," 183).

80 Breman, *The Village on Java and the Early-Colonial State*, 42.

81 De Wolff van Westerrode, quoted in Henley, "Custom and Koperasi." *Padi* is unhusked rice.

82 Boomgaard, "The Javanese Village as a Cheshire Cat," 296; Henley, "Custom and Koperasi."

83 Furnivall, *Netherlands India*, 389, emphasis in the original, cited in Henley, "Custom and Koperasi."

84 Boeke, "Objective and Personal Elements," 298; Ellen, "The Development of Anthropology," 315; Schoffer, "Dutch 'Expansion' and Indonesian Reactions," 90; Wertheim, *Indonesian Economics*, 32, 39, 44. Wertheim, *Indonesian Economics* discusses the shifts in Boeke's thinking about difference, the debates he stimulated, and the limited influence of his theories on colonial policy. See also Henley, "Custom and Koperasi."

85 See Wertheim, *Indonesian Economics*, 32.

86 Boeke, "Objective and Personal Elements," 294. For iterations of the faith in community in British India, see Cowen and Shenton, *Doctrines of Development*; Dewey, "Images of the Village Community"; Mosse, "Colonial and Contemporary Ideologies of 'Community Management.' "

87 Boeke, "Village Reconstruction," 303; Wertheim, *Indonesian Economics*, 44–46.

88 Wertheim, *Indonesian Economics*, 42.

89 Boeke, "Village Reconstruction," 309–15; Wertheim, *Indonesian Economics*, 45–6.

90 These debates are discussed in Henley, "Custom and Koperasi," 7; Wertheim, *Indonesian Economics*, 17, 21.

91 Wertheim, *Indonesian Economics*, 52–53. Kahin, *Nationalism and Revolution*, 22–23.

92 De Kat Angelino, cited in Wertheim, *Indonesian Economics*, 56.

93 Van Vollenhoven's students also conducted *adat* studies on Java, where the two modes of construing difference coexisted.

94 Burns, "The Myth of Adat," 98–101.

95 Ibid., 8, 56; Sonius, introduction to *Van Vollenhoven*, xxxii.

96 Burns, "The Myth of Adat," 78–79, 93–94, 97.

97 Ibid., 9, 97; Sonius, introduction to *Van Vollenhoven*, xxxiii.

98 Sonius, introduction to *Van Vollenhoven*, li.

99 Burns, "The Myth of Adat," 15, 35.

100 Ibid., 14, 33, 21–22.

101 Van Vollenhoven cited in Burns, "The Myth of Adat," 21, and see 34.

102 Van Vollenhoven cited in ibid., 15. See also Sonius, introduction to *Van Vollenhoven*, xxx.

103 Ellen, "The Development of Anthropology," 318–19; Lev, "Colonial Law," 65.

104 Burns, "The Myth of Adat," 83, 102.

105 Ibid., 104.

106 See Winichakul, *Siam Mapped*, on the changes wrought by territorialized notions of sovereignty in Siam. On personalized rule in the archipelago, see Anderson, "The Idea of Power"; Elson, "*International Commerce*"; and Reid, "Political 'Tradition' in Indonesia."

107 Burns, "The Myth of Adat," 83; Ellen, "The Development of Anthropology," 320.

108 Fasseur, "Cornerstone and Stumbling Block," 40; Lev, "Colonial Law," 64.

109 Lev, "Colonial Law," 64, 65.

110 Davidson and Henley, "Introduction: Radical Conservatism."

111 Burns, "The Myth of Adat," 3, 8; Ellen, "The Development of Anthropology," 317–19; Elson, "International Commerce," 156; M. B. Hooker, *Adat Law in Indonesia*, 1; Lev, "Colonial Law," 66; Sonius, introduction to *Van Vollenhoven*, lx–lxiii. See Nordholt, "The Making of Traditional Bali," on the "discovery" of traditional Bali and its bureaucratic reformation, which began in the nineteenth century and intensified under the Ethical policy.

112 Lev, "Colonial Law," 71.

113 Ibid., 72.

114 Fasseur, "Cornerstone and Stumbling Block," 55.

115 Bourchier, *Lineages of Organicist Political Thought in Indonesia*.

116 Lev, "Colonial Law," 71. For a study of realignments of colonial racial division along axes of class and spatial location in postcolonial Africa, see Mamdani, *Citizen and Subject*.

117 Bowen, "On the Political Construction of Tradition"; Davidson and Henley, "Introduction: Radical Conservatism."

118 Fitzpatrick, "Land, Custom, and the State in Post-Suharto Indonesia."

119 Lev, "Colonial Law," 70; Reid, "Political 'Tradition' in Indonesia," 25. Jamie Davidson and David Henley note that Supomo was exposed to fascist ideas as a student in the Netherlands and developed an intellectual admiration for German national socialism ("Introduction: Radical Conservatism"). Japanese nationalists absorbed organicist ideas from similar European sources and influenced Indonesian nationalists during the occupation. For extended discussion, see Bourchier, *Lineages of Organicist Political Thought in Indonesia*. On the influence of the German Historical School of Economics on Dutch debates over *adat* and land rights, see Kahn, *Constituting the Minangkabau*.

120 Bourchier, *Lineages of Organicist Political Thought in Indonesia*; Reid, "Political 'Tradition' in Indonesia," 25.

121 Reid, "Political 'Tradition' in Indonesia," 26–27. See also Anderson, "The Idea of Power."

122 Anderson, "Old State, New Society," 480.

123 Ibid., 482.

124 In *A Modern History of Southeast Asia*, Clive Christie describes these movements and their manipulation by the Dutch as they attempted to hold onto the
Indies.

125 Anderson, "Old State, New Society," 483.

126 Anderson, "The Idea of Power," 73.

127 Anderson, "Old State, New Society," 485–86.

128 Ibid., 486.

129 Hefner, *The Political Economy of Mountain Java*; Robinson, *The Dark Side of
Paradise*, 273, 281, 282–85. Anderson, *The Spectre of Comparisons*, 303, 315,
discusses the position of Indonesian Chinese.

130 Anderson, "Indonesian Nationalism," 12. See also Robinson, *The Dark Side of
Paradise*, 281.

131 Anderson, "Indonesian Nationalism," 13.

132 Ibid., 11–15. On New Order violence, see also Siegel, *A New Criminal Type in
Jakarta*; and Vickers, "Reopening Old Wounds," 10.

133 Anderson, "Indonesian Nationalism," 10.

134 Ibid., 11–15.

135 Fitzpatrick, "Land, Custom and the State."

136 Foucault, "Right of Death and Power over Life." See also Agamben, "The
Camp as the *Nomos* of the Modern." In *Race and the Education of Desire*, Ann
Stoler explores how this calculus relates to racial ideologies and practices of
government in colonial and contemporary settings (84–88).

137 Criminality is examined by James Siegel in *A New Criminal Type in Jakarta*.

138 Quoted in Pemberton, *On the Subject of "Java,"* 313.

139 Gus Dur is the nickname of Abdurrahman Wahid, president of Indonesia
from 1999 to 2001.

140 See Anderson, "Indonesian Nationalism," 12; Hefner, *Civil Islam*, 63; Robinson, *The Dark Side of Paradise*.

141 Agamben, "The Camp as the *Nomos* of the Modern."

142 Nancy Peluso, in "Weapons of the Wild," describes how the Indonesian military used tactics of psychological warfare to incite Kalimantan Dayaks to violently expel their Chinese neighbors in the 1960s. Indonesia's military, or
factions of it, have played a role in engineering ethnic and religious conflict
post-Suharto, a fact recognized by the World Bank among others. See World
Bank, *Support for Poor and Disadvantaged Areas*, 4.

143 The direction of the discussion was not condoned by USAID, the meeting's hosts. It emerged unexpectedly. Suripto's written paper for the seminar did not mention executions (Suripto, "Permasalahan dan Upaya Penanggulangan Illegal Logging"). Controversies surrounding Suripto are discussed in Human Rights Watch, *Without Remedy*, 15 n.47.

144 See the interviews reported in MacDougall, "The Technocratic Model," 1178–81. MacDougall applauds the New Order approach as a "highly functional strategy of government" in the context of economic crisis when supported by a sufficient degree of coercion (1183).

145 V. Hooker, "The New Order," 60–64. Hooker contrasts Suharto's speeches with those made by Sukarno: intimate, inspirational, prone more to telling stories and elucidating dilemmas than to issuing instructions. See also Langenberg, "The New Order State."

146 Breman, *The Village on Java and the Early-Colonial State*. See also Boomgaard, "The Javanese Village as a Cheshire Cat."

147 V. Hooker, "The New Order," 66.

148 On New Order patronage, see Feit, "Repressive-Developmentalist Regimes in Asia"; Hart, "Agrarian Change"; King, "Indonesia's New Order," 109–11. See Mbembe, *On the Postcolony*, 39–52, on the use of gifts funded with aid dollars to institutionalize domination in sub-Saharan Africa, where they helped to socialize state power and privatize public prerogatives. These arrangements unraveled under structural adjustment and caused the state apparatus to implode.

149 Government-through-patronage could also provoke unexpected reversals. See Jim Schiller's account of how New Order development intersected with the mobilization of the mass Islamic organization Nahdatul Ulama and the merchant class in Java Schiller, "State Formation and Rural Transformation."

150 Anderson, *The Spectre of Comparisons*, 300.

151 Anderson, "Old State, New Society"; Tanter, "Oil, IGGI and US Hegemony."

152 Li, "Compromising Power."

153 Dove and Kammen, "Vernacular Models of Development," 620.

154 Schiller, "State Formation and Rural Transformation," 401. See also Li, "Compromising Power"; and Peluso, *Rich Forests, Poor People*. The intimate and compromised relations between state and citizens in the context of develop-

ment interventions are described for India by Gupta, "Blurred Boundaries";
Gupta, *Postcolonial Developments.*

155 Schiller, "State Formation and Rural Transformation."

2. PROJECTS, PRACTICES, AND EFFECTS

1 Schrauwers, "Houses, Hierarchy, Headhunting and Exchange."

2 Henley, *Jealousy and Justice.* Henley stresses the desire for incorporation into the VOC's quasi-state regime as a corrective to accounts which stress upland peoples' apparent "genius for managing without states" (Reid, "Inside Out," 80–81) and their love for the freedom and autonomy of "nonstate" spaces (see J. Scott, *Seeing Like a State*). See also Li, "Relational Histories."

3 Henley, *Nationalism and Regionalism,* 36.

4 Ibid., 31–32.

5 Ibid., 38.

6 Ibid., 50.

7 Henley, *Fertility, Food and Fear,* 222–35, 409–11, 528–29.

8 The groups are labeled with their historical names. Some of the Pekawa later became known as Da'a. The group named Tawaelia is located in present day Sedoa. The source of Figure 1 is Kaudern 1925:33, reproduced in Henley, *Fertility, Food and Fever,* 223. Compare figure 1 with map 2.

9 Language groups are described in Noorduyn 1991. Henley (*Nationalism and Regionalism*) and Schrauwers (*Colonial "Reformation"*) discuss the role of missionaries in ethnogenesis.

10 Enslavement also followed from failure to pay debts or fines. On slavery in Central Sulawesi, see Acciaioli, *Searching,* 71; Schrauwers, "Houses, Hierarchy, Headhunting and Exchange"; and Schrauwers, "H(h)ouses, E(e)states and Class," 87–90.

11 Acciaioli, *Searching,* 68; Henley, *Fertility, Food and Fever,* 76–77, 593–95; Schrauwers, "Houses, Hierarchy, Headhunting and Exchange"; Schrauwers, "H(h)ouses, E(e)states and Class," 89.

12 Aragon, *Fields of the Lord,* 73–89.

13 In *In the Realm of the Diamond Queen,* Anna Tsing reports men's travels in Kalimantan in similar terms.

14 Henley, *Fertility, Food and Fever,* 82–85, 227–34.

15 The pan-Indonesian pattern of migration from hinterlands to coasts is described in Reid, "Inside Out." On piracy in Central Sulawesi, see Velthoen, " 'Wanderers, Robbers and Bad Folk.' "

16 Aragon, *Fields of the Lord*, 106–7; Henley, *Fertility, Food and Fever*, 227.

17 Henley, *Fertility, Food and Fever*, 29.

18 For accounts of highland-coastal relations in Sulawesi, see Aragon, *Fields of the Lord*; Atkinson, *The Art and Politics of Wana Shamanship*; George, *Showing Signs of Violence*; Li, "Relational Histories"; Nourse, *Conceiving Spirits*; Schrauwers, "Houses, Hierarchy, Headhunting and Exchange"; Schrauwers, *Colonial "Reformation"*; and Velthoen, " 'Wanderers, Robbers and Bad Folk.' "

19 Acciaioli, *Searching*, 71–73, 76; Henley, *Jealousy and Justice*; Schrauwers, "Houses, Hierarchy, Headhunting and Exchange."

20 Acciaioli, *Searching*, 83n44. Acciaioli does not describe the form of this pressure. See also Schrauwers, *Colonial "Reformation,"* 46.

21 Acciaioli, *Searching*, 84; Weber, Faust, and Kreisel, "Colonial Interventions," 411.

22 Henley, *Fertility, Food and Fever*, 47.

23 Schrauwers, *Colonial "Reformation,"* 47–48.

24 Ibid., 53.

25 Adriani cited in ibid., 50.

26 These arguments are developed by Schrauwers in *Colonial "Reformation."* See Aragon, *Fields of the Lord*, 107–9, and Acciaioli, *Searching* on the Salvation Army mission assigned to the hills around Palu and Kulawi.

27 Aragon, *Fields of the Lord*, 100–104; Schrauwers, *Colonial "Reformation,"* 32, 46–47.

28 Englenberg cited in Schrauwers, *Colonial "Reformation,"* 48.

29 Adriani cited in Henley, *Fertility, Food and Fever*, 591. Toraja is the generic label the Dutch used for Sulawesi highlanders.

30 Henley, *Fertility, Food and Fever*, 584–95. See also Dove, "The Agroecological Mythology."

31 Weber, Faust, and Kreisel, "Colonial Interventions," 414.

32 Henley, *Fertility, Food and Fever*, 84, 352–59, 546–50; Weber, Faust, and Kreisel, "Colonial Interventions," 414.

33 Aragon, *Fields of the Lord*, 101; Henley, *Fertility, Food and Fever*, 384; Weber, Faust, and Kreisel, "Colonial Interventions," 417.

34 Bigalke, "Dynamics of the Torajan Slave Trade in South Sulawesi."

35 Crawfurd, *A Descriptive Dictionary of the Indian Islands and Adjacent Countries,* 194. Thanks to David Henley for this reference.

36 Aragon, *Fields of the Lord,* 63.

37 Cameron, *The Conservation Band-Aid,* 74, 79–80.

38 Weber, Faust, and Kreisel, "Colonial Interventions," 422–24.

39 Schrauwers, "The Miser's Store," 28–29.

40 Weber, Faust, and Kreisel, "Colonial Interventions," 423.

41 Dove, "The Agroecological Mythology."

42 Henley, *Fertility, Food and Fever,* 516–21, 567–72.

43 Ibid., 476–79, 528–29.The exception was a forest band in the foothills close to the coast (409).

44 Ibid., 476.

45 Valentyn cited in Acciaioli, *Searching,* 65.

46 Henley, *Fertility, Food and Fever,* 487.

47 Ibid., 484.

48 Grove, *Green Imperialism*; Henley, *Fertility, Food and Fever,* 581. Environmental catastrophism and its use to justify draconian interventions is explored in Leach and Mearns, "Environmental Change and Policy"; and Watts, "Black Acts."

49 Quoted in Henley, *Fertility, Food and Fever,* 484.

50 Quoted in ibid., 486.

51 Ibid.

52 Ibid., 581.

53 Ibid., 560.

54 Weber, Faust, and Kreisel, "Colonial Interventions," 416–17. Three rangers were employed to survey forests in 1926 in search of teak. They found none, although they thought ebony had commercial prospects. In "Genealogies of the Political Forest," Nancy Peluso and Peter Vandergeest explore colonial debates about state claims to forest outside Java (776–77). Some contemporary Sulawesi highlanders claim to still recognize and respect Dutch forest boundaries established for watershed protection, while they reject New Order forest boundaries designed for timber extraction and territorial control.

55 Henley, *Fertility, Food and Fever,* 560.

56 Schrauwers, *Colonial "Reformation,"* 72.

57 Foucault, "Governmentality," 93.

58 Henley, *Fertility, Food and Fever*, 310.

59 Quoted in ibid., 230.

60 Ibid. Henley has an extended discussion of the different profiles of malaria at different elevations, and the high mortality associated with migration, resettlement in a new disease environment, and the clearing of new land (264–74).

61 Ibid., 230 and chapter 8.

62 Ibid., 233.

63 Ibid., 234.

64 Ibid., 235.

65 Haba, *Resettlement and Sociocultural Change*, 159; Weber, Faust, and Kreisel, "Colonial Interventions," 418.

66 Cited in Weber, Faust, and Kreisel, "Colonial Interventions," 419.

67 Ibid.

68 Haba, *Resettlement and Sociocultural Change*, 162–63.

69 Weber, Faust, and Kreisel, "Colonial Interventions," 417.

70 Aragon, *Fields of the Lord*, 57–59, 141.

71 Bugis is the name of an ethnolinguistic cluster with its own internal variations. Bugis seafarers had a reputation as pirates and were the original "Bugimen" of Europe's scary tales. They migrated throughout the Indonesian archipelago and beyond as traders, fishers, and farmers. On Bugis migration to Central Sulawesi, see Acciaioli, *Searching*; Acciaioli, "Kinship and Debt."

72 Aragon, *Fields of the Lord*, 142–43.

73 Ibid., 141–49; Velthoen, "Mapping Sulawesi in the 1950's."

74 The experience of being labeled alien and primitive is evocatively described in Tsing, *In the Realm of the Diamond Queen*. In a preface to *Masyarakat Terasing di Indonesia*, a book about *masyarakat terasing* by the anthropologist Koentjaraningrat, the Minister for Social Affairs contrasted the strangeness of *masyarakat terasing* to the positively valued, comforting homogeneity of "ordinary, average, Indonesians as a whole" (*bangsa Indonesia secara rata-rata dalam keseluruhan*). The book's cover and several photographs depict near-naked West Papuans engaged in exotic dances and unfamiliar tasks. Each chapter presents a "tribe," isolated and apparently without history.

75 Department of Social Affairs, *Isolated Community Development*, 4. This En-

glish publication translates *masyarakat terasing* as "isolated communities," but the term *terasing* has a richer set of meanings equally integral to the program logic: (1) secluded, separated, isolated; (2) exotic, very strange. Associated terms include *difference, deviation,* and *alienation.* See Echols and Shadily, *Kamus Indonesia-Inggris.*

76 Haba, *Resettlement and Sociocultural Change,* 55n7.

77 These characteristics are widely shared by "ordinary" villagers making the selection of targets for the program a matter of compromise (see Li, "Compromising Power").

78 Colchester, "Unity and Diversity." The Depsos position on primitives was repeated by senior officials when I conducted an evaluation of the program in 1997–98. "Estranged" people were not part of the New Order program to rule through cultural difference described in Kahn, *Constituting the Minangkabau;* Pemberton, *On the Subject of "Java";* and Schrauwers, *Colonial "Reformation,"* although they might qualify after they had been civilized.

79 I reviewed many university reports in 1997–98. The program was modified in the 1990s to permit "estranged" people to remain on their ancestral land, although they were limited to the standard two hectares, ruling out swidden. See Li, Arifin, and Achadiyat, *Design for the Evaluation of the Program for Isolated Communities,* for a report on Depsos resettlement in Kalimantan and Sulawesi. See also Suparlan, *Orang Sakai Di Riau.* After the severe critique by members of Indonesia's indigenous rights movement, emboldened by *reformasi,* the program was renamed the Program for Isolated Communities, Kelompok Adat Terpencil, or KAT. It acquired a shiny new Web site, but its assumptions and practices were little changed. See Duncan, "From Development to Empowerment."

80 Transmigration commenced in the colonial period when the goal was to supply plantation labor. The rationale shifted over time. See Hardjono, "Transmigration"; and Stoler, *Capitalism and Confrontation in Sumatra's Plantation Belt.*

81 Haba, *Resettlement and Sociocultural Change,* 45, 169, 367; Hoppe and Faust, *Transmigration and Integration,* 19.

82 Transmigration official interviewed by STORMA, *Processes of Destabilization,* 36. The department encountered this problem when transmigrants who were slated for relocation because their settlement overlapped with a mining

concession organized to protest. See Sangaji, *Buruk INCO Rakyat Digusur*, 171–84.

83 By 1998, official statistics show a total of 342,135 transmigrants relocated to Central Sulawesi, Sulawesi Tengah, *Propinsi Sulawesi Tengah Dalam Angka*. In Napu, six hundred families were placed at three sites directly next to the boundaries of the park (ANZDEC, *Environmental Management*, 20; Schweithelm, Wirawan, Elliott, and Khan, *Sulawesi Parks Program*, 39–42).

84 The infection of transmigrants with schistosomiasis was recognized as a public health scandal. In one site, thirty-seven people—17 percent of the residents—were infected within two years of resettlement, and at least fifty people were reported to have died of the disease in the first decade. See ADB, *Evaluasi Kinerja Secara Kualitatif*, 50–55; YTM, "Konservasi Yang Anti Rakyat," 9; YTM, *Notulensi Dialog Dodolo*.

85 ANZDEC, *Social Analysis*, 21; Hoppe and Faust, *Transmigration and Integration*; STORMA, *Socio-Economic Aspects of Village Communities*; TNC, *Laporan Kegiatan*, 46–57; YTM, "Konservasi Yang Anti Rakyat," 9.

86 On the misreading of conservation zones as natural or wild, see Cronon, "The Trouble with Wilderness"; and Neumann, "Ways of Seeing Africa."

87 Moniaga, "Toward Community-Based Forestry."

88 World Wildlife Fund, *Lore Lindu National Park Management Plan*, 36. Compare the private, heritable property rights attached to durian, a fruit tree that can live for a century deep inside a forest (Peluso, "Fruit Trees and Family Trees").

89 ANZDEC, *Environmental Management*, 17. See also Schweithelm, Wirawan, Elliott, and Khan, *Sulawesi Parks Program*, 51. Cameron, *The Conservation Band-Aid*, 85–87, found that coffee continued to be planted during the 1980s, and coffee land within the park was bought and sold, testimony to villagers' conviction that their rights were real.

90 See also Aragon, *Fields of the Lord*, 63.

91 ANZDEC, *Social Analysis*, 78, 81–82. In Central Sulawesi overall, 2,706 households were moved into thirty resettlement sites under the Depsos program in the period 1971–94, and a further 7,200 households were classified as still-to-be developed (Department of Social Affairs, *Isolated Community Development*, 89–92). Several hundred additional Da'a families were moved to Palolo resettlement sites by the Forest Department.

92 Quoted by Haba, *Resettlement and Sociocultural Change*, 358. Among modes of intimidation reported by Haba was the labeling of uncooperative groups as "communist."

93 Department of Social Affairs, *Isolated Community Development*, 89–92.

94 Tsing, *In the Realm of the Diamond Queen*. For a discussion of marginality that situates my perspective in relation to that of Indonesia scholars Anna Tsing, John Pemberton, Joel Kahn, and others, see Li, "Marginality, Power and Production."

95 Hill farmers resettled from the Kulawi hills to the Palolo Valley had a slightly different experience. See Aragon, *Fields of the Lord*, 304. Haba found that Da'a hill farmers disputed the idea that valley dwellers were superiors to emulate. "Local accounts," he found, "encode more specific patterns of migration and set forth more fine-grained differentiating criteria of cultural distinction" (*Resettlement and Sociocultural Change*, 74). In Palu and Palolo, hill and valley farmers are separated by a religious divide as the valleys became Muslim before the colonial period while the hills later became Christian.

96 Events in Rahmat were consistent with those in other Depsos resettlements for Da'a, studied by Haba in *Resettlement and Sociocultural Change*.

97 See also Aragon, *Fields of the Lord*, 303. For the enduring relevance in 1990s Tentena of identities pegged to the original hillside hamlets resettled a century ago, see Schrauwers, *Colonial "Reformation,"* 62.

98 Panca Sila is the state ideology that promises social justice and religious tolerance.

99 In the section of Rahmat originally allocated to the Da'a, of 148 households, 63 had no land. In another section there were 80 registered households, many of them absentee landlords living in Palu. Out of 80, 20 households were landless. Another indication of the land problem is the people per square kilometer in the Palolo resettlement villages: in Rahmat, the number was 245 (YTM, "Konservasi Yang Anti Rakyat," 8).

100 See Li, "Compromising Power"; and Li, Arifin, and Achadiyat, *Design for the Evaluation of the Program for Isolated Communities*. See also Aragon, *Fields of the Lord*, 303. Haba found that some resettlers assessed their previous lives as "still backward and traditional," while others valued the absence of landowners, wage labor, and domination (*Resettlement and Sociocultural Change*, 160, 305–10).

101 His statement that "we had always lived in these hills" occludes the unsettled past of his people, the Kaili subgroup Rarangganau, originally from the hills east of Palu, who were targets of multiple resettlement programs since the colonial period. See Haba, *Resettlement and Sociocultural Change*, 159–60; Henley, *Fertility, Food and Fever*, 234–35.

102 From a taped interview conducted with Arianto Sangaji in 2003, transcribed by YTM and edited to reduce repetition.

103 J. Scott argues in *Seeing Like a State* that ruling regimes expect resettlement to increase the malleability of populations and to thwart collective protest (235, 253).

3. FORMATIONS OF CAPITAL AND IDENTITY

1 E-mail from a friend, February 12, 2003. I later quizzed her about the encounter, and about the officer's proposed solution. What prompted her to write to me was the overlap between the officer's unsolicited analysis of the agrarian dimension of the conflict and the analysis I had offered in discussions with her a few months before.

2 For accessible accounts of the Poso conflict, see Aragon, "Communal Violence"; Human Rights Watch, *Breakdown*.

3 White, "Problems in the Empirical Analysis of Agrarian Differentiation," 20.

4 See Lucas and Warren, "The State, the People, and Their Mediators." The tenure situation in the state-claimed forest zone is explored in Contreras-Hermosilla and Fay, "Strengthening Forest Management."

5 Customary rights activists in the province argued there was no historical evidence for a Raja's dominion over land in the interior; there was evidence that local, autonomous groups exercised customary rights over land and regulated their own affairs, practices that continue in some areas (YTM, "Menunggu Pengakuan Hak Masyarakat Adat").

6 Davidson and Henley, "Introduction: Radical Conservatism"; Fitzpatrick, "Land, Custom and the State."

7 Sangaji, "The Masyarakat Adat Movement in Indonesia," 15.

8 Land allocation to corporations and the attendant corruption and coercion are discussed in Lucas and Warren, "The State, the People, and Their Mediators," 96–99.

9   Sangaji, *Menuju Pengelolaan* TNLL, 11.

10 See ANZDEC, *Social Analysis*, 81–82; Sitorus, *Land, Ethnicity, and the Competing Power*, 14.

11 Burkard, *Stability or Sustainability?* 30.

12 Gunter Burkard discusses the Headman's land selling in this village, an especially egregious case (ibid., 35).

13 Customary rights advocates seek to mitigate this risk by promoting collective rather than individual tenure (Lynch and Harwell, *Whose Natural Resources?*).

14 See also Burkard, *Stability or Sustainability?*; Ruf, "From Tree-Crop Planting to Replanting."

15 Rapid commoditization and accumulation of land in frontier zones was reported in the highlands of Vietnam and Thailand (De Koninck and Dery, "Agricultural Expansion"; Hirsch, *Political Economy of Environment in Thailand*). The general pattern is discussed in Elson, *The End of the Peasantry in Southeast Asia*.

16 ANZDEC, *Social Analysis*, 24; Lumeno, *Sistem Pemilikan*.

17 Bureau of Statistics data compiled by Sangaji (*Rumput Kering*, 16–17).

18 See Li, "Images of Community." In "Cultivating Cacao," Jill Belsky and Stephen Siebert describe the attempt of leaders in the isolated village of Moa to prevent covillagers from selling their land in a context where villagers considered land under cacao to be privately owned.

19 Schrauwers discusses the application of this policy in Central Sulawesi and the impossibility of maintaining separation in practice ("The Miser's Store," 29–30). See also Davidson and Henley, "Introduction: Radical Conservatism."

20 Schrauwers, Colonial *"Reformation,"* 21, 73–77. On New Order patronage, see also Hart, "Agrarian Change."

21 Burkard, *Stability or Sustainability?*, 29.

22 In the villages surrounding the park, closely monitored by conservationists, there was an overall population increase of 60 percent in the period 1980–2000. By 2001, migrants from outside Central Sulawesi, mainly Bugis from South Sulawesi and Javanese transmigrants, comprised 21 percent of the population in the subdistricts bordering the park: Sigi Biromaru, 23 percent; Palolo, 23 percent; Kulawi, 14 percent; Lore Utara (comprising Napu and Besoa), 30 percent; Lore Selatan (Bada), 3 percent (Maertens, Zeller, and Birner, *Explaining Agricultural Land Use*, 5).

23 Acciaioli, "Kinship and Debt"; Ruf, "From Tree-Crop Planting to Replanting"; Ruf and Yoddang, "The Sulawesi Cocoa Boom."

24 Maertens, Zeller, and Birner, *Explaining Agricultural Land Use*, 3; Ruf and Yoddang, "The Sulawesi Cocoa Boom."

25 Ruf, "From Tree-Crop Planting to Replanting."

26 My findings on processes of land transfer are consistent with other studies in Palolo and Napu. See Burkard, *Stability or Sustainability?*; Sitorus, *Land, Ethnicity, and the Competing Power*; Sitorus, "*Revolusi Cokelat*." See also Li, "Local Histories, Global Markets."

27 Sitorus, "*Revolusi Cokelat*," 10.

28 Burkard, *Stability or Sustainability?*, 4.

29 This heterogeneity was reflected in a village-by-village demographic survey (Yayasan Kayu Riva, *Survei Demogaphi*). Besides the subethnic groups already mentioned, there were Rampi, Seko, and Pada people from South Sulawesi who arrived as slaves before colonial conquest, or fled epidemics, notably in 1918 (Acciaioli, *Searching*, 102n57, 103; Aragon, *Fields of the Lord*, 76).

30 Acciaioli, *Searching*. In the 1990s, Putromo Paada reports (*Migrasi dan Konflik*, 98–100), Lindu people refused to work for the Bugis as a protest against their appropriation of Lindu land and labor.

31 Ruf found that 35 percent of Bugis migrants to the cacao frontier started out with very low capital, at most a few days' food. Early arrivals were able to acquire land at very low prices. Later waves of migrants into the same area had to pay much higher prices for land at third- or fourthhand, and more of them came with capital (Ruf, "From Tree-Crop Planting to Replanting," 35).

32 Pak Silo, taped interview, 2003.

33 Lindu, *Keputusan Bersama Lembaga Adat dan Pemerintah Desa se Dataran Lindu*.

34 The Lindu elite did not adhere to a two-hectare limit. A survey by YTM found that Lindu people, Bugis, and Kulawi migrants owned land roughly proportionate to the size of their populations, but within each group land ownership was unequal, with a few large landowners and many near landless (Sugiharto, Hasan, and Yabu, *Masalah Agraria*). Nevertheless, there was truth in the Lindu perception that, in the aggregate, it was outsiders who had taken over their land.

35 See Acciaioli, "Grounds of Conflict"; and Paada, *Migrasi dan Konflik*, 105, for Bugis perspectives.

36 On the success of measures to prevent escalation of conflicts at Lindu, see Acciaioli, "Grounds of Conflict"; and Paada, *Migrasi dan Konflik*, 109. Processes of escalation are further discussed in chapter 7.

37 Schrauwers, *Colonial "Reformation,"* 87–88.

38 Acciaioli, *Searching*, 88; Aragon, *Fields of the Lord*, 279, 301.

39 Schrauwers, *Colonial "Reformation,"* 84.

40 Aragon, *Fields of the Lord*; Haba, *Resettlement and Sociocultural Change*.

41 Schrauwers, *Colonial "Reformation,"* 5. On the high educational status of the Pamona and their aspirations for government jobs, see Sangaji, *Rumput Kering*.

42 On the symbolism of headhunting and its contemporary resonance, see *Headhunting and the Local Imagination in Southeast Asia*, edited by Janet Hoskins, and Peluso and Harwell 2001. On persistent view of highlanders as headhunters, see Henley, *Nationalism and Regionalism*, 28; Schrauwers, "Houses, Hierarchy, Headhunting and Exchange."

43 Aragon, "Communal Violence"; Hefner, *Civil Islam*.

44 Aditjondro, "Kerusuhan Poso"; Aragon, "Communal Violence." Struggles over high office were also a factor in violent conflicts in Maluku (ICG, *Indonesia: Overcoming Murder and Chaos in Maluku*). See also Vel, "Tribal Battle in Remote Island."

45 Sangaji, *Rumput Kering*, 35–41.

46 See Peluso and Watts, "Violent Environments," for a critique of neo-Malthusian explanations for conflict.

47 In 2000, the three senior executive positions in Poso District were indeed occupied by prominent members of the Habibie-linked association for Muslim intellectuals, ICMI (Sangaji, *Rumput Kering*, 38–39).

48 YTM, "Segregasi Masyarakat Poso," 16.

49 Sangaji, *Rumput Kering*, 36.

50 Aditjondro, "Kerusuhan Poso"; Sangaji, "Pasukan Terlatih dan Perubahan Pola Kekerasan di Poso."

51 Sangaji, "Kegagalan Keamanan di Poso."

52 Human Rights Watch, *Breakdown*; ICG, *Indonesia Backgrounder*.

53 Cacao and the recovery of territory figured prominently in journalistic accounts of the conflict, such as McCall, "Indonesia: Spirit of Jihad." Refugees reported that their cacao had been cut down or was being harvested by "thieves" (*Kompas*, "Hidup dari Transmigrasi ke Transmigrasi"). See also Aragon, "Communal Violence."

54 YTM, "Segregasi Masyarakat Poso."

55 *Kompas*, "Mengembalikan Citra Poso," "Poso Kembali Mencekam."

56 On cramped spaces, see Rose, *Powers of Freedom*, 280.

4. RENDERING TECHNICAL?

1 Maertens, Zeller, and Birner, *Explaining Agricultural Land Use*, 6.

2 Schweithelm et al., *Sulawesi Parks Program*, 27.

3 Cameron, *The Conservation Band-Aid*, vii.

4 TNC, *An Integrated Sulawesi Conservation Area*.

5 ANZDEC, *Environmental Management*, 17.

6 ADB, *Report and Recommendation*, ii.

7 Ibid., 4.

8 Ibid., 7, 11.

9 Ibid., 2.

10 ADB, *Summary Environmental Impact Assessment*, 5.

11 ADB, *Report and Recommendation*, 24. The province was ranked twenty-third of twenty-seven for poverty according to the national composite Human Development Index (ADB, *Report and Recommendation*, 2).

12 ADB, *Report and Recommendation*, 25.

13 ADB, *Report and Recommendation*, 65.

14 ADB, *Summary Environmental Impact Assessment*, 4, 6.

15 ADB, *Report and Recommendation*, 26.

16 ADB, *Summary Environmental Impact Assessment*, 11.

17 ANZDEC, *Social Analysis*, 24.

18 ADB, *Report and Recommendation*, 31.

19 E. Brown, "Grounds at Stake in Ancestral Domains"; Enters, *The Token Line*. In "Cultivating Cacao," Belsky and Siebert report that farmers in Kulawi understood the ecological benefits of growing cacao under shade in mixed gardens but still grew it as a monocrop in full sun to maximize short-run profit.

20 ADB, *Report and Recommendation*, 13.

21 Ibid., 65–66.

22 Cameron, *The Conservation Band-Aid*, 110, found that poor households in a park border village in Kulawi obtained up to 56 percent of their cash income from rattan.

23 ANZDEC, *Social Analysis*, 26.

24 ADB, *Report and Recommendation*, 18, 27, 36.

25 ANZDEC, *Social Analysis*, 28.

26 ADB, *Report and Recommendation*, 13, emphasis mine.

27 ANZDEC, *Social Analysis*, 22.

28 ADB, *Summary Environmental Impact Assessment*, 12.

29 ANZDEC, *Social Analysis*, 78–80.

30 Ibid., 28.

31 ADB, *Summary Environmental Impact Assessment*, 7.

32 ADB, *Report and Recommendation*, 12.

33 Ibid., 27.

34 ANZDEC, *Environmental Management*, 19. On Indonesia's illegal logging networks, see McCarthy, *"Wild Logging"*; Obidzinski, *Logging in East Kalimantan, Indonesia.*

35 ADB, *Report and Recommendation*, 27.

36 ADB, *Summary Environmental Impact Assessment*, 12.

37 ADB, *Report and Recommendation*, 20, 51–58.

38 ANZDEC, *Social Analysis*, 37.

39 Ferguson, *The Anti-Politics Machine*, 225.

40 ADB, *Report and Recommendation*, 71.

41 ADB, *Summary Environmental Impact Assessment*, 15. The costing is justified in ADB, *Report and Recommendation*, 66–67.

42 The project's failures were fully exposed in the midterm evaluation reports, the product of a rather effective participatory process. There was no coverup, and no construction of project success. See ADB, *Evaluasi Kinerja Secara Kualitatif;* ADB, *Hasil Evaluasi;* ADB, *Mid-Term Evaluation;* and ADB, *Project Review Mission.* The evaluation concluded that ADB should take its share of responsibility for invalid assumptions, failure to recognize risks, and for proposing no workable link between development and conservation (ADB, *Evaluasi Kinerja Secara Kualitatif,* 148–49).

43 *Nuansa Pos*, "Pimpro CSIADP Diminta Bayar Upah Kerja Jalan"; *Nuansa Pos*, "Buntut Kasus Proyek CSIADP di Sadaunta Lore Lindu."

44 CARE, *Project Evaluation*, 7.

45 See Levang, "From Rags to Riches in Sumatra," for a study of the rapid demise of an expert-designed agroforestry project planned to combine food crops with rubber for farmer "self-sufficiency." Farmers, finding the biodiverse farming system too labor-intensive, switched to monocrop rubber combined with wage labor.

46 Burkard, *Stability or Sustainability?*, 24; CARE, *Protection of Tropical Forests*, 11–13. In "Shifting Cultivation and 'Deforestation,' " Arild Angelsen discusses the illogic of intensifying agriculture as a means to keep farmers out of forests.

47 CARE, *Project Evaluation*, 6.

48 Dedicated cacao farmers did not use *mapalus*, preferring to use family labor or paid workers (Burkard, *Stability or Sustainability?*, 21).

49 CARE, *Report on the Interim Evaluation*, 15, 19, 36.

50 Ibid., 19, 36.

51 Ibid., 20; CARE, *Protection of Tropical Forests*, 10, 28.

52 CARE, *Project Evaluation*, 13, 17, 23–24.

53 Birner and Mappatoba, *Community Agreements on Conservation in Central Sulawesi*, 14–15.

54 Schweithelm et al., *Sulawesi Parks Program*, iii.

55 TNC, *Lore Lindu National Park, Indonesia Program Information Sheet*.

56 Schweithelm et al., *Sulawesi Parks Program*, 39–47.

57 Ibid., 4.

58 Ibid., 4, 52, 76.

59 Ibid., 95.

60 Ibid., 76–79.

61 TNC, *Lessons Learned*, 7.

62 TNC later proposed to work with the cacao boom to support high-value, organic cacao in return for conservation contracts. The park Director rejected this plan, arguing that cacao was already too prevalent in and around the park and threatened biodiversity (TNC, *Lessons Learned*; TNC, *Building Conservation Capacity*, 22). TNC recognized "that the opportunities for alternative economic activities are extremely limited" (TNC, *Building Conservation Capacity*, 23).

63 Dove, "So Far from Power, So Near to the Forest."

64 Mama Yonas, taped interview, 2003.

65 *Kompas*, "Kepala Balai Taman Nasional Lore Lindu."

66 Sangaji, *Politik Konservasi*.

67 YTM, *Dokumentasi*.

68 Ibid.

69 STORMA, *Processes of Destabilization*, 31.

70 Alam, "Katu Tribe Allowed to Retain Forest Home." On the Katu case, see Sangaji, *Politik Konservasi*, and D'Andrea, *Coffee, Custom, and Capital*.

71 A good summary of these arguments is Sangaji, *Menuju Pengelolaan TNLL*, a booklet published by WALHI and distributed to villagers around the park.

72 Scientists sent from Jakarta to verify Katu's claims later conducted transect studies comparing Katu's land to the nearby transmigration zone and confirmed the Katu's land was more biodiverse. I do not know why the comparator transect was outside the park.

73 CARE, *Report on the Interim Evaluation*, 47.

74 TNC, *TNC Lessons Learned*, 11–12. TNC argued that backlash against the ADB made it a conservation risk (TNC, *Building Conservation Capacity*, 7).

75 His comments probably referred to TNC's attempt to work with the ADB in 1999 to form "enterprise groups" to receive project funds. These funds were tied rather directly to conservation contracts. The funds never materialized. See TNC, *TNC Lessons Learned*, 12.

76 By the standards of the U.S. Congressional Financial Advisory Commission (the Meltzer Commission), at least 70 percent of ADB's projects in Indonesia were assessed as not likely to produce lasting economic or social benefits, that is, U.S.$11.36 billion of Indonesia's U.S.$16 billion ADB debt (DTE, "Evaluating the ADB in Indonesia").

77 Harley, *TNLL: Bebani Utang*; WALHI, *Laporan Hasil Monitoring Proyek*.

78 In 2003, action to reclaim this land was ongoing through a legal process and direct action. Villagers attempting to occupy the land were attacked by a mobile police brigade.

5. POLITICS IN CONTENTION

1 See Conklin and Graham, "The Shifting Middle Ground." Points of agreement and divergence between NGO activists pursuing these agendas, and

between NGOS and farmers' movements, are discussed in Lucas and Warren, "The State, the People, and Their Mediators."

2   Because this dispute became bitter and personalized, I have kept the identities of the various parties intentionally vague, and focused on the underlying issues. For a representative sample of positions, see Abbas, Siera, and Awang, *Interaksionisme*; CARE, *Protection of Tropical Forests*, 43–47; Faisal and Montesori, "Orang Dongi-Dongi"; FKKM, *Pertemuan di FKKM*; Laban, "Prospek Negatif"; Laban, Thamrin, and Cougar, *Sumbangan*; Laudjeng, "Jangan Cemarkan"; Sangaji, *Menuju Pengelolaan TNLL*; TNC, *TNC Lessons Learned*, 33–35; Top FM, *Dongi-Dongi, Fenomena, Masalah, Solusi*; WALHI, *Kontroversi Dongi Dongi*; WALHI, *Lembaran Fakta*; and WALHI, *Pendudukan Dongi Dongi*. See also postings to FKKM@yahoogroups.com, ADAT@yahoogroups.com, and KPSHK @yahoogroups.com, as well as news reports in *Nuansa Pos, Radar Sulteng, Suara Pembaruan*, and *Kompas*. My account also draws on interviews with representatives of TNC, CARE, ADB; the provincial planning agency BAPPEDA; WALHI, YBHR, FKTNLL, YTM, Katopasa and Yayasan Pekurehua; leaders of the Free Farmers Forum; and villagers of Sedoa, Watumaeta, Dongi-Dongi, and Rahmat in May–June 2003.

3   Ortner, "Resistance."

4   Li, Arifin, and Achadiyat, *Design for the Evaluation of the Program for Isolated Communities*.

5   In the original: *Anda Masuki Wilayah Kedaulatan Forum Petani Merdeka*.

6   I use the capitalized *Farmers* to refer to members of the Free Farmers Forum resident at Dongi-Dongi. The designation Farmer is crucial to their self-positioning. Opponents argue that they are not farmers but loggers.

7   I recorded the dialogue, later transcribed and published in YTM, "Menakar Keinginan Warga Dongi-Dongi." The politician's position in this encounter was complex. He was tasked by the District Head to help persuade the Farmers to accept resettlement. He was accompanied by officials from the transmigration department. His stated goal was to find out which resettlement site would suit the people best, in terms of their cultural preferences. He also had a business interest, since he heads an NGO that undertakes "social preparation" for government resettlement projects on a contract basis. As a politician in the era of *reformasi*, he also sought popular support.

8   The association with GAM was reported by a Farmer present when the District Head made this statement.

9   Eviction was again threatened in 2003 in a formal edict (Governor, *Keputusan Gubernur*). The edict noted that the illegal activities logging and settlement in the park had to be stopped because they were reducing "the authority of the government" (*kewibawaan pemerintah*). In September 2003, a thousand people from Dongi-Dongi marched on the Governor's office in Palu to protest against the edict and continued corruption in the resettlement program (*Radar Sulteng*, "Kantor Gubernur Diserbu").

10 Many of these arguments were made during the public dialogue with the politician described above and received applause from the assembled Farmers.

11 "Why Are Hill People Being Returned to the Hills?" was the title of an article in a national newspaper, one of a four-part series on Dongi-Dongi. See Montesori, "Kenapa Orang Gunung Dekembalikan ke Gunung?"

12 Laban, "Tragedi Dongi-Dongi Q-sruh Pandang Konservasi," 64. TNC, aware that downstream issues had more traction in public opinion than biodiversity, provided scientific confirmation of the risk of flooding and put a monetary value on water from the park at U.S.$8.9 million per year (TNC, *Lore Lindu Water Resources Valuation Study*).

13 Abdon Nababan, in "Respon Untuk Cermatan Kasus Dongi Dongi," wrote astutely of the grist provided by the Dongi-Dongi case to debates among activists weighing conservation, land rights, and social justice.

14 The dynamic between the NGOs, the "e-mail war," the hardening of positions, and the moratorium on NGO contact with villagers were described by Wibowo, a university researcher from Java working with STORMA, during a dialogue session at which members of the forum and other parties presented their perspectives. The transcript of this meeting is thirty single-spaced pages of dense debate (FKKM, *Pertemuan di FKKM*).

15 See Abbas, Siera, and Awang, *Interaksionisme*; and Laban, Thamrin, and Cougar, *Sumbangan*.

16 Sangaji, *Menuju Pengelolaan TNLL*; WALHI, *Kontroversi Dongi Dongi*.

17 See *Kompas*, "Kepala Balai Taman Nasional Lore Lindu"; and *Koran Tempo*, "Kepala Taman Nasional Robek Piagam WALHI." The Director viewed Dongi-Dongi as a situation in which weak and ignorant people were being used (ADB,

Mid-Term Evaluation, appendix 14; Laban, "Prospek Negatif"). He described capitalism and individualism as a virus spreading among villagers. He advocated a return to communal forms of ownership and management he imagined to be customary (Laban, "Tragedi Dongi-Dongi Q-sruh Pandang Konservasi").

18 Laban, Thamrin, and Cougar, *Sumbangan*, 56.

19 *Koran Tempo*, "Kepala Taman Nasional Robek Piagam WALHI"; Laban, *Pernyataan Sikap*; WALHI, *Kontroversi Dongi Dongi*.

20 This argument evades a key tension between indigenous rights and land rights platforms. Since villagers everywhere contest the state's claim to land in the name of their customary rights, attempts by landless people to reclaim land from the state or state-sponsored corporations routinely come up against customary claimants. They would have clear rights only if they happened to be in their ancestral place. One speaker at a discussion about Dongi-Dongi described the framing of claims based on who lived where hundreds of years ago the "disease of indigenism" (*penyakit keaslian*), out of step with the common need of poor people (*rakyat kecil*) for land in a context where powerful people monopolize it (FKKM, *Pertemuan di FKKM*). See also Li, "*Masyarakat Adat*, Difference, and the Limits of Recognition"; and Sangaji, "The Masyarakat Adat Movement in Indonesia."

21 Top FM, *Dongi-Dongi, Fenomena, Masalah, Solusi*.

22 Malkki, "National Geographic."

23 The case for land reclaiming by leverage was made in relation to Dongi-Dongi in newspaper articles by Agus Firdaus ("Petani Dongi-Dongi Pasca Reklaiming"). For an accessible overview of KPA's position, see Lucas and Warren, "The State, the People, and Their Mediators."

24 Since it was the mountain people Christianized by missionaries who later came to occupy the indigenous slot, it is true that Palu NGOs espousing the indigenous cause often work with Christians, but they are not exclusive. YTM, for example, has worked with Muslim Javanese transmigrants threatened with seizure of their land (Sangaji, *Buruk INCO Rakyat Digusur*).

25 *Nuansa Pos*, "WALHI Sulteng Perlu Memberikan Pemahaman FPM Dongi Dongi"; Laban, Thamrin, and Cougar, *Sumbangan*, 109.

26 *Kompas*, "Kepala Balai Taman Nasional Lore Lindu."

27 See Katopasa, "Pejabat Wali Kota Palu, Melakukan Praktek Illegal Logging," and "60–100 Unit Chain Saw Setiap Hari Beroperasi di Dongi-Dongi"; Laban, "Prospek Negatif." A WALHI report named the villagers, Forest Department officials, and senior members of the police and army involved in logging in Palolo and Dongi-Dongi (WALHI, *Laporan Tim Investigasi*).

28 Sargeant, "Update: Birding Logistics in the National Parks of Northern Sulawesi."

29 The utopic vision of Dongi-Dongi was described by a member of the pro-farmer alliance in a newspaper article (Firdaus, "Petani Dongi-Dongi Pasca Reklaiming").

30 A Golkar party worker informed me that there were 6,800 Da'a in Palolo, outnumbering the original valley dwellers, the Kaili Ija (4,500), and migrant groups such as Bugis, Torajan, and resettled Kulawi hill farmers. I did not confirm these numbers, though their significance to party organizers is noteworthy.

31 Laban, Thamrin, and Cougar, *Sumbangan*, 75–76.

32 Ibid., 75.

33 E-mails between Duncan Neville of TNC and Sangaji of YTM on July 16 and 17, 2001, were widely circulated and posted to several newsgroups.

34 The reference could be to one of the covenants of the ADB loan, which states, "The Borrower shall not allow any project or activity . . . that would have an adverse environmental impact on the Park." An ADB report noted that "major encroachment and illegal harvesting in Dongi-Dongi area" were not in compliance with this Covenant (ADB, *Project Review Mission*, appendix 6).

35 CARE, *Report on the Interim Evaluation*, 26; CARE, *Protection of Tropical Forests*, appendix 3, outcome 1.

36 CARE, *Report on the Interim Evaluation*, 38, 50, 46.

37 See ADB, *Evaluasi Kinerja Secara Kualitatif*, 129; ADB, *Hasil Evaluasi*, 10; and ADB, *Mid-Term Evaluation*, especially appendix 14, contributed by the park Director.

38 See my discussion of diverse deployments of *adat* in Central Sulawesi, including the elite ethnopolitics emerging in the wake of the legislation on regional autonomy (Li, "Adat in Central Sulawesi").

39 Bernstein, "Taking the Part of Peasants?" 69.

1   Dutton, "Engaging Communities," 25.

2   Ibid., 27.

3   Ibid., 32.

4   TNC, *TNC Lessons Learned*, i.

5   TNC, *Draft Management Plan*, 2/1; TNC, *TNC Lessons Learned*, 14.

6   I cite the draft with permission of TNC's Palu office. The management plan finally signed by the Ministry of Forests in 2004 was scaled down and, according to a TNC staff member, "more pragmatic." TNC's intellectual leadership in defining the "philosophy" guiding the preparation of the plan was acknowledged in a report (TNC, *TNC Lessons Learned*, 14).

7   TNC, *TNC Lessons Learned*, 27.

8   Ibid., 25. Note that TNC's "threat analysis" using Landsat images showed a reduction in forest canopy of less than 1 percent between 1983 and 2003. The "threat" highlighted by TNC was the increased rate of forest loss during that period (ADB, *Mid-Term Evaluation*, annex 1 and 2).

9   TNC, *Building Conservation Capacity*, 9.

10   TNC, *Draft Management Plan*, 2/67–68. This conclusion echoed that of foresters in Java, dubious about poverty alleviation (Peluso, *Rich Forests, Poor People*).

11   TNC, *TNC Lessons Learned*, 12.

12   TNC, *Draft Management Plan*, 2/75.

13   TNC, *TNC Lessons Learned*, 30.

14   TNC, *Building Conservation Capacity*, 20.

15   TNC, *Draft Management Plan*, 2/12.

16   Ibid., 2/13.

17   Ibid., 2/20.

18   Ibid., 2/90; TNC, *TNC Lessons Learned*, 26.

19   TNC, *Draft Management Plan*, 2/13. See also 2/89.

20   TNC, *TNC Lessons Learned*, 26.

21   CARE, *Report on the Interim Evaluation*, 45; TNC, *Building Conservation Capacity*, 34; TNC, *TNC Lessons Learned*, 34–35.

22   TNC, *TNC Lessons Learned*, 26.

23   TNC, *Building Conservation Capacity*, 9.

24 TNC, *TNC Lessons Learned*, i.

25 TNC, *Draft Management Plan*, 2/20. See also 2/71.

26 TNC, *TNC Lessons Learned*, 33. See the critique of comanagement by Benda-Beckmann and Benda-Beckmann in "Community Based Tenurial Rights."

27 TNC, *Draft Management Plan*, 1/2. I do not know whether the Director General wrote or approved the preface, which appeared in the draft under his name.

28 Ibid., 2/100–101.

29 TNC, *Draft Management Plan*, 2/92–93. TNC insisted that villagers who participated in mapping teams must understand that the team had "no authority to suggest relocation of boundaries" (TNC, *Building Conservation Capacity*, 20).

30 TNC, *Draft Management Plan*, 2/108.

31 Ibid., 2/100; TNC, *TNC Lessons Learned*, 33.

32 As Jonathan Padwe astutely observed in his comments on a draft of this manuscript, "this seems almost exactly backward. Conflict was the cause of lack of participation in the past; acceptance, correctly arranged, guarantees participation."

33 TNC, *Draft Management Plan*, 2/102. The passage is a quote from a TNC document of 1998. The reference to boundary revision here was specious: no procedure for boundary revision was proposed in 1998 or in the 2001 draft.

34 Mitchell, *Rule of Experts*.

35 TNC, *Draft Management Plan*, 2/185.

36 Ibid., 2/185.

37 Ibid., 2/95.

38 Ibid., 2/100.

39 Ibid., 2/65, 2/178.

40 Ibid., 2/69.

41 Boomgaard, "Introducing Environmental Histories of Indonesia"; Henley, *Fertility, Food and Fever*.

42 TNC, *Draft Management Plan*, 2/67.

43 Ibid., 2/167.

44 Ibid., 2/84–86.

45 Ibid., 2/90.

46 Ibid., 2/91, chart 14.1.

47 Ibid., 2/105.

48 Ibid., 2/107.

49 Ibid., 2/66.

50 Ibid., 2/155.

51 Ibid., 2/149.

52 Ibid., 2/157. On the replacement of swidden with cacao in Moa, see Belsky and Siebert, "Cultivating Cacao."

53 TNC, *Draft Management Plan*, 2/156.

54 Ibid.

55 Ibid., 2/157–59.

56 Ibid., 2/69.

57 Ibid., 2/103.

58 In this case, maps and legibility were not unilateral instruments of control imposed by states and resisted by the populace. On countermapping, see Peluso, "Whose Woods Are These?"

59 This risk was also observed in CARE, *Report on the Interim Evaluation*, 41.

60 TNC, *Draft Management Plan*, 2/20.

61 TNC, *Draft Management Plan*, 1/67, 76. The figure of 26 percent anthropogenic forest includes the two enclave areas, but significantly exceeds them.

62 Ibid., 1/54–61.

63 The report was an appendix to TNC, *Building Conservation Capacity*.

64 CARE, *Protection of Tropical Forests*, 6. The governmental project of engaging people in new practices as a way to create environmental subjects is closely examined in Agrawal, *Environmentality*.

65 CARE, *Report on the Interim Evaluation*, 21.

66 ADB, *Mid-Term Evaluation*, annex 14.

67 Sedoa, for example, reported illegal loggers in its territory and threatened to apprehend them if the authorities did not intervene.

68 TNC, *TNC Lessons Learned*, 33.

69 TNC, *Draft Management Plan*, 2/103.

70 TNC, *TNC Lessons Learned*, 27.

71 TNC, *Draft Management Plan*, 2/178.

72 TNC, *Participatory Conservation Planning Manual*, 2, emphasis in original.

73 This figure appeared as chart 8.2 in TNC, *Draft Management Plan*, 2/51.

74 TNC, *Draft Management Plan*, 3/4.

75 TNC, *Participatory Conservation Planning Manual*, 7.

76 TNC, *Building Conservation Capacity*, 36.

77 TNC, *Participatory Conservation Planning Manual*, 12.

78 TNC, *Building Conservation Capacity*, 37.

79 TNC, *Participatory Conservation Planning Manual*, 18.

80 TNC, *Draft Management Plan*, 3/8–9.

81 TNC, *Building Conservation Capacity*, 37; TNC, *Draft Management Plan*, 3/127–28.

82 TNC, *Participatory Conservation Planning Manual*, 21.

83 TNC, *Draft Management Plan*, 3/129.

84 Ibid., 3/12–26.

85 Ibid., 3/27–41 and 95–106.

86 Ibid., 3/43.

87 Ibid., 3/69.

88 Ibid., 3/69, 78.

89 Ibid., 3/127–28.

90 TNC, *Kesepakatan Konservasi*, 25; TNC, *TNC Lessons Learned*, 16.

91 TNC, *Building Conservation Capacity*, 38.

92 Ibid., 39; TNC, *Kesepakatan Konservasi*, 14.

93 TNC, *Kesepakatan Konservasi*, 15–16.

94 Ibid., 16.

95 Ibid., 15, 30.

96 Ibid., 18–19.

97 Ibid., 28.

98 TNC, *Building Conservation Capacity*, 39.

99 On villager calculations of benefits versus costs in village monitoring, see Burkard, *Stability or Sustainability?*, and Burkard, *Natural Resource Management*, 13, 14. Burkard also noted the potential for reporting enemies more than friends, intensifying conflict.

100 Sedoa, "Peraturan Desa Sedoa."

101 TNC, *Building Conservation Capacity*, 34.

102 Ibid., 41.

103 TNC, *Laporan Kegiatan Pemetaan*, 33.

104 The influence of "the Katu case" in stimulating Watumaeta leaders to make claims on the park was noted in Burkard, *Stability or Sustainability?*, and in Burkard, *Natural Resource Management*, 15. TNC reported that in Watumaeta, members of the village elite were selling coffee land within the park to mi-

grants even as they talked of recovering ancestral land (TNC, *Laporan Kegiatan Pemetaan*, 30–33). On land reclaiming organized by a village Headman in Palolo, see Sitorus, "*Revolusi Cokelat.*"

105 See Birner and Mappatoba, *Community Agreements on Conservation in Central Sulawesi*, 23.

106 TNC, *Laporan Kegiatan Pemetaan*, 33.

107 TNC, *TNC Lessons Learned*, 12.

108 Ibid., 15.

109 Ibid., 14.

110 TNC, *Draft Management Plan*, 2/58.

111 This figure originally appeared, in a slightly different form, as chart 10.2 in TNC, *Draft Management Plan*, 2/61.

112 YTM, *Pertemuan Konsultasi*, table 1.

113 In a subsequent meeting with villagers organized by YTM, the park Director demonstrated that he had an astute grasp of processes around the park, and villagers' concerns. Yet his proposals did not address them. He urged people to voluntarily uproot their coffee and cacao inside the park, to improve the sustainable harvesting of rattan and *damar*, save indigenous rice strains, make and market bark cloth for tourists, collect wild honey, preserve medicinal plants, restock endangered bird populations, learn about the role of the park in watershed protection, and recover pride in themselves through their customary resource management regimes (Laban, "Membangun Gerakan Komunitas Lokal, Menuju Konservasi Radikal").

114 Behoa, *Kesepakatan Konservasi*; Behoa, *Kesepakatan Lembaga*. The negative effects of park exclusion on the people of Besoa were recorded in the transcripts of several "dialogues" with park authorities in which villagers described their bitter experiences in very concrete terms (YTM, *Dialog Kebijakan*).

115 Quoted in YTM, *Notulensi Dialog Masyarakat Mataue*.

116 Burkard, *Stability or Sustainability?* and *Natural Resource Management*, 6.

117 Burkard, *Stability or Sustainability?*, 33.

118 See Tsing, "Becoming a Tribal Elder," for a vivid account of the ascription of nature loving to Kalimantan villagers. On the role of scarcity, see Ellen, "What Black Elk Left Unsaid."

119 TNC, *Building Conservation Capacity*, appendix.

120 Lindu, *Keputusan Bersama Lembaga Adat dan Pemerintah Desa se Dataran Lindu.*

121 Birner and Mappatoba, *Community Agreements on Conservation in Central Sulawesi.*

122 Peters, "Encountering Participation and Knowledge in Development Sites," 7.

7. DEVELOPMENT IN THE AGE OF NEOLIBERALISM

1 See the World Bank's Social Development Web sites in Washington and Jakarta. A subcategory labeled "Community-Driven Development" was a U.S.$7 billion portfolio at the bank in 2004. For a critical review by bank staff, see Mansuri and Rao, "Community-Based and -Driven Development."

2 This expression appeared in Woolcock, "Social Capital and Economic Development," 187.

3 Guggenheim, *Crises and Contradictions*, 2, 8. Further phases and offshoots of the program were scheduled to receive 25 percent of all World Bank lending to Indonesia in the period 2004–7 and were a cornerstone of the Country Assistance Strategy (World Bank, *Indonesia: Country Assistance Strategy* [2004], ii).

4 Guggenheim, *Crises and Contradictions*, 2.

5 Ibid., 3.

6 Ibid., 2.

7 In 2001–2, a bank staff member from Washington was already investigating its replicability (Edstrom, *Indonesia's Kecamatan Development Project*).

8 Guggenheim et al., *Indonesia's Kecamatan Development Program*, 4.

9 World Bank, *Second Kecamatan Development Project*, 20.

10 World Bank, *Community Recovery*, vii.

11 Rose, *Powers of Freedom*, 176. Pat O'Malley describes use of this strategy to govern aboriginal populations in Australia ("Indigenous Governance"). The present book has shown the multiple ways in which community was invoked in the context of struggles over resources, but I do not elaborate on this aspect here. For a sample of literature on this topic, see Jenson, "Claiming Community"; Li, "Images of Community"; Moore, "Clear Waters and Muddied Histories"; Watts, "Development and Governmentality."

12 Rose, *Powers of Freedom*, 176, 189; J. Scott, *Seeing Like a State.*

13 Rose, *Powers of Freedom*, 136.

14 Ibid., 177.

15 Ibid., 172. For colonial and contemporary examples, see Agrawal and Gibson, "Enchantment and Disenchantment"; Chatterjee, "Community in the East"; Cowen and Shenton, *Doctrines of Development*, 56–57; Dewey, "Images of the Village Community"; Mosse, "Colonial and Contemporary Ideologies of 'Community Management' "; Robertson, *People and the State*.

16 Rose, *Powers of Freedom*, 172, emphasis in original.

17 Ibid., 135.

18 Ibid., 174, 178.

19 Responsibilization is exemplified by the Grameen Bank and others that require people to form groups and take collective responsibility for loan repayments.

20 Rose, *Powers of Freedom*, 175.

21 Green, "Participatory Development and the Appropriation of Agency," 69, emphasis original. Green provides a useful critical analysis of empowerment and participation in theory and practice.

22 Chambers, foreword to Blackburn and Holland, *Who Changes?*, xvi. For Robert Chambers, the frontiers of improved development in the 1990s were practical and institutional—not political or economic. They centered on personal attitudes. See Francis, "Participatory Development at the World Bank," for a critique of a World Bank account of the heroic odyssey and personal transformations associated with the adoption of participation and the experience of listening to the "voices of the poor."

23 Elinor Ostrom's work on crafting institutions was an important influence. See Agrawal, "Common Property Institutions"; Cleaver, "Insititutions, Agency and the Limitations of Participatory Approaches to Development."

24 Pretty and Ward, "Social Capital and the Environment," 209.

25 For these authors, the neoliberal agenda to promote entrepreneurship through group formation was explicit. Support must be designed to make groups independent because "creating dependent citizens rather than entrepreneurial citizens reduces the capacity of citizens to produce capital" (Pretty and Ward, "Social Capital and the Environment," 220).

26 See L. Brown and Fox, "Accountability within Transnational Coalitions."

27 Hulme and Edwards, "Conclusion: Too Close to the Powerful, Too Far from the Powerless?" 277.

28 In the preface and introduction to *Civil Society and the Political Imagination in Africa*, John and Jean Comaroff review the history of the civil society concept and the conjuncture in southern Africa in which it again came to the fore.

29 Howell and Pearce, "Civil Society," 78.

30 Biggs and Neame, "Negotiating Room to Maneuver," 49; Howell and Pearce, "Civil Society," 80–81.

31 For a striking example, see Blair, "Donors, Democratisation and Civil Society."

32 Bebbington and Riddell, "Heavy Hands," 110–11; Blair, "Donors, Democratisation and Civil Society"; Edwards, Hulme, and Wallace, "Increasing Leverage for Development," 9.

33 Antlöv, "Indonesian Civil Society," 15.

34 Ibid., 16.

35 Ibid., 19–23.

36 A similar tension was present in an Australian Aid document that cautioned against imposing Western liberal democratic values on Indonesian civil society, then listed criteria for selecting the kinds of civil society organizations Australian Aid should support, and the skills they needed to learn (IDSS, *Strategic Choices for Working with CSOS in Indonesia*).

37 Antlöv, "The Making of Democratic Local Governance in Indonesia."

38 DiZirega cited in Edmunds and Wollenberg, "A Strategic Approach." Edmunds and Wollenberg provide a useful critique of stakeholder processes based on their experience in Kalimantan.

39 Antlöv, "Not Enough Politics!" 84.

40 Ibid., 86n1.

41 World Bank, *Local Capacity*, 41. See also Evers, *Resourceful Villagers, Powerless Communities*, 11, 15; and World Bank, *Social Capital, Local Capacity, and Government*, 36.

42 World Bank, *Social Capital, Local Capacity, and Government*, 13.

43 Ibid., 3.

44 Evers, *Resourceful Villagers, Powerless Communities*. See also Antlöv, "Not Enough Politics!"; and Antlöv, "Village Government."

45 There was also frank recognition of corruption within bank projects. See Guggenheim, *Crises and Contradictions.*

46 Guggenheim, *Crises and Contradictions*; Woodhouse, *Village Corruption in Indonesia.*

47 World Bank, *Indonesia: Country Assistance Strategy* (2001), 6.

48 Ibid., i–ii, 17, 24.

49 Rose, *Powers of Freedom*, 141–42.

50 World Bank, *Indonesia: Country Assistance Strategy* (2001), 28.

51 Ibid., ii.

52 BPS, BAPPENAS, and UNDP, *The Economics of Democracy.*

53 World Bank, *Indonesia: Country Assistance Strategy* (2001), 28, 26. The role of the social development program in ensuring access to "development" in the context of bank-enforced competition and "selectivity" was further emphasized in the subsequent CAS (28). A bank study of decentralization recommended a role for the central government in defining standards that lower levels of government must meet, pushing responsibility downward (World Bank, *Decentralizing Indonesia*). The proposition that properly designed decentralization would make political and administrative elites more accountable, rather than intensify the authoritarian tendencies of "predatory networks of patronage," is critically examined in Hadiz, "Decentralization and Democracy in Indonesia."

54 World Bank, *Second Kecamatan Development Project*, 3.

55 Ibid., 5.

56 Guggenheim et al., *Indonesia's Kecamatan Development Program*, 2.

57 Ibid., 9.

58 World Bank, *Third Kecamatan Development Project.*

59 For details on how the concept of social capital was mobilized and measured in the bank studies, see World Bank, *Social Capital, Local Capacity, and Government.*

60 Bebbington, et al. "Exploring Social Capital."

61 Guggenheim, *Crises and Contradictions*, 34.

62 Putnam, *Making Democracy Work*, 167; quoted in Wetterberg, *Crisis, Social Ties, and Household Welfare*, 3.

63 Harriss, *Depoliticizing Development*, 97.

64 Woolcock, "Social Capital and Economic Development."

65 Michael Woolcock makes these arguments at length. I find his argument circular: prosperous societies have good stocks of social capital; poor, unequal, and violent societies have low stocks, and little prospect of increasing them. As with material capital, those who have shall receive more (ibid., 155, 182). See Fine, "The Developmental State Is Dead"; Hart, "Development Critiques in the 1990s"; Watts, "Development Ethnographies"; and especially Harriss, *Depoliticizing Development*, for critiques of the bank's use of social capital.

66 Harriss, *Depoliticizing Development*, 110.

67 Guggenheim, *Crises and Contradictions*, 37.

68 Evers, *Resourceful Villagers, Powerless Communities*, 8.

69 World Bank, *Local Capacity*, 15.

70 Guggenheim, *Crises and Contradictions*, 21.

71 World Bank, *Local Capacity*, 41.

72 Guggenheim, *Crises and Contradictions*, 22.

73 Ibid., 22–23.

74 World Bank, *Social Capital, Local Capacity, and Government*, 63–64.

75 Evers, *Resourceful Villagers, Powerless Communities*, 47, 53. See also Gupta, "Blurred Boundaries."

76 Evers, *Resourceful Villagers, Powerless Communities*, 57.

77 Ibid., 49; World Bank, *Local Capacity*, 51.

78 Evers, *Resourceful Villagers, Powerless Communities*, 60.

79 Block grants had been used under the New Order and during the 1997–98 crisis, but without such tight control (Guggenheim, *Crises and Contradictions*).

80 World Bank, *Second Kecamatan Development Project*, 6; World Bank, *Kecamatan Development Program Phase One*, 6–8, 20–21.

81 World Bank, *Kecamatan Development Program Phase One*, 8, 24.

82 Edstrom, *Indonesia's Kecamatan Development Project*, 2. Guggenheim et al., *Indonesia's Kecamatan Development Program*, still listed poverty alleviation as KDP's prime objective (6).

83 World Bank, *Second Kecamatan Development Project*, 3.

84 Guggenheim et al., *Indonesia's Kecamatan Development Program*, 9; Woodhouse, *Village Corruption in Indonesia*, 3; World Bank, *Second Kecamatan Development Project*, 13.

85 Guggenheim, *Crises and Contradictions*, 38.

86 Ibid., 39, 40.

87   World Bank, *Second Kecamatan Development Project*, 4–5.

88   World Bank, *Kecamatan Development Program Phase One*, 15.

89   World Bank, *Kecamatan Development Program Phase One*, 54.

90   Guggenheim, *Crises and Contradictions*, 7.

91   Woodhouse, *Village Corruption in Indonesia*, 18.

92   World Bank, *Kecamatan Development Program Phase One*, 54.

93   Woodhouse, *Village Corruption in Indonesia*, 1.

94   World Bank, *Second Kecamatan Development Project*.

95   Evers, *Legal Assistance Program for KDP Communities*, 15–16; World Bank, "Village Justice in Indonesia."

96   World Bank, *Kecamatan Development Program Phase One*, 52.

97   Evers, *Legal Assistance Program for KDP Communities*, 14.

98   World Bank, *Kecamatan Development Program Phase One*, 53.

99   Rose, *Powers of Freedom*, 73, emphasis original.

100 Guggenheim, *Proposal to the Norwegian Trust Fund*, 4.

101 Woodhouse, *Village Corruption in Indonesia*, 6.

102 Ibid., 42.

103 Ibid., 4–5.

104 Ibid., 35–39.

105 Evers, *Legal Assistance Program for KDP Communities*; Woodhouse, *Village Corruption in Indonesia*.

106 World Bank, *Idea Note, Justice for the Poor*, 4; World Bank, *Village Justice in Indonesia*.

107 Evers, *Legal Assistance Program for KDP Communities*, 5–8.

108 Guggenheim, *Proposal to the Norwegian Trust Fund*. The eventual sample size was six hundred (Guggenheim, e-mail to author, October 29, 2005).

109 World Bank, *Kecamatan Development Program Phase One*, 9.

110 Guggenheim, *Crises and Contradictions*, 33.

111 World Bank, *Second Kecamatan Development Project*, 20. In 2004, 40 percent of districts opted to provide matching grant funds to KDP. KDP proposed to make matching contributions from districts a requirement for those districts to retain access to KDP funds after an initial three-year period (Guggenheim et al., *Indonesia's Kecamatan Development Program*, 12, 16).

112 Story collected by Enurlaela Hasanah, retold in Guggenheim, *Crises and Contradictions*, 1–2.

113 Evers, *Legal Assistance Program for* KDP *Communities*, 10.

114 World Bank, *Kecamatan Development Program Phase One*, 40–44.

115 Discussion of KDP at a seminar at the World Bank in Jakarta in which I presented a paper on "Government through Community," September 2002.

116 Guggenheim, *Crises and Contradictions*, 33.

117 Ibid.

118 Ferguson, *The Anti-Politics Machine*, 270.

119 World Bank, *Village Justice in Indonesia*.

120 See ICG, *Indonesia: Managing Decentralization and Conflict*, for a comparable study in South Sulawesi.

121 Madden and Barron, *Violence and Conflict Resolution*, 69; World Bank, *Indonesia: Country Assistance Strategy* (2004), 1; World Bank, *Support for Poor and Disadvantaged Areas*.

122 Barron, Smith, and Woolcock, *Understanding Local Level Conflict Pathways*, 1.

123 Ibid. See also Barron and Madden, *Beyond Structural Factors*; Madden and Barron, *Violence and Conflict Resolution*; C. Smith, *The Roots of Violence*; Tajima, *Mobilizing for Violence*; Welsh, *Mobbing for Justice*.

124 In *The Roots of Violence*, Claire Smith describes past customary regimes in Kalimantan in these terms. Madden and Barron describe the attenuated mediation skills of villagers in *Violence and Conflict Resolution*.

125 Barron, Smith, and Woolcock, *Understanding Local Level Conflict Pathways*, 10.

126 On methodological individualism in bank social science, see Harriss, *Depoliticizing Development*; on the crafting of institutions, see Agrawal, "Common Property Institutions."

127 C. Smith, *The Roots of Violence*, 45.

128 Barron, Smith, and Woolcock, *Understanding Local Level Conflict Pathways*, 33.

129 Ibid., 34.

130 Ibid., 30, 31.

131 Ibid., 36, 37.

132 Ibid., 35.

133 Ibid., 34. See also C. Smith, *The Roots of Violence*, 48–50.

134 See Tajima, *Mobilizing for Violence*.

135 The risks are described in C. Smith, *The Roots of Violence*; Tajima, *Mobilizing for Violence*, 29. Bank social experts planned a controlled study of the risks and

benefits of using KDP-style mechanisms for conflict management (Barron et al., *Do Participatory Development Projects Help*).

136 World Bank, "Support for Poor and Disadvantaged Areas," 3.

137 Ibid., 5, 38.

138 Ibid., 8.

139 Ibid., 8.

140 Ibid., 7.

141 Ibid., 31.

142 Ibid., 22.

143 Lucas and Warren, "The State, the People, and Their Mediators," 115n106; World Bank, *Land Management and Policy Development Project*.

144 World Bank, *Indonesia: Country Assistance Strategy* (2004), annex G. Madden and Barron stress the need for "good growth" that offers equitable benefits to different population groups (*Violence and Conflict Resolution*, 74–76). They point out that bank support for transmigration—a program to promote growth—left a legacy of conflict that continued to be played out decades later. Yet the CAS made no mention of the need to ensure that growth was "good" rather than bad. Obviously there are diverse views on these matters within the bank and some awkward disjunctions.

145 World Bank, *Support for Poor and Disadvantaged Areas*, 4.

146 Ibid., 25.

147 Reports cited in Human Rights Watch, *Without Remedy*, 29. See also Lucas and Warren, "The State, the People, and Their Mediators."

148 WALHI, *A Violent Start of the Year for Indonesian Communities*.

149 Lucas and Warren, "The State, the People, and Their Mediators."

150 Human Rights Watch, *Without Remedy*, 19.

151 Ibid., 47.

152 Ibid., 20.

153 Ibid., 3, 55. The report cites Chip Fay and Martua Sirait's finding that the Forest Department failed to follow its own procedures for gazetting forest land ("Reforming the Reformists," 139). By 2002 only 68 percent of the state-claimed forest estate had been gazetted. Where it was gazetted, the legal requirement for notification of local communities was often violated. Thus rights to the ungazetted or improperly gazetted land continue to be vested in

customary communities, and grants of this land to logging corporations, plantations, and others are properly described as seizures.

154 Human Rights Watch, *Without Remedy*, 3–4.

155 Ibid., 4–5, 20.

156 Ibid., 3, 30, 33–44.

157 Ibid., 32.

158 Ibid., 63.

159 Ibid.,29.

160 Ibid., 31, 52.

161 Ibid., 33–35, 50–52.

162 See also Hadiz, "Decentralization and Democracy in Indonesia"; ICG, *Indonesia: Natural Resources and Law Enforcement*; McCarthy, *"Wild Logging"*; McCarthy, "Changing to Gray."

163 Bank social scientists have studied the negotiations and struggles that go into the production of their own policy narratives. See Bebbington, "Exploring Social Capital"; Guggenheim, *Proposal to the Norwegian Trust Fund*; Guggenheim, *Crises and Contradictions*. For superb analyses of policy processes, and the work it takes to maintain the apparent coherence of development programs, see Fairhead and Leach, *Misreading the African Landscape*; Fairhead and Leach, *Science, Society and Power*; and Mosse, "Is Good Policy Unimplementable?"

164 Foucault, "Questions of Method," 81.

165 Hadiz, "Decentralization and Democracy in Indonesia," 702.

CONCLUSION

1 Foucault, "Governmentality," 100.

2 See Peluso, "Coercing Conservation."

3 Cooke and Kothari, "The Case for Participation as Tyranny," 14–15.

4 Cleaver, "Insititutions, Agency and the Limitations of Participatory Approaches to Development," 54.

5 Rahnema, "Participation," 123. See also Cruikshank, *The Will to Empower*.

6 Translated from the original circulated by FKTNLL@palu.wasantara.net.id on February 5, 2002.

7 Foucault, "Questions of Method."

8   J. Scott, *Seeing Like a State.*

9   Cliffe, Guggenheim, and Kostner, *Community-Driven Reconstruction*, 1.

10 The approach is described in Cliffe, Guggenheim, and Kostner, *Community-Driven Reconstruction*. Noer Fauzi of the Consortium for Agrarian Reform (personal communication, June 2003) expressed concern about KDP moving into conflict zones where the government was weak and there was no coordination with social movements whose visions for how to reconstruct society diverged from World Bank priorities. The project appraisal document for SPADA duly noted that bank activities in conflict zones might be opposed on "nationalist" grounds (World Bank, *Support for Poor and Disadvantaged Areas*, 41).

11 Cliffe, Guggenheim, and Kostner, *Community-Driven Reconstruction*, 20.

12 World Bank, *Conflict and Recovery in Aceh*, 4.

13 See Escobar, *Encountering Development*, 225–26; Esteva, "Development," 22. For arguments against generalized antistatism, see Jeffrey and Lerche, "Stating the Difference"; and Nugent, "Building the State, Making the Nation."

14 Anton Lucas and Carol Warren explore tensions between NGOs and mobilized farmers ("The State, the People, and Their Mediators").

15 A rally held by the Forum was attacked by enforcers (YTM, "Rakyat Bangkit Pejabat Tersesat").

16 Hansen and Stepputat, *States of Imagination*, 2.

17 Mamdani, *When Victims Become Killers*; Mbembe, *On the Postcolony.*

18 See Potter and Lee, *Tree Planting in Indonesia*, on farmer assessment of the costs and benefits of oil-palm in Kalimantan. See Bebbington and Bebbington, "Development Alternatives" for responses to "alternative" development in the Andes, and Cowen and Shenton, *Doctrines of Development*, on alternative development as a reiteration of trusteeship.

Abbas, M. Nafsir, Tasrief Siera, and San Afri Awang, eds. *Interaksionisme Simbolik Dongi-Dongi*. Jogjakarta: Debut, 2002.

Acciaioli, Greg. "Grounds of Conflict, Idioms of Harmony: Custom, Religion, and Nationalism in Violence Avoidance at the Lindu Plain, Central Sulawesi." *Indonesia* 72 (2001): 81–112.

———. "Kinship and Debt: The Social Organisation of Bugis Migration and Fish Marketing at Lake Lindu, Central Sulawesi." In *Authority and Enterprise among the Peoples of South Sulawesi*, edited by R. Tol, K. v. Dijk, and G. Acciaioli. Leiden: KITLV, 2000.

———. *Searching for Good Fortune: The Making of a Bugis Shore Community at Lake Lindu, Central Sulawesi*. PhD diss., Australian National University, 1989.

ADB. *Evaluasi Kinerja Secara Kualitatif dan Substantif pada Posisi Pertengahan (Mid Term) Proyek CSIADCP*. Vol. 1, *Laporan Induk*. Palu: CSIADCP (Provincial Coordination Unit, BAPPEDA), 2002.

———. *Hasil Evaluasi Kinerja Kualitatif Mid-Term Proyek CSIADC: Kesimpulan dan Usulan/ Rekomendasi Tindak Lanjut Secara Global*. Palu: CSIADCP (Provincial Coordination Unit, BAPPEDA), 2002.

———. *Mid-Term Evaluation of CSIADCP Performance in Qualitative and Substantive Terms*. Vol. 2, *Annexes*. Palu: CSIADCP (Provincial Coordination Unit, BAPPEDA), 2002.

———. *Project Review Mission, CSIADCP*. Tokyo: Asian Development Bank, 2002.

———. *Report and Recommendation of the President to the Board of Directors on a*

Proposed Loan to the Republic of Indonesia for the Central Sulawesi Integrated Area Development and Conservation Project. Tokyo: Asian Development Bank, 1997.

———. *Summary Environmental Impact Assessment of the Central Sulawesi Integrated Area Development and Conservation Project in the Republic of Indonesia.* Tokyo: Asian Development Bank, 1997.

Aditjondro, George. *Kerusuhan Poso dan Morawali, Akar Permasalahan dan Jalan Keluarnya.* Palu: Yayasan Tanah Merdeka, 2004.

Agamben, Giorgio. "The Camp as the *Nomos* of the Modern." In *Violence, Identity, and Self Determination,* edited by H. De Vries and S. Weber. Stanford, Calif.: Stanford University Press, 1997.

Agrawal, Arun. "Common Property Institutions and Sustainable Governance of Resources." *World Development* 29 (2001): 1649–72.

———. *Environmentality: Technologies of Government and the Making of Subjects.* Durham, N.C.: Duke University Press, 2005.

Agrawal, Arun, and Clark Gibson. "Enchantment and Disenchantment: The Role of Community in Natural Resource Conservation." *World Development* 27 (1999): 629–50.

Alam, Tanra. "Katu Tribe Allowed to Retain Forest Home." *Jakarta Post,* August 3, 1999.

Allen, John. *Lost Geographies of Power.* Oxford: Blackwell, 2003.

Anderson, Benedict. "The Idea of Power in Javanese Culture." In *Culture and Politics in Indonesia,* edited by C. Holt. Ithaca, N.Y.: Cornell University Press, 1972.

———. "Indonesian Nationalism Today and in the Future." *New Left Review,* no. 235 (1999): 3–17.

———. "Old State, New Society: Indonesia's New Order in Comparative Historical Perspective." *Journal of Asian Studies* 42 (1983): 477–96.

———. *The Spectre of Comparisons: Nationalism, Southeast Asia, and the World.* London: Verso, 1998.

Angelsen, Arild. "Shifting Cultivation and 'Deforestation': A Study From Indonesia." *World Development* 23 (1995): 1713–29.

Antlöv, Hans. "Indonesian Civil Society in Search of Engagement, Diversity and Accountability." Unpublished manuscript, 2002.

———. "The Making of Democratic Local Governance in Indonesia." In *Southeast Asian Responses to Globalization: Restructuring Governance and Deepening Democ-*

racy, edited by F. K. W. Loh and J. Ojendal. Honolulu: University of Hawai'i Press, 2005.

——. "Not Enough Politics! Power, Participation and the New Democratic Polity in Indonesia." In *Local Power and Politics in Indonesia: Decentralization and Democratization*, edited by E. Aspinall and G. Fealy. Singapore: Institute of Southeast Asian Studies, 2003.

——. "Village Government and Rural Development in Indonesia: The New Democratic Framework." *Bulletin of Indonesian Economic Studies* 39 (2003): 193–214.

ANZDEC. *Environmental Management and Biodiversity Conservation in the Lore Lindu Bioregion*. Palu: Asian Development Bank, 1997.

——. *Social Analysis and Community Development*. Palu: Asian Development Bank, 1997.

Aragon, Lorraine. "Communal Violence in Poso, Central Sulawesi: Where People Eat Fish and Fish Eat People." *Indonesia* 72 (2001): 45–80.

——. *Fields of the Lord: Animism, Christian Minorities, and State Development in Indonesia*. Honolulu: University of Hawai'i Press, 2000.

Atkinson, Jane. *The Art and Politics of Wana Shamanship*. Berkeley: University of California Press, 1989.

Barron, Paddy, and David Madden. *Beyond Structural Factors: The Importance of Culture in Conflict Resolution in Indonesia*. Cambridge, Mass.: Kennedy School of Government, Harvard University, 2002.

Barron, Patrick, Claire Smith, and Michael Woolcock. *Understanding Local Level Conflict Pathways in Developing Countries: Theory, Evidence and Implications from Indonesia*. Social Development Papers, Conflict Prevention and Reconstruction, No. 19. Washington: World Bank, 2004.

Barron, Patrick, Rachael Diprose, David Madden, Claire Smith, and Michael Woolcock. *Do Participatory Development Projects Help Villagers Manage Local Conflicts? A Mixed Methods Approach to Assessing the Kecamatan Development Project, Indonesia*. Washington: World Bank, 2004.

Bebbington, Anthony. "Reencountering Development: Livelihood Transition and Place of Transformation in the Andes." *Annals of the Association of American Geographers* 90 (2000): 495–520.

Bebbington, A., and D. Bebbington. "Development Alternatives: Practice, Dilemmas and Theory." *Area* 33 (2001): 7–17.

Bebbington, Anthony, and Roger Riddell. "Heavy Hands, Hidden Hands, Holding

Hands? Donors, Intermediary NGOs and Civil Society Organisations." In *NGOs, States and Donors: Too Close for Comfort?*, edited by D. Hulme and M. Edwards. New York: St. Martin's Press / Save the Children, 1997.

Bebbington, Anthony, Michael Woolcock, Scott Guggenheim, and Elizabeth Olson. "Exploring Social Capital Debates at the World Bank." *Journal of Development Studies* 40, no. 5 (2002): 33–64.

Behoa. *Kesepakatan Konservasi Masyarakat Adat Desa Doda, Bariri, Hanggira dan Lempe*. Behoa: Lembaga Adat Robo Behoa, 2000.

———. *Kesepakatan Lembaga Adat Robo Behoa, Lembaga Adat Desa, Pemerintah Desa dan Toko Masyarakat dalam hal Pelanggaran Adat Orang Behoa di Desa Doda, Bariri, Haggira, Lempe*. Behoa: Lembaga Adat Robo Behoa, 2000.

Belsky, Jill M., and Stephen F. Siebert. "Cultivating Cacao: Implications of Sungrown Cacao on Local Food Security and Environmental Sustainability." *Agriculture and Human Values* 20 (2003): 277–85.

Benda-Beckmann, Franz von, and Keebet von Benda-Beckmann. "Community Based Tenurial Rights: Emancipation or Indirect Rule? In *Papers of the XIth International Congress of the Commission on Folk Law and Legal Pluralism, Moscow August 18–22, 1997*, edited by K. v. Benda-Beckmann and H. F. Finkler. N.p., 1999.

Bernstein, Henry. "Taking the Part of Peasants?" In *The Question of Food: Profits Versus People?*, edited by H. Bernstein, B. Crow, M. Mackintosh, and C. Martin. New York: Monthly Review, 1990.

Berry, Sara. *No Condition Is Permanent: The Social Dynamics of Agrarian Change in Sub-Saharan Africa*. Madison: University of Wisconsin Press, 1993.

Bhabha, Homi. "Of Mimicry and Man: The Ambivalence of Colonial Discourse." In *Tensions of Empire: Colonial Cultures in a Bourgeois World*, edited by F. Cooper and L. Stoler. Berkeley: University of California Press, 1992.

Bigalke, T. "Dynamics of the Torajan Slave Trade in South Sulawesi." In *Slavery, Bondage and Dependency in Southeast Asia*, edited by A. Reid. St. Lucia: University of Queensland Press, 1983.

Biggs, Stephen, and Arthur Neame. "Negotiating Room to Maneuver." In *Beyond the Magic Bullet: NGO Performance and Accountability in the Post–Cold War World*, edited by M. Edwards and D. Hulme. West Hartford, Conn: Kumarian, 1996.

Birner, Regina, and Marhawati Mappatoba. *Community Agreements on Conservation* in Central Sulawesi: A Coase Solution to Externalities or a Case of Empowered Deliberative Democracy? Palu: STORMA, 2002.

Black, I. "The 'Lastposten': Eastern Kalimantan and the Dutch in the Nineteenth and Early Twentieth Centuries." *Journal of Southeast Asian Studies* 16 (1985): 281–91.

Blair, Harry. "Donors, Democratisation and Civil Society: Relating Theory to Practice." In *NGOS, States and Donors: Too Close for Comfort?*, edited by D. Hulme and M. Edwards. New York: St. Martin's Press / Save the Children, 1997.

Boeke, J. H. "Objective and Personal Elements in Colonial Welfare Policies" (1927). In *Indonesian Economics: The Concept of Dualism in Theory and Policy*, edited by W. F. Wertheim. The Hague: W. Van Hoeve Publishers, 1961.

——. "Village Reconstruction" (1952). In *Indonesian Economics: The Concept of Dualism in Theory and Policy*, edited by W. F. Wertheim. The Hague: W. Van Hoeve Publishers, 1961.

Boomgaard, Peter. "Colonial Forest Policy in Java in Transition, 1865–1916." In *The Late Colonial State in Indonesia: Political and Economic Foundations of the Netherlands Indies 1880–1942*, edited by R. Cribb. Leiden: KITLV, 1994.

——. "Introducing Environmental Histories of Indonesia." In *Paper Landscapes: Explorations in the Environmental History of Indonesia*, edited by P. Boomgaard, F. Colombijn, and D. Henley. Leiden: KITLV, 1997.

——. "The Javanese Village as a Cheshire Cat: The Java Debate against a European and Latin American Background." *Journal of Peasant Studies* 18 (1991): 288–304.

Bourchier, David. *Lineages of Organicist Political Thought in Indonesia*. PhD diss., Monash University, Melbourne, 1996.

Bowen, John R. "On the Political Construction of Tradition: Gotong Royong in Indonesia." *Journal of Southeast Asian Studies* 45 (1986): 545–61.

BPS, BAPPENAS, and UNDP. *The Economics of Democracy: Financing Human Development in Indonesia*. Jakarta: BPS, BAPPENAS, UNDP, 2004.

Breman, Jan. *Taming the Coolie Beast: Plantation Society and the Colonial Order in Southeast Asia*. Delhi: Oxford University Press, 1989.

——. *The Village on Java and the Early-Colonial State*. Rotterdam: Comparative Asian Studies Program, 1980.

Briggs, Morgan. "Empowering NGOs: The Microcredit Movement through Foucault's Notion of Dispositif." *Alternatives* 26 (2001): 233–58.

Brown, Elaine C. "Grounds at Stake in Ancestral Domains." In *Patterns of Power and Politics in the Philippines: Implications for Development*, edited by J. F. Eder and R. L. Youngblood. Tempe: Arizona State University, 1994.

Brown, L. David, and Jonathan Fox. "Accountability within Transnational Coalitions." In *The Struggle for Accountability: The World Bank, NGOS, and Grassroots Movements*, edited by L. D. Brown and J. Fox. Cambridge, Mass.: MIT Press, 1998.

Burchell, Graham. "Peculiar Interests: Civil Society and Governing 'the System of Natural Liberty.'" In *The Foucault Effect: Studies in Governmentality*, edited by G. Burchell, C. Gordon and P. Miller. Chicago: University of Chicago Press, 1991.

Burkard, Gunter. *Natural Resource Management in Central Sulawesi: Past Experience and Future Prospects*. Palu: STORMA, 2002.

——. *Stability or Sustainability? Dimensions of Socio-economic Security in a Rain Forest Margin*. Palu: STORMA, 2002.

Burns, Peter. "The Myth of Adat." *Journal of Legal Pluralism* 28 (1989): 1–127.

Cameron, Peggy. *The Conservation Band-Aid: A Case Study from Indonesia*. Masters thesis, Dalhousie University, Halifax, Nova Scotia, 1994.

CARE. *Project Evaluation of Agriculture and Natural Resources Protection of Tropical Forest through Environmental Conservation on Marginal Lands (PTF-ECML) and Biodiversity Conservation for Lore Lindu National Park (BCNP) in South, Southeast, and Central Sulawesi*. Jakarta: CARE International Indonesia, 2000.

——. *Protection of Tropical Forests through Ecological Conservation of Marginal Land (PTF-ECML) Project, Phase II 2001–2005, Second Annual Report*. Jakarta: CARE International Indonesia, 2003.

——. *Report on the Interim Evaluation of CARE International Indonesia Project: Protection of Tropical Forests through Environmental Conservation of Marginal Lands (PTF-ECML) Phase II*, prepared by Oyvind Sandbukt and Rudy Syaf Palu: CARE, 2002.

Chakrabarty, Dipesh. *Provincializing Europe: Postcolonial Thought and Historical Difference*. Princeton, N.J.: Princeton University Press, 2000.

Chambers, Robert. Foreword to *Who Changes? Institutionalizing Participation in Development*, edited by J. Blackburn and J. Holland. London: Intermediate Technology Publications, 1998.

Chatterjee, Partha. "Community in the East." *Economic and Political Weekly* 33, no. 6 (1998): 277–82.

——. *The Nation and Its Fragments: Colonial and Postcolonial Histories.* Princeton, N.J.: Princeton University Press, 1993.

Christie, Clive J. *A Modern History of Southeast Asia: Decolonization, Nationalism and Separatism.* London: Tauris, 1996.

Clarke, John. *Changing Welfare, Changing States: New Directions in Social Policy.* London: Sage, 2004.

Cleaver, Frances. "Insititutions, Agency and the Limitations of Participatory Approaches to Development." In *Participation: The New Tyranny?*, edited by B. Cooke and U. Kothari. London: Zed Books, 2001.

Cliffe, Sarah, Scott Guggenheim, and Markus Kostner. *Community-Driven Reconstruction as an Instrument in War-to-Peace Transitions.* Social Development Papers, Conflict Prevention and Reconstruction, No. 7. Washington: World Bank, 2003.

Colchester, Marcus. "Unity and Diversity: Indonesian Policy towards Tribal Peoples." *Ecologist* 16, no. 2–3 (1986): 89–98.

Comaroff, John, and Jean Comaroff. "Preface and Introduction." In *Civil Society and the Political Imagination in Africa*, edited by J. Comaroff and J. Comaroff. Chicago: University of Chicago Press, 1999.

——. *Ethnography and the Historical Imagination.* Boulder, Colo.: Westview, 1992.

Conklin, Beth, and Laura Graham. "The Shifting Middle Ground: Amazonian Indians and Eco-Politics." *American Anthropologist* 97 (1995): 695–710.

Contreras-Hermosilla, Arnoldo, and Chip Fay. *Strengthening Forest Management in Indonesia through Land Tenure Reform: Issues and Framework for Action*: Forest Trends, 2005.

Cooke, Bill, and Uma Kothari. "The Case for Participation as Tyranny." In *Participation: The New Tyranny?*, edited by B. Cooke and U. Kothari. London: Zed Books, 2001.

Cooper, Frederick, and Randall Packard, eds. *International Development and the Social Sciences.* Berkeley: University of California Press, 1997.

Cowen, Michael, and Robert Shenton. *Doctrines of Development.* London: Routledge, 1996.

Crawfurd, John. *A Descriptive Dictionary of the Indian Islands and Adjacent Countries.* London: Bradbury and Evans, 1856.

Crehan, Kate. *Gramsci, Culture, and Anthropology.* Berkeley: University of California, 2002.

Cronon, William. "The Trouble with Wilderness; or, Getting Back to the Wrong Nature." In *Uncommon Ground*, edited by W. Cronon. New York: W. W. Norton and Company, 1996.

Cruikshank, Barbara. *The Will to Empower: Democratic Citizens and Other Subjects.* Ithaca, N.Y.: Cornell University Press, 1999.

Crush, Jonathan. "Introduction: Imagining Development." In *Power of Development*, edited by J. Crush. London: Routledge, 1995.

D'Andrea, Claudia. *Coffee, Custom, and Capital: Territorialization and Adat Identity in Central Sulawesi's Lore Lindu National Park.* PhD diss., University of California, Berkeley, 2003.

Davidson, Jamie S., and David Henley. "Introduction: Radical Conservatism—The Protean Politics of Adat." In *The Revival of Tradition in Indonesian Politics: The Deployment of Adat from Colonialism to Indigenism*, edited by J. Davidson and H. David. London: Routledge, in press.

De Koninck, Rodolphe, and Steve Dery. "Agricultural Expansion as a Tool of Population Redistribution in Southeast Asia." *Journal of Southeast Asian Studies* 28, no. 1 (1997): 1–26.

Dean, Mitchell. " 'Demonic Societies': Liberalism, Biopolitics, and Sovereignty." In *States of Imagination: Ethnographic Explorations of the Post Colonial State*, edited by T. B. Hansen and F. Stepputat. Durham, N.C.: Duke University Press, 2001.
———. *Governmentality: Power and Rule in Modern Society.* London: Sage, 1999.

Department of Social Affairs. *Isolated Community Development: Data and Information.* Jakarta: Directorate for Development of Isolated Communities, 1994–95.

Deventer, C. T. van. "A Welfare Policy for the Indies" (1902). In *Indonesian Economics: The Concept of Dualism in Theory and Policy*, edited by W. F. Wertheim. The Hague: W. Van Hoeve Publishers, 1961.

Dewey, Clive. "Images of the Village Community: A Study in Anglo-Indian Ideology." *Modern Asian Studies* 6 (1972): 291–328.

Dillon, Michael. "Sovereignty and Governmentality: From the Problematics of the 'New World Order' to the Ethical Problematic of the World Order." *Alternatives* 20 (1995): 323–68.

Dirks, Nicholas. *Castes of Mind: Colonialism and the Making of Modern India.* Princeton, N.J.: Princeton University Press, 2001.

Dove, Michael. "The Agroecological Mythology of the Javanese and the Political Economy of Indonesia." *Indonesia* 39 (1985): 1–35.

———. "So Far from Power, So Near to the Forest: A Structural Analysis of Gain and Blame in Tropical Forest Development." In *Borneo in Transition: People, Forests, Conservation, and Development*, edited by C. Padoch and N. L. Peluso. Kuala Lumpur: Oxford University Press, 1996.

Dove, Michael R., and Daniel M. Kammen. "Vernacular Models of Development: An Analysis of Indonesia under the 'New Order.'" *World Development* 29 (2001): 619–39.

Drayton, Richard. *Nature's Government: Science, Imperial Britain, and the "Improvement" of the World*. New Haven, Conn.: Yale University Press, 2000.

Dreyfus, Hubert L., and Paul Rabinow. *Michel Foucault: Beyond Structuralism and Hermeneutics*. Brighton: Harvester, 1982.

DTE. "Evaluating the ADB in Indonesia: The Operation Was a Success, but the Patient Died." *Down to Earth: IFIs Factsheet* 12 (2001).

Duncan, Christopher R. "From Development to Empowerment: Changing Indonesian Government Policies Toward Indigenous Minorities." In *Civilizing the Margins: Southeast Asian Government Policies for the Development of Minorities*, edited by C. R. Duncan. Ithaca, N.Y.: Cornell University Press, 2004.

Dupont, Danica, and Frank Pearce. "Foucault contra Foucault: Rereading the 'Governmentality' Papers." *Theoretical Criminology* 5, no. 2 (2001): 123–58.

Dutton, Ian. "Engaging Communities as Partners in Conservation and Development." *Van Zorge Report*, May 2001, 24–32.

Echols, John M., and Hassan Shadily. *Kamus Indonesia-Inggris*. 3rd ed. Jakarta: PT Gramedia, 1989.

Edmunds, David, and Eva Wollenberg. "A Strategic Approach to Multistakeholder Negotiations." *Development and Change* 32 (2001): 231–53.

Edstrom, Judith. *Indonesia's Kecamatan Development Project: Is It Replicable? Design Considerations in Community Driven Development*. Social Development Paper No. 39. Washington: World Bank, 2002.

Edwards, Michael, David Hulme, and Tina Wallace. "Increasing Leverage for Development: Challenges for NGOs in a Global Future." In *New Roles and Relevance: Development NGOs and the Challenge of Change*, edited by D. Hulme and T. Wallace. Bloomfied, Conn.: Kumarian, 2000.

Ellen, Roy F. "The Development of Anthropology and Colonial Policy in the Netherlands, 1800–1960." *Journal of the History of the Behavioural Sciences* 12 (1976): 303–24.

——. "What Black Elk Left Unsaid: On the Illusory Images of Green Primitivism." *Anthropology Today* 2, no. 6 (1986): 8–12.

Elson, R. E. *The End of the Peasantry in Southeast Asia: A Social and Economic History of Peasant Livelihood.* London: MacMillan, 1997.

——. "International Commerce, the State, and Society: Economic and Social Change." In *The Cambridge History of Southeast Asia*, edited by N. Tarling. Cambridge: Cambridge University Press, 1992.

Enters, Thomas. *The Token Line: Adoption and Non-Adoption of Soil Conservation Practices in the Highlands of Northern Thailand: Paper Presented at the International Workshop on Soil Conservation Extension.* June 4–11, 1995, Chiang Mai, Thailand.

Escobar, Arturo. *Encountering Development: The Making and Unmaking of the Third World.* Princeton, N.J.: Princeton University Press, 1995.

Esteva, Gustavo. "Development." In *The Development Dictionary: A Guide to Knowledge as Power*, edited by W. Sachs. London: Zed Books, 1992.

Evers, Pieter. *Legal Assistance Program for KDP Communities: A First Assessment of the Legal Assistance Pilot Project in Central Java and North Sumatra (August–October 2001).* Jakarta: World Bank, 2001.

——. *Resourceful Villagers, Powerless Communities: Rural Village Government in Indonesia.* Jakarta: World Bank, 2000.

Fairhead, James, and Melissa Leach. *Misreading the African Landscape: Society and Ecology in a Forest-Savanna Mosaic.* Cambridge: Cambridge University Press, 1996.

——. *Science, Society and Power: Environmental Knowledge and Policy in West Africa and the Caribbean.* Cambridge: Cambridge University Press, 2003.

Faisal, Elly Burhaini, and Jeis Montesori. "Orang Dongi-Dongi, Lore Lindu (1–3)." *Suara Pembaruan*, August 13–15, 2003.

Fasseur, C. "Cornerstone and Stumbling Block: Racial Classification and the Late Colonial State in Indonesia." In *The Late Colonial State in Indonesia: Political and Economic Foundations of the Netherlands Indies, 1880–1942*, edited by R. Cribb. Leiden: KITLV, 1994.

Fay, Chip, and Martua Sirait. "Reforming the Reformists in Post-Soeharto Indonesia." In *Which Way Forward? People, Forests and Policy Making in Indonesia*, edited by C. P. Colfer and I. A. P. Resosudarmo. Washington: Resources for the Future, copublished by CIFOR and ISEAS, 2002.

Feit, Herb. "Repressive-Developmentalist Regimes in Asia." *Alternatives* 7 (1981): 491–506.

Ferguson, James. *The Anti-Politics Machine: "Development," Depoliticization, and Bureaucratic Power in Lesotho.* Minneapolis: University of Minnesota Press, 1994.

——. "Paradoxes of Sovereignty and Independence: 'Real' and 'Pseudo' Nation-States and the Depoliticization of Poverty." In *Siting Culture: The Shifting Anthropological Object*, edited by K. F. Olwig and K. Hastrup. London: Routledge, 1997.

Fine, Ben. "The Developmental State Is Dead—Long Live Social Capital?" *Development and Change* 30 (1999): 1–19.

Firdaus, Agus. "Petani Dongi-Dongi Pasca Reklaiming." *Nuansa Pos*, March 11–23, 2002.

Fitzpatrick, Daniel. "Land, Custom and the State in Post-Suharto Indonesia: A Foreign Lawyer's Perspective." In *The Revival of Tradition in Indonesian Politics: The Deployment of Adat from Colonialism to Indigenism*, edited by J. S. Davidson and D. Henley. London: Routledge, forthcoming.

FKKM. *Pertemuan di FKKM, Diskusi Solusi Dongi-Dongi.* Palu: FKKM Sulawesi Tengah, 2003.

Foucault, Michel. "Afterword: The Subject and Power." In *Michel Foucault: Beyond Structuralism and Hermeneutics*, edited by H. L. Dreyfus and P. Rabinow. Brighton: Harvester, 1982.

——. "Governmentality." In *The Foucault Effect: Studies in Governmentality*, edited by G. Burchell, C. Gordon and P. Miller. Chicago: University of Chicago Press, 1991.

——. "Questions of Method." In *The Foucault Effect: Studies in Governmentality*, edited by G. Burchell, C. Gordon, and P. Miller. Chicago: University of Chicago Press, 1991.

——. "Right of Death and Power over Life." In *The Foucault Reader*, edited by P. Rabinow. New York: Pantheon Books, 1984.

——. *Power/Knowledge: Selected Interviews and Other Writings, 1972–1977.* Sussex: Harvester, 1980.

Francis, Paul. "Participatory Development at the World Bank: The Primacy of Process." In *Participation: The New Tyranny?*, edited by B. Cooke and U. Kothari. London: Zed Books, 2001.

Furnivall, J. S. *Netherlands India: A Study of Plural Economy* (1939). Cambridge: Cambridge University Press, 1967.

Geertz, Clifford. *Negara: The Theatre State in Nineteenth-Century Bali*. Princeton, N.J.: Princeton University Press, 1980.

George, Kenneth. *Showing Signs of Violence: The Cultural Politics of a Twentieth-Century Head Hunting Ritual*. Berkeley: University of California Press, 1996.

Goldman, Michael. *Imperial Nature: The World Bank and Struggles for Social Justice in the Age of Globalization*. New Haven, Conn.: Yale University Press, 2005.

Gordon, Colin. "Governmental Rationality: An Introduction." In *The Foucault Effect: Studies in Governmentality*, edited by G. Burchell, C. Gordon, and P. Miller. Chicago: University of Chicago Press, 1991.

Governor. *Keputusan Gubernur Sulawesi Tengah Nomor 188.44/1500/RO. Kumpang-6-ST/2003 Tentang Pembentukan Tim Penanganan Terpadu Taman Nasional Lore Lindu Sulawesi Tengah*. Palu, 2003.

Green, Maia. "Participatory Development and the Appropriation of Agency in Southern Tanzania." *Critique of Anthropology* 20, no. 1 (2000): 67–89.

Grove, Richard. *Green Imperialism: Colonial Expansion, Tropical Island Edens and the Origins of Environmentalism, 1600–1860*. Cambridge: Cambridge University Press, 1995.

Guggenheim, Scott. *Crises and Contradictions: Understanding the Origins of a Community Development Project in Indonesia*. Jakarta: World Bank, 2004.

——. *Proposal to the Norwegian Trust Fund for Environmentally and Socially Sustainable Development*. Jakarta: World Bank, 2002.

Guggenheim, Scott, Tatag Wiranto, Yogana Prasta, and Susan Wong. *Indonesia's Kecamatan Development Program: A Large-Scale Use of Community Driven Development to Reduce Poverty*. Jakarta: World Bank, 2004.

Gupta, Akhil. "Blurred Boundaries: the Discourse of Corruption, the Culture of Politics, and the Imagined State." *American Ethnologist* 22 (1995): 375–402.

——. *Postcolonial Developments*. Durham, N.C.: Duke University Press, 1998.

Haba, Johanis. *Resettlement and Sociocultural Change among the "Isolated Peoples" in Central Sulawesi, Indonesia: A Study of Three Resettlement Sites*. PhD diss., University of Western Australia, Perth, 1998.

Hadiz, Vedi R. "Decentralization and Democracy in Indonesia: A Critique of Neo-Institutional Perspectives." *Development and Change* 35 (2004): 697–718.

Hall, Stuart. "Cultural Identity and Diaspora." In *Identity: Community, Culture, Difference*, edited by J. Rutherford. London: Lawrence and Wishart, 1990.

——. "On Postmodernism and Articulation: An Interview with Stuart Hall." In

Stuart Hall: Critical Dialogues in Cultural Studies, edited by L. Grossberg, D. Morley, and K.-H. Chen. London: Routledge, 1996.

Hannah, Matthew. *Governmentality and Mastery of Territory in Nineteenth-Century America*. Cambridge: Cambridge University Press, 2000.

Hansen, Thomas Blom, and Finn Stepputat. "Introduction: States of Imagination." In *States of Imagination: Ethnographic Explorations of the Post Colonial State*, edited by T. B. Hansen and F. Stepputat. Durham, N.C.: Duke University Press, 2001.

Hardjono, Joan. "Transmigration: Looking to the Future." *Bulletin of Indonesian Economic Studies* 22, no. 2 (1986): 28–53.

Harley. *TNLL: Bebani Utang*. Palu: WALHI, 2001.

Harriss, John. *Depoliticizing Development: The World Bank and Social Capital*. London: Anthem, 2002.

Hart, Gillian. "Agrarian Change in the Context of State Patronage." In *Agrarian Transformations: Local Processes and the State in Southeast Asia*, edited by G. Hart, A. Turton, and B. White. Berkeley: University of California Press, 1989.

——. "Development Critiques in the 1990s: Culs de Sac and Promising Paths." *Progress in Human Geography* 25 (2001): 649–58.

Hefner, Robert. *Civil Islam: Muslims and Democratization in Indonesia*. Princeton, N.J.: Princeton University Press, 2000.

——. *The Political Economy of Mountain Java: An Interpretive History*. Berkeley: University of California, 1990.

Henley, David. "Custom and Koperasi: The Cooperative Ideal in Indonesia. In *The Revival of Tradition in Indonesian Politics: The Deployment of Adat from Colonialism to Indigenism*, edited by J. S. Davidson and D. Henley. London: Routledge, forthcoming.

——. *Fertility, Food and Fever: Population, Economy and Environment in North and Central Sulawesi, 1600–1930*. Leiden: KITLV, 2005.

——. *Jealousy and Justice: The Indigenous Roots of Colonial Rule in Northern Sulawesi*. Amsterdam: VU University Press, 2002.

——. *Nationalism and Regionalism in a Colonial Context: Minahasa in the Dutch East Indies*. Leiden: KITLV, 1996.

Hindess, Barry. "The Liberal Government of Unfreedom." *Alternatives* 26: 93–111, 2001.

Hirsch, Philip. *Political Economy of Environment in Thailand*. Manila: Journal of Contemporary Asia Publishers, 1993.

Hoben, Allan. "Paradigms and Politics in Ethiopia." In *The Lie of the Land: Challenging Received Wisdom on the African Environment*, edited by M. Leach and R. Mearns. London: International African Institute, 1996.

Hooker, M. B. *Adat Law in Indonesia*. Oxford: Oxford University Press, 1978.

Hooker, Virginia M. "The New Order: Standardisation of Language." *Prisma* (1990): 54–67.

Hoppe, Michael, and Heiko Faust. *Transmigration and Integration in Indonesia: Impacts on Resource Use in the Napu Valley, Central Sulawesi*. Palu: STORMA, 2004.

Hoskins, Janet, ed. *Headhunting and the Local Imagination in Southeast Asia*. Stanford, Calif.: Stanford University Press, 1996.

Houben, V. J. H. "Profit versus Ethics: Government Enterprises in the Late Colonial State." In *The Late Colonial State in Indonesia: Political and Economic Foundations of the Netherlands Indies 1880–1942*, edited by R. Cribb. Leiden: KITLV, 1994.

Howell, Jude, and Jenny Pearce. "Civil Society: Technical Instrument or Social Force for Change?" In *New Roles and Relevance: Development NGOS and the Challenge of Change*, edited by D. Hulme and T. Wallace. Bloomfield, Conn: Kumarian, 2000.

Hugenholtz, W. R. "The Land Rent Question and Its Solution, 1850–1920." In *The Late Colonial State in Indonesia: Political and Economic Foundations of the Netherlands Indies 1880–1942*, edited by R. Cribb. Leiden: KITLV, 1994.

Hulme, David, and Michael Edwards. "Conclusion: Too Close to the Powerful, Too Far from the Powerless?" In *NGOS, States and Donors: Too Close for Comfort?*, edited by D. Hulme and M. Edwards. New York: St. Martin's Press/Save the Children, 1997.

Human Rights Watch. *Breakdown: Four Years of Communal Violence in Central Sulawesi*. New York: Human Rights Watch, 2002.

——. *Without Remedy: Human Rights Abuse and Indonesia's Pulp and Paper Industry*. New York: Human Rights Watch, 2003.

Hüsken, Frans. "Declining Welfare in Java: Government and Private Inquiries, 1903–1914." In *The Late Colonial State in Indonesia: Political and Economic Foundations of the Netherlands Indies, 1880–1942*, edited by R. Cribb. Leiden: KITLV, 1994.

ICG. *Indonesia Backgrounder: Jihad in Central Sulawesi*. Jakarta: International Crisis Group, 2004.

——. *Indonesia: Managing Decentralization and Conflict.* Jakarta: International Crisis Group, 2003.

——. *Indonesia: Natural Resources and Law Enforcement.* Jakarta: International Crisis Group, 2001.

——. *Indonesia: Overcoming Murder and Chaos in Maluku.* Jakarta: International Crisis Group, 2000.

IDSS. *Strategic Choices for Working with CSOS in Indonesia.* Victoria: International Development Support Services (IDSS) for ACCESS (Australian Community Development and Civil Society Strengthening Scheme), AUSAID, 2002.

James, Deborah, and Albert Schrauwers. "An Apartheid of Souls: Dutch and Afrikaner Colonialism and Its Aftermath in Indonesia and South Africa—An Introduction." *Itinerario* 27, no. 3–4 (2003): 49–80.

Jeffrey, Craig, and Jens Lerche. "Stating the Difference: State, Discourse and Class Reproduction in Uttar Pradesh, India." *Development and Change* 31 (2000): 857–78.

Jenson, Steffen. "Claiming Community: Local Politics on the Cape Flats, South Africa." *Critique of Anthropology* 24, no. 2 (2004): 179–207.

Kahin, George McTurnan. *Nationalism and Revolution in Indonesia.* Ithaca, N.Y.: Cornell University Press, 1952.

Kahn, Joel. *Constituting the Minangkabau: Peasants, Culture and Modernity in Colonial Indonesia.* Oxford: Berg, 1993.

Katopasa. "60–100 Unit Chain Saw Setiap Hari Beroperasi di Dongi-Dongi." Press release. Palu: Yayasan Katopasa and Yayasan Jambata. May 11, 2002.

——. "Pejabat Wali Kota Palu, Melakukan Praktek Illegal Logging." Press release. Palu: Yayasan Katopasa, May 10, 2002.

King, Dwight. "Indonesia's New Order as a Bureaucratic Polity, a Neopatrimonial Regime, or a Bureaucratic Authoritarian Regime: What Difference Does It Make?" (1979). In *Interpreting Indonesian Politics: Thirteen Contributions to the Debate,* edited by B. Anderson and A. Kahin. Ithaca, N.Y.: Cornell Modern Indonesia Project, Cornell University, 1982.

Koentjaraningrat, ed. *Masyarakat Terasing di Indonesia.* Jakarta: Gramedia with Departmen Sosial, 1993.

Kompas. "Hidup dari Transmigrasi ke Transmigrasi," November 7, 2001.

——. "Kepala Balai Taman Nasional Lore Lindu: WALHI Dukung Perambahan Hutan," October 26, 2002.

——. "Mengembalikan Citra Poso," September 18, 2001.

——. "Poso Kembali Mencekam." June 27, 2001.

Koran Tempo. "Kepala Taman Nasional Robek Piagam WALHI," October 26, 2002.

Kuitenbrouwer, Maarten. *The Netherlands and the Rise of Modern Imperialism.* Oxford: Berg, 1992.

Laban, Banjar Yulianto. "Membangun Gerakan Komunitas Lokal, Menuju Konservasi Radikal." In *Dialog Kebijakan Tentang Taman Nasional Lore Lindu (TNLL) dan Orang (Toi) Behoa, 16 November 2000,* edited by YTM. Palu: Yayasan Tanah Merdeka, 2000.

——. "Tragedi Dongi-Dongi Q-sruh Pandang Konservasi." In *Interaksionisme Simbolik Dongi-Dongi,* edited by M. N. Abbas, T. Siera, and S. A. Awang. Jogjakarta: Debut, 2002.

——. *Pernyataan Sikap BTNLL Terhadap Kasus Perubahan Fungsi TNLL di Dongi-Dongi.* Palu: Balai Taman Nasional Lore Lindu, July 9, 2001.

——. "Prospek Negatif Penebangan Liar di Taman Nasional Lore Lindu." *Indonesia Nature Conservation Newsletter (INCL)* 5 (10–11), 2002.

Laban, Banjar Yulianto, Tanty Thamrin, and Shadiq Dicky Cougar. *Sumbangan Terhadap Deforestasi dan Pelecehan Hak Masyarakat Adat To Tawelia Sedoa.* Palu: Forum Kemitraan Taman Nasional Lore Lindu (FKTNLL), 2002.

Langenberg, Michael Van. "The New Order State: Language, Hegemony and Ideology." In *State and Civil Society in Indonesia,* edited by A. Budiman. Clayton, Victoria: Monash University, 1990.

Latour, Bruno. *We Have Never Been Modern.* Cambridge, Mass.: Harvard University Press, 1993.

Laudjeng, Hedar. "Jangan Cemarkan TAP MPR/IX/2001." fktnll@yahoogroups.com, May 9, 2002.

Leach, Melissa, and Robin Mearns. "Environmental Change and Policy: Challenging Received Wisdom in Africa." In *The Lie of the Land: Challenging Received Wisdom on the African Environment,* edited by M. Leach and R. Mearns. London: International African Institute, 1996.

——, eds. *The Lie of the Land: Challenging Received Wisdom on the African Environment.* London: International African Institute, 1996.

Lev, Daniel S. "Colonial Law and the Genesis of the Indonesian State." *Indonesia* 40 (1985): 57–74.

Levang, Patrice. "From Rags to Riches in Sumatra: How Peasants Shifted from

Food Self-Sufficiency to Market-Oriented Tree Crops in Six Years." *Bulletin of Concerned Asian Scholars* 29, no. 2 (1997): 18–30.

Li, Tania Murray. "Adat in Central Sulawesi: Contemporary Deployments." In *The Revival of Tradition in Indonesian Politics: The Deployment of Adat from Colonialism to Indigenism*, edited by J. S. Davidson and D. Henley. London: Routledge, forthcoming.

——. "Articulating Indigenous Identity in Indonesia: Resource Politics and the Tribal Slot." *Comparative Studies in Society and History* 42, no. 1 (2000): 149–79.

——. "Beyond 'the State' and Failed Schemes." *American Anthropologist* 107 (2005): 383–94.

——. "Compromising Power: Development, Culture and Rule in Indonesia." *Cultural Anthropology* 14, no. 3 (1999): 1–28.

——. "Images of Community: Discourse and Strategy in Property Relations." *Development and Change* 27 (1996): 501–27.

——. "Local Histories, Global Markets: Cocoa and Class in Upland Sulawesi." *Development and Change* 33 (2002): 415–37.

——. "Marginality, Power and Production: Analysing Upland Transformations." In *Transforming the Indonesian Uplands: Marginality, Power and Production*, edited by T. M. Li. London: Routledge, 1999.

——. "*Masyarakat Adat*, Difference, and the Limits of Recognition in Indonesia's Forest Zone." *Modern Asian Studies* 35 (2001): 645–76.

——. "Relational Histories and the Production of Difference on Sulawesi's Upland Frontier." *Journal of Asian Studies* 60, no. 1 (2001): 41–66.

Li, Tania Murray, Haswinar Arifin, and Anto Achadiyat. *Design for the Evaluation of the Program for Isolated Communities*. Jakarta: Directorate of Isolated Community Development, Department of Social Affairs, with the support of UNDP Jakarta and UN Department of Economic and Social Affairs, New York, 1998.

Lindblad, J. Thomas. "The Contribution of Foreign Trade to Colonial State Formation in Indonesia, 1900–1930." In *The Late Colonial State in Indonesia: Political and Economic Foundations of the Netherlands Indies, 1880–1942*, edited by R. Cribb. Leiden: KITLV, 1994.

Lindu. *Keputusan Bersama Lembaga Adat dan Pemerintah Desa se Dataran Lindu, No. 32/DL/LA/KPTS/X.PD/2001*. Lindu: Lembaga Adat dan Pererintah Desa, 2001.

Locher-Scholten, Elsbeth. "Dutch Expansion in the Indonesian Archipelago Around

1900 and the Imperialism Debate." *Journal of Southeast Asian Studies* 25, no. 1 (1994): 91–111.

Lucas, Anton, and Carol Warren. "The State, the People, and Their Mediators: The Struggle over Agrarian Law Reform in Post-New Order Indonesia." *Indonesia* 76 (2003): 87–126.

Ludden, David. "India's Development Regime." In *Colonialism and Culture*, edited by N. B. Dirks. Ann Arbor: University of Michigan Press, 1992.

Lumeno, Ferdinand. *Sistem Pemilikan Tanah Dan Tingkat Kemampuan Ekonomi Di Desa Lelio, Kolori, Lengkeka, Kageroa Dan Tuare Kecamatan Lore Selatan Kabupaten Poso Sulawesi Tengah.* Palu: Yayasan Tanah Merdeka, 2000.

Lynch, Owen, and Emily Harwell. *Whose Natural Resources? Whose Common Good? Towards a New Paradigm of Environmental Justice and the National Interest in Indonesia.* Jakarta: Lembaga Studi dan Advokasi Masyarakat (ELSAM), 2002.

MacDougall, John James. "The Technocratic Model of Modernization: The Case of Indonesia's New Order." *Asian Survey* 16 (1978): 1166–83.

Madden, David, and Paddy Barron. *Violence and Conflict Resolution in "Non-Conflict" Regions: The Case of Lampung, Indonesia.* Social Development Paper No. 2. Jakarta: World Bank, 2004.

Maertens, Miet, Manfred Zeller, and Regina Birner. *Explaining Agricultural Land Use in Villages Surrounding the Lore Lindu National Park in Central Sulawesi, Indonesia.* Palu: STORMA, 2002.

Malkki, Liisa. "National Geographic: The Rooting of Peoples and the Teritorialization of National Identity among Scholars and Refugees." *Cultural Anthropology* 7, no. 1 (1992): 24–44.

Mamdani, Mahmood. *Citizen and Subject: Contemporary Africa and the Legacy of Late Colonialism.* Princeton, N.J.: Princeton University Press, 1996.

——. *When Victims Become Killers: Colonialism, Nativism, and the Genocide in Rwanda.* Princeton, N.J.: Princeton University Press, 2001.

Mansuri, Ghazala, and Vijayendra Rao. "Community-Based and -Driven Development: A Critical Review." *World Bank Research Observer* 19, no. 1 (2004): 1–39.

Massey, Doreen. "Power Geometry and a Progressive Sense of Place." In *Mapping the Futures: Local Cultures, Global Change*, edited by J. Bird, B. Curtis, T. Putnam, G. Robertson, and L. Tickner. London: Routledge, 1993.

Mbembe, Achille. *On the Postcolony.* Berkeley: University of California Press, 2001.

McAfee, Kathleen. "Selling Nature to Save It? Biodiversity and Green Developmentalism." *Environment and Planning D: Society and Space* 17 (1999): 133–54.

McCall, Chris. "Indonesia: Spirit of Jihad Keeps Divided Communities on a War Footing." *South China Morning Post*, December 11, 2001.

McCarthy, John. "Changing to Gray: Decentralization and the Emergence of Volatile Socio-legal Configurations in Central Kalimantan, Indonesia." *World Development* 32 (2004): 1199–1223.

——. *"Wild Logging": The Rise and Fall of Logging Networks and Biodiversity Conservation Projects on Sumatra's Rainforest Frontier*. Bogor: Center for International Forestry Research, 2000.

McClure, Kirstie. "Taking Liberties in Foucault's Triangle: Sovereignty, Discipline, Governmentality, and the Subject of Rights." In *Identities, Politics, Rights*, edited by A. Sarat and T. Kearns. Ann Arbor: University of Michigan, 1995.

Mehta, Uday. "Liberal Strategies of Exclusion." In *Tensions of Empire: Colonial Cultures in a Bourgeois World*, edited by F. Cooper and L. Stoler. Berkeley: University of California Press, 1997.

Mitchell, Timothy. *Colonizing Egypt*. Berkeley: University of California Press, 1988.

——. *Rule of Experts: Egypt, Technopolitics, Modernity*. Berkeley: University of California Press, 2002.

Moniaga, Sandra. "Toward Community-Based Forestry and Recognition of *Adat* Property Rights in the Outer Islands of Indonesia." In *Legal Frameworks for Forest Management in Asia: Case Studies of Community/State Relations*, edited by J. Fox. Honolulu: East-West Center Program on Environment, 1993.

Montesori, Jeis. "Kenapa Orang Gunung Dekembalikan ke Gunung?" *Suara Pembaruan*, October 1, 2001.

Moore, Donald S. "Clear Waters and Muddied Histories: Environmental History and the Politics of Community in Zimbabwe's Eastern Highlands." *Journal of Southern African Studies* 24 (1998): 377–403.

——. "Subaltern Struggles and the Politics of Place: Remapping Resistance in Zimbabwe's Eastern Highlands." *Cultural Anthropology* 13, no. 3 (1998): 1–38.

——. *Suffering for Territory: Race, Place, and Power in Zimbabwe*. Durham, N.C.: Duke University Press, 2005.

Mosse, David. "Colonial and Contemporary Ideologies of 'Community Management': The Case of Tank Irrigation Development in South India." *Modern Asian Studies* 33 (1999): 303–38.

———. "Is Good Policy Unimplementable? Reflections on the Ethnography of Aid Policy and Practice." *Development and Change* 35 (2004): 639–71.

Nababan, Abdon. "Respon Untuk Cermatan Kasus Dongi Dongi." adat@yahoo groups.com, August 24, 2001.

Neumann, Roderick P. "Ways of Seeing Africa: Colonial Recasting of African Society and Landscape in Serengeti National Park." *Ecumene* 2 (1995): 149–69.

Noorduyn, Jacobus. *A Critical Survey of Studies on the Languages of Sulawesi.* Leiden: KITLV Press, 1991.

Nordholt, Henk Schulte. "The Making of Traditional Bali: Colonial Ethnography and Bureaucratic Reproduction." In *Colonial Subjects: Essays on the Practical History of Anthropology*, edited by P. Pels and O. Salemink. Ann Arbor: University of Michigan Press, 1999.

Nourse, Jennifer. *Conceiving Spirits: Birth Rituals and Contested Identities among Lauje of Indonesisa.* Washington: Smithsonian Institution Press, 1999.

Nuansa Pos. "Buntut Kasus Proyek CSIADP di Sadaunta Lore Lindu—Taman Nasional: Anggota Dewan Marah, Masyarakat Lore Ditipu." December 30, 2002.

———. "Pimpro CSIADP Diminta Bayar Upah Kerja Jalan." December 28, 2002.

———. "WALHI Sulteng Perlu Memberikan Pemahaman FPM Dongi Dongi," November 8, 2002.

Nugent, David. "Building the State, Making the Nation: The Bases and Limits of State Centralization in 'Modern' Peru." *American Anthropologist* 96 (1994): 333–69.

O'Malley, Pat. "Indigenous Governance." *Economy and Society* 25 (1996): 310–26, 1996.

O'Malley, Pat, Lorna Weir, and Clifford Shearing. "Governmentality, Criticism, Politics." *Economy and Society* 26 (1997): 501–17.

Obidzinski, K. *Logging in East Kalimantan, Indonesia: The Historical Expedience of Illegality.* Amsterdam: PhD diss, University of Amsterdam, 2002.

Ortner, Sherry B. "Resistance and the Problem of Ethnographic Refusal." *Comparative Studies in Society and History* 37, no. 1 (1995): 173–91.

Paada, Putromo. *Migrasi dan Konflik Daerah Tujuan: Kasus Desa Tomado di Enclave Taman Nasional Lore Lindu Sulawesi Tengah.* Masters thesis, Universitas Hasanuddin, Makassar 2001.

Pels, Peter. "The Anthropology of Colonialism: Culture, History, and the Emergence of Western Governmentality." *Annual Review of Anthropology* 26 (1997): 163–83.

Pels, Peter, and Oscar Salemink, eds. *Colonial Subjects: Essays on the Practical History of Anthropology*. Ann Arbor: The University of Michigan Press, 1999.

Peluso, Nancy. "Coercing Conservation? The Politics of State Resource Control." *Global Environmental Change* 3 (1993): 199–217.

——. "A History of State Forest Management in Java." In *Keepers of the Forest*, edited by M. Poffenberger. West Hartford, Conn.: Kumarian, 1990.

——. "Fruit Trees and Family Trees in an Anthropogenic Forest: Ethics of Access, Property Zones, and Environmental Change in Indonesia." *Comparative Studies in Society and History* 38 (1996): 510–48, 1996.

——. *Rich Forests, Poor People: Resource Control and Resistance in Java*. Berkeley: University of California Press, 1992.

——. "Weapons of the Wild: Strategic Uses of Violence and Wildness in the Rain Forests of Indonesian Borneo." In *In Search of the Rain Forest*, edited by C. Slater. Durham, N.C.: Duke University Press, 2003.

——. "Whose Woods Are These? Counter-Mapping Forest Territories in Kalimantan, Indonesia." *Antipode* 27 (1995): 383–406.

Peluso, Nancy Lee, and Peter Vandergeest. "Genealogies of the Political Forest and Customary Rights in Indonesia, Malaysia, and Thailand." *Journal of Asian Studies* 60 (2001): 761–812.

Peluso, Nancy, and Michael Watts. "Violent Environments." In *Violent Environments*, edited by N. Peluso and M. Watts. Ithaca, N.Y.: Cornell University Press, 2001.

Peluso, Nancy, and Emily Harwell. "Territory, Custom, and the Cultural Politics of Ethnic War in West Kalimantan, Indonesia." In *Violent Environments*, edited by N. Peluso and M. Watts. Ithaca, N.Y.: Cornell University Press, 2001.

Pemberton, John. *On the Subject of "Java."* Ithaca, N.Y.: Cornell University Press, 1994.

Peters, Pauline. "Encountering Participation and Knowledge in Development Sites." In *Development Encounters: Sites of Participation and Knowledge*, edited by P. Peters. Cambridge, Mass.: Harvard University Press, 2000.

Pigg, Stacy Leigh. "Inventing Social Categories through Place: Social Representations and Development in Nepal." *Comparative Studies in Society and History* 34 (1992): 491–513.

Polanyi, Karl. *The Great Transformation* (1944). Boston: Beacon, 1957.

Potter, Lesley, and Justin Lee. *Tree Planting in Indonesia: Trends, Impacts and Directions*. Bogor: Center for International Forestry Research (CIFOR), 1998.

Pretty, Jules, and Hugh Ward. "Social Capital and the Environment." *World Development* 29 (2001): 209–27.

Procacci, Giovanna. "Social Economy and the Government of Poverty." In *The Foucault Effect: Studies in Governmentality*, edited by G. Burchell, C. Gordon, and P. Miller. Chicago: University of Chicago Press, 1991.

Putnam, Robert D. *Making Democracy Work: Civic Traditions in Modern Italy.* Princeton, N.J.: Princeton University Press.

Radar Sulteng. "Kantor Gubernur Diserbu." September 30, 2003.

Rahnema, Majid. "Participation." In *The Development Dictionary: A Guide to Knowledge as Power*, edited by W. Sachs. London: Zed Books, 1992.

Reid, Anthony. "Inside Out: The Colonial Displacement of Sumatra's Population." In *Paper Landscapes: Explorations in the Environmental History of Indonesia*, edited by P. Boomgaard, F. Colombijn, and D. Henley. Lieden: KITLV, 1997.

——. "Political 'Tradition' in Indonesia: The One and the Many." *Asian Studies Review* 22, no. 1 (1998): 23–38.

Robertson, A. F. *People and the State: An Anthropology of Planned Development.* Cambridge: Cambridge University Press, 1984.

Robinson, Geoffrey. *The Dark Side of Paradise: Political Violence in Bali.* Ithaca, N.Y.: Cornell University Press, 1995.

Roe, Emery M. "Development Narratives, or Making the Best of Blueprint Development." *World Development* 19 (1991): 287–300.

Rose, Nikolas. *Powers of Freedom: Reframing Political Thought.* Cambridge: Cambridge University Press, 1999.

Rostow, Walter. *The Stages of Growth: A Non-Communist Manifesto.* Cambridge: Cambridge University Press, 1960.

Ruf, François. "From Tree-Crop Planting to Replanting: A New Turning-Point for the Sulawesi Cocoa Boom." In *Workshop on the Future of Indonesian Cocoa Through Replanting and Pest Disease Control*, edited by CIRAD-ASKINDO. Jakarta: CIRAD-ASKINDO, 1997.

Ruf, François, and Yoddang. "The Sulawesi Cocoa Boom and Its Crises." *Plantations, Recherche, Developpement* (July–August 1999): 248–53.

Sangaji, Arianto. *Buruk INCO Rakyat Digusur: Ekonomi Politik Pertambangan Indonesia.* Jakarta: Pustaka Sinar Harapan, 2002.

——. "The Masyarakat Adat Movement in Indonesia: a Critical Insider's View." In

The Revival of Tradition in Indonesian Politics: The Deployment of Adat from Colonialism to Indigenism, edited by J. S. Davidson and D. Henley. London: Routledge, forthcoming.

——. *Menuju Pengelolaan TNLL Berbasis Masyarakat*. Palu: WALHI, 2001.

——. "Kegagalan Keamanan di Poso." *Kompas*, November 11, 2005.

——. "Pasukan Terlatih dan Perubahan Pola Kekerasan di Poso." *Kompas*, October 17, 2003.

——. *Politik Konservasi: Orang Katu Di Behoa Kakau*. Bogor: KpSHK, 2002.

——. *Rumput Kering di Balik Anyir Darah: Konteks Sosial Dari Trajedi Kemanusiaan Poso*. Palu: Yayasan Tanah Merdeka, 2003.

Sargeant, Dave. "Update: Birding Logistics in the National Parks of Northern Sulawesi." Worldtwitch Web site, worldtwitch.virtualave.net/sulawesi_sargeant.htm, August 21, 2001.

Schiller, Jim. "State Formation and Rural Transformation: Adapting to the 'New Order' in Jepara." In *State and Civil Society in Indonesia*, edited by A. Budiman. Victoria: Monash University, 1990.

Schoffer, I. "Dutch 'Expansion' and Indonesian Reactions: Some Dilemmas of Modern Colonial Rule (1900–1942)." In *Expansion and Reaction: Comparative Studies in Overseas History*, edited by H. L. Wesseling. Leiden: Leiden University Press, 1978.

Schrauwers, Albert. "The 'Benevolent' Colonies of Johannes van den Bosch: Continuities in the Administration of Poverty in the Netherlands and Indonesia." *Comparative Studies in Society and History* 43 (2001): 298–328.

——. *Colonial "Reformation" in the Highlands of Central Sulawesi, Indonesia, 1892–1995*. Toronto: University of Toronto Press, 2000.

——. "H(h)ouses, E(e)states and Class: On the Importance of Capitals in Central Sulawesi." *Bijdragen, tot de Taal-, Land- en Volkenkunde* 160–61 (2004): 72–94.

——. "Houses, Hierarchy, Headhunting and Exchange: Rethinking Political Relations in the Southeast Asian Realm of Luwu." *Bijdragen tot de Taal-, Land- en Volkenkunde* 153 (1997): 311–35.

——. "The Miser's Store: Property and Traditional Law in the Governance of the 'Native' Economy." *Journal of Peasant Studies* 29, no. 2 (2002): 24–46.

Schweithelm, James, Nengah Wirawan, Joanna Elliott, and Asmeen Khan. *Sulawesi Parks Program Land Use Survey and Socio-Economic Survey: Lore Lindu Na-*

tional Park and Morawali Nature Reserve. Directorate General of Forest Protection and Nature Conservation, Ministry of Forestry, Government of Indonesia and The Nature Conservancy, 1992.

Scott, David. "Colonial Governmentality." *Social Text*, no. 43 (1995): 191–220.

Scott, James C. *Seeing Like a State: How Certain Schemes to Improve the Human Condition Have Failed*. New Haven, Conn.: Yale University Press, 1998.

Sedoa. *Peraturan Desa Sedoa, No 15/KDS-Perdes/II/2003, 2003*. Village council document.

Sider, Gerald. "When Parrots Learn to Talk, and Why They Can't: Domination, Deception, and Self-Deception in Indian-White Relations." *Comparative Studies in Society and History* 29 (1987): 3–23.

Siegel, James. *A New Criminal Type in Jakarta: Counter-Revolution Today*. Durham, N.C.: Duke University Press, 1998.

Sitorus, Felix. *"Revolusi Cokelat": Social Formation, Agrarian Structure, and Forest Margins in Upland Sulawesi, Indonesia*. Palu: STORMA, 2002.

——. *Land, Ethnicity, and the Competing Power: Agrarian Dynamics in Forest Margin Communities in Central Celebes, Indonesia*. Palu: STORMA, 2002.

Skaria, Ajay. "Shades of Wildness: Tribe, Caste, and Gender in Western India." *Journal of Asian Studies* 56 (1997): 726–45.

Slater, David. "Rethinking the Spatialities of Social Movements: Questions of (B)orders, Culture, and Politics in Global Times." In *Cultures of Politics, Politics of Cultures: Revisioning Latin American Social Movements*, edited by S. E. Alvarez, E. Dagnino, and A. Escobar. Boulder, Colo.: Westview, 1997.

Smith, Claire. *The Roots of Violence and Prospects for Reconciliation: A Case Study of Ethnic Conflict in Central Kalimantan, Indonesia*. Social Development Papers, Conflict Prevention and Resolution, No. 23. Washington: World Bank, 2005.

Smith, Gavin. *Confronting the Present: Towards a Politically Engaged Anthropology*. Oxford: Berg, 1999.

Sonius, H. W. J. Introduction to *Van Vollenhoven on Indonesian Adat Law*, edited by J. F. Holleman. The Hague: Martinus Nijhoff, 1981.

Stoler, Ann Laura. *Capitalism and Confrontation in Sumatra's Plantation Belt, 1870–1979*. New Haven, Conn.: Yale University Press, 1985.

——. *Carnal Knowledge and Imperial Power: Race and the Intimate in Colonial Rule*. Berkeley: University of California Press, 2002.

——. "Making Empire Respectable: The Politics of Race and Sexual Morality in Twentieth-Century Colonial Cultures." *American Ethnologist* 16 (1989): 634–61.

——. "Rethinking Colonial Categories: European Communities and the Boundaries of Rule." In *Colonialism and Culture*, edited by N. B. Dirks. Ann Arbor: University of Michigan Press, 1992.

——. "Sexual Affronts and Racial Frontiers: European Identities and the Cultural Politics of Exclusion in Colonial Southeast Asia." *Comparative Studies in Society and History* 34 (1992): 514–51.

——. *Race and the Education of Desire: Foucault's History of Sexuality and the Colonial Order of Things.* Durham, N.C.: Duke University Press, 1995.

Stoler, Ann Laura, and Frederick Cooper. "Between Metropole and Colony: Rethinking a Research Agenda." In *Tensions of Empire: Colonial Cultures in a Bourgeois World*, edited by F. Cooper and A. L. Stoler. Berkeley: University of California Press, 1997.

STORMA. *Processes of Destabilization and Conditions of Stability of Rainforest Margins in Indonesia: Report on the Field Visit in Palu.* Palu: STORMA, 1999.

——. *Socio-Economic Aspects of Village Communities in and around Lore-Lindu National Park.* Palu: STORMA, 1999.

Sugiharto, Hariyanto Hasan, and Nurdin Yabu. *Masalah Agraria di Dataran Lindu, Kecamatan Kulawi, Kabupaten Donggala, Sulawesi Tengah.* Palu: Yayasan Tanah Merdeka, 2002.

Sulawesi Tengah. *Propinsi Sulawesi Tengah Dalam Angka.* Palu: 1998.

Suparlan, Parsudi. *Orang Sakai Di Riau: Masyarakat Terasing Dalam Masyarakat Indonesia.* Jakarta: Yayasan Obor Indonesia, 1995.

Suripto. "Issue, Permasalahan dan Upaya Penanggulangan Illegal Logging." Paper presented at Natural Resource Management Seminar, Jakarta, August 18, 2002.

Tajima, Yuhki. *Mobilizing for Violence: The Escalation and Limitation of Identity Conflicts: The Case of Lampung, Indonesia.* Jakarta: World Bank, 2004.

Tanter, Richard. "Oil, IGGI and US Hegemony: Global Pre-Conditions." In *State and Civil Society in Indonesia*, edited by A. Budiman. Victoria: Monash University, 1990.

Thomas, Nicholas. *Colonialism's Culture: Anthropology, Travel and Government.* Princeton, N.J.: Princeton University Press, 1994.

TNC. *An Integrated Sulawesi Conservation Area: Indonesia Program Information Sheet 10.* Palu: TNC, 2000.

———. *Building Conservation Capacity and Partnerships at Lore Lindu National Park, Sixth and Final Report to National Resources Management II Program*, USAID. Palu: The Nature Conservancy, 2002.

———. *Draft Management Plan, Lore Lindu National Park*. Palu: Taman Nasional Lore Lindu/The Nature Conservancy, 2002.

———. *Kesepakatan Konservasi Masyarakat di Lima Desa sekitar TN Lore Lindu*. Palu: The Nature Conservancy, 2002.

———. *Laporan Kegiatan Pemetaan Bersama Masyarakat di 10 (sepuluh) Desa Sekitar TNLL*. Palu: The Nature Conservancy, 2001.

———. *Lessons Learned from Compatible Enterprise Development Initiatives at Lore Lindu National Park*. Palu: The Nature Conservancy, 2001.

———. *Lore Lindu National Park*, Indonesia Program Information Sheet 1. Jakarta: TNC, n.d.

———. *Lore Lindu Water Resources Valuation Study*. Palu: The Nature Conservancy, 2001.

———. *Participatory Conservation Planning Manual*. Palu: The Nature Conservancy, 2003.

———. *TNC Lessons Learned from Building Conservation Capacity and Partnership at Lore Lindu National Park*. Palu: The Nature Conservancy, 2002.

Top FM. *Dongi-Dongi, Fenomena, Masalah, Solusi: Pengakuan Yang Terlambat*. Transcript of radio talk show. Palu: Radio Nugraha Top FM, July 17, 2002.

Tsing, Anna Lowenhaupt. "Becoming a Tribal Elder, and Other Green Development Fantasies." In *Transforming the Indonesian Uplands: Marginality, Power and Production*, edited by T. M. Li. London: Routledge, 1999.

———. *In the Realm of the Diamond Queen: Marginality in an Out-of-the-Way Place*. Princeton, N.J.: Princeton University Press, 1993.

Valverde, Mariana. "'Despotism' and Ethical Liberal Goverance." *Economy and Society* 25 (1996): 357–72.

Vandergeest, Peter, and Nancy Lee Peluso. "Territorialization and State Power in Thailand." *Theory and Society* 24 (1995): 385–426.

Vel, Jacqueline. "Tribal Battle in Remote Island: Crisis and Violence in Sumba (Eastern Indonesia)." *Indonesia* 72 (2001): 141–58.

Velthoen, Esther. "Mapping Sulawesi in the 1950's." In *Indonesia in Transition: Work in Progress*," edited by H. S. Norholt and G. Asnan. Yogyakarta: Pustaka Pelajar, 2003.

——. " 'Wanderers, Robbers and Bad Folk': The Politics of Violence, Protection and Trade in Eastern Sulawesi, 1750–1850." In *The Last Stand of Asian Autonomies: Responses to Modernity in the Diverse States of Southeast Asia and Korea, 1750–1900*, edited by A. Reid. New York: St. Martin's Press, 1997.

Vickers, Adrian. "Reopening Old Wounds: Bali and the Indonesian Killings—A Review Article." *Journal of Asian Studies* 57 (1998): 744–85, 1998.

WALHI. *A Violent Start of the Year for Indonesian Communities*. Jakarta: WALHI, 2004.

——. *Laporan Tim Investigasi Wilayah Tongoa-Kamarora dan Dongi-Dongi (Kawasan TNLL), 18–20 July 2002*. Palu: WALHI, 2002.

——. *Lembaran Fakta: Taman Nasional Lore Lindu*. Jakarta: WALHI, 2001.

——. *Pendudukan Dongi Dongi Oleh Forum Petani Merdeka (FPM)*. Jakarta: WALHI, 2001.

——. *Kontroversi Dongi Dongi*. Jakarta: WALHI, 2001.

——. *Laporan Hasil Monitoring Proyek CSIADCP di Kabupaten Poso dan Kabupaten Donggala, Propinsi Sulawesi Tengah*. Palu: WALHI, 2001.

Watts, Michael. " 'A New Deal in Emotions': Theory and Practice and the Crisis of Development." In *Power of Development*, edited by J. Crush. London: Routledge, 1995.

——. "Black Acts." *New Left Review* 9 (2001): 125–39.

——. "Development and Governmentality." *Singapore Journal of Tropical Geography* 24 (2003): 6–34.

——. "Development Ethnographies." *Ethnography* 2 (2001): 283–300.

Weber, Robert, Heiko Faust, and Werner Kreisel. "Colonial Interventions on the Cultural Landscape of Central Sulawesi by 'Ethical Policy': Impacts of the Dutch Rule in Palu and Kulawi, 1905–1942." *Asian Journal of Social Science* 31 (2003): 398–434.

Welsh, Bridget. *Mobbing for Justice: Variation in Vigilante Killings in Indonesia*. World Bank Seminar Presentation, Jakarta, December 15, 2003.

Wertheim, W. F. Introduction to *Indonesian Economics: The Concept of Dualism in Theory and Policy*, edited by W. F. Wertheim. The Hague: W. Van Hoeve Publishers, 1961.

Wesseling, H. L. "The Giant That Was a Dwarf, or the Strange History of Dutch Imperialism." In *Theory and Practice of European Expansion Overseas: Essays in Honour of Ronald Robinson*, edited by A. Porter and R. Holland. London: Frank Cass, 1989.

Wetterberg, Anna. *Crisis, Social Ties, and Household Welfare: Testing Social Capital Theory with Evidence from Indonesia.* Jakarta: World Bank, 2005.

White, Benjamin. "Problems in the Empirical Analysis of Agrarian Differentiation." In *Agrarian Transformations: Local Processes and the State in Southeast Asia,* edited by G. Hart, A. Turton, and B. White. Berkeley: University of California Press, 1989.

Wilder, Gary. "Practicing Citizenship in Imperial Paris." In *Civil Society and the Political Imagination in Africa,* edited by J. Comaroff and J. Comaroff. Chicago: University of Chicago Press, 1999.

Williams, Raymond. *Keywords.* London: Fontana, 1976.

Winichakul, Thongchai. *Siam Mapped: A History of the Geo-Body of a Nation.* Honolulu: University of Hawai'i Press, 1994.

Woodhouse, Andrea. *Village Corruption in Indonesia: Fighting Corruption in the World Bank's Kecamatan Development Program.* Jakarta: World Bank, 2005.

Woolcock, Michael. "Social Capital and Economic Development: Toward a Theoretical Synthesis and Policy Framework." *Theory and Society* 27 (1998): 151–208.

World Bank. *Community Recovery through the Kecamatan Development Project: Appraisal Document.* Jakarta: World Bank, 2005.

——. *Conflict and Recovery in Aceh: An Assessment of Conflict Dynamics and Options for Supporting the Peace Process.* Jakarta: World Bank, 2005.

——. *Decentralizing Indonesia: A Regional Public Expenditure Review Overview Report.* Jakarta: World Bank, 2003.

——. *Idea Note, Justice for the Poor: Program for the Reform of Legal Institutions in the Local Environment.* Jakarta: World Bank, 2002.

——. *Indonesia: Country Assistance Strategy.* Jakarta: World Bank, 2001.

——. *Indonesia: Country Assistance Strategy.* Jakarta: World Bank, 2004.

——. *Kecamatan Development Program Phase One: Final Report 1998–2002.* Jakarta: Ministry of Home Affairs (Community Development Agency), KDP National Secretariat and National Management Consultants, World Bank, 2002.

——. *Land Management and Policy Development Project: Appraisal Document.* Jakarta: World Bank, 2004.

——. *Local Capacity and Its Implications for Development: The Case of Indonesia, A Preliminary Report.* Jakarta: World Bank, 1999.

——. *Second Kecamatan Development Project: Appraisal Document.* Jakarta: World Bank, 2001.

——. *Social Capital, Local Capacity, and Government: Findings from the Second Indonesian Local Level Institutions Study: Overview Report.* Jakarta: World Bank, 2002.

——. *Support for Poor and Disadvantaged Areas: Project Appraisal Document.* Jakarta: World Bank, 2005.

——. *Third Kecamatan Development Project: Appraisal Document.* Jakarta: World Bank, 2003.

——. *Village Justice in Indonesia: Case Studies on Access to Justice, Village Democracy and Governance.* Jakarta: World Bank, 2004.

World Wildlife Fund. *Lore Lindu National Park Management Plan, 1981–1986.* Bogor: World Wildlife Fund for the Directorate of Nature Conservation, Republic of Indonesia, 1981.

Yayasan Kayu Riva. *Survei Demogaphi: Pola Perubahan Populasi dan Pengaruhnya Terhadap Manajmen Taman Nasional Lore Lindu.* Palu: The Nature Conservancy/Balai Taman Nasional Lore Lindu, 2001.

YTM. *Dialog Kebijakan Tentang Taman Nasional Lore Lindu (TNLL) dan Orang (Toi) Behoa, 16 November 2000.* Palu: Yayasan Tanah Merdeka, 2000.

——. *Dokumentasi Kasus Masyarakat Adat Katu 1997 s/d 1999.* Palu: Yayasan Tanah Merdeka, 1999.

——. "Konservasi Yang Anti Rakyat." *Seputar Rakyat* 1, no. 6 (2003): 7–9.

——. "Menakar Keinginan Warga Dongi-Dongi." *Seputar Rakyat* 1, no. 6 (2003): 14–17.

——. "Menunggu Pengakuan Hak Masyarakat Adat." *Seputar Rakyat* 1, no. 2 (2002): 3–6.

——. *Notulensi Dialog Dodolo dengan Balai Taman Nasional Lore Lindu (BTNLL) dan Dinas Kesejateraan Sosial, Balai Desa Dodolo, 5 Agustus 2003.* Palu: Yayasan Tanah Merdeka, 2003.

——. *Notulensi Dialog Masyarakat Mataue dan Balai Taman Nasional Lore Lindu, Balai Desa Mataue, 14 Agustus 2003.* Palu: Yayasan Tanah Merdeka, 2003.

——. *Pertemuan Konsultasi Masyarakat di Sekitar Taman Nasional Lore Lindu (TNLL), Toro, 27–30 September 2000, Laporan Proseding.* Palu: Yayasan Tanah Merdeka, 2000.

——. "Rakyat Bangkit Pejabat Tersesat." *Seputar Rakyat* 1, no. 1 (2002): 10–11.

——. "Segregasi Masyarakat Poso." *Seputar Rakyat* 2, no. 2 (2004): 13–17.

Ford Foundation, 237–238

Forest boundaries: and class formation, 106–107, 122; in colonial period, 39–40, 43–44, 72–76; and illegal logging, 55–56, 168, 179, 184–185, 187, 207, 217, 223, 265; in the New Order, 51, 58, 60–61, 84–94, 98–99, 101, 334 n.153; and timber concessions, 58, 89, 92, 99, 102, 161, 174–175, 264–266. *See also* Conservation

Foucault, Michel, 5–19, 25–28, 34, 54, 59, 270, 285 n.4, 287 n.22, 288 n.28

Free Farmers Forum, 150–154, 156–191

Furnivall, J. S., 35, 40, 44, 47

Goldman, Michael, 287 n.23

Government: practice of, 5–19, 270; and governmental rationality (governmentality), 6, 12–13, 18, 27, 34, 56, 59, 61, 270. *See also* Rendering technical

Governor of Central Sulawesi, 4, 93, 98, 102, 111, 149, 153–154, 276, 280, 319 n.9

Gramsci, Antonio, 19, 22–27, 270

Grove, Richard, 13, 73

Guggenheim, Scott, 231, 248, 253–255

Haba, Johanis, 63, 104, 309 nn.95, 100

Hadiz, Vedi, 269, 330 n.53

Hall, Stuart, 22, 24, 147, 292 n.75

Hart, Gillian, 291 n.67

Henley, David, 62–64, 72–75, 300 n.119, 303 n.2, 306 n.60

Hindess, Barry, 14, 289 n.77

Human Rights Watch (HRW), 265–266

India, 12–14, 35, 52, 297 n.71, 299 n.86

Indigenous people: as contested identity, 112–116, 145–150, 159–160, 168–175, 190; and resource management, 199–207, 225; and rights advocates, 4, 50, 115, 147–149, 168–173, 279. *See also* Adat; Katu; Land; Lindu Lake

Islam. *See* Muslims

Japanese occupation, 52, 76–77, 79, 300 n.119

Java, 24, 31–48, 52, 55, 57, 76, 132, 233, 282. *See also* Transmigration

Kahin, George, 38

Kaili, 86, 164, 174, 320 n.101, 321 n.30. *See also* Da'a

Kalimantan, 86, 157, 165, 183, 264, 301 n.142

Katu, 145–150. 169–172, 177, 188–189, 195, 200–201, 205, 207, 226

Kecamatan Development Program (KDP), 230–269

Kruyt, Albert, 67–68, 72, 74–75, 107, 117, 120, 282

Kulawi Valley, 63–67, 71, 76–78, 99–102, 112, 164, 185, 203–204, 212, 219. *See also* Lindu Lake; Tompi

Labor: as basis for land rights, 20, 82–86, 98–100, 104, 116, 173–174; and class formation, 19–22, 108, 112–114, 160, 165, 179, 185; forced, in colonial period, 32, 36–44, 62, 70–71, 79

Land: conflict in the 1960s, 8, 53; customary rights to, 4, 23, 39–40, 48–
52, 82–86, 98–108, 115–116, 145–
150, 217–219, 224–226, 310 n.5, 320
n.20, 334 n.153; private accumula-
tion/dispossession of, 19–22, 39,
44, 89, 91–116, 182–183, 309 n.99,
312 n.34; and Raffles' tenure studies,
35–37; state allocation of, 80–94,
100–103, 153; and struggles in Sulawesi highlands, 142–55, 156–191,
194–199, 213, 217–219, 225, 262–
266. *See also* Agrarian Law; Consortium for Agrarian Reform; Labor
Latour, Bruno, 17
Law: and private property, 20, 41, 54,
83, 97–100, 116, 160; as tactic to
govern conduct, 16, 35, 94, 107, 195–
199, 209, 213–216, 240–241. *See
also* Adat; Agrarian Law; Apartheid;
Conservation Law of 1990
Lev, Daniel, 37, 50–51
Lindu Lake, 23, 26, 63, 114–116, 147–
148, 171–172, 176–177, 180, 212,
226
Lore Lindu National Park, 10, 29, 84–
85, 91, 191, 114, 123–229
Ludden, David, 13, 15

Maps: as state claims to territory, 39,
82, 84, 101, 153, 175, 199–206, 215,
299 n.106, 323 n.29; villagers' coun-
termaps, 145–147, 176, 178, 205,
218–219, 224, 324 n.58. *See also* Forest boundaries
Marx, Karl, 17, 19–20
Massey, Doreen, 28

Masyarakat adat. See Indigenous
people
Masyarakat terasing. See Department of
Social Affairs
Mbembe, Achille, 13, 16
Mental guidance: as the New Order
keyword, 58, 121, 178
Migrant: as identity contrasted to
"local," 77–78, 97–98, 105, 111–116,
160, 173–174, 309 n.95. *See also*
Bugis; Department of Social Affairs;
Transmigration
Military: and economic gain, 53, 55,
102–103, 120, 133, 179, 256–257,
264. *See also* New Order; Violence
Mill, J. S., 14
Minahasa, 36, 62–63, 67, 71–72, 79,
120
Mission. *See* Christians
Mitchell, Timothy, 10–11, 199
Moore, Donald, 286 n.6, 292 n.83, 293
n.92
Mosse, David, 335 n.163
Mouffe, Chantal, 289 n.30
Muslims: and colonial policy, 69, 117;
conflict with Christians, 96–97,
116–122; and the New Order, 55–56,
118. *See also* Bugis

Napu Valley, 63, 65–66, 74; Bugis
migration to, 103–104, 109–116,
119, 122; and conservation, 213–214,
217–220; and Dongi-Dongi, 168,
170–171, 175, 181; transmigration to,
82–84, 100. *See also* Sedoa,
Watumaeta
Native, as legal category, 32, 44–45

Tradition (*continued*)
tionists, 200–206, 224–227; by
"ethical" reformers, 42–51; by
Farmers at Dongi-Dongi, 169, 181–
182; by Raffles, 35; by Van den
Bosch, 36–38; by World Bank, 230–
262
Transmigration, 81–84, 119, 160, 262,
307 nn.80, 82, 308 nn.83, 84, 311
n.22, 334 n.144
Trusteeship, 4–10, 15, 21–25; critique,
278–283
Tsing, Anna, 86, 303 n.13, 306 n.74,
309 n.94, 326 n.118

USAID, 55, 125, 194

Vandergeest, Peter, 39, 305 n.54
Village: as administrative unit, 57; reg-
ulation of 1906, 42–43. *See also*
Community; Tradition
Violence: and capitalism, 19–22, 97; at
Dongi-Dongi, 181, 184–187; and
eviction, 92, 99, 142–145, 195; and

improvement, 5, 8, 12–18, 34, 53–56,
66–70, 78, 86, 301 n.142; rendered
technical, 256–264. *See also* New
Order; Poso
VOC, 32, 36, 38, 44–45, 62, 73, 293 n.3,
303 n.2
Vollenhoven, Cornelis Van, 48–51, 97,
282, 299 n.93

WALHI, 147–154, 167, 170–171, 177,
180, 265
Watts, Michael, 16, 286 n.6, 305 n.48
Watumaeta, 111–112, 218–219, 325
n.104
Woolcock, Michael, 331 n.65
World Bank, 230–269. *See also*
Neoliberalism
World Wildlife Fund, 125

Yayasan Tanah Merdeka (WTM), 145–
149, 162, 167–168, 170–171, 180,
187, 223–225, 279–280. *See also*
Sangaji, Arianto

TANIA MURRAY LI is a professor of anthropology and Senior Canada Research Chair in Political Economy and Culture in Asia-Pacific at the University of Toronto. She is the author of *Malays in Singapore: Culture, Economy, and Ideology* and the editor of *Transforming the Indonesian Uplands: Marginality, Power, and Production.*

Library of Congress Cataloging-in-Publication Data

Li, Tania, 1959–

The will to improve : governmentality, development, and the

practice of politics / Tania Murray Li.

p. cm.   Includes bibliographical references and index.

ISBN 978–0–8223–4008–9 (cloth : alk. paper)

ISBN 978–0–8223–4027–0 (pbk. : alk. paper)

1. Economic development—Political aspects.

2. Sulawesi Tengah (Indonesia)—Economic policy.

I. Title. HD82.L483 2007   338.9598'4—dc22

2006035585